THE POLITICS OF SONGS IN EIGHTEENTH-CENTURY BRITAIN, 1723–1795

Poetry and Song in the Age of Revolution

Series Editors: Michael Brown
John Kirk
Andrew Noble

Titles in this Series

1 United Islands? The Languages of Resistance
John Kirk, Andrew Noble and Michael Brown (eds)

2 Literacy and Orality in Eighteenth-Century Irish Song
Julie Henigan

3 Cultures of Radicalism in Britain and Ireland
John Kirk, Michael Brown and Andrew Noble (eds)

Forthcoming Titles

James Orr, Poet and Irish Radical
Carol Baraniuk

Reading Robert Burns: Texts, Context, Transformations
Carol McGuirk

www.pickeringchatto.com/poetryandsong

THE POLITICS OF SONGS IN EIGHTEENTH-CENTURY BRITAIN, 1723–1795

BY

Kate Horgan

PICKERING & CHATTO
2014

Published by Pickering & Chatto (Publishers) Limited
21 Bloomsbury Way, London WC1A 2TH

2252 Ridge Road, Brookfield, Vermont 05036-9704, USA

www.pickeringchatto.com

All rights reserved.
No part of this publication may be reproduced,
stored in a retrieval system, or transmitted in any form or by any means,
electronic, mechanical, photocopying, recording, or otherwise
without prior permission of the publisher.

© Pickering & Chatto (Publishers) Ltd 2014
© Kate Horgan 2014

To the best of the Publisher's knowledge every effort has been made to contact
relevant copyright holders and to clear any relevant copyright issues.
Any omissions that come to their attention will be remedied in future editions.

BRITISH LIBRARY CATALOGUING IN PUBLICATION DATA

Horgan, Kate, author.

The politics of songs in eighteenth-century Britain, 1723–1795. – (Poetry and song in the age of revolution)
1. Political ballads and songs – Great Britain – 18th century – History and criticism. 2. Great Britain – Politics and government – 1714 – 1820.
I. Title II. Series
782.4'2'0941'09033-dc23

ISBN-13: 9781848934795
e: 9781781440957

This publication is printed on acid-free paper that conforms to the American
National Standard for the Permanence of Paper for Printed Library Materials.

Typeset by Pickering & Chatto (Publishers) Limited
Printed and bound in the United Kingdom by CPI Books

CONTENTS

Acknowledgements	vii
List of Figures	ix
Introduction	1
1 The Heart of the Lion: The 'Princely Song' and the Transmission of Richard.	29
2 The Psalms that Bind: 'Sternhold and Hopkins', the 'Old Hundredth' and the Ballad.	61
3 Songs as Philippics: The 'Harmodium Melos' and the 'Io Paean' of Revolution.	93
4 Song and Pikes in Sheffield: The Trial of James Montgomery.	129
Afterword	171
Notes	175
Works Cited	221
Index	247

ACKNOWLEDGEMENTS

I would like to thank Professor Gillian Russell, who guided me through the PhD upon which this book is based and has been an unfailing support. I cannot thank Gillian enough for the knowledge and wisdom she has shared with me over the years and for showing me a new way into the past that has been both illuminating and inspiring. Thank you to Jon Mee, Nigel Leask and Kevin Gilmartin for their thoughtful comments on my work and to the editors of this series, Michael Brown, John Kirk and Andrew Noble. Special thanks to Glen Rose for her invaluable proofreading.

Sophie Horgan and Jonathan McCabe provided extraordinary assistance in the preparation of the manuscript and I owe them both a huge debt of gratitude for their good humour and fortitude. Put simply, I could not have done this without you. My parents have always encouraged my educational endeavours and I am immensely grateful for their unconditional love and support over the years. Roger Ellis has always been an inspiration, with an uncanny knack for popping up when least expected! Together with Andrea MacIntyre, he showed me immense kindness during my stay in Sheffield and beyond. Thanks to my aunts – Allyson Strong for her regular brown paper parcels and cheering texts and Lisa Gorringe for her interest and encouragement. The practical advice of Marty Collins was also very much appreciated. My grandparents, though long gone, continue to shape the things that I do, for which I am grateful.

Three dear friends in particular have played a very important role in my life during the completion of this project: Annmarie Elijah, Vivien Silvey and Melody Broome. I would also like to thank and acknowledge the support of Erica Woolman. Moglet and Angus, my darling feline friends, have their paw-prints all over this work and have been constant companions. Also, to the many other friends and colleagues that are too numerous to mention here, I offer my heartfelt thanks.

Finally, I would like to thank Pickering & Chatto for publishing this work.

LIST OF FIGURES AND TABLES

Figure 2.1: Title page of the 1749 edition of *The Whole Book of Psalms* – 'Sternhold and Hopkins' — 69
Figure 2.2: 'God Save the King' as printed in the *Gentleman's Magazine* in October 1745 — 87
Figure 3.1: 'Homer singing his verses to the Greeks'. Print by James Gillray, published by Hannah Humphrey, 1797 — 100
Figure 3.2: A Song Sung at the Anniversary of the Revolution of 1688 — 124
Figure 3.3: A New Song, Sung by Mr Dignum at the Anniversary of the Revolution of 1688 — 125
Figure 4.1: Title page of the *Patriot*, 1792 — 132
Figure 4.2: Handbill of 'A Serious Lecture' and 'Hymn', 1794 — 146
Figure 4.3: Woodcut detail from the title page of the *Patriot* — 167
Figure 4.4: Portrait of James Montgomery — 170

Table 1.1: Historical Songs from Volume Three of *A Collection of Old Ballads* (1725) — 44

INTRODUCTION

In October 1789, just months following the fall of the Bastille and the beginning of the French Revolution, the following report was printed in London newspapers:

> It being customary for the Gardes du Corps at Versailles to give an entertainment to any new regiment that arrives there, the Regiment de Flandres was on Thursday last sumptuously entertained with a dinner by the corps in the palace. After dinner their Most Christian Majesties judged proper to honour the company with their presence, and condescended to shew their satisfaction at the general joy which prevailed among the guests. On their appearance the music instantly played the favourite song of 'O Richard, O mon Roi', and the company, joining in chorus, seemed to unite all ideas in one unanimous sentiment of loyalty and love for the King, and nothing was heard for some time but repeated shouts of Vive le Roi, within and without the palace. In the height of their zeal they proceeded to tear the national cockades from their hats, and trampled them under their feet. The Gardes du Corps supplied themselves with black cockades, in the room of those they had treated with such disdain. The news of these proceedings soon reached Paris, where a general ill humour visibly gained ground.[1]

The 'favourite song' of 'O Richard, ô mon Roi' was taken from the highly successful comic opera *Richard Coeur de Lion* by Michel-Jean Sedaine (1719–97) which premiered on 21 October 1784, with the music by André-Ernest-Modeste Grétry.[2] The opera took as its central episode the story of the rescue of King Richard the Lionheart from captivity in a castle in Austria by his faithful minstrel Blondel. In her study of French Revolutionary songs, Laura Mason observes that when reports of this extravagant dinner and entertainment reached Paris a populace already struggling with severe bread shortages became inflamed.[3] Soon after, on 5 October 1789, the Parisian market women would march on Versailles and the royal family were ignominiously returned to the capital. Mason points out that initial reports had focused upon the trampling of the black cockade as an affront to the revolution – it was not until a year later, in 1790, that testimony given before the municipal courts concerning the march on Versailles revived an awareness that the song, 'O Richard', was part of the demonstration of loyalty of the guards to their King.[4] Shortly after the hearings finished, the Comédie-Italienne performed Sedaine's opera and from this point, argues Mason, 'O Richard' became the 'royalist anthem' functioning as an answer to the popular revolutionary song 'Ça Ira' ('that will go') and maintaining a more consistent popularity than the *Marseillaise*.[5] Marvin A. Carlson and James H. Johnson also note instances of the performance of 'O Richard' such as in 1791, when an actor at the Comédie-Italienne replaced the word 'Richard' with 'Louis' in a verse from the song 'O Richard' so that the words ran:

> Oh Louis, oh my king!
> With our love we faithfully embrace you,
> And the law that's written on our hearts
> Dedicates us to serve your cause.[6]

The significance of the song, 'O Richard', would have resonated with British readers of the London papers that carried reports of the infamous dinner. Adaptations of the French opera, *Richard Coeur De Lion*, had been performed at the royal theatres of Drury Lane and Covent Garden in 1786 and actually overlapped by a week.[7] The Drury Lane production, translated by John Burgoyne, enjoyed considerable success with thirty-three performances in the first season and a total of one hundred and fourteen performances over a period of eleven years.[8] In 1789, Blondel's song of loyalty to a King from the distant past spoke to the present crisis, at a time when the future of the monarchy in France was deeply uncertain and amidst fears of the spread of revolution.

The enduring resonance of the Richard-Blondel story forms the vehicle by which this book explores the politics of song in British eighteenth-century and Romantic culture. Richard Coeur de Lion, or Richard the Lionheart as he is known in English, functions here in three ways: he provides the thematic device of singing to the king at the heart of each chapter; he is the figure through which the book begins its exploration of the politics of songs in Chapter One; and finally, as this newspaper report shows, he introduces the context of songs of the French revolution and their circulation in Britain. A thorough-going account of political songs in Britain during the 1790s, equivalent to Mason's, has yet to be written, despite the fact that songs have often featured as evidentiary material. Francis Place (1771–1854), a member of the London Corresponding Society in the 1790s and described by E. P. Thompson as 'the greatest archivist' of the early movement for parliamentary reform, pioneered the use of such evidence.[9] Place was acutely aware of the importance of the songs that he knew as an apprentice boy because they marked the progress of working people, who would later come to be defined as the working-class, toward respectability. In 1819, with the aid of 'Mr Tijou' and Richard Hayward, he recorded the words to thirty-two bawdy songs in a manuscript, together with the 'flash ballads' of his youth:

> The Following songs and specimens of songs, are all of them from, ballads bawled about the streets, and hung against the walls. It will seem incredible that such songs should be allowed but it was so.[10]

Place registers a sense of the ubiquity and ephemerality of songs here, with their disappearance during the course of his lifetime a source of wonder. The series 'Poetry and Song in the Age of Revolution', of which this book is a part, therefore provides a valuable opportunity to consider long forgotten songs and their traditions in the British context.

The need for this has been demonstrated by the important work that has already contributed to our understanding of the importance of songs in eighteenth-century political life such as E. P. Thompson's seminal *Making of the English Working Class* (1963), Iain McCalman's *Radical Underworld* (1988), Gillian Russell's *Theatres of War* (1995) and John Barrell's *Imagining the King's Death* (2000).[11] McCalman's study alerted us to songs as a mode of communication in the 'free and easy' taverns and debating societies, including the fact that followers of the ultra-radical Thomas Spence composed political songs to the tunes of popular folk ballads.[12] James Epstein's work includes songs as part of a range of symbolic practices including radical toasting and dining which were an important part of political discourse and sociability.[13] Michael T. Davis has pointed to the value of an 'interface' between the 'history of politics' and the 'history of music' for understanding the power of songs as tools of political resistance, examining the assimilation of French revolutionary songs such as 'Ça Ira' into British radical culture.[14] The threat of the transmission of radical ideas posed by the orality of radical song and their recurring tropes has been highlighted in Michael Scrivener's work on John Thelwall's songs for the London Corresponding Society (LCS), and his well-known anthology of democratic verse from the period, *Poetry and Reform* (1992).[15] The adaptability of well-known melodies was a key feature of the political song culture of the period and is demonstrated by the singing of 'O Richard' to the King Louis. Scrivener's insight into the 'omnipresent' nature of political songs during the eighteenth century in Volume One of *United Islands?* (2012) makes the valuable point that songs were so 'material' and 'commonplace' as to be excluded from the aesthetic domain, a concern which is also taken up in this book.[16]

Complementing this has been a small body of work exploring loyalist song in the 1790s. Mark Philp's analysis of the letters sent to the Association for Preserving Liberty and Property against Republicans and Levellers, revealed many examples of contributors who sought to offer an antidote to the 'poison' of Thomas Paine's *Rights of Man* (1791–2) by demonstrating their loyalty through song.[17] In the later collection *Resisting Napoleon* (2006) Philp included a chapter on 'Music and Politics, 1793–1815' observing the 'crucial' but 'little discussed' role that songs and music played in fostering the loyalty of the British public during the war.[18] Notable exceptions to this include the work of Vic Gammon, who has examined the role of British songs in constructing a negative image of Napoleon during the revolutionary wars, and Robin Ganev whose *Songs of Protest, Songs of Love* (2009) deals with Hannah Moore's efforts to combat the effect of street ballads on the poor by producing ballads as part of the Cheap Repository Tracts series.[19] Once again emphasizing the importance of melody, Ganev points out that the Bishop of London, Bielby Porteous, advised Moore to set her ballads to 'easy, popular, vulgar tunes' such as 'Chevy Chase' and 'Two Children in the Wood'.[20]

The series in which this volume is part addresses a gap in the cultural history of music and the configuration of ballad scholarship within the discipline of English literary studies. Paul Langford observed in 1989 that 'the potential of eighteenth-century music studies beyond musicology has yet to be exploited', and as recently as 2005 Jeffrey Jackson and Stanley Pelkey began their introduction to a collection of interdisciplinary essays on music and history with the question: 'why haven't historians and musicologists been talking to one another?'[21] The new cultural history of music has also sought to address this gap and has been described by Jane Fulcher in *The Oxford Handbook of the New Cultural History of Music* (2011) as a 'new synthesis' of methodologies drawn from 'the new cultural history' and 'new musicology' of the 1980s, providing a 'new sensitivity to the symbolic realm and 'a deeper understanding of surrounding forces and their dynamics' in the study of music.[22] As yet, however, this 'new cultural history of music' is mainly concerned with elite forms of music-making and has not significantly engaged with the history of the ballad as it intersects with literary studies and political song. From the perspective of literary studies, Patricia Fumerton and Anita Guerrini have noted that scholarship on the ballad has also been characterized by disciplinary and temporal boundaries. Echoing Jackson and Pelkey, they have called for 'scholars from different historical periods and different academic boundaries to talk to one another'.[23]

The political song, which has fallen through this gap in research, has yet to be extensively explored or theorized as a discreet category. The period associated with the ascendancy of Sir Robert Walpole has been viewed as the last high point of the broadside ballad as topical political song. Milton Percival's 1916 *Political Ballads Illustrating the Administration of Sir Robert Walpole* was influential in forming this narrative, arguing that 'as the newspaper grew and strengthened, the ballad withered and decayed'.[24] For Percival, the political ballad had a highly journalistic function in the transmission of topical news and was antithetical to a 'literary point of view'.[25] Paula McDowell's 2006 essay on the political balladry of the Walpole period, which appeared in a special edition of *Eighteenth Century* devoted to ballads and songs in the eighteenth century, explicitly addressed the category of the political ballad in its topical permutation and its exclusion from the category of the 'literary' in both ballad collections and scholarship itself as the century progressed. In doing so McDowell initiated an important discussion about the relationship between the political ballad and the literary ballad which encompassed a consideration of the ballad revival.[26]

This book will develop and expand the parametres of this discussion to include, in particular, the 1790s. While I indicated previously that a comprehensive account of the political songs of this decade remains to be written, Scrivener's insights into the 'omnipresent' nature of songs during the eighteenth century demonstrates the difficulties of such an aim, and as such I can only hope to make a partial contribution to such a study. In the course of researching this work it became evident that songs are often particularly resistant to conventional temporal boundaries and periodization. It became clear that it was necessary to establish the long durée of the politics of song in the eighteenth century in order to understand the contexts in Britain after 1789. This long durée is examined in relation to a number of key themes and case studies beginning with an exploration of the 'politics of song' in the 1725 publication of 'The Princely Song of Richard Cordelion', in the third volume of the seminal *Collection of Old Ballads* (1723–5). This particular song illustrates the long-standing popularity of King Richard's story for ballad-writers and singers, a history that was revived in the contexts of the French Revolution and its aftermath, in both Britain and France. The book considers the ballad history of King Richard in its own right, which has received little attention from scholars, as well as using that history as exemplary of the long durée of the politics of song, illustrating how the topical contexts in which it was revived could interact with deeply embedded histories and continuities.

Together with Joseph Addison's essays on the ballads 'Chevy Chase' and 'Two Children in the Wood' in the *Spectator*, scholars have viewed the *Collection of Old Ballads* as marking the beginning of the 'ballad revival', the scholarly and polite interest in balladry which began during the eighteenth century.[27] This development marked the beginning of the codification and elevation of certain ballads as 'literary', contributing eventually to the formalizing of the discipline of 'English Literature', presaging Romanticism and the development of folklore studies in the nineteenth century. A more capacious eighteenth-century understanding of ballads as song sung in the streets thus began to be narrowed during this period and there was also a similar narrowing in what constituted a ballad's political meaning, the ballad increasingly being seen as apolitical and timeless. This book deliberately uses the term 'song' in its title, rather than ballad which has a different valence, in order to capture some of this capaciousness. It also interprets the category of 'song' in broader terms than has often been the case, bringing to the fore the relationship between topical songs, classical songs, psalms and hymns. While this exploration is necessarily partial and incomplete, the book aims to provide a compelling narrative of interconnections.

A cornerstone argument is that the song-forms of this period were malleable and intersected with each other: ballad and hymn tunes could be set to topical lyrics to address issues of the day, and 'narrative ballads' could function topically in certain situations. The 'politics of songs' of the title therefore refers to two processes at work: the malleability of songs in this period; and the cultural politics surrounding the efforts of key figures of the ballad revival, including Thomas Percy (1729–1811) and Joseph Ritson (1752–1803), who were involved in the cataloguing, categorizing and defining of songs in their printed works. In this way the book will demonstrate the limitations of defining the political song primarily in relation to topicality. This introductory chapter will proceed by outlining the currency of the story of Richard and Blondel in eighteenth-century antiquarian and music scholarship. It will then draw upon Plato as a way of theorizing the malleability which is the 'politics of songs'. Two sections following this will provide an overview of the ballad revival and the formation of scholarship on the ballad, beginning with the period from Addison to Wordsworth and the later emergence of ballad studies into the nineteenth century. Finally, the chapter will conclude with an overview of the structure and themes of the book. In line with the inter-disciplinary nature of the series and the injunctions of Fumerton and Guerrini, the book combines the perspectives of literary studies and political history with detailed archival analysis to suggest some of the reasons why songs featured so significantly in the politics and culture of the revolutionary decade.

Richard the Lionheart

Richard Plantagenet (1157–99), as ruler of the Angevin Empire, was King of a realm that included Britain and France. He became King of England in 1189 and ruled until his premature death during battle in 1199.[28] As a historical figure he is known as the 'absent King' and while he was away leading the second crusade an alternative King-figure, and icon of balladry, emerged in the mythical figure of Robin Hood.[29] While an extensive scholarship is attached to Robin Hood, the story of Richard and Blondel has remained unexplored, despite the fact that it was already well-known in eighteenth-century Britain before the stage productions of 1786. The poet and bluestocking, Anna Williams (1706–83), who lived in the household of Samuel Johnson, provided an account of Blondel's rescue of Richard entitled 'Blondiaux' in her poetic miscellany of 1766.[30] Williams offers the most concise summary of the story. In his long search for Richard, who had failed to return to England from the crusade, Blondel had arrived at the castle of the Duke of Austria where an unknown prisoner was being held:

> one day he placed himself over-against a window of the tower in which King Richard was kept, and began to sing a French song which they had formerly composed together. When the King heard the song, he knew that the singer was Blondel, and when half of it was sung, he began the other half and completed it.[31]

Blondel and Richard's singing to each other illustrates the power of song to penetrate the formidable structure of the castle walls: it has an emancipating force. It is this singing which leads to Richard's freedom from captivity because, having identified his sovereign, Blondel then returns to England to summon the barons on a rescue mission.

A year later, Williams's account was cited in the second edition of Thomas Percy's (1729–1811) 'Essay on the Ancient English Minstrels' which introduced Volume One of his influential *Reliques of Ancient English Poetry* (1767).[32] Percy presented a 'more antiquated' account of the story, describing Richard as 'the great restorer and hero of Chivalry ... and also the distinguished patron of Poets and Minstrels'.[33] According to Percy, English minstrelsy had thrived under Richard's reign owing to the influence of the multitudes of Provençal Bards whom he invited to court upon assuming the throne in England. The account of his rescue by Blondel had itself been 'rescued from oblivion by an ingenious lady' (Anna Williams) and was a 'remarkable fact which ought to be recorded for the honour of poets and their art'.[34] The ramifications of Percy's use of Richard in his theory of minstrelsy are explored further in Chapter One. Percy also noted the 'curious Provençal song', said to be authored by Richard and printed by Horace Walpole in *A Catalogue of Royal and Noble Authors* (1758), as 'not destitute of pathetical and sentimental beauties'.[35]

Accounts of Richard's rescue by Blondel were also reproduced in the two works of the 1770s that marked the beginning of music scholarship as a separate discipline with its own historiography: John Hawkins's *General History of the Science and Practice of Music* (1776) and Charles Burney's *General History of Music* (1776–89). Hawkins's account appeared first, in the second of five volumes, where he provided evidence that Richard was skilled in the art of poetry and rectified his omission from Bishop Thomas Tanner's (1674–1735) *Bibliotheca Brittanicus*, a catalogue of British writers before 1600 published in 1748.[36] To this end, Burney cited the work of the Italian scholar Giovanni Crescimbeni (1663–1728) who had referred to Richard's writings in Volume Two of his *Commentari della Volgar Poesia* (1710).[37] Following Crescimbeni's lead, Horace Walpole visited the Laurentine library in Florence, where he had uncovered the 'curious Provençal song'.[38] More significantly, however, the late seventeenth century scholar Thomas Rymer (1642/3–1713) is described by Hawkins as 'the first of our countrymen' to assert that Richard was a writer.[39] In *A Short View of Tragedy* (1693) Rymer had refuted the medieval chronicler Roger of Hoveden's (*d.* 1201/2) characterization of Richard as a mere propagandist who had paid his retinue of troubadours to sing his praises in the streets.[40] The 'incontestible proof' for Hawkins that Richard was 'of the class of poets ... termed Provençal' was the account of his rescue by Blondel present in Fauchet and Favyn, both of which had been cited by Percy.[41] It was important for Hawkins to demonstrate that Richard was a legitimate 'poet' because this strengthened a genealogy of national music; however, as Hoveden's dissent from this narrative demonstrates, Richard's significance had long been a focus of contestation.

Charles Burney's (1726–1814) treatment of Richard's rescue by Blondel appeared in 1782 in the second volume of his four volume *General History*.[42] Like Hawkins, Burney quoted a lengthy excerpt from the account of Claude Fauchet, but also drew upon the hitherto unnoticed old French romance titled *La Tour Tenebreuse, or The Black Tower*, originally published in Paris in 1705, which contained the song of Richard and Blondel written in the language of Provence.[43] Burney also noted that Jean Baptiste de Sainte-Palaye's *Histoire Litteraire des Troubadours* (1774), translated by Susanna Dobson as *The Literary History of the Troubadours* (1777), contained the French version of the 'Song of Complaint' by Richard, printed in Walpole's earlier *Royal Catalogue*.[44] Burney's research at the Vatican Library enabled his most original contribution: the music and words to a song composed by the troubadour Guacelm Anselm Faidit upon Richard's death, which he had found amongst manuscripts bequeathed by the queen of Sweden.[45] In 1793 the Reverend Richard Eastcott drew heavily upon Burney in his account of the story of Blondel's rescue of Richard in *Sketches of the Origins, Progress and Effects of Music*.[46]

When considering this eighteenth-century scholarship, the question arises as to why the rescue story was treated as a 'remarkable fact' for Percy, and as historical evidence for Hawkins and Burney? By contrast, twentieth century historians have viewed the story of Richard's rescue by Blondel as one of many legends surrounding Richard Plantagenet.[47] Part of the answer to this can be found in eighteenth-century conceptions of music's power that continued to be influenced by Ancient Greece. The Greeks had an understanding of music that emphasized its effects upon the character and behaviour of the individual. Louis Harap notes that the Greeks were preoccupied with both the technical nature of music, investigated mathematically by Pythagoras, and with how music affected the character of the individual and society, or the *ethos* of music.[48] As Edward Lippman observes, long before such concepts are expressed explicitly in philosophy they appear as part of myths of musical magic in cases where music exerts an irresistibly powerful force.[49] The most well-known of these myths is the story of Orpheus. Following the death of his wife Eurydice, Orpheus moves the gods with his powerful music and they grant his wish to allow her to leave the underworld on the condition that he does not look back.[50] Orpheus is also able to charm the natural world with his music. Burney, in true enlightenment fashion, was skeptical about many of the claims for music's supernatural powers as represented in the Orpheus story, although a belief in the healing powers of music upon the body remained current in the eighteenth century.[51] In relation to Blondel's rescue of Richard, there was a plausibility to the story because the song of Richard and Blondel functioned like a code rather than being magical in a strictly supernatural sense. In other words, the power of the song represented the 'ethos' of music in action through the loyalty and fealty Blondel demonstrated in singing to his King – music in this respect was not merely reflective of politics but was able to effect change.

The Politics of Songs

Of the Greek writings on music relating to 'ethos', it is those of Plato (*c.* 429 BC– 347 BC) which are foregrounded here because of his belief in the power of song to affect the workings of the state. Lippman describes Plato's work as the definitive expression of ideas of the 'ethos' of music.[52] In the *Republic* the dialogue between Glaucon and Socrates turns to a discussion of song. Socrates observes that song is comprised of three things, 'words, *harmonia*, and rhythm'.[53] By *harmonia*, Socrates means a kind of scale, or series of intervals upon which a melody could be based. Different harmonia were thought to accord with different characteristics and emotional states. Socrates tells Glaucon that two *harmoniai* are suitable for the republic: the 'Dorian' which 'imitates the sounds and cadences of a man who is brave in deeds of war'; and the 'Phrygian' which will 'imitate those of a man engaged in peaceful activities, acting of his own will … in accordance with his intelligence, without excessive conceit, but behaving … with restraint and moderation'.[54]

Plato advocates a pedagogical practice that will promote a harmonious balance of the soul for the citizens of his ideal republic. Socrates and Glaucon discuss the importance of a proper education that includes gymnastics and 'mousikē' – not instrumental music, but rather a combination of music with dance or song. The two elements of gymnastics and mousikē must be in harmony to produce a good citizen. As Glaucon observes, 'Those who practise nothing but gymnastics turn out more ferocious than is proper, while those who practice nothing but mousikē become softer than is really good for them'.[55] Drawing upon the qualities of both the Dorian and the Phrygian, Socrates explains that 'the soul that is harmonized is temperate and brave'.[56] The need to educate men upon this principle and for this education to continue through appropriate instructors is linked to the broader preservation of the state. Socrates tells Glaucon, 'In our city, then, Glaucon, we shall constantly need the services of such as instructor, if the constitution is to be preserved', to which he replies, 'Nothing could be needed more urgently'.[57]

The connection between the regulation of the state through law and the regulation of music is made explicit in a later passage when Socrates warns Adeimantus of the danger of innovation in gymnastics and music:

> When someone says that people praise more highly the song that is most newly come to minstrels' lips they should fear that people might easily suppose the poet to mean not just new songs, but a new style of song ... Styles of music are nowhere altered without change in the greatest laws of the city: so Damon says, and I concur.[58]

As is clear in the above quote, Damon, 'the Athenian', informed Plato's discussions of the moral effects of music and its ability to shape social and political structures.[59] In the *Laws*, Plato's last work, the discussion between the Athenian and Megillus demonstrates the strictness with which Plato conceived of the regulation of songs. The Athenian reflects upon the ancient laws which ruled the common people, under which the types and forms of music were strictly controlled.[60] Types of songs included, hymns, lamentations, paeans, the Dionysian dithyramb and the *nomoi*, a word that also meant 'law'.[61] The melody of one type of song was not allowed to be used for another type of song. The Athenian explains that these rules were to be governed by special judges rather than by the shouts and clapping of the people.[62] Later when songs came to be mixed – 'lamentations with hymns and paeans with dithyrambs' – the lawlessness in music led to a rejection of the laws of the state.[63] The mixing of well-known melodies with political lyrics was, of course, a characteristic of songs that functioned politically in the eighteenth century.

Vanessa Agnew explores Platonic continuities in eighteenth-century musical culture in her 2008 monograph, *Enlightenment Orpheus* (2008). Agnew refers to the 'musical traveler' as 'an heir to the Neo-platonist tradition that emphasized music's utilitarian character', or its ability to produce direct effects on the listener such as treating disease and regulating labour.[64] Drawing upon the pervasive myth of Orpheus, Agnew conceptualizes eighteenth-century engagement with neo-platonic thought, as 'Orphic discourse'.[65] The musical voyages she examines include those of Burney, who traveled through the German states conducting research for his histories of music (and whose researches in the Vatican library unearthed the song to Richard); and the state-sponsored voyage of Captain James Cook to the Pacific, which resulted in encounters with Polynesian music. Remembering that the music-making of Orpheus produced powerful effects upon his listeners, Agnew examines 'orphic discourse' in the accounts of travelers as they crossed borders and encountered the music of different nations. Her extraordinary study concludes that neo-platonist ideas of musical utility continued on into the nineteenth century.[66] This argument is a significant break from standard accounts of the rise of what is termed 'autonomous music', or music valued as an art form in its own right, a perspective which has influenced how the song culture of the eighteenth century has been evaluated. Lydia Goehr's influential account of the rise of autonomous music dates a decisive shift in 1800 when instrumental music began to undergo a process of canonization and was no longer dependent upon words, or valued for its utilitarian and ceremonial functions as part of the rituals of court, church and state.[67] While this book does not consider songs in relation to the development of 'autonomous music' more generally, Goehr's arguments and more importantly those of Agnew, are useful for conceptualizing the politics of song in the eighteenth century, specifically in terms of its utilitarian significance and its potential value and role in the state.

An important text that illustrates these dimensions of song is Thomas Gray's 1757 poem 'The Bard', which was quickly established as a canonical work on autonomous aesthetic grounds but which is foregrounded here as a poem about the power of political song. 'The Bard' presents a kind of spatial reversal of Blondel's singing up to Richard in his castle. For it is the bard who stands on high, on a rock watching King Edward I's army descending 'down the steep of Snowdon's shaggy side'. Gray offers a vision of the bard that would become iconic:

> Robed in the sable garb of woe,
> With haggard eyes the Poet stood;
> (Loose his beard, and hoary hair
> Stream'd, like a meteor, to the troubled air)
> And with a Master's hand, and Prophet's fire,
> Struck the deep sorrows of his lyre.[68]

The bard sings a curse, the opening lines of which form the beginning of the poem: 'Ruin seize thee ruthless King!'[69] The source of his sorrow is, as Gray informs the reader in a note introducing the poem, 'A tradition current in Wales, that Edward the First, when he completed the conquest of that country, ordered all the Bards, that fell into his hands, to be put to death'.[70] Roger Lonsdale traces Gray's source for this to Thomas Carte's *General History of England*, published in 1750. According to Carte, Edward ordered the Bards to be hanged because they would put those 'remains of the Antient Britains in mind of the valiant deeds of their ancestors' and had the potential to incite sedition.[71] The figure of the bard as a poet has been extensively investigated by Katie Trumpener, in *Bardic Nationalism* (1997), and Maureen McLane, in *Balladeering, Minstrelsy, and the Making of British Romantic Poetry* (2008), two studies which are concerned with the formation of British Romanticism. In the context of my book however, Gray's bard exemplifies the idea of the song and the 'poet' who sings it as having 'orphic' power to effect change, a subject which has fallen outside the scope of literary history and the parallel historiography of music as an autonomous art form as addressed by Agnew.

A variation on this idea is also expressed by Andrew Fletcher of Saltoun (1653–1716) who made the observation that 'if a man were permitted to make all the ballads, he need not care who should make the laws of a nation', demonstrating the currency of the Platonic belief in the ability of songs to affect the constitution of the state in the eighteenth century.[72] Similarly, Fletcher's fellow

Scotsman, David Herd, prefaced his two volume collection of Scottish songs, published in 1776, with a reflection upon the importance of songs in the political life of the state:

> And trivial as his idea of a song may be, the statesman has often felt this paultry engine affecting the machine of government; and those who are versant in history can produce instances of popular songs and ballads having been rendered subservient to great revolutions both in church and state.[73]

Herd's use of 'subservient' here is in the sense of *serving* the cause of revolutions. The perception of triviality that he identified has, however, continued to occlude a consideration of his emphasis on the political efficacy of songs. Songs defined as 'political' because of their reference to topical details have been dismissed as 'real' literature because of their perceived failure to endure beyond their own context, and readings of literary 'ballads' as political songs have been overshadowed by their status as aesthetic and nostalgically evocative texts. The next section will offer a brief outline of the ballad revival with these issues in mind.

The Ballad Revival – Addison to Wordsworth

The beginning of the eighteenth-century 'ballad revival' is widely taken to be the publication in 1711 of Joseph Addison's three *Spectator* essays on 'Chevy Chase' and 'Two Children in the Wood'.[74] Addison praises the ballads for their simplicity and artlessness, describing the 'old song' of 'Chevy Chase' as 'the favourite ballad of the common People of England' which is 'full of the majestic simplicity which we admire in the greatest of the ancient poets'.[75] Notable here is the way his terminology slips from 'old song' to 'favourite ballad'. Addison supports this 'judgement' with the 'practice and authority of Virgil' comparing several verses of 'Chevy Chase' with verses from Virgil's *Aeneid*.[76] He contrasts the pleasing simplicity of these ballads to the unfavourable productions of 'gothick wit' of writers such as Cowley and those who rely upon epigrams, puns and conceits which are not to the taste of the common people.[77] According to Addison, the enduring popularity of 'Chevy Chase' amongst the common people is an index of its quality:

> for it is impossible that anything should be universally tasted and approved by a Multitude, tho' they are only the Rabble of a Nation, which hath not in it some peculiar Aptness to please and gratifie the Mind of Man.[78]

Addison's references to Homer and Virgil are doubly significant here because they lead to his reading of 'Chevy Chase' as a political song which can be seen as a precursor to 'God Save the King': 'The greatest modern criticks have laid it down as a rule, that an heroic Poem should be founded upon some important precept of morality, adapted to the constitution of the country in which the poet writes'.[79] Echoing the French critic Rene Le Bossu, Addison observes that the purpose of Homer's *Iliad* was to act as a cautionary tale about the dangers of disunity for the group of separate city states that comprised Greece:

> As Greece was a Collection of many Governments, who suffered very much among themselves, and gave the Persian Emperor, who was their common Enemy, many Advantages over them by their mutual Jealousies and Animosities; Homer, in order to establish among them an Union, which was so necessary for their Safety, grounds his Poem upon the Discords of the several Grecian Princes who were engaged in a Confederacy against an asiatick Prince.[80]

Book One of the *Iliad* opens with the rage of Achilles: 'Rage – Goddess, sing the rage of Peleus's son Achilles'.[81] The rage stems from a disagreement with King Agamemnon concerning the spoils of war and the fate of the captured maidens Chryseis and Briseis, which leads to Achilles withdrawing his forces. Addison reads 'Chevy Chase' as providing a similar lesson for the feuding English and Scottish noblemen of the middle ages. The ballad narrates the bloody battle between the Douglas family and the Percys, the last four lines, according to Addison, offering the 'precept' to deter men from 'unnatural contentions':

> God save the King, and bless the Land
> In Plenty, Joy, and Peace;
> And grant henceforth that foul Debate
> 'Twixt Noblemen may cease[82]

Addison's reading of 'Chevy Chase' as a parable on national unity comes following the *Act of Union* in 1707 which created Great Britain through the union of England, Scotland and Wales. The quotation of the phrase 'God save the King' from 'Chevy Chase' is prescient here, given the role of the song 'God Save the King' in the Jacobite rebellion of 1745. Addison's reading of 'Chevy Chase' as a political song is a point which has been neglected, however, as the narrative of the ballad revival has emphasized his elevation of the aesthetic qualities of 'Chevy Chase' and its re-definition as literature.

In this narrative, Addison's framing of 'Chevy Chase' and 'Two Children in the Wood' in the classical tradition of Homer and Virgil marked a turning point in legitimating this literature of the 'common people' and was cited by the 1723 three volume collection of *Old Ballads*, and by Thomas Percy's 1765 *Reliques*. Percy's *Reliques*, and the legitimation of the ballad, in turn influenced William Wordsworth and Samuel Taylor Coleridge's *Lyrical Ballads* of 1798. In his preface to the *Lyrical Ballads*, published in 1800 and 1802, Wordsworth outlined his aim to select 'incidents and situations from common life ... in a selection of the language really used by men'.[83] Wordsworth quoted a stanza from the 'Babes in the Wood', a version of 'Two Children in the Wood', to illustrate 'poetry in which the language closely resembles that of life and nature' and in order to counter Samuel Johnson's criticism of the ballad revival.[84] Johnson had parodied Thomas Percy in the following stanza which implied that interest in the ballad was simply a celebration of the banal: 'I put my hat upon my head,/ And walked into the Strand,/And there I met another man /Whose hat was in his hand'.[85] For Wordsworth, however, Johnson's parody was 'a mode of false criticism' and an unfair basis for comparison.[86] Wordsworth's appropriation and use of Addison in the preface to the *Lyrical Ballads* illustrates how, by 1798, a literary theory of the ballad was increasingly coming to occlude understandings of its political meanings and value.

Definitional and historical questions concerning the categories 'ballad' and 'song' were crucial in the making of Thomas Percy's *Reliques of Ancient English Poetry* (1765). As Nick Groom has documented in great detail, Percy corresponded with a wide range of antiquarians, including William Shenstone, seeking advice on the composition of the text.[87] On 24 April 1761 Shenstone wrote to ask:

> do you make any Distinction betwixt a Ballad, and a Song; and so confine yourself to the Former? With the common people, I believe, a Song becomes a ballad as it grows in years; as they think an old serpent becomes a Dragon, or an old Justice, a Justice of Quorum. For my own part, I who love by means of different words to bundle up distinct Ideas, am apt to consider a Ballad as containing some little story, either real or invented. Perhaps my notion may be too *contracted* –Yet, be this as it will, it may not be of much Importance to consult / Etymology on this occasion, as it will be necessary herein to follow the ordinary opinion of the world, at Last. Again, if you admit what I call Songs, you must previously acquaint me, within what Date you think it best to circumscribe yourself: And this will lay you under difficulties when I come to teize you with Horace's argument – demo unum, demo etiam unum, Dum cadat eluses etc. For what will become of the new 'William and Margarett', 'Leinster fam'd for Maidens fair' and many more of a good stamp, which it will touch you nearly, to omit? Again, what will you determine as to old renowned songs, that perhaps have little or no Merit; and would not have existed to this day, but for the tunes with which they are connected?[88]

Shenstone's Latin quotation is from the Epistle to Augustus in Horace's second book of epistles.[89] The epistle encompasses a discussion on literary value and how it should be determined. In addressing Augustus, Horace observes that the Romans' veneration of him as Emperor is the opposite to the way judgements are formed in relation to other things, including poetry, where an attitude prevails of 'Favouring the old, despising the new, loathing all / That has not completed its time and vanished from earth'.[90] To probe this further, Horace constructs a discussion and poses the question: what constitutes 'old'? If a one hundred year limit is imposed what must happen with those poets who fall short by a month or a year? His imagined interlocutor responds that those poets who fall just short would be included as 'old' and thus considered great. The substance of Horace's response is that such gradual inclusions would eventually lead to the collapse of the argument that the passage of time is the determinant of greatness. C.O. Brink notes that 'Horace regards this as a false problem, since he does not believe that poetic virtue resides in age'.[91]

Shenstone observes that for the common people 'ballads' are determined by the passage of time and the accretion of meanings resulting in exaggerations and a tendency to romanticize the past as grander than the present – where 'an old serpent becomes a Dragon or an old Justice becomes a Justice of Quorum'. This forms a counterpoint to Shenstone's understanding of 'songs' as new or contemporaneous with his own time. As examples he cites the song 'William and Margaret' which was written by David Mallet sometime around 1724 and was, as Mallet informs us, inspired by a common ballad'; and Thomas Tickell's 'Lucy and Colin' which was printed in 1725 and was an imitation of 'William and Margaret' set in Ireland.[92] Shenstone implies that a distinction between ballads and songs based solely upon the passage of time is false or at least not entirely satisfactory, and in this sense he goes beyond Horace by pointing to the difficulties of a taxonomy based upon 'ancientness' in addition to the allocation of intrinsic value to 'ancientness'. Shenstone proposes another means of making the distinction through narrative, but concedes that this also may be unsatisfactory for being 'too contracted' – presumably because new songs such as 'William and Margaret' are also based upon a narrative. Bearing in mind that Shenstone quoted Horace to Percy amidst the rage for 'ancient poetry', fuelled by the publication in 1760 of James MacPherson's *Fragments of Ancient Poetry* and the later Ossian poems, which were eventually revealed to be fakes, his comments can be read as a hint to Percy not to place value upon ballads solely because of their perceived 'ancientness'.[93] He thus verges on teasing Percy by proposing newer songs which fall outside a cut-off date in order to demonstrate the arbitrariness of such a measure through time. Finally, Shenstone raises a further complicating variable through the category of 'old songs' that have endured because of their 'tunes' rather than their intrinsic merit.

That Percy did not entirely ignore Shenstone's advice is reflected in the full title the work: *Reliques of Ancient English Poetry: Consisting of Old Heroic Ballads, Songs, and other pieces of our Earlier Poets, (chiefly of the lyric kind) Together with some few of later Date*; and in the inclusion of both 'William and Margaret' and 'Lucy and Colin' in Volume Three of the *Reliques*, as well as Shenstone's well known song 'Jemmy Dawson' in Volume One.[94] While Percy acknowledged Shenstone in his Preface as well as his other antiquarian correspondents, he failed to acknowledge Cluer Dicey, the largest printer of broadsides and ephemera in Britain at this time. Dicey had given Percy access to his 'old Stock ballads', those ballads that in the seventeenth century had been owned by a syndicate known as the 'ballad partners', which as perennial favourites, could be reprinted time and again and guarantee the partners' financial return on their stock.[95] As Paula McDowell has discussed, this was a significant omission, and one which helped instantiate a hierarchy of Percy's ballads as literary texts more valuable than the songs of the street.[96] In a letter to Shenstone, Percy described Dicey as 'an acquaintance ... of a much lower stamp' but also acknowledged that he was 'the greatest printer of ballads in the Kingdom'.[97] McDowell has shown that Percy's theory of English minstrelsy, articulated in the essay which introduced Volume One of his *Reliques*, valorized a heroic *oral* tradition of minstrelsy as superior to print and the products of the press owned by Dicey, and which made up the Roxburghe and Pepys collections of ballads. Chapter One examines the politics of Percy's approach to ballads and his theory of English minstrelsy through his treatment of Richard the Lionheart. Building on the work of McDowell and Philip Connell, the chapter brings forth new material which demonstrates that Percy's theory of minstrelsy was deeply politicized and interpreted as such by Joseph Ritson through the lens of the Norman Yoke.[98]

The importance of Percy to the narrative of English Literature as it informed Romanticism was once again emphasized by Wordsworth in the 'Essay Supplementary to the Preface' which introduced the two-volume edition of his poems in 1815. Further expounding on the poetic theory outlined in the 'Preface' to *Lyrical Ballads*, Wordsworth gave a 'hasty retrospect of the poetical literature ... for the greater part of the last two Centuries'.[99] He situates the *Reliques* as a work which 'redeemed' the poetry of the country from the unfeeling works of the neo-classical movement typified by Pope. Of Pope's efforts at translating the moon-light scene from the *Iliad* Wordsworth writes that 'a blind man, in the habit of attending accurately to descriptions casually dropped from the lips of those around him, might easily depict these appearances with more truth'.[100] Though James Thomson had come close to achieving feeling through this in his rendering of nature in the *Seasons* poems, for Wordsworth it took Percy's *Reliques* to unlock true poetic feeling and redeem English poetry.[101]

Albert B. Friedman, author of the seminal 1960s study *The Ballad Revival*, examined the influence of Wordsworth's critical reassessment and the broader lineage of the ballad claimed by the Romantic movement. Friedman was the first critic to draw attention to readings of Addison as a proto-romantic as anachronistic, pointing out that the ballad papers were part of a larger essay on true and false wit that extended from numbers fifty-eight to sixty-three of the *Spectator*.[102] Rather than anticipating the break with neo-classicism so celebrated by Wordsworth, Friedman contends that the *Spectator* essays were 'conceived in full support of orthodox neo-classicism'.[103] He further notes that it was by 'an extension of neoclassic tenets' that Addison became the 'momentary champion of popular poetry' rather than through a rejection of them.[104] The classical parallels Addison established between 'Chevy Chase' and Virgil were ridiculed by William Wagstaff and the critic and playwright John Dennis on the basis that he had extended these tenets too far and had mistaken simplicity for vulgarity. This is one example Friedman uses to demonstrate that 'the ballad revival is not altogether emancipated from the dead hands of the romantic critics', or those who read Addison as a precursor to Romanticism.[105] Another example is his criticism of nineteenth-century scholars John Hales and Frederick Furnivall, who printed a version of Percy's infamous old folio manuscript in 1867–8. In their essay on the ballad revival attached to Volume Two, Hales and Furnivall described a poetic wasteland, 'a valley of dry bones' which was regenerated by the *Reliques*, echoing Wordsworth.[106] Friedman makes an important methodological point by complicating the teleological narrative of romanticism that plots a course from the ballad scholarship of Addison to Percy to Wordsworth.

Following Friedman, this book also seeks to complicate this narrative further by extending the category of 'song' to include psalms and hymnody, focusing specifically in Chapter Two on the dominant printed version of the psalms in the eighteenth century, commonly known as 'Sternhold and Hopkins'. The importance of the song form of the psalm in the eighteenth century can also be illustrated in relation to the reception of Addison's ballad papers. John Dennis attacked Addison's ballad essays in a piece entitled 'Of Simplicity in Poetical composition, in Remarks on the 70th Spectator'. His response took the form of a letter addressing Henry Cromwell who had questioned whether Addison had been writing about 'Chevy Chase' in jest or in earnest. The substance of Dennis's argument was that Addison had been writing neither in jest nor in earnest because his premises were nonsensical. Dennis claims that Addison's praise of the similarities between 'Chevy Chase' and Virgil's *Aeneid* was akin to comparing the metrical translation of Psalm 148 present in Thomas Sternhold and John Hopkins's *Whole Book of Psalms* with the hymn in the fifth book of John Milton's *Paradise Lost*:

> Thus we see, that in spight of the pretended resemblance, the old Dogrel is contemptible, and *Virgil is incomparable* and inimitable. One might with a great deal more Justice pretend, that there is a resemblance between the 148th Psalm of *Sternhold,* and that admirable Hymn of *Milton* in the Fifth Book of *Paradise Lost*. And yet we need only transcribe them both, and place them together here, to convince the Reader, that the one is bald, and vile, and wretched, and the other great and exalted Poetry.[107]

Dennis quotes the entire hymn from Milton, and Sternhold and Hopkins's version of Psalm 148, to prove his point that where one is translated doggerel the other is a work of genius, and that though they make use of the same 'figures' there is no more resemblance between them than there is between 'Light and Darkness, heat and Cold, life and death, heaven and earth'.[108]

'Sternhold and Hopkins' became a synonymous term for doggerel and 'bad' poetry from the mid-sixteenth century and a fruitful source for cheap joke chapbooks in the eighteenth century, known as 'Joe Miller's Jests'. Just as the ballad came to be implicated in a new formulation of literary value, and as scholars such as Dianne Dugaw and Steve Newman have pointed out, its reappraisal was crucial in establishing the canon and tenets of literary criticism, so 'Sternhold and Hopkins' also came to be used as a measure of value.[109] Ballads and psalms were linked as part of this process of the construction of the 'literary', yet the psalm has rarely been discussed in ballad scholarship and the literary history of this period more generally. The psalms also have a much more fundamental relationship to the trope of singing to the King, as they were ostensibly written by David, the minstrel King, to be sung to the praise of God the heavenly King. As shown in Chapter Two, the psalms formed an important ritualistic role in the affairs of church and state. Their very ubiquity meant that psalm tunes and texts could be mixed and conscripted into political causes, a process which Plato identified as potentially leading to the breakdown of the law and constitution. This book will argue that the history of the psalm is crucial to an understanding of the politics of song in this period in its 'Orphic' sense and that the psalm is an important context for the song and ballad and vice versa.

Beyond the Ballad Revival

Francis James Child, the nineteenth-century scholar who produced eight volumes of *English and Scottish Ballads* (1857–8), developed a conception of the ballad that would come to dominate scholarship. In the preface to the 1860 edition of this text he referred to two classes of ballads: the *ancient* ballads of England and Scotland, gathered from oral tradition, which his volumes purported to reproduce as the 'true popular ballads'; and the words of the professional ballad-maker, that made up the bulk of garlands and broadsides and belonged to 'artificial literature, – of course to an humble department'.[110] Child considered broadsides, and thus printed ballads, as part of this 'humble department' and did not hide his disdain for the Roxburghe and Pepys broadside collections. In a letter of 25 August 1872 to his mentor, the Danish ballad scholar Sven Grundtvig, Child refers to some of the difficulties of his taxonomy and states his opinion on the majority of broadsides:

> We cannot of course exclude all ballads which have not been taken from the mouths of the people – nor perhaps include all such. The oldest Robin Hood ballads are derived from MS., and very many other of the best and oldest, and on the other hand some ballads written in comparatively recent times, especially historical ones, are

found in the mouths of the people. The immense collections of Broadside ballads, the Roxburghe and Pepys, of which but a small part has been printed, doubtless contain some ballads which we should at once declare to possess the popular character, and yet on the whole they are veritable dung-hills, in which, only after a great deal of sickening grubbing, one finds a very moderate jewel.[111]

In his article 'Ballad Poetry' published in Johnson's *New Universal Cyclopedia* in 1877, Child took great pains to define 'popular' as 'not in the sense of something arising from and suited to the lower orders of a people' but as indicating a class of ballad that existed 'anterior to the appearance of the poetry of art' when the people existed as one and were not divided by 'political organization and book-culture into markedly distinct classes'.[112] Child defines the ballad, therefore, as apolitical, a characteristic evident in his description of the popular ballad as a naturalized expression of 'the people as an individual' rather than an individual man, with the 'fundamental characteristic' being 'the absence of subjectivity and of self-consciousness'.[113]

The notion that ballads were orally transmitted, pre-modern and apolitical, would become the central tenet of Folklore studies as it developed in the late nineteenth and early twentieth centuries.[114] The influential folklorist Cecil Sharp, an avid field collector of ballads tunes 'from the mouths' of people in rural Somerset and the Appalachian Mountains, expounded this view and a theory of transmission that relied upon continuity, variation and selection.[115] Sharp was attracted to the Appalachian people because of their isolation from influences which would corrupt the folksongs. He was thus guided by ideas of rural oral purity which would later be the source of much contention. Though Sharp's work is beyond the scope of this book, it represents one outcome, Child's being another, of hierarchies that were first articulated in the eighteenth century – the value of ancient ballads over 'modern' songs and the superiority of oral transmission over printed broadsides.[116]

A significant amount of scholarship has dismantled the binary opposition between oral transmission and print culture entrenched in these assumptions. Robert Thomson's groundbreaking 1974 PhD thesis found that a large portion of 'stock ballads' owned and printed by a syndicate of ballad partners in the seventeenth century also constituted the English folksong repertoire, demonstrating that oral transmission and printed transmission were interdependent.[117] Similarly, Adam Fox points to the way the three media of speech, script and print infused and interacted with each other in sixteenth and seventeenth century England.[118] Fox cites the ballad of 'Chevy Chase' as an example of this, noting that the song would have been carolled aloud and learned by heart, but that it also circulated in manuscript and was included in the folio manuscript upon which Percy ostensibly based his *Reliques*. The song also appeared in print, as evident in Stationers's Company records over the course of the sixteenth century.[119] In Volume Two of this series, *Literacy and Orality in Eighteenth-Century Irish Song* (2012), Julie Henigan also questions in similar terms the dichotomy between orality and print in the Irish song tradition.

The work of Dianne Dugaw and Paula McDowell has focused upon recovering songs that have been marginalized or all but forgotten in the wake of these hierarchies of value. Dugaw's pioneering *Warrior Women* (1989) recovered a tradition of songs that employed the motif of the warrior woman which she described as the 'broadside hits' for the lower classes which reached the height of their popularity in the eighteenth century[120] In her examination of the output of the Jacobite printer, Francis Clifton (fl. 1716–24), Paula McDowell focused on the topical political ballads that were excluded from eighteenth and nineteenth century ballad collections, particularly Percy's and Child's, broadening our understanding of the diverse cultural roles of balladry.[121] In his discussion of political songs of the 1790s, Michael Scrivener notes the avoidance of any consideration of the genre of political song in the work of Percy and later John Aikin, who produced an anthology and discussion of song genres entitled *Essays on Song Writing* in 1772. Scrivener points out that given Aikin's background as a prominent literary intellectual within middle-class liberal Dissenting circles, this could be no accident and that such an omission points to an aesthetic system that had become 'thoroughly naturalized' with the developing Romantic aesthetic.[122]

Those nineteenth-century collections that *do* focus on the kind of topical political material foregrounded by McDowell and Scrivener emphasize the point that the rise of polite 'literature' led to a diminished understanding of the political nature and complexity of eighteenth-century songs. Thomas Wright in the preface to his *England Under The House of Hanover* (1849) would lament:

> Unfortunately, no one, as far as I have been able to discover, had made any considerable collection of political songs, satires, and other such tracts, published during the last century and the present. This is a circumstance much to be regretted, for it is a class of popular literature which is rapidly perishing, although the time is not yet past when such a collection might be made with considerable success.[123]

Notably, Wright does not use the term 'ballads' in his work, referring only to political 'songs', an indication of how, by the mid-nineteenth century, ballads had been linked with the timeless and the apolitical. William Walker Wilkins answered Wright's call with his 1860 two volume work *Political Ballads of the Seventeenth and Eighteenth Centuries*. Again, Wilkins pointed to the gap that had developed between the study of 'literature' and modern songs:

> Whilst every other department of literature has been thoroughly explored, amplified, and variously illustrated, our modern political songs and ballads – the best illustrations of history – constitute the solitary exception to the general rule'.[124]

Echoing Shenstone, Wilkins identifies 'literature' with ballads, and songs as being contemporary and topical, although he does not exclude the category of the 'political ballad' referring to 'modern political songs and ballads'. The two reasons Wilkins offers for this neglect are the diffuse scattering of such material and that fact that it was lacking in literary merit.[125] For Wilkins, the value of political ballad lay in its connection with the voice of the people and he proposes a suspension of the 'ordinary rules of criticism' in order to judge the value of the songs from a historical perspective. The historian Thomas Macaulay who had drawn upon ballads in his *History of England* was an exemplar of this and Wilkins describes him as 'the only native historian who has thought them worthy of, his particular study and use'.[126]

Moving into the twentieth century, Milton Percival's collection of *Political Ballads Illustrating the Administration of Sir Robert Walpole* (1916) acknowledged that 'the attempt to regard these ballads from a literary point of view is likely to be encountered at the very outset by the incredulous query of whether they are literature'.[127] Percival categorizes political ballads into three groups. The first were ballads written by those of 'considerable literary ability', such as William Pulteney who produced political ballads for the opposition and John, Lord Hervey who wrote for the Walpole's ministry; the second group, referred to as a 'grub street brotherhood' composed by lesser politicians; and the lowest group written for the 'good Christian people that lived round Paul's steeple and which preserve 'the mood and temper of the masses'.[128] Percival situates the political ballad in relation to the newspaper and the pamphlet pointing to their 'journalistic function' during a time when newspapers were too expensive for most people owing to the stamp acts.[129] With the rise of the newspaper, the broadside ballad, according to Percival, experienced a decline as the newspaper took on the role of commenting on topical events. Percival's collection therefore represents the apogee of the view of the politics of song, as consisting in its topical, newsworthy value. This book not only challenges the prevailing view of the politics of song as being defined by topical content or context by conceptualizing a broader, more inclusive, 'Orphic' politics of song; it also challenges Percival's narrative of decline by pointing to the presence of songs in newspapers, an aspect of song textuality which has yet to be significantly explored.

The value of these songs that fell outside of the categories 'literary' or folkloric, began to be recognized by twentieth-century historians who were interested in evidence of working class culture. Charles Harding Firth, known for his published collection of navy songs, read a paper titled 'The Ballad History of the Reigns of Henry VII And Henry VIII' before the Royal Society on 21 November 1907, beginning with the observation that:

> Ballads are useful as a supplement to graver historical authorities, and throw light upon the history of the past which we could not derive from other sources. It is generally not difficult to know what the great men of any day – the nobles, and statesmen, and men of letters – thought about the events which happened in their time. We have their letters, or their speeches, or their biographies; but it is difficult to know what the common people who formed the mass of the nation thought and it is important to know this too.[130]

Since the publication of E. P. Thompson's *The Making of the English Working Class* (1963), which drew upon ballads as evidence in his explication of the growth of working-class consciousness between 1780–1832, and his later collection of essays, *Customs in Common* (1991) which included an essay on 'Rough Music', such material has been part of a broader methodological aim to write 'history from below', drawing upon sources that attempt to shine light on the 'common people', to use Firth's image.[131] Roy Palmer's numerous collections from the 1970s, including his 1974 *A Touch on the Times: Songs of Social Change*, and Martha Vicinus's 1975 *Broadsides of the Industrial North* with its regional focus, are two such examples.[132] Palmer's later anthology *The Sound of History: Songs and Social Comment* (1988) upbraided historians for neglecting 'ballad evidence'.

The idea of certain structures underpinning 'the ballad' has been used as a categorization strategy since the advent of ballad scholarship. The emphasis upon narrative noted by Shenstone developed into the idea of the 'impersonal narrative' as a characteristic of the ballad, emphasized by Child and the later scholar George Kittredge. However much difficulty has emerged with categorization strategies that engage with the idea of the 'popular', and this is evident in both Wilkins and Percival. For Wilkins the popular does not include material written by those close to court. He points to the poems included in the four volume *Collection of State Poems* by 'Buckingham, Rochester, and other exalted personages' as *not* 'exponents' of the 'popular mind'.[133] Wilkins included a lengthy quote from Robert Blakey's 1855 *The History of Political Literature* to support this: 'The popular song is easy, simple, and born of the incidents of the day. It is the intellectual personification of the feelings and opinion of a people'.[134] By contrast, Milton Percival's first category of the political ballad writers included politicians and persons of rank.

Defining the 'popular' in relation to the political is still an ongoing and fraught issue. Peter Burke's *Popular Culture in Early Modern Europe*, first published in 1978 and reissued in 2009, defined popular culture as the culture of 'ordinary people' below the level of the elite and charted the separation between the elites and the lower classes by 1800.[135] Tim Harris, while acknowledging the work of E. P. Thompson and Burke in encouraging scholars to consider the 'humbler ranks', raised the conceptual problem that the term 'popular culture' describes the culture of the non-elite in a way that contributed to a misleading sense of homogeneity. Harris 'problematises' the 'two tier model of cultural conflict' by pointing to instances of *vertical* rather than horizontal, cultural alignment; that is alignments which cut across class and were based on religion, gender or regional identity.[136]

In terms of Romantic literary studies, the turn to the historical contextualization of texts advocated by Marilyn Butler in the early 1980s has led to an increasing interest in the popular and the use of this material in a way that illuminates canonical imaginative literature.[137] In the seminal *Oxford Companion to the Romantic Age* (1999), Iain McCalman describes Romanticism as 'a notoriously slippery concept of modern history' and calls for a 'historical recovery' that enables us to 'recontextualize' and enlarge the canon by 'shifting our angles of vision'.[138] Maureen McLane's *Balladeering, Minstrelsy and the Making of British Romantic Poetry* (2008) provides one such shifting angle of vision. She observes that 'to think of British Romantic poetry' is to inevitably recall Wordsworth, Shelley and Burns and iconic poems such as 'the Tyger' and 'Ode to a Nightingale', but that 'ballads and songs' such as 'Chevy Chase' and 'Barbara Allen' are 'equally constitutive of poetry in the Romantic era'.[139] More recently, the emergence of a discourse of 'the popular' in the Romantic period has been explored in the collection edited by Philip Connell and Nigel Leask, *Romanticism and Popular Culture in Britain and Ireland* (2009). In their introduction, Connell and Leask observe that the English literary canon and 'Romantic theory' is 'historically dependent upon an objectifying distinction between high and low', in order to explain the neglect of popular culture within the category of Romanticism.[140]

As these studies show, the 'angles of vision', to use McCalman's term, have been considerably broadened since Friedman made his criticism of Wordsworth and the nineteenth-century romantic critics. However the role of the 'ballad' as being 'constitutive of the poetry of the Romantic era', to quote McLane, continues to be the dominant narrative. Taking a different approach, this book subsumes the ballad within the category of 'song', and examines issues of canonicity in relation to texts such as the psalms of 'Sternhold and Hopkins', which fall outside the domain of the 'literary'. Those songs that challenge the dominance of the ballad in both studies of popular culture and literary history, by disrupting its definitions and chronology, have been anthologized in collections as 'political songs and ballads' since the nineteenth century, yet they have not been theorized in a way that recognizes their own underlying tradition and structure. This book looks to Plato to provide such a theory; as previously discussed, the politics of song can be defined as that mixing of styles that Plato sought to ban from his ideal republic.

24 *The Politics of Songs in Eighteenth-Century Britain, 1723–1795*

Chapter Outline

My argument begins with the 'Princely Song of Richard Cordelion', which tells the story of how King Richard's fight with a lion led to the appellation of the 'Lionheart'. Chapter One examines the politics of this song in the context of its publication in Volume Three of the *Collection of Old Ballads* (1723–5) a key text of the ballad revival, as discussed. The anonymous editor reads the song as a satire on Richard's sexuality – the King 'not having lived with his Queen in that loving manner which would have become so pious a Prince'.[141] The question of the anonymous editor's identity has remained unanswered. This chapter makes a contribution to a more complete understanding of his political identity by demonstrating the influence of the Whig historian Paul de Rapin-Thoyras upon the editor's interpretation of the 'Princely Song'. It will also be shown that the source for the 'Princely Song' was a sixteenth-century *Garland* collection by Richard Johnson. The cultural politics at play in the transmission of the 'Princely Song' and the role of Richard Johnson is explored in the relation to work of two key figures of ballad scholarship at this time, Thomas Percy and Joseph Ritson. Percy's account of the ancient minstrels as part of an aristocratic courtly tradition, and his co-option of Richard the Lionheart as a 'minstrel king' who facilitated this, was fiercely contested by Ritson, who pointed to a counter-tradition of popular song amongst the vulgar which was represented in print in the collections of men such as Richard Johnson. This chapter brings to the fore the politics embedded in the ballad revival and ends in 1786 when the 'Princely Song' was reprinted in newspapers, revealing its porous capacity as a topical text and a song with a longer political resonance.

Another important minstrel king for men and women of the eighteenth century was King David, thought to have been the author of the body of texts known as the Psalms of David. Chapter Two investigates the role of print and the Stationers' Company monopoly in perpetuating the 'authorized', quasi-legal status of the most widespread translation of the psalms used in the Church of England, the sixteenth-century translation by Thomas Sternhold and John Hopkins, known most commonly as 'Sternhold and Hopkins'. From this ubiquitous text, which was frequently bound to the back of the Book of Common Prayer and family bibles, emerged the psalm tune and text known as the 'Old Hundredth'. 'Sternhold and Hopkins' became implicated, along with the ballad, in the politics of literary value, though the text has not featured in literary histories of the ballad which maintain a secular focus. John Dennis's observations on the questionable literary value of 'Sternhold and Hopkins' are further explored in this chapter along with a number of commentaries surrounding psalmody, including Thomas Warton's call for the removal of 'Sternhold and Hopkins' from the liturgy in his *History of English Poetry* (1774). 'Sternhold and Hopkins' was bound up with complex questions of national identity in the eighteenth century, retaining for Warton associations with the puritan fanaticism of the sixteenth-century, but also functioning to consolidate the song-culture and identity of the Church of England as distinct from those Dissenting sects, including Methodism on the margins of the church, which embraced a more expansive hymnody. 'Sternhold and Hopkins' and the 'Old Hundredth' were deeply embedded into the fabric of everyday life in this period, providing another context in which to frame and understand national song and the emergence of the national anthem, 'God Save the King'. The role of both of these songs in the celebrations of the King's recovery from illness in 1789 is foregrounded as a topical instance of singing to the king in which the unifying power of song functions to overcome a longer and more complex politics outlined in this chapter.

Chapter Three begins with a key image of the psalms, of God putting songs into the people's mouths, in the context of state celebrations of the 1688 Revolution which were staged in 1788. Following the fall of the Bastille, these celebrations took place amidst calls by the 'New Whigs' – to use Edmund Burke's term – for the reform of the electoral system and another attempt by Dissenting groups, in May of that year, to repeal the Test and Corporations Act. Richard Price's speech to the Revolution Society entitled *A Discourse on the Love of Our Country*, delivered on the birthday of William III on 4 November 1789, articulated both of these aims in a *tour de force* of patriotic sentiment. This chapter examines Edmund Burke's response to Price in the *Reflections on the Revolution in France* (1790) and to the reformist agenda of the New Whigs in his *Appeal from the Old to the New Whigs* (1791) through the metaphors of song and sound that he employs. Burke states that Price 'philippizes and chaunts his prophetic song'.[142] Demosthenes had denounced the prophesies of the Delphic oracle for 'philippizing' in favour of Philip of Macedon in his attempts to warn the citizens of Athens of Philip's ambition to conquer Greece. This chapter uncovers a more specific relationship between philippizing and singing by drawing upon the scholarship of Robert Lowth who compared the classical song by Callistratus, known as the 'Harmodium Melos', with a philippic. The 'Harmodium Melos' emerges a potent example of the power of song as a form of political communication in ancient Greece and Rome. The song appeared in *The Learned Banqueters* by Athenaeus (fl. AD 200) and tells the story of the murder of the tyrant Hipparchus by the lovers Harmodius and Aristogeiton. Lowth had emphasized that the song functioned to maintain the civil life of the polity because it ensured that the populace were aware of their liberties, being widely known in Athens and sung at every banquet, in the streets and 'in the meanest assemblies of the common people'.[143] This chapter demonstrates that the 'Harmodium Melos' functioned as an emblematic political song in the eighteenth century in both scholarship and in the context of the club culture of political associations, a point which has not been noted in ballad scholarship. Political songs that were influenced by its iconography continued to have the function that Lowth identified in the context of the Revolution Society and in radical and political culture in 1789.

The final chapter focuses on the politics of song in the crisis decade of the 1790s. The use of political songs as evidence in the treason trials in 1794 draws upon Platonic understandings of the power of music to affect the constitution of the state. Olivia Smith, who charts the challenge to the hegemony of language between 1790 and 1819, regarded material such as the chapbook and the ballad as essentially tangential to forms of political participation such as the petition. She writes that, 'while the audience read chap-books and ballads it was considered to have a distinct and subordinate province. Although such material might express ideas about political events, it was not regarded as an attempt to participate in public life'.[144] However, the treason trials show that this material was indeed seen as having political value and potency.

Chapter Four considers the trope of singing to the King in the context of radical Sheffield culminating in the trial of James Montgomery for seditious libel in 1795 for printing 'A patriotic Song by a Clergyman of Belfast'. The songs of radical Sheffield included Joseph Mather's version of 'God Save Great Thomas Paine', one of many versions that circulated which performed the treasonous overthrow of the monarch and re-imagined a republican political order. In the treason trial of LCS secretary Thomas Hardy, Montgomery was identified as the author of a hymn sung at an anti-war meeting that was held on the day appointed by royal proclamation for a General Fast in support of the war.[145] Montgomery's employer, Joseph Gales, the printer of the local newspaper, the *Sheffield Iris*, was named as the printer of the hymn. Gales, who played a key part in the Sheffield radical movement, absconded to America under the threat of prosecution just prior to the London treason trials, to be eventually joined by his wife Winifred, leaving Montgomery to run the newspaper and printing business with Gales's sisters. Montgomery thus became the scapegoat for Gales and for those Sheffield reformers who together with Hardy had escaped prosecution, when he was found guilty of seditious libel in 1795.

The reference to Belfast in the song for which Montgomery was tried points to the broader network of song connections that this chapter uncovers. This network includes the emergence of 'Ça Ira' in the trial of the Scottish radical Thomas Muir and the response to this by the radical group, the United Irishmen. Chapter Four also traces the circulation of 'A Patriotic Song by a Clergyman of Belfast' from a United Irish songbook, to newspapers in England, and finally to William Pitt's 'green bag' as the basis for a state prosecution. In more recent times the song has appeared in Michael Scrivener's 1992 anthology, *Poetry and Reform*.[146] A series of other poems by its suspected author, Thomas Stott of Dromore, have also appeared in Betty Bennett's *British War Poetry in the Age of Romanticism 1793–1815*.[147] However, the version of this text sold as a 'song' and its role in the prosecution and persecution of Montgomery have remained obscured. In being able to draw these connections, this book owes much to the pioneering efforts of Bennett, who in compiling her collection, conceived of the literary output of the romantic period as encompassing the kind of topical verse so often dismissed as doggerel and for which earlier scholars found themselves apologizing.

The other significant influence on my discussion of the politics of song in the 1790s and in relation to the central trope of the book of singing to the King is John Barrell's *Imagining the King's Death* (2000). Barrell outlined the new interpretation of England's Statute of Treasons (25 Edward III) that was developed in response to the political climate of the 1790s, when for the first time, the 'lower orders' became part of the agitation for parliamentary reform alongside those elite reformers who were more in the mould of 'commonwealth men'. The first clause of the statute provided that high treason was committed 'when a man doth compass or imagine the death of our lord the King'. Barrell demonstrates that a shift occurred in the legal interpretations of the word 'imagine' to allow for 'modern' or 'French' treason. Whereas 'imagine' had traditionally been interpreted in a 'purposive sense' and was related to an action upon the King's body, the modern treasons necessitated that 'imagine' be interpreted more broadly as an attack upon the constitution, which could encompass those who may not have had direct designs on the body of the King but wished to overthrow the body politic.[148] The idea of imagining could also be extended to representations such as songs, playbills, pamphlets, and caricatures, all of which fall within Barrell's extraordinarily dense account. It was in this way that evidence such as the song to the tune of 'Vicar of Bray' could be included in Hardy's trial – as part of the prosecution's attempt to prove the conspiracy not only upon the actual body of the King but upon the political order. This final chapter brings into focus the particular importance of song in relation to the political order, as evident in the experiences of James Montgomery in the context of the 1790s and as part of the broader politics of song that the book maps.

1 THE HEART OF THE LION: THE 'PRINCELY SONG' AND THE TRANSMISSION OF RICHARD

On 27 October 1786 the London newspaper, the *Morning Post and Daily Advertiser*, printed 'A Princely Song of Richard Cordelion, and of his bold Courage and lamentable Death'.[1] The next day this same song, with the exception of two stanzas, was printed in the *Morning Chronicle and London Advertiser*.[2] Over the course of some twenty-two stanzas, taking up more than a column, the song tells the story of King Richard as 'a noble Christian warrior' who sets off on a crusade to free Jerusalem. The King marches forth with his 'noble knights and gentlemen' but his soldiers begin to die for want of victuals. Upon seeking aid from the Duke of Austria, Richard is instead taken ransom. Despite his situation as a prisoner, he kills the Duke's son, 'with one small Box l'th'ear', following an insult, and is subsequently thrown into a 'dungeon deep' to meet his punishment in the jaws of a lion 'all in rage'. However, the daughter of the Duke has fallen in love with Richard and decides to save his life by secretly conveying to him a weapon concealed in her rich embroidered silk scarf. He uses his secret weapon to slay the lion and 'with valiant courage' pulls out its heart. Following this act of valour, 'which made the duke and all his Lords/ In fearful manner start', Richard obtains his freedom and returns to England, having promised the Duke's daughter that he will return to marry her. Upon raising an English army, however, he is diverted 'to pass the seas of Acon walls' and returns to the battles of the crusade.[3] There Richard is slain by a poisoned arrow before he can fulfill the marriage promise. The Duke's daughter becomes bent on seeking revenge for his death and when the murderer is found, she commands that his skin be stripped from bone. Dying broken-hearted, she is buried in the same grave as her beloved. The song ends with the question 'Did ever Princess end her Life/ Thus for her true Love's sake?'

The context for the printing of this song was the performance of the play *Richard Coeur de Lion*, an adaptation of Jean Michel Sedaine's opera by the army officer and playwright John Burgoyne for Drury Lane, and by Leonard McNally for Covent Garden.[4] However, the song was not actually taken from these plays. It had another history of transmission through the ballad and song scholarship of the eighteenth century.

In tracing the transmission of this song as a text printed in newspapers, as part of song collections, and as a broadside, this chapter will explore the politics of the 'Princely Song' through a range of print media and performance contexts. While this historical approach gives rise to a complicated chronology, it is valuable in recovering the politics of the song as it intersects with a long cultural memory and history that continued to resonate in topical contexts such as the operatic performances. The first part of the chapter explores the context of the publication of the 'Princely Song' in the influential three volume *Collection of Old Ballads* (1723–5). The anonymous editor of the *Collection* provided historical commentaries for the 'old ballads' as a framing device for his elite readership, while maintaining a mocking attitude to any literary or antiquarian pretensions. The *Collection* has been situated as an important work in the ballad revival and the editor's ambivalence toward his texts has been read as reflecting the transition of the ballad from a low cultural form to the subject of antiquarian inquiry.[5] Part One adds to this view of the *Collection* by revealing that the editor's commentaries are influenced by the work of Whig historian Paul de Rapin-Thoyras (1661–1725) and that Whig historiography underpins the editor's ambivalence toward the 'Princely Song', which he reads as a satire upon Richard's marriage, implying that the King was a 'sodomite'. The editor thus subverts the 'Dorian' characteristics of the song, remembering that in Platonic theory the Dorian was a song style which imitated the sounds and cadences of the man who is brave in war, in marked contrast to Rapin's veneration of the Saxon King Alfred. The 'Princely Song' was transmitted from the *Collection* to circulate as a broadside from the press of William Dicey, as discussed in Part Two, demonstrating that the song was also accessible in a much cheaper form. Part Three moves back in time to the Jacobean period in order to trace the transmission of the 'Princely Song' from Richard Johnson's (fl. 1592–1622) 1620 text, *The Golden Garland*, to the *Collection*. The song's status as part of Johnson's *Golden Garland* is foregrounded because this text, as well as Johnson's 1612 *Crowne Garland* collection, was the source for all of the historical songs in the third volume of the *Collection*. The approach in ballad history which has focused upon ballads as single text entries in the registers of the Stationers' Company has obscured the importance of the Johnson *Garlands* and by extension, Johnson himself – notwithstanding the difficulties in categorizing Johnson as an 'author' or compiler. Part Four discusses the cultural politics at play in Thomas Percy's transmission of the lionheart story through Shakespeare rather than Richard Johnson in his 'Essay on Ancient Metrical Romances'; and his adoption of the Blondel story as part of his theory of English minstrelsy in the second edition of the *Reliques* published in 1767. Percy's theory was heavily criticized by Joseph Ritson, who argued that Percy had fundamentally confabulated fiction and history in calling French court minstrels 'English minstrels', obscuring the politics of the Norman Yoke and the true nature of English song as a *popular* tradition. Finally, the chapter returns to the context with which it opened, 1786, when the 'Princely Song' was printed in the newspapers as a way of engaging with the topicality of the opera as adapted by the Irishman Leonard MacNally, the recent failed attempt upon the King's life and British foreign relations with France. This chapter argues that this history of the transmission of the 'Princely Song' across the eighteenth century, with roots in the seventeenth century, is valuable as a case study which highlights the porosity and fluidity of songs as they circulate through different print media and become imbued with political meaning. Richard the Lionheart has been completely neglected in ballad studies, with much more attention being devoted to Robin Hood, the outlaw King figure who also emerged during Richard the Lionheart's reign.[6] This chapter addresses this neglect and establishes the trajectory of the book, which moves from the 'Old Whig' political identity of the editor of the *Collection* to the mobilization of radical political songs following the French Revolution.

The Collection

A version of the 'Princely Song of King Richard Cordelion, and of his bold Courage, and lamentable Death' appeared in Volume Three of *A Collection of Old Ballads Corrected from the Best and Most Ancient Copies Extant. With Introductions Historical, Critical, or Humorous. Illustrated with Copper Plates*, printed by 'J. Roberts' in 1725.[7] The previous volumes had been printed in 1723, also by Roberts. By the 1720s, James Roberts was established as a prolific London trade publisher, having inherited the print business of Richard and Abigail Baldwin in 1714, which had been firmly aligned with the Whig interest.[8] Michael Treadwell observes that following the decisive 1714 political victory of the Whigs, the business grew in importance.[9]

The work of Dianne Dugaw and Nick Groom has shown that the significance of the *Collection* was immense because it informed Thomas Percy's later composition of the *Reliques of Ancient English Poetry*, though Percy did not formally acknowledge his use of the text.[10] More recently, William St. Clair has argued that the *Collection* was published in order to secure copyright over its content.[11] A licensing regime had existed in the seventeenth century which enabled a consortium of stationers, who became known as 'the ballad partners', to group together to purchase the copyrights of ballads.[12] St. Clair argues that following the collapse of this licensing regime, and in the transitional period following the introduction of the first copyright law – the 1710 Statute of Ann (8 Ann Cap. 19) – a large number of these ballads were published in the *Collection* for the purpose of re-establishing copyright.[13] In spite of the work of these scholars, however, the identity of the editor of the *Collection* remains in question. This first section of the chapter will examine the complex voice of the editor and his mock antiquarianism in presenting a collection of old songs in the form of a book for an elite audience. His use of the history of Paul de Rapin-Thoyras to frame the 'Princely Song' so that it may be considered valuable as a satire, points to the role of an 'Old Whig' persona in the editor's identity, consistent with the Whig publishing context of Roberts. This dimension of the *Collection* has yet to be noted and is presented here as a contribution to the important question of the editor's identity.

The most distinctive feature of the *Collection* is the voice of the anonymous editor in the prefaces that introduce the three volumes, and in the introduction which frames each song as a historical text to be investigated. The understanding of ballads as songs, rather than literary artifacts, previously highlighted by Albert Friedman, is evident in the editor's interchangeable use of the terms 'ballad' and 'song' throughout his prefaces. In Volume One the editor begins by reflecting upon how his preface is different from conventional prefaces and dedications, where a 'servile' author must 'beg' his readers not to damn his work:

> As for my Part, I have not been accustomed to servile Fawning, and begging the Question; and am fully determin'd not to begin now. I would always put myself upon the Level with a Reader, and think myself under no manner of Obligation: I have his Money, and he has my works; and I am sure he may keep the one in his study, much longer than I shall the other in my Pocket. If there be any beauties in this Book, 'tis certainly his Business to find them out; and if there ben't – why, he can't say I cheated him: I never pretended to give him more than an old Song.[14]

By emphasizing the commercial transaction of a reader exchanging money for the book, the editor can dispense with the convention of apologizing for his work and as Paula McDowell observes, he makes no attempt to hide his own economic motives.[15] By situating himself as an equal – or 'level' – the editor has no 'obligation' to flatter the reader. However, the register of the editor's address is complex and multivalent; while he downplays the literary pretensions of these 'old songs', and shifts responsibility to the reader to find the 'beauties' in the book, the fact that they *are* collected in a book which was 'bound in calf' and sold for three shillings demonstrates that the songs are framed and presented for an elite readership.[16] The editor's shifting, and at times defensive, tone thus reflects his uncertain role as a mediator of these 'old songs'.

In spite of this recognition that 'old songs' may be judged worthless, the editor attempts to point to the value of ballads with evidence that a number of 'poets' were actually ballad-writers. Homer, for example, 'the very prince of poets, if we may trust ancient Records, was nothing more than a blind ballad singer'.[17] Homer's 'ballads' were 'collected' and 'connected' by 'somebody' who 'gave us the Iliad and Odysseys'; gesturing to the editor's own role as a potential canonizer.[18] A genealogy of 'ballad writers' stretching from the ancients to the Restoration is represented in the engraved frontispiece of six busts: Homer, Pindar, Anacreon, Horace, Sir John Suckling and Abraham Cowley. The editor asserts that it would be an 'endless' task to prove that the 'poets' of the frontispiece were 'ballad-writers' and stresses their shared role in the homosocial, convivial culture of the alehouse noting that 'Anacreon would never sit down contented without his Bottle and his Song'.[19]

This classical lineage is bolstered by a comparison between the 'ballad-makers' as a 'more ancient, more numerous, and more noble Society than the boasted Free-Masons'.[20] Noticeable here is the unstable terminology, shifting from 'ballad writers' to 'ballad makers', implying an artisanal crafting of ballads.[21] The term 'ballad-maker' could be employed in a pejorative way to indicate a composer or writer of lower status and ability. Henry Carey (1687–1743), famous for his 1717 ballad 'Sally in the Alley', demonstrates this in the preface to the second volume of his 1728 *Six Songs for Conversation*, a text in which he set existing verse to music.[22] Carey complains that

> part of the generous Reception my former performances met with, open'd the mouth of envy against me, and gave my enemies opportunity to brand me with the title of ballad-maker; which at that time did me no small prejudice among the undiscerning mankind.[23]

Much like the editor of the *Collection*, however, Carey reports that upon further reflection he realized that 'the greatest poets have made ballads' and that the most 'eminent musicians' have set music to them.[24] Carey discusses the meaning of the word 'ballad' as implying a song sung at a ball but as understood to mean 'any song, where two or more verses are sung to the same tune'. Like the editor of the *Collection*, Carey also notes the importance of ballads as aids to conviviality and sociability – if it were not for 'ballad makers', he warns, company would 'grow insipid and dull' as ballads are 'helps to conversation'.[25]

In addition to 'ballad maker', the editor of the *Collection* also employs the term 'song-enditer'. Nathan Bailey's *Universal Etymological Dictionary*, first published in 1721, points to the French derivation of the word: 'To Endite [*enditer*, F.] to compose or write the matter of a letter, &c. See *To indict*'.[26] The relationship between 'enditer' and the specific legal meaning of 'indict' is elaborated in Richard Burn's *The Justice of the Peace and Parish Officer* (1756):

> Indictment cometh of the French word *enditer*, and signifieth in law, an accusation found by an inquest of twelve of more upon their oath. And as the *appeal* is ever the suit of the party, so the indictment is always the suit of the king.[27]

The legal connotations of 'endite' suggest an idea of inscription as fixing a song for posterity, making it part of a textual record, as well as a view of the ballad writer as the amanuensis of history, its 'indicter', not its author. Pindar and Homer were both song-enditers because they recorded heroic events for posterity:

> It was the custom of these *Song-Enditers* thus to transmit to their Children the glorious Actions which happen'd in their days. And I believe it never was used more than amongst the English in Times of old. For we may very reasonably suppose, that one half at least of their works are lost; and we have still one half of whatever is remarkable in History, handed down to us in Ballads.[28]

An example of the ability of ballads to transmit history, and another use of the term 'song enditer', appears on the title page of the *Collection* in a quote drawn from the prologue of Nicholas Rowe's 1714 play *Jane Shore*:

> Let no nice sir despise the hapless Dame,
> Because Recording BALLADS chaunt her Name.
> Those Venerable Ancient Song-Enditers
> Soar'd many a Pitch above our modern Writers.
> With rough Majestick Force they mov'd the heart,
> And Strength and Nature made amends for Art[29]

As Gillian Russell has observed, the play of Jane Shore was a 'hybrid product' of elite and popular traditions in the eighteenth century and had long been transmitted by ballad singers and chapmen.[30] Indeed, 'The lamentation of Jane Shore' appears in Volume One of the *Collection*.[31] In drawing this quotation from Rowe's prologue, the *Collection* once more makes a claim for the value of ballads, but in a way that simultaneously reveals their lowly status: the quote demands that Jane Shore's presence in 'recording ballads' should provide no reason to despise her. Rowe's praise of the song-enditers' ability to move the heart with 'strength' and 'nature' rather than 'art' registers the shift in taste that followed Addison's praise of the simplicity of the old song 'Chevy Chase' against the 'epigrammatical turns and points of wit' of the modern, metaphysical poets.[32]

Addison had confessed to his compulsion to study and admire ballads in his *Spectator* essays, and a particular facet of the antiquarian persona of the editor of the *Collection* that should be foregrounded are his addresses to fellow antiquarian gentlemen readers. At the end of Volume One appears an advertisement for the second volume 'now preparing for the press', promising a great number of songs 'more antique' and upon 'far older subjects'. The advertisement also carries an address to readers asking them to send ballads to James Roberts:

> If any admirer of old Ballads has any scarce ones by him, Copies of which he would have preserved, he is desired to send them directed to Mr. Roberts near the Oxford Arms in Warwick-Lane, and at the same time if he pleases, directions where the songs should be return'd after the compiler of this Collection has taken a copy of them.[33]

In Volume Two, the editor thanks 'those gentlemen who were so kind as to send us what old Ballads they had in their possession'.[34] The editor conscripts these antiquarian 'gentlemen' into the composition of the text, possibly mockingly, as part of what Dianne Dugaw dubs his facetious persona.[35] The question of the sources used in the composition of the *Collection*, and the source of the 'Princely Song', comes into focus in my later discussion on the transmission of Richard Johnson.

The question of the editor's identity has remained unsolved. Mary Segar pointed out that the sale catalogue of the library of literary scholar Dr Richard Farmer, in the possession of antiquarian and collector Francis Douce (1757–1834), referred to the *Collection* as 'Philips Collection of Ballads'.[36] This information was recorded on the copy of the *Collection* owned by Douce, who also noted that Joseph Ritson had recorded a similar statement of Farmer's attribution to Philips on his copy.[37] As a result of this information, William Lowndes's nineteenth century *Bibliographer's Manual* named the editor as Ambrose Philips and the current English Short Title Catalogue also lists Philips.[38] However, Lillian de la Torre Bueno strongly disputed the attribution of Ambrose Philips, with one of her many objections being that Phillips had a reputation for dedicatory servility that was completely at odds with the tone of the editor.[39] Henry Carey had even dubbed him 'Namby Pamby' Philips in recognition of this.[40] Robert Thomson later agreed with Bueno's assessment that Philips was unlikely to be the editor.[41] He pointed to an article in the *Gentleman's Magazine* of January 1823 by Joseph Haslewood, writing under the pseudonym 'Eu. Hood', which suggested that the editor's identity was David Mallet, the Scottish author who had modernized the ballad 'Fair Margaret's Misfortune' into the enormously successful 'William and Margaret', which was included in Volume Three of the *Collection*.[42] Thomson points out that if the editor had been Philips, it is unlikely that he would have included Mallet's version of 'William and Margaret' without an acknowledgment.

While Thomson expressed little hope about the possibility of ever positively identifying the editor of the *Collection*, that does not preclude us from forming a more complete picture of his political identity, which brings us to the editor's introduction to the 'Princely Song' in Volume Three. The editor provides a lengthy history of Richard's reign and then purports to separate fact from fiction and to correct the misleading 'romantick' notions connected with it:

> The Story of the King's Reign to an unprejudic'd reader, must appear very romantick; yet, spite of this, he is cry'd up by the legend Writers for his holy Expedition. Our Poet writ the following song as a Satyr upon those pious Encomiums: and to that end has made his Story much more romantick than it actually was. The point he seems mostly to dwell upon is, the Love of the lady, who saves his Life, which we may plainly see is design'd for the highest Piece of satyr upon that Monarch's Life, he not having lived with his Queen in that loving manner which would have become so pious a Prince, or which so virtuous a Princess as she really was, might have expected. This

I thought necessary to premise, to prevent the petty Cavils of Witlings and Wou'd-be Criticks, who, not capable of examining such a Piece, might judge it by its first outward Appearance, which indeed is but very indifferent. And had the Song really been no better than a first Sight of it would perswade us, yet would I have inserted it, intending these Books not barely for a Collection of Ballads, but for the Instruction of those who have not Leisure or Inclination to search historical Transactions: and who may, I hope, learn as much from these Abridgements, as may give them a tolerable Insight into the history of their Country.[43]

The editor makes a new claim for the song's value by framing it as a satire that calls into question Richard Coeur de Lion's heroism and the narrative of chivalry – the Doric characteristics of the song. In this reading, the central plank of the satire is the 'love of a lady who saves his life' which, according to the editor, is a gross exaggeration and thus a comment upon Richard's conjugal relationship with his wife Queen Berengaria of Navarre – 'he not having lived with his Queen in that loving manner which would have become so pious a Prince, or which so virtuous a Princess, as she really was, might have expected'. In the context of the 'Princely Song' it is the love of Richard that inspires the Duke of Austria's daughter to convey to him a secret weapon which enabled him to save his life in the encounter with the lion. Richard died in battle before he could return to marry her, and despite avenging his death by ordering the grisly execution of his assailant, her grief remained inconsolable:

> Yet ended not this Ladies Grief,
> For him she lov'd so dear,
> Deep Sorrows even broke her heart,
> As plainly did appear
> And both were buried in one Grave
> Thus true love's end you hear,
> That died for our Saviour, &c.
>
> Did ever Lady for her Love,
> More Strangely undertake?
> Did ever Daughter in this kind,
> A grieved Father make?
> Did ever Princess end her Life
> Thus for her true Love's sake?
> And all for our Saviour, &c.[44]

The tune to the song is given as 'You Batchelors' which also potentially lends a significance to the editor's reading. As indicated previously in the quote from Henry Carey, tunes were often shared by numerous songs and sometimes took on different names as a result of a particularly successful broadside.[45] 'You batchelors that brave it' is the first line of the ballad 'The Lamentation of a new-married man, briefly declaring the sorrow and grief that comes by marrying a young wanton wife'. In this ballad a newly married man describes the loss of his freedom to his demanding wife. This ballad appears in the Roxburghe and Pepys collections of ballads from the seventeenth century which have been digitized as part of the English Broadside Ballad Archive at the University of California.[46] The Roxburghe and Pepys versions are sung to the tune of 'where is my true love' which may, therefore, be the same song as 'you batchelors'.[47] The idea attached to the tune, of a reluctant husband, may have informed the editor's reading of the 'Princely Song' as a satire on Richard's marriage.

The question of Richard's sexuality came under much scrutiny in the twentieth century when, in 1948, J. H. Harvey claimed that he was 'breaking the conspiracy of silence surrounding the popular hero Richard' that had supposedly kept him closeted.[48] John Gillingham has dated this as the earliest explicit reference to Richard's sexuality, but notes that 'one or two eighteenth-century authors may have thought Richard was homosexual'.[49] Gillingham points to the work of Laurence Echard who produced the first volume of his *History of England* in 1707 and to the more well-known fifteen volume *History of England* by the Huguenot historian Paul de Rapin-Thoyras, published in England from 1723.[50]

The editor of the *Collection* was familiar with Echard's *History* as he refers to it in his introduction to the 'Doleful death of Queen Jane', printed in Volume Two.[51] Rapin refers to Richard's neglect of his wife and his 'sins against nature' in a passage in Volume Three of his history:

> In fine, if Credit is to be given to what certain Historians say of him, an *unbridled Lust* hurried him on, not only to neglect the Queen his Wife in order to abandon himself to an infamous Debaucher, but even to commit Sins against Nature. It is affirmed, that a poor Hermit took the Freedom to upbraid him with that detestable Crime before his whole Court, and to conjure him, in the Name of God, to reflect on the Destruction of *Sodom*.[52]

The 'detestable crime' which would cause Richard to reflect upon the 'destruction of sodom' was, of course, sodomy. The criminalization of sodomy and the oppression of homosexuality at this period achieved sanction from a misinterpretation of the Bible, where the 'sin' of sodomy was seen as the cause of God's destruction of the cities of Sodom and Gomorrah in the book of Genesis.[53] The inability to even enunciate the word 'sodomy', as evident in Rapin's passage, was also reflected in legal discourse. In his *Commentaries* on English law, William Blackstone (1723–80), the judge and legal authority, refers to 'the infamous crime against nature' which is 'a crime not fit to be named', noting that as a capital offence, it reflected the law of God and the 'destruction of two cities by fire from heaven'.[54] While modern historians have queried Rapin's interpretation, for my purposes Rapin's history forms an important context for the *Collection* and the framing of the 'Princely Song'.[55]

Not only was Rapin's history deeply inflected with the politics of his own age, but his own personal experiences placed him at the front, quite literally, of the English Revolution of 1688. Hugh Trevor-Roper has recounted that following the revocation of the Edict of Nantes in France in 1685, which rescinded Protestant rights, Rapin sought refuge in England. This proved difficult, as England was then under the rule of the openly Catholic James II. Attempts to convert Rapin saw him leave the country for the safety of the Protestant Netherlands, where he became an officer in William of Orange's army.[56] Rapin was part of William's forces that landed at Torbay in the revolution of 1688 that saw James II and his heir banished and the perceived threat of Catholic tyranny quashed. Consequently, the history that Rapin produced was deeply influenced by this Whiggish context, Roper describing it as the 'first systematic "Whig interpretation"' of England's history, and one that became a standardized authority until it was surpassed by David Hume's (1711–76) *History of England*, the first volume of which was published in 1754.[57]

Rapin's narrative stressed the central tenet of Whig thought: that the Anglo-Saxons had brought with them a mixed system of government and the model of a parliamentary system.[58] As outlined by Christopher Hill in his seminal account of the theory of the Norman Yoke, this idea, however inaccurate, had enormous historical significance.[59] The narrative of the Norman Yoke proposed that when the Anglo-Saxons were conquered by the Normans under King William in 1066, the people lost their liberties and government.[60] Though some concessions were granted under Norman rule, such as the Magna Carta, Hill explains that 'the tradition of lost Anglo-Saxon freedom was a stimulus to ever more insistent demands upon the successors of the Norman usurpers'.[61] This narrative is clearly at work in Rapin's history with his idealization of the Anglo-Saxon form of government. Roper notes that 'the English constitution that was vindicated in 1688 was, according to Rapin, the identical constitution which the Anglo-Saxons had brought with them from Germany'.[62]

Unsurprisingly then, Rapin's treatment of Richard, a Norman King who ruled from 1189–99, was in stark contrast to the treatment of the Anglo-Saxon King Alfred (AD 848/9–99). Simon Keynes has pointed out that Rapin's *History* helped to foster the cult of King Alfred in the early eighteenth century with Rapin referring to Alfred as 'Alfred the Great' and idealizing him as 'a just, learned, and religious Prince, a Lover of his subjects and an indefatigable promoter of arts, sciences, justice and religion'.[63] Moreover Alfred used his power 'for the good and benefit of his subjects', unlike Richard, who levied heavy taxes in order to pursue his crusades.[64] Rapin makes it clear that Alfred's revenue came from his hereditary estate, noting 'it was not customary, in those days, for princes to levy taxes upon the people, in order to squander money in luxury and extravagancies'.[65] The editor of the *Collection* describes Alfred in strikingly similar terms to Rapin in the introduction to the song 'King Alfred and the Shepherd', which appears in Volume One. He observes that Alfred

> was a just, wise, and pious prince, of a very liberal Education; endowments uncommon in those early days: and besides the arts of war and government, he understood several of the sciences; and, amongst other, music and poetry to a perfection.[66]

Alfred presented an idealized model of Kingship which was mobilized by the Whig 'patriots' in opposition to the administration of Prime Minister Robert Walpole and the 'court Whigs' of George I. Walpole had come to power in 1721 and was to maintain an oligarchical grip on government until 1742.[67] J. G. A. Pocock has written of the complex 'varieties of Whiggism' during the eighteenth century, which included the distinctions between Whigs such as Walpole and those 'old Whigs' who opposed him by defining themselves as part of an older tradition and employing the adjectives 'patriot', 'true' or 'real' Whigs.[68] Walpole's power was consolidated and concentrated thanks to measures such as the Septennial Act of 1716, which lengthened the terms of parliament to seven years, a measure at odds with the Anglo-Saxon ideal of annual parliaments and the 'Commonwealthman tradition' of the seventeenth century which stressed the need for more frequent parliaments.[69] Such distinctions would also come into play later in the century in Burke's appeal to the 'old Whigs', discussed in Chapter Three. Frederick, Prince of Wales, became an important figure and patron of the opposition 'patriot' Whigs, including the writers James Thomson and Richard Glover who wrote the political ballad 'Admiral Hosier's Ghost'.[70] By 1737 the Prince of Wales was in open hostility against his father and the government and, as Christine Gerrard has shown, the identification of Frederick as King Alfred which had begun in poetry of the 1720s and continued in the 1730s, reached its height in 1740 when James Thomson and David Mallet produced their masque *Alfred* for the Prince, from which the song 'Rule Britannia' emerged.[71] As with 'God Save the King', discussed in the next chapter, 'Rule Britannia' achieved a status akin to a national anthem in the eighteenth century, and Mallet's involvement in *Alfred* lends support to Thompson and Hood's suggestion that he was the editor of the *Collection*. The composite identity of King Alfred and Prince Frederick further demonstrates the potency and politicization of Rapin's history at this time.

David Hume took a very dim view of Rapin's 'Old Whig' partiality and styled his own history against this as impartial and more disinterested. Writing to James Oswald in a letter dated 28 June 1753, he observed:

> The more I advance in my undertaking, the more am I convinced that the History of England has never yet been written, not only for style, which is notorious to all the world, but also more matter; such is the ignorance and partiality of all our historians. Rapin, whom I had an esteem for, is totally despicable. I may be liable to the reproach of ignorance, but I am certain of escaping that of partiality.[72]

In the volume where Hume dealt with Richard the First he reached similar conclusions to Rapin about the failure of Richard's rule. Hume contended that Richard was a profligate monarch who had squandered his finances and government in pursuing the crusades not for religious motives, but for military prowess:

> the King, impelled more by the love of military glory than by superstition, acted, from the beginning of his reign, as if the sole purpose of his government had been the relief of the holy land, and the recovery of Jerusalem from the Saracens.[73]

While acknowledging that Richard's reign was 'very oppressive and somewhat arbitrary, by the high taxes which he levied' Hume nonetheless observed that Richard acquired 'the appeallation of the lion-hearted, "*coeur de lion*" because of his military talents and that 'no man even in that romantic age, carried personal courage and intrepidity to a greater height'.[74] Hume's characterization of the Lionheart acknowledges the narrative of his heroism, in contrast to Rapin's history which is used by the editor of the *Collection* to deconstruct this narrative in his framing of the 'Princely Song' as a satire on Richard's sexuality and a subversion of the Dorian tradition.

The use of Rapin's history to frame the 'Princely Song' and 'King Alfred and the Shepherd' highlights the importance of the 'Old Whig' identity adopted by the editor. This context has not been recognized because the *Collection* has primarily been foregrounded as an important text in literary historiography as a precursor to Thomas Percy's 1765 *Reliques of Ancient English Poetry*, which presents a more serious 'antiquarian' and high-cultural engagement with the ballad. The *Collection*, however, is an important text in its own right because of its politicization of songs as 'history'. In the case of the 'Princely Song', the editor established a new value for the song as a satire for a readership who could afford to purchase the three shilling calf-skin bound volume. Despite this, the 'Princely Song' also continued to have an important history as a popular broadsheet which followed its publication in the *Collection*.

The Single Sheet

The song is also one of the many 'old ballads' listed in the 1754 trade catalogue of William and Cluer Dicey, which also lists holdings of maps, prints, copy-books, drawing-books, histories, old ballads, broad sheet and other patters, and garlands that were printed and sold at their warehouse 'opposite the South Door of Bow-Church in Bow Church-Yard, London'.[75] The catalogue lists the ballad titles alphabetically and the 'Princely Song', from Volume Three of the *Collection*, appears as 'King Richard, Sir-nam'd Coeurdelion' amidst several other ballads about Kings. The broadside carries the imprint of 'William Dicey Northampton' in the Madden Collection, housed at the University of Cambridge.[76]

We know that Dicey drew his broadside from the *Collection* because the song is framed by using passages of the editor's commentary. For example, the broadside of the 'Princely Song' carries the following note to the readers:

> Note, As the Use of these old Songs is very great, in respect that many children never would have learn't to Read had they not took a delight in poring over Jane Shore or Robin Hood, &c. which has insensibly stole into them a curiosity and desire of reading other the like Stories, till they have improved themselves more in a short time than perhaps they would have done in some years at school: in order still to be useful, I promist to affix an Introduction, in which I shall point out what is Fact and what is Fiction in each Song; which will (as may be readily suppos'd) give not only Children, but Persons of more ripe years, an insight into the reality, intent, and design, as well as many times the Author and Time when such Song was made, which has not hitherto been explain'd.

The observation that 'several fine Historians are indebted to Historical ballads for all their learning', which appears in the equivalent passage in the *Collection*, has been excised in Dicey's broadsheet version of the 'Princely Song' and the sarcasm of the editor is replaced by the sincere purpose of supplying 'not only children, but persons of more ripe years' with a correct historical context.

Dianne Dugaw has also noted that Dicey drew broadsheets from the *Collection*, and that this same passage, which she describes as 'unironic' and 'deadpan', was used for a broadsheet version of the ballad 'Chevy Chase', drawn from Volume One of the *Collection*.[77] Her argument is that this was part of a marketing strategy of the Diceys, designed to present ballads as antique for a popular audience, because both Dicey and later Percy 'transformed ironic and playful comments into earnest commentary'.[78] Dugaw points to the revision of the headnote accompanying the broadside ballad 'Maudlin, the Merchant's daughter of Bristol', which had appeared in Volume Three of the *Collection*, as further evidence of this, contending that the changed headnote of the broadside 'implies an unmistakably more wholehearted acceptance of the historicity and value of the ballad than what we find in the facetious remarks of *A Collection of Old Ballads*'.[79]

In Dicey's version of 'A Princely Song of King Richard', however, which is not considered by Dugaw, there is no change in the song's commentary and it is presented as a satire in exactly the same way as it is in the *Collection*. The historical introduction outlining the history of Richard Coeur de Lion which appears next to the picture is reproduced verbatim from the *Collection*, including the satirical framing of the song. This ballad does not entirely fit Dugaw's schema, therefore, and suggests that the concerns of the editor of the *Collection* and of Dicey in reprinting the ballad verbatim, were the same.

The Dicey family played a key role in the eighteenth-century ballad trade. Dicey, together with his partner Robert Raikes, established the newspaper the *Northampton Mercury*, together with a printing business at Northampton in

1720.[80] The two partners went their separate ways in 1725 when William Dicey became the sole proprietor of the Northampton press and all imprints from this point at Northampton carried solely his name until his death in 1756.[81] The year 1725 was also when the third volume of the *Collection* was printed, the source for Dicey's version of the song. Despite the listing of the song amongst the 'old ballads' in the trade catalogue of 1754, it is impossible to pinpoint a specific time-frame for the printing of the Dicey broadsheet version because the imprint carries no date and it could have conceivably been issued many times between the printing of the *Collection* in 1725 and 1754. William Dicey maintained this Northampton press until his death, in addition to assuming control of a printing press and warehouse in Bow Street London, which came to be managed by his son Cluer.[82]

The sphere of Dicey's influence was considerable and continued to grow throughout the eighteenth century thanks to his innovative distribution strategy and his willingness to diversify his trade. In a publication marking the bi-centenary of the *Northampton Mercury* in 1920, Sir Ryland Adkins points to Dicey's canny use of 'travelling agents' and quack medicine to ensure that the business was not solely dependent upon the delivery of newspapers:

> So 'the men that carry the news' tramped from village to village, delivering the paper at hall and grange and rectory. How could that be a 'business proposition?' By itself it was not. The men that carried the news also carried pill and other quack medicines. Chap-books were quickly added, the crime broadsides came not infrequently and, as the printers became booksellers and stationers, there was plenty of work for the travelling agents.[83]

Robert Thomson added much detail to this sketch by pointing out that the 'travelling agents' were actually chapmen.[84] It was customary for printers to sell quantities of ballads and chapbooks to chapmen who would travel around the country selling these and other items. Instead of selling ballads and chapbooks to chapmen, however, Dicey and Raikes employed them as distributors of their newspaper the *Northampton Mercury*. In addition to their distribution duties, the chapmen were also employed to collect news and advertisements and were given ballads and chapbooks to sell to people who could not afford the newspaper.[85] Dicey and Raikes thus capitalized upon the mobility of the chapmen and their extensive routes in the country-side to distribute a range of printed goods which appealed to different sections of the market. Under this arrangement, instead of pocketing their takings, the chapmen would have given them to their employers, Dicey and Raikes.[86] It is conceivable then, that the 'Princely Song' formed part of a chapman's pack which was sold alongside *Northampton Mercury* and 'Bates Pectoral Drops' – the medicine which Dicey held an interest in.

The song would eventually find its way from travelling alongside the newspaper to inside the newspaper, as the beginning of this chapter has shown. Though the early twentieth century ballad scholar, Milton Percival has noted that in the eighteenth century, 'as the newspaper grew and strengthened, the ballad withered and decayed', the case of the 'Princely Song' suggests a different process, of absorption and redefinition as part of the newspaper, rather than eclipse.[87]

The Garlands

What was the source for the 'Princely Song' as reproduced in Volume Three of the *Collection* and by Dicey? Its reproduction points to the use of a seventeenth century song collection by Richard Johnson (*fl.* 1592–1622) entitled *The Golden Garland of Princely pleasures and delicate Delights Wherein is contained the Histories of many of the Kings, Queenes Princes, Lords, Ladies, Knights and Gentlewomen of this Kingdom.*[88] The earliest surviving copy of this garland is dated 1620, though the imprint states that this is the third time imprinted. The 'Princely Song' to the tune of 'You Batchelors that Brave it' is the third song in Part One of the *Golden Garland* which contains a total of seventeen songs on historical subjects. Of these seventeen songs eleven are reprinted in the *Collection*. Three of these eleven songs appear in Volume Two of the *Collection*, and the remaining songs, including the 'Princely Song', appear in Volume Three.[89] While it is possible that this song text was sent to 'Mr. Roberts', as requested in the advertisement, it is perhaps more likely that the call for ballads was part of the collegial antiquarian persona constructed by the editor/compiler as a kind of marketing device. Richard Johnson's seventeenth-century texts therefore present evidence of a different type of transmission, though this is disguised when the editor of the *Collection* reprints individual songs such as 'The Princely Song' as if they were sent to him by one of the many correspondent collectors.

Further evidence of this can be found in the liberal borrowing from an earlier collection of songs by Richard Johnson printed in 1612, entitled *A Crowne Garland of Goulden Roses. Gathered out of Englands royall garden. Being the lives and strange fortunes of many great personages of this Land*, and a reprint of this text from 1659.[90] As the title suggests, the first half is comprised of songs about royal figures with miscellaneous songs comprising the second part. The editor of the *Collection* also borrowed heavily from the *Crowne Garland*, using seven of the first ten historical songs across the three volumes of the *Collection*.[91] One of these songs, 'The Life and death of famous Thomas Stukely, an English gallant in the time of Queene Elizabeth, who ended his days in a battaile of Kings in Barbarie' was issued as a broadside numerous times across the seventeenth and early eighteenth centuries, though there is no record of this song recorded as a separate entry in the Stationers' Company registers.[92] So while it is possible that this broadside version found its way to the editor of the *Collection*, the inclusion of the other songs points to his use of the *Crowne Garland* as the primary source. The idea that the *Collection* was composed of old ballads that had resurfaced through the work of diligent correspondents was perhaps more 'romantic' than the idea that much of the editor's 'reserved material' of historical ballads was drawn from *The Golden Garland*, and *The Crowne Garland*.

In Volume Three of the *Collection*, seventeen of the first nineteen songs can be traced to the Johnson *Garlands*.[93]

Table 1.1: Historical Songs from Volume Three of A Collection of Old Ballads (1725)

Historical Songs from Volume Three of *A Collection of Old Ballads* (1725)	Golden Garland, 1620	Crowne Garland, 1612	Crowne Garland, 1659 ed.
I. A Song of the strange Lives of two young Princes in England, who became two Shepherds on Salisbury Plain, and were afterwards restored to their former Estates.	X		
II. A Princely Song of King Richard Cordelion, and of his bold Courage, and lamentable Death.	X		
III. A Song of the Deposing of King Richard II. and how after many Miseries, he was murder'd in Pomfret Castle.	X		
IV. A Song of the Wooing of Queen Catherine, by Owen Tudor, a young Gentleman of Wales. Translated out of the Welsh.	X		
V. The Life and Death of the Great Duke of Buckingham, who came to an untimely End, for consenting to the deposing of the two gallant young Princes, King Edward the Fourth's Children.		X	
VI. A Song of the Life and Death of King Richard the Third, who, after many Murthers by him committed upon the Princes and Nobles of this Land, was slain at the Battel of Bosworth in Leicestershire, by Henry the Seventh, King of England.	X		
VII. The Story of Ill-May-Day, in the Time of King Henry the Eighth, and why it was so called; and how Queen Katherine begged the Lives of Two thousand London Apprentices.			X
VIII. A Song of an English Knight, that married the Royal Princess, Lady Mary, Sister to King Henry the Eighth, which Knight was afterward made Duke of Suffolk.	X		
IX. A Princely Song of the Six Queens that were married to Henry the Eighth, King of England.			X
X. A lamentable Ditty on the Death of Lord Guilford Dudley, and the Lady Jane Grey, that for their Parents Ambition, in seeking to make these two young Princes King and Queen of England, were both beheaded in the Tower of London.	X		
XI. The lamentable Complaint of Queen Mary for the unkind Departure of King Philip, in whose Absence she fell sick and died.			X
XII. The most rare and excellent History of the Dutchess of Suffolk's Calamity.			X
XIII. A joyful Song of the deserved Praises of good Queen Elizabeth, how Princely she behaved herself at Tilbury Camp in Essex, in Eighty-eight, when the Spaniards threatened the Invasion of this Kingdom.	X		
XIV. A lamentable Ditty on the Death of Robert Devereux, Earl of Essex, who was beheaded in the Tower of London on Ash-Wednesday, 1600/1.*			
XV. A lamentable Ballad on the Earl of Essex's Death.*			
XVII. The Life and Death of Queen ELIZABETH.†		X	

Historical Songs from Volume Three of *A Collection of Old Ballads* (1725)	Songs of Richard Johnson		
	Golden Garland, 1620	Crowne Garland, 1612	Crowne Garland, 1659 ed.
A short and sweet Sonnet made by one of the Maids of Honour, upon the death of Q. Elizabeth, which she sewed upon a Sampler of Red Silk.‡		X	
XVIII. An excellent Song made of the Successors of King Edward the IVth.			X
XVIII. A Servant's Sorrow for the Loss of his late Royal Mistress Queen Anne, who deceas'd at Hampton - Court the 2d of May, 1618.§			X

* The three fields in this row have been deliberately left blank to indicate that this song from the *Collection* is not present in any of the *Garland* editions.
† The numeral 'XVI' does not appear in the text – the numbering jumps straight from 'XV' to 'XVII'.
‡ 'A short and sweet Sonnet...' is unnumbered within the *Collection*.
§ The numeral 'XVIII' appears twice; the two different titles, however, refer to entirely separate songs.

This forms the entire portion of the volume devoted to historical songs. The reprinting of 'The Princely Song' and the songs from the Johnson *Garlands* in *The Collection* thus presents the transmission of songs from one collection into another collection in *addition* to the republication of songs which circulated as broadsheets, which were represented as individual title entries in the Stationers' Company registers. From the early eighteenth century, therefore, transmission was not simply a matter of single sheets being collected as books but of collections recycling and reconfiguring previous collections. This has perhaps been overlooked because the most important work on the process of ballad transmission has tracked the progress of ballads as individual entries in the registers of the Stationers' Company. Robert Thomson's seminal study, for example, draws upon the entries of the ballad partners in the Stationers' Registers during the seventeenth century, highlighting three significant entries in the Registers when the partners entered a large number of ballads: 1 June 1629, 13 March 1656 and 1 March 1675.[94] Thomson found that the various 'folksongs' listed in these entries demonstrated that the idea of 'folksong' as reliant upon oral transmission within non-literate rural communities could not be sustained and that the print tradition played an important role in its transmission.[95] The registers showed that the 'oral' tradition coexisted and was undoubtedly influenced by a printed tradition that had its origins in the trade relationship developed by the ballad partners.[96] Tessa Watt employed a similar methodology to Thomson in her use of the Stationers' Company registers to trace the continuity of 'godly songs' during the period 1550–1640.[97] Watt determined the percentage of religious ballads as a figure of the total number of ballad entries in the register by looking at the title of each entry.[98]

Richard Johnson is best known for *The Seven Champions of Christendom*, a prose romance about the deeds of St George which was printed in two parts in 1596 and 1597.[99] As Naomi Liebler notes, the text was reprinted five times during the period 1596–1639 with eleven more printings between 1639 and 1696, and had an almost continual record of print in abridged and bowdlerized forms until the 1930s.[100] Given the extraordinary continuity of this print history, Jennifer Fellows observes that *The Seven Champions* has the potential to 'further our understanding of the popular culture of over three centuries' but it has been much neglected by literary history.[101]

Very little is known of Johnson's life – his baptismal certificate is dated 24 May 1573 and he is thought to have died in 1659.[102] Yet Liebler points to Johnson's ability to combine existing stories into texts to form a bricolage as a reflection of the times and genres in which he worked:

> While no great case should be made for Johnson as an original thinker or stylistic innovator, it is important to remember that the genres in which he worked were those that specifically relied upon the familiar, even the repetitive, for their enormous appeal and popularity ... Formula, cliché, homage and reiteration were the tools of every popular writer's trade, including Shakespeare's, and including as well that of ecclesiastical writers; these forms work together, happily sharing space on any reader's bookshelves, aligned during the Elizabethan period with other immensely popular forms of middle-class reading material, such as broadsides and ballads.[103]

Scholars have been cautious concerning Johnson's authorship of texts, however, because of identified instances of plagiarism.[104]

This issue relating to Johnson's authorship is made even more complex by the printing history of the two garland collections. The *Crowne Garland* was entered into the Stationers' Register on 18 February 1612 for John Wrighte, who would later become one of the ballad partners.[105] Later editions were published in 1631, 1659 and 1692. Part Two of these later editions, starting from the 1631 edition, came to include songs which had been printed in earlier collections and which circulated as broadsides. In his introduction to the reprinted edition of the *Crowne Garland*, which the Percy Society published in 1842, William Chappell notes that the song 'A most rare and excellent History of the Dutchess of Suffolks Calamity', was from Thomas Deloney's 1607 *Strange Histories*.[106] Given this information, we can tell that the earliest edition of the *Crowne Garland* used by the editor of the *Collection* was the 1631 edition, because these later songs are also included.

The 'Princely Song', fits closely with Johnson's *Seven Champions*, as a celebration of chivalric might. Like St George, the central protagonist of the *Seven Champions*, Richard is celebrated for his prowess as a soldier – to the extent that he comes to be folded into the St George mythos in a ballad called 'Saint George's Commendation', which was published as a broadside in 1612.[107] This broadside was printed many times over the course of the seventeenth and eighteenth centuries and found its way into the Pepys and Roxburghe collections as well as Volume One of the *Collection*.[108] It was also issued under the title of 'St

George and the Dragon' and was entered into the Stationers' Register in 1657 and again in 1675.[109] 'Saint George's Commendation' is actually less about Saint George and more a cataloguing of other heroes, to whom the reader is invited to make a comparison. It begins by instructing the reader to read 'old histories' to learn of Saint George's feats before boasting of the knights that followed him:

> Why doe you boast of Arthur and his Knights,
> Knowing how many men have endured fightes,
> Besides King Arthur, and Lancelot du Lake,
> Sir Tristan de Lionel, that fought for Ladyes sake:
> Read old Histories, and then thou shalt see,
> Saint George, Saint George the Dragon made to flee;
> S. George for England, S. Dennis is for France,
> Sing Hony soit qui mal y panse[110]

The chorus of the ballad returns to Saint George's central act of heroism, the slaying of the dragon, at the end of each stanza and also includes the phrase 'Hony soit qui mal y panse', (shame of him who thinks this evil) which became the motto of the Order of the Garter and surrounded the royal coat of arms. Stanza ten of the 1612 ballad, reprinted by Rollins from the Pepys collection, deals with the exploits of Richard the First and gives a summary of the narrative heart of *Richard Cordelion*:

> *Richard* the first, King of this Land,
> He gored the Lion with his naked hand:
> The Duke of *Austria* nothing did he feare,
> He killed his sonne with a boxe on the eare:
> Besides, his famous actes done in the Holy land.
> S. George, saint George the Dragon did withstand;
> St. George for England, &c. [111]

Notably, in this stanza Richard gores the Lion with his bare hands whereas the 'Princely Song' involves the subplot of the daughter of the Duke of Austria who secretly conveys to Richard an instrument that will save his life. In the 'Princely Song' Richard pulls out the lion's heart *after* he has thrust the knife into the lion's throat, the display of the heart making 'the Duke and all his Lords,/ in fearful manner start,/To see this Royal *English* King/To play so brave a Part'. In a way, Richard is *playing* the part of hero as it is through this action that he is able to claim his freedom through the 'Law of Arms' – trial by ordeal. This plot device functions to bind him to the Duke's daughter, which is the point of incongruity that informs the satirical reading of the song offered in the *Collection* and in William Dicey's broadsheet version.

'Saint George's Commendation' appears in Volume One of the *Collection* as 'St. George and the Dragon' and contains some variations from the Pepys edition. Most notably, the stanza devoted to Richard is excised. In his introduction to 'St. George and the Dragon' the editor reaches the limits of his ability to draw upon history:

> I should think my Collection very imperfect, was this old Panegyrick upon our English saint and Patron to be omitted. His adventures were many and various, and even those variously related. Where-ever any Historical Circumstances are omitted, or thro' Length of Time, and the Error of Writers, are misrepresented; I shall endeavor to set them in the fairest Point of Light I possibly can. But in the Case of Saints, we must have recourse to Legends; those, I must confess, are something out of my way.[112]

It is fitting then that the editor uses the next song, 'The Seven Champions of Christendom', which as indicated previously was closely associated with Richard Johnson, to provide further historical details surrounding St George.

> In my former Argument, I refused to give the History, or rather the fable of St. George; but lest any of my readers should be unacquainted with it, I have inserted the following Ballad; where they'll not only find his History but that of the other six Champions of Christendom with it; and the Account is, I believe; as authentic as any we have extant. The only Thing I have to object to the Poet here, is his Partiality; for he has bestow'd Half the Song upon our English hero, whilst the other six have but one Half between them all.[113]

While they remain unacknowledged, the texts of Richard Johnson inform the editor's disquiet over the difficult relationship between ballads and history. In turning now to histories *of* the ballad, both Richard Coeur de Lion and Richard Johnson continue to feature in the politics of transmission.

From Richard to Minstrelsy

In the third volume of his *Reliques of Ancient English Poetry*, first published in 1765, Thomas Percy also printed the ballad of 'St George's Commendation' from the Pepys collection, though under the title 'St George For England'. Percy interprets the Ballad as a 'burlesque' on the style of old ballads; 'particularly of the rambling transitions and wild accumulation of unconnected parts'.[114] Unlike the version in the *Collection*, Percy's version *does* include the stanza concerning Richard I. However the 'Princely Song' does not appear in any of the three volumes or editions of the *Reliques*. Percy's *Reliques* transmit Richard in a different way – through his theory of national minstrelsy, representing a different kind of politics.

As previously indicated, the influence of the *Collection* on Percy's *Reliques* has been well established in the scholarship of Groom, Dugaw and McDowell; in addition to the old 'folio manuscript' which Percy had found, this was a key, yet unacknowledged, source.[115] Not only did Percy reproduce many of the individual songs contained in the *Collection*, but he also adopted the style of producing the historical annotations and introductions to the ballads. As Cleanth

Brooks notes, Percy depended most heavily upon Richard Farmer when he was compiling the *Reliques* and Farmer lent Percy many books.[116] Percy wrote to Farmer on 9 October 1763:

> In my petty researches I have pickt up an illustration of a passage in Shakespear, which whether it is new or not you must inform me for I have not one annotator at hand. 'Tis in *King John*, Act 1. In the Bastard's speech are these Lines, speaking of Rich I.
>
> Against whose fury and unmatched force
> The awelesse lion could not wage the fight
> Nor keepe his princely heart from Richard's hands.
> He that perforce robs lions of their hearts
> May easily win a woman's.
>
> This alludes to the fabulous history of Rich. Coeur de Lion, in an old metrical Romance, Imprinted for W. de Worde 1528. 4to black Letter and retail'd in the ballad of Richd Cordelion printed in the Collection 12° vo. 3^d p.11. *I intend to make a great use of this remark in my preface, if it is unblown upon, which I beg you will inform me.*[117]

As Brooks notes, Percy did go on to make use of this passage in his essay 'On the Ancient Metrical Romances' which introduced the third volume of the 1765 *Reliques*.[118] In this essay, which has received little attention from scholars compared with the 'Essay on the Ancient Minstrels' attached to Volume One, Percy argued for the importance and revival of the metrical romances that celebrated the feats of chivalry. Percy's use of this passage occurs in the context of his discussion about the need for a collection of metrical romances in order to 'throw new light' on the history of English poetry. Romances, he claims, have been greatly neglected in favour of the 'tedious allegories of Gower, or the dull and prolix legends of Lydgate', referring to the poets John Gower (*d.* 1408) and John Lydgate (*c.* 1370–c. 1449).[119] Percy favours the revival of romances through song: 'Should the public encourage the revival of some of those ancient Epic songs of Chivalry, they would frequently see the rich ore of an Ariosto or a Tasso, tho' buried it may be among the rubbish and dross of barbarous times'.[120] To illustrate this point and to lend credibility the idea of reviving romances he notes that Chaucer and Spenser 'abound' with allusions to the old Romances as does Shakespeare: 'In his play of KING JOHN our great dramatic poet alludes to an exploit of Richard I, which the reader will in vain look for in any true history'.[121] Percy quotes the same paragraph that he had written to Farmer about and then an extended excerpt from the 'old Romance' of *Kynge Rycharde cuer du Lyon* printed in 1528 in order to demonstrate the origin of Shakespeare's reference: 'the fact here referred to, is to be traced to its source only in the old Romance of Richard Ceur de Lyon, in which his encounter with a Lion makes a very shining figure'.[122] Percy then quotes a lengthy passage from this text that describes Richard's encounter with the lion.

As the above extract demonstrates, Percy primarily looks to Shakespeare rather than to the *Collection*, or Richard Johnson, in order to legitimate his call for the reassessment of old Romances. Where he *does* mention Richard Johnson in the *Reliques*, it is in the introduction to the ballad that opens 'book three' of the third volume of the *Reliques* entitled 'The Birth of St. George'.[123] Here, Percy acknowledges that the incidents described in this ballad 'are chiefly taken from the old story-book of the *Seven Champions of Christendom*; which tho' now the play-thing of children, was once in high repute'.[124] Before stating 'the author' of this romance was 'one Richard Johnson, who lived in the reigns of Elizabeth and James', Percy looks to canonical sources, quite literally, to contextualize the popularity of the story.[125] He quotes a line from the satires of Joseph Hall (1574–1656) printed in 1597: 'Bp. Hall' in his satires ... ranks '"St. George's sorrel, and his cross of blood" among the most popular stories of his time'.[126] He also notes that Spenser 'borrowed hints' from the song, as shown by 'an ingenious critic'.[127] The 'ingenious critic' was Percy's friend and scholarly adviser, Thomas Warton, who made his reputation with a 1754 publication *Observations on the Faerie Queene of Spenser*.[128] The most important point to emerge from the introduction to 'The Birth of St George' however, is that Percy downplays Richard Johnson as a derivative transmitter, pointing out that he copied the story from earlier metrical romances: 'The Seven Champions tho' written in a wild inflated style, contains some strong Gothic painting; which seems, for the most part, copied from the metrical romances of former ages'.[129] Finally, Percy makes it clear that he includes this ballad reluctantly: 'It cannot be denied, but that a great part of the following ballad is modern: for which reason it would have been thrown to the end of the volume, had not its subject procured it a place here'.[130] Like Johnson's work, it dates from the seventeenth century and cannot therefore be considered as 'ancient' as Percy would have preferred.

Both the editor of the *Collection* and Percy are therefore engaged in obscuring Richard Johnson – the former as part of his attempt to construct himself as an antiquarian collector receiving ballads as single texts from correspondents, the latter as part of his attempt to establish an ancient lineage of metrical romances and minstrels. The editor of the *Collection* is wary of the ability of ballads to convey history, and he uses his introductions to correct various historical inaccuracies. Percy however, to a certain extent, rehabilitates the history passed down by the minstrels. According to Percy, the bards and the scalds originally had the function as historians at court, recording the victories of warriors and the royal genealogy of princes; however, as history became 'more stable' in prose, the songs of the bards and scalds became more fictitious:

> It was not probably till after the historian and the bard had been long disunited, that the latter ventured at pure fiction. At length when their business was no longer to instruct or inform, but merely to amuse, it was no longer needful for them to adhere

to truth. Then began fabulous and romantic songs which for a long time prevailed in France and England before they had books of Chivalry in prose. Yet in both these countries the minstrels still retained so much of their original institution, as frequently to make true events the subject of their songs; and indeed, as during the barbarous ages, the regular histories were almost all writ by the Monks, the memory of events was preserved and propagated among the ignorant laity by scarce any other means than the popular songs of the Minstrels.[131]

Percy notes that his manuscript contains several poems of this kind and cites Dr Grey's findings that the story of Richard pulling out the lion's heart is referred to in Rastell's chronicle 'as proof that the old metrical Romances throw light on our old writers in prose: many of our ancient Historians have recorded fictions of Romance'. For Percy, songs predate yet continue to inform the romances and history:

> It is well known to Historians, that when William the Conqueror with his Normans marched down to the battle of Hastings, they animated themselves by singing (in some popular Romance or Ballad) the exploits of Roland, the great hero of Chivalry.[132]

Percy's call for a reappraisal of the romance accords with his theory of minstrelsy articulated in the first volume of the *Reliques*. The theory of minstrelsy is predicated upon an elevation of 'the ancient', or the middle-ages, over the Elizabethan and Jacobean. Percy's minstrels were 'the genuine successors of the bards who united the arts of Poetry and music and sung verses to the harp of their own composing ... at the houses of the great'.[133] He even uses the story of King Alfred assuming the disguise of a minstrel in order to gain access to the camp of the Danish invaders as evidence of proof of the esteem with which minstrels were held at this time.[134] During the reign of Elizabeth I, however, the minstrels had sunk so low as to be classed alongside 'rogues and vagabonds' in the statute to prevent vagrancy passed in the thirty-ninth year of her rule, and, according to Percy, this 'put an end to the profession'.[135] The minstrels did not compose for publication and the extant copies of their works were 'doubtless taken down from their mouths', as opposed to the 'new race of ballad-writers' that succeeded them 'who wrote narrative songs merely for the press'.[136] Percy concludes his essay by reiterating the replacement of minstrelsy with the songs of the late Elizabethan and Jacobean ballad-writers.

> Towards the end of Queen Elizabeth's reign ... the genuine old Minstrelsy seems to have been extinct, and thenceforth the ballads that were produced were wholly of the latter kind, and these came forth in such abundance, that in the reign of James I. they began to be collected into little Miscellanies under the name of Garlands, and at length to be written purposely for such collections.[137]

Recent scholars including Paula McDowell have noted the hierarchy Percy establishes in this essay, and which is evident in the passages quoted above, between oral and manuscript culture which pre-dates the print culture of the late sixteenth century.[138] The specifics of this, in terms of the transmission of the ballads collected by Richard Johnson and the figure of Richard Coeur de Lion, are foregrounded in this chapter. In the footnote to Percy's concluding statement, he lists the two Johnson garlands – *The Crowne Garland* and *The Golden Garland* – along with several others including Thomas Deloney's garland collections and Martin Parker's garland collection.[139] Richard Johnson was one of the 'new race of ballad writers' who replaced the minstrels and wrote purely for the press. As previously discussed, Percy's mention of Johnson's *Seven Champions* in Volume Three of the *Reliques*, in connection with 'the birth of St George', was to point out its derivative nature and to pre-date it in line with favoured 'ancient' genealogy. While Percy is correct that Johnson might be seen as a compiler of legends rather than an originator, the point is that, in connection with his broader theory of minstrelsy, Johnson represents a point of rupture, or a turning point between the ancient and the modern. Percy's decision not to include the 'Princely Song' in his *Reliques*, despite drawing upon many other songs from the *Collection*, can therefore be read as consistent with his theory of minstrelsy, because it was not an 'ancient song' and moreover, it had been politicized through the framework of Rapin's Whig history in the *Collection*.

A much enlarged version of Percy's essay on minstrelsy appeared in the second edition of the *Reliques* published in 1767 which was also printed as part of a separate collection of his *Four Essays* published that same year.[140] Here, Richard I makes an appearance as a patron of minstrelsy, in a way which bolsters Percy's earlier observations published in the 'Essay on Metrical Romance'. The role of Richard I is introduced as the first 'particular fact' following the conquest:

> After the Norman conquest I have not met with any very particular fact concerning the Minstrels, till we come down to the reign of Richard the First: and under him their profession seems to have revived with additional splendour. Richard, who was the great restorer and hero of Chivalry, was also the distinguished patron of Poets and Minstrels: He was himself of their number, and some of his verses are still extant.[141]

Percy directs the reader to Horace Walpole's *Catalogue of Royal Authors* for these verses, despite the fact that Walpole had been less than complimentary about Richard Coeur de Lion.[142] Richard emerges as part of the theory of English Minstrelsy through example and appropriation. According to Percy, Richard invited 'multitudes' of Provençal bards to his court and 'loaded them with honours and rewards'.[143] This functioned to encourage an indigenous minstrelsy:

> the distinction and respect which Richard showed to men of this profession, although his favours were chiefly heaped upon foreigners, could not but recommend the profession itself among his own subjects: and therefore we may conclude that English Minstrelsy would, in a peculiar manner, flourish in his time.[144]

Importantly, this is the first time in Percy's essay that he uses the term 'English minstrelsy'. Richard thus emerges as the first staging post upon which Percy mounts his post-Norman Conquest theory of minstrelsy.

Another 'fact' used by Percy to support his theory is an account of Blondel's rescue of Richard through song:

> The distinguished service which Richard received from one of his Minstrels, in rescuing him from his cruel and tedious captivity, is a remarkable fact which ought to be recorded for the honour of poets and their art. This fact has lately been rescued from oblivion, and given to the world in very elegant language by an ingenious lady.[145]

The 'ingenious lady' was Anna Williams, whose 1766 account of the story has been discussed in the introduction. Williams was part of the Johnson household and Samuel Johnson was also an important influence on the *Reliques*, writing its dedication to the Countess of Northumberland, Percy's patron.[146] In 1766 Anna Williams's *Miscellanies in Prose and Verse* was published, which contained an account of Richard's rescue by 'Blondiaux'.[147] Williams's source was President Fauchet's *Recueil de l'origine de Langue et Poesie Françoise, Ryme et Romans*, printed in Paris by Mamert Patisson in 1581.[148] Percy, demonstrating his own antiquarian credentials, reproduces a 'more antiquated relation of the same event' by quoting from Book Five of the English translation of French historian Andrew Favine's *Theatre of Honour and Knighthood*, printed in London in 1623. In his account of Richard, Favine referred to an 'ancient manuscript of old poesies' and it was this that enabled Percy to produce a 'more antiquated relation' of the same event.[149]

Percy faced opposition to his theory in 1766, in a paper read to the Society of Antiquaries by 'Mr Pegge' which was later published in the journal of the society. Pegge argued against Percy's contention that the minstrels would have flourished amongst the Saxons because of the influence of the Britons and the Danes: 'we cannot reasonably argue from the modes and customs either of the Britons or Danes to those of the Saxons'.[150] He also refuted Percy's use of the 'evidence' that King Alfred assumed a minstrel disguise in order to gain access to the Danish camp by pointing out that other chroniclers made no mention of this: 'This is a most notable story, and Rapin might justly stile it the boldest resolution that ever entered into the thoughts of a prince. But then it is of a very doubtful authority'.[151] It was possibly in response to this critique that Percy sought to bolster the *post*-Conquest part of his argument through reference to Richard I.

The most damaging opposition to Percy's theory of minstrelsy came from Joseph Ritson (1752–1803), who critiqued Percy in his 'Essay on National Song', published in 1783.[152] A conveyancing lawyer by profession, Ritson spent his leisure time pursuing antiquarian interests including ballad collecting, editing and literary scholarship. His meticulous scholarship and, at times, irascible disposition led to a number of disputes with other scholars including Percy and Warton. As Marilyn Butler observes, Ritson defined the ballad as 'a popular democratic form' which resonated with his politics as a committed republican in the revolutionary decade of the 1790s.[153] Ritson pointed out that the only real evidence Percy had for this period related to the existence of French court minstrels:

> Without attempting to controvert the slightest fact laid down by the learned prelate, one may be well permitted to question the propriety of his inferences, and, indeed, his general hypothesis. Every part of France, but more especially Normandy, seems to have formerly abounded in minstrels ... Many of these people, we can easily suppose, attended England; and perhaps were provided for, or continued to gain a subsistence by their professional art among the settlers. The constant intercourse which so long subsisted between the two countries, that is, while the English monarchs had possessions in France, afforded the French and Norman minstrels constant opportunities of a free and unexpensive passage into England, where they were certain of a favourable reception and liberal rewards from the king, his barons, and other Anglo-Norman subjects. French or Norman minstrels, however, are not English ones.[154]

In refuting Percy's argument, Ritson makes a further distinction between court minstrels and men who made a livelihood by singing to the 'illiterate vulgar' who would have been precluded from singing at court and in the 'houses of the great' because of the language barrier between Saxon and French (the language of court and government) which reflected the social hierarchy at this time. There was no record of the songs these men sang because, according to Ritson, they themselves were illiterate:

> There is not the least proof that the latter [Percy's English minstrels] were a respectable society, or that they even deserve the name of a society. That there were men in those times, as there are in the present, who gained a livelihood by going about from place to place, singing and playing to the illiterate vulgar is doubtless true; but that they were received into the castles of the nobility, sung at their tables, and were rewarded like the French minstrels, does not any where appear, nor is it at all credible. The reason is evident. The French tongue alone was used at court, and in the households of the Norman barons (who despised the saxon manners and language), for many centuries after the conquest, and continued till, at least, the reign of Henry VIII. The polite language of both court and country, and as well known as the English itself: a fact of which (to keep to our subject) we need no other evidence than the multitude of French poems and songs to be found in every library. The learned treatise above noticed might therefore with more propriety have been intitled 'An essay on the ancient French Minstrels', whom the several facts and anecdotes there related alone concern.[155]

Ritson foregrounds a continuing popular song culture here that was transmitted by travelling men who entertained the 'vulgar', as opposed to Percy's minstrels who were a part of the culture of the court and nobility.

Ritson counters practically every claim Percy made about English minstrelsy, including his attempts to date certain songs and to excavate a pre-Elizabethan tradition. Whereas Percy marks the Elizabethan period as a point of decline, Ritson views it as a point of origin and discredits Percy's lack of real evidence: 'We now arrive at the time of Queen Elizabeth; in which we are to look for the origin of the modern English song; not a single composition of that nature, with the smallest degree of poetical merit, being discoverable at any preceding period'.[156] Ritson further observes that the 'ancient' black letter copies of 'the more common English ballads', such as those in the Pepys collection, are not older than the sixteenth century.[157] Dispensing with the idea of ballads being passed down from the ancient minstrels through an oral manuscript tradition, Ritson describes a commercial print context for their production: 'these ballads were originally composed for public singers by profession, and perhaps immediately for printers, booksellers, or those who vended such like things'.[158] While acknowledging the difficult question of authorship, he points to the importance of Richard Johnson as part of this popular tradition:

> But whether they were, in every case, first published in single sheets, and not, till afterwards collected into *Garlands*, or whether they made their first appearance in such collections, does not clearly appear. Thomas Deloney and Richard Johnson, writers by profession of amusing books for the populace, were famous ballad-makers about this period. And could we be assured that they were the real authors of the *Garlands*, or collections published under their respective names, we might be able to refer most of the ballads in the present collection to the one or the other.[159]

The importance of Ritson to this argument is to demonstrate that the print history and mode of dissemination of balladry was inextricably linked to political meaning and contestation. This is in line with Philip Connell's work on the politicized nature of the study of 'Ancient' poetry in the later eighteenth century. Connell observes that the alignment of the Norman conquest with the modern national character was 'strikingly at odds with the immemorialist commonplaces of eighteenth-century Whig thought, which continued to maintain a degree of continuity between the Anglo-Saxons in the post-conquest periods'.[160] The radical version of the 'Norman Yoke', in which the Norman invasion of 1066 signaled the end of the rights of the people guaranteed by Saxon government, gained currency in the 1770s in the wake of Obadiah Hulme's 1771 essay on the origins of the English Constitution, *An Historical Essay on the English Constitution*. Recalling Rapin, Hulme identified the Saxons as to whom 'the English are indebted to for their constitution, or mode of government; introduced into England, about the year four hundred and fifty'.[161] With the invasion of the Normans under William the Conqueror in 1066 the elective power of the people was eventually destroyed. William 'reversed the Saxon form of government which was founded upon the common rights of mankind, and established an arbitrary power, in himself'.[162] James Burgh's *Political Disquisitions*, published in 1774 and deeply influential amongst reformers, also held up the ideal example of the Saxons, whose parliaments, or *witena gemots*, were held annually from the time of King Alfred.[163] For Ritson, Percy's seamless incorporation of Richard into his theory of English minstrelsy ignored the political rupture of the Norman Yoke and mistakenly conflated the culture of the tyrannical Norman invaders with the indigenous song culture of the people.

While the 'Princely Song' does not appear in Ritson's collection, it had previously been picked up by Thomas Evans (1742–84), a bookseller who capitalized upon the success of Percy by printing his own collection as 'Evans's edition' of *Old Ballads, Historical and Narrative* in 1777.[164] Evans viewed his work as a supplement to Percy's, informing his readers that none of the ballads appeared in Percy's collection and directing them to Percy's essay on minstrelsy.[165] Ritson's antiquarian interests would eventually take a different turn and focused upon the outlaw King-figure from Richard's reign, Robin Hood. In 1795 he published a volume of songs relating to Robin Hood which was informed by his own radical politics and provides another example of the long cultural memory of balladry being deployed as political song in a topical context.[166] Radical political songs in the context of 1795 are further examined in Chapter Four. This permeation of politics into the ballad can be explored through tracking its transmission through a variety of print media and performance contexts; as well as song collections and broadsides, 'Princely Song' can be seen, in 1786, to find its way into the medium of the newspaper, a format closely tied to cultural identity and political feeling, as discussed below.

The Newspaper

Richard the Lionheart, a figure of shifting complexity, appeared in the stage productions of the two royal theatres, Drury Lane and Covent Garden, in 1786, which thereby led to review and discussion in the popular newspapers of the time, not only of the performances but also within the wider context of the balladry on that theme. In the stage version adapted by Leonard MacNally for the Theatre Royal Covent Garden, the essence of the story of Blondel's rescue of Richard is used to reunite the thwarted lovers Lauretta and Florestan and to free the imprisoned Richard so that he can be re-united with his wife Berengaria. The ode which Blondel sings to establish Richard's identity is that 'which love for Berengaria inspired Richard's breast'.[167] In contrast to the interpretation of the 'Princely Song' as a satire, Richard emerges as a passive figure at the centre of intersecting plot devices which affirm the heterosexual romances. This was also the case in the Drury Lane version, adapted by John Burgoyne, where Blondel is ascribed a minor role as one of the King's men and rescuers rather than the singer of the all important song-signal that leads to Richard's rescue. This role is given to Matilda who sings a song which she had composed with Richard in the early days of their courtship in order to establish his identity.[168]

The MacNally Covent Garden production began slightly earlier than the Drury Lane version and incurred the wrath of the *Morning Post* and the *Morning Chronicle*, the two papers that would reprint the 'Princely Song'. The *Post* quipped on 18 October 1786 that 'a recent representation is sufficient to convince the public, that if a King has the heart of a lion, a Poetaster can terribly mangle him with a feather'.[169] Both papers depicted MacNally, an Irishman, as a toady who sought and depended upon Royal favour, the *Post* observing on 19 October 1786 that 'Richard of Covent-Garden, although *heart* of Lion, will find himself indebted to the humanity and protection of George the Third, even for a temporary existence in his native land'.[170] The *Morning Chronicle* went even further with an ironic tribute to MacNally's excessive loyalism:

> As far as his intention went, he deserves commendation and thanks, and if violent professions of loyalty, elaborate encomiums on our free constitution, and our national virtue and integrity, profuse compliments to the female sex, and pointed severities on those, who would not die to preserve their monarch from slavery, entitle a writer to a more than ordinary share of approbation, no man living has a better claim to it, than the gentleman who avows *Richard Coeur De Lion*, performed yesterday evening.[171]

The presence of the King at the Royal Command performance of 19 October gave the paper even more ammunition for invective:

> The King attended the new opera on the third night! No trifling compliment to the Author this, whether we view it in an honourable or a lucrative light. But after the eulogiums upon Royalty, and the invectives against regicide, could our Monarch do less? In return for the sentiments of loyalty, with which the author has interspersed *Richard Coeur De Lion*, it would be but justice to knight him. What a potent recommendation to the publick would it prove for this Gentleman's future dramas to have been produced by – Sir Leonard MacNally.[172]

In terms of the political alliances of these newspapers, MacNally was attacked by both the Whig and ministerial interest. In 1786 the *Morning Post* was a ministerial paper, while Arthur Aspinall and Lucyle Werkmeister report that the *Morning Chronicle* had been started in the Whig interest and remained so until 1788.[173] Unlike its representation in the *Collection* and in the Dicey broadsheet, the 'Princely Song' as represented in these newspapers contains no surrounding commentary presenting it as a satire. The commentary surrounding the song was that of the newspaper itself, the context of 1786, representing the song's transmission into yet another medium of print as it intersected with the oral performance contexts of the stage.

MacNally's background as an Irishman evidently informed these attacks on his excessive loyalism. Born into a Catholic family in Dublin in 1752 he converted to Protestantism in the 1760s.[174] He began his career as a lawyer in Dublin before coming to London in the late 1770s, becoming involved in journalism and producing several works for the theatre including a stage version of *Robin Hood* performed at Covent Garden in 1784.[175] Thomas Bartlett also notes that MacNally wrote several pamphlets at this time which drew attention to the plight of Ireland.[176] MacNally returned to Dublin in 1790 and became involved with radical politics as a member of the United Irishmen; however, soon after he began to act as a paid government informer, providing regular reports on the group's activities using the signature 'J. W'.[177] Bartlett's study reveals the depth of MacNally's duplicity and treachery, which was not uncovered during his lifetime. In acting as defence counsel for members of the United Irishmen, for example, on numerous occasions he secretly revealed the defence strategies to the prosecution.[178] Bartlett has raised the question as to whether scrutiny of MacNally's creative output in the 1780s might offer any clues to his later role as informer. While a reading of his plays as a window into his psychology would be problematic, these newspaper reports of him playing minstrel to the King, in an attempt to gain patronage, seem particularly prescient.[179] The republication of the 'Princely Song' in the *Morning Post* and *Morning Chronicle* in the context of their attacks on MacNally also takes on an added topical significance as another way of undermining him, pointing to a reactivation of the song as a satire on courage as it was understood in the *Collection*.

The assassination attempt on George III during the summer of 1786 was also part of the topical context that informed the reception of the play and which MacNally deliberately drew upon to speak to his audience and, as the *Morning Chronicle* suggests, the King himself. George III experienced a surge in popularity following the ill-fated attempt of Margaret Nicholson to assassinate him with a dessert knife, as he alighted from his carriage at St. James's Palace, on 2 August 1786.[180] Nicholson was subsequently declared insane and committed to Bedlam for the rest of her life. The *Morning Chronicle* observed 'her Majesty seemed to be sensibly affected, when she heard those passages in the opera that alluded to a recent and well-known event'.[181]

The other important political event occupying much column space and informing the stage productions and the reprinting of the song was the Anglo-French treaty of 1786, also known as the 'Eden Treaty', after the principle negotiator for Britain, William Eden. Described by W. O. Henderson as 'one of the most important agreements of the eighteenth century', the treaty marked a decisive break from the previous agreement, the 1713 treaty of Utrecht, which followed the controversial peace of Utrecht in 1712.[182] Under the 1713 treaty, France was highly protectionist and focused on reducing foreign imports to protect native markets, and Britain had failed to ratify articles eight and nine of the treaty which would have guaranteed reciprocal freedom of trade between the two nations.[183] As both France and Britain faced huge amounts of national debt, the advantages of a trade alliance became desirable, offering the chance to negotiate the setting of duties for different imports and the opportunity to capture revenue from the thriving smuggling market.[184] The treaty was signed on 26 September 1786 amidst much controversy. The treaty provided a language of trade, imports and exports in which to speak of the play. The *General Advertiser* observed that 'of all the insignificant and nonsensical baubles ever imported from France *Coeur de Lion* is the most contemptible'.[185] A further reference to the treaty features in the description of the royal attire at the command performance:

> The King was dressed in a velvet blue suit. Her majesty wore a silk pompadore gown; and each of the Princesses a white one, likewise of silk; which may be considered as a proof of their superior taste, as well as of their benevolence in encouraging the silk trade, which the whimsical fashion of muslin and cotton gowns has reduced to the most deplorable condition.[186]

The fact that the 'pompadore' gown was made of silk is significant, as silk was a point of contention in the negotiations of mid-August 1786, when the French wanted the British to waive their prohibition on the importation of French silks. However, as Marie Donaghy records, this was a non-negotiable point with Eden's trump card being that the potential for popular protest by the silk workers would cause the British Parliament to reject the treaty altogether.[187] The Eden treaty lasted just 7 years until 1793 when England and France went to war.

The newspapers also took the opportunity to capitalize on the publicity and controversy of the rival productions by printing songs from the operas.[188] The songs from the stage productions were printed in separate song books which ran to multiple editions and found their way into multi-volume songsters *The Banquet of Thalia* (1788) and *The Busy Bee* (1790).[189] The music publishers Longman and Broderip and John Preston also made two entries into the Stationers' Registers which copyrighted music connected with the plays.[190] Milton Percival has noted that in the eighteenth century, 'as the newspaper grew and strengthened, the ballad withered and decayed'.[191] In the case of the 'Princely Song', however, the newspaper presented a new form of print in which the song could be revived and re-mediated amidst the flurry of printing activity created by *Richard Coeur de Lion*.

Conclusion

This chapter has traced the transmission of the 'Princely Song' across the eighteenth century through a number of different print media as a case study of the politics of song. It began with the seminal *Collection of Old Ballads* in which the 'old Whig' identity of the editor informed the framing of the 'Princely Song' as a satire on Richard's marriage, an interpretation which would then inform the broadsheet version produced by William Dicey. An analysis of the composition of the *Collection* reveals that the origins of the 'Princely Song', and many of the other songs printed in Volume Three, were the garland song collections of the Jacobean writer Richard Johnson, an important transmitter of the St. George legend which also came to enfold the story of Richard's encounter with the Lion in ballad representations. Johnson's source texts were obscured, however, as the editor of the *Collection*, adopting an antiquarian persona, writes of receiving songs sent in by 'gentlemen' correspondents. While the influence of the *Collection* on Thomas Percy's *Reliques of Ancient English Poetry* has been often noted, this chapter has shown that Percy's transmission of Richard the Lionheart, as part of his theory of minstrelsy which extended beyond the Norman Conquest, functioned to obscure Richard Johnson and the 'Princely Song'. For Percy, Johnson was part of the 'new race' of 'modern' ballad writers from the late Elizabethan period whose printed works marked the end of the largely oral tradition of the 'ancient minstrels'. This was vigorously contested by Joseph Ritson who pointed out that Percy effaced the popular print tradition of songs, of which Richard Johnson was part. The politics of song again emerges in this schism between the two with Ritson pointing out that Percy's English minstrels who had supposedly been encouraged by Richard the Lionheart's patronage and had performed in the 'houses of the great', would have actually been the Norman minstrels of the court and aristocracy. In the tradition of the 'Old Whig' historiography which had venerated the pre-Conquest era of the Saxons and King Alfred, Ritson called Percy to account for mystifying this distinction. The 'Princely Song' once again found circulation in book form as part of Thomas Evans's collection of *Old Ballads* in 1777 which marketed itself as a supplement to Percy by containing the songs that had not been used in his *Reliques*. Finally, the printing of the 'Princely Song' in the *Morning Post* and the *Morning Chronicle* in October 1786 indicates the song's topical relevance as the rival patent theatres both staged productions of the play *Richard Coeur De Lion*. This chapter has revealed the politics and porosity of the song in terms of the macro historiographical concerns of Whiggish history, spanning to the time of King Alfred, and the micro political concerns of 1786, following the recent attack on the King by Margaret Nicholson and in the wake of the Anglo-French treaty. The 'Princely Song' is not a canonical text – it was relegated to Volume Three of the *Collection* and overlooked by Percy. However, the song reveals the multivalent and multitextual ways in which songs functioned politically in the eighteenth century. The next chapter will continue to explore the relationship between a single song in the context of a broader collection through its focus on the hundredth psalm and the psalms of 'Sternhold and Hopkins', which became implicated in the politics of literary value. This will move us to the next occasion of singing to the King in 1788.

2 THE PSALMS THAT BIND: 'STERNHOLD AND HOPKINS', THE 'OLD HUNDREDTH' AND THE BALLAD

In the eighteenth century, the names 'Sternhold and Hopkins', referring to the metrical psalter, were familiar to English men and women of all classes. Thomas Sternhold and John Hopkins had paraphrased the Old Testament Book of Psalms from Hebrew prose into verse in the mid-sixteenth century. Their translation was still so well-known two centuries later that Thomas Paine could use it to make a joke about 'natural' hierarchy in the first part of *Rights of Man*: 'Whether the archbishop precedes the duke, or the duke the bishop, it is I believe, to the people in general, somewhat like Sternhold and Hopkins, or Hopkins and Sternhold; you may put which you please first'.[1] The title page of 'Sternhold and Hopkins' referred to the psalms as 'laying apart all ungodly songs and ballads which tend only to the nourishing of vice and corruption of youth', but the link between the 'songs' of the Bible and their secular equivalents persisted. This chapter explores this connection in the context of the eighteenth century, when 'Sternhold and Hopkins' as signifiers of both the 'old' and the 'old' way of singing, came to be implicated in the role of ballads and songs in the evolving politics of literary value. The one hundredth psalm, which emerged from 'Sternhold and Hopkins' as the 'Old Hundredth' at the turn of the eighteenth century, forms the focus of my examination of the intersection between the cultural politics of 'Sternhold and Hopkins' and the ballad. Accounts of the rise of the ballad in eighteenth-century literary culture have yet to consider the coeval role of 'Sternhold and Hopkins', which, as this chapter will show, both informed and helped shape the formative role of the ballad in literary culture.

The study of the metrical psalms of Sternhold and Hopkins in the eighteenth century has been confined to the context of church history and the development of the hymn as a related form of religious song.[2] While the hymn is an important corollary to the metrical psalm, this chapter confines itself to 'Sternhold and Hopkins' because of the belief that the text was especially authorized, or 'allowed', by the Church of England, a status that the hymn did not enjoy. In his *Social History of English Music*, published in 1964, E. D. Mackerness made the observation that the discussion of parochial music of the eighteenth century should be of interest to the student of 'social history'.[3] Since then investigations of the psalmody of the period have focused upon the musicological features and performance practice of 'parochial psalmody', also known as West Gallery music.[4] Sally Drage characterizes this music as 'written and performed by amateurs' as opposed to professional musicians who were often connected with the cathedrals as organists or choir masters.[5] Vic Gammon has defined parochial psalmody as 'vernacular church music of the eighteenth and nineteenth century', framing parochial psalmody as a new 'plebeian style' of performance, which reflected the fact that the church choirs and bands that were formed during this period were comprised of artisans.[6] The 'plebeian style' was characterized by the singing of the psalms in a loud, full-throated way which became the subject of much complaint. In 1787, for example, William Vincent wrote that 'parochial music is at present confined to psalmody, which, from the general manner of performing it, is become an object of disgust, instead of rational delight and edification'.[7] In the third volume of his *History of Music*, Charles Burney complained that the reverence for the psalms had been lost because of the 'wretched manner' in which they were performed.

> There can be no objection to sober and well-disposed villagers meeting, at their leisure hours, to practice Psalmody together, in private, for their recreation, but it seems as if their public performance might be dispensed with during divine service, unless they had acquired a degree of excellence far superior to what is usually met with in parish churches, either in town or country where there is no organ.[8]

Burney expressed a wish that the performance of amateur village singers be restricted to the home.

Gammon draws upon E. P. Thompson's patrician-plebeian model of social relations in his framing of parochial psalmody in relation to commentators such as Burney and Vincent.[9] Thompson had argued that in the social relations between the patricians and the plebs, an accommodating reciprocity functioned.[10] Customary 'plebeian' behaviours were tolerated, such as the rioting of a crowd in response to food shortages, and the performance of 'rough music' in rituals of humiliation to punish individuals who had violated community norms.[11] 'Rough music' was loud and cacophonous and might involve, for example, the violent hitting of tin-cans outside an offender's house during a Skimmington ride. Thompson's complex model allowed for plebeian agency through customary culture, though always within a larger framework of cultural hegemony maintained by the patrician elite. In framing parochial psalmody as a 'plebeian' musical style, Gammon also emphasizes the idea of plebeian agency, going so far as to say that 'the church lost control of the music that went on within its own walls'.[12] He also draws upon the concept of 'licence' to frame parochial psalmody as part of the range of customary behaviours identified by Thompson which operated within the framework of reciprocity: 'This licence was extended from food riots to violent football matches, from rough music to church music'.[13] According to Gammon, in the second half of the nineteenth century this licence gave way to more elite musical taste and the church choirs and bands were forced out of the church by the Oxford movement.[14] 'Lower class forms of musical expression' had been disciplined 'and the parish church attempted to become an imitation of the cathedral'.[15] In his work on parochial psalmody, Gammon explicitly states that his interest is in the 'usage of the music' as opposed to its 'origin': 'I take the view that it is not the origin of music that is important, it is its usage that is of crucial interest'.[16]

While acknowledging the important contribution to this area Gammon's work has made, this chapter foregrounds the role of 'Sternhold and Hopkins' as the text of the psalms to which music was performed as an important and neglected point of origin. It is the contention here that music and text cannot be separated, the 'Old Hundredth' describing a set of lyrics drawn from 'Sternhold and Hopkins' and an accompanying tune. An emphasis upon the performance style of eighteenth-century parochial psalmody has led to a significant point being overlooked: this was the belief that 'Sternhold and Hopkins' was an 'allowed' text.

It was not until a ruling in 1820 that the question of the status of 'Sternhold and Hopkins' was clarified in the case of Cotterill v Holy and Ward, heard before the Chancery Court of the diocese of York. Thomas Cotterill, the curate at St. Paul's Church in Sheffield from 1817–23, was taken to court by Daniel Holy and Samuel Broomhead Ward for introducing,

> of his own pretended authority into the Public performance of divine service ... a certain selection of hymns and a metrical version of Psalms not set forth or allowed by law to be used in Churches or Chapels of the establishment of the Church of England or by any competent authority whatsoever.[17]

The hymns and metrical psalms that Cotterill used were his own authored and translated *Selection of Psalms and Hymns*, first published in 1810.[18] In the preface to the eighth edition of the text, published in 1819 and reprinted in 1829, he defended his right to use his own text rather than the 'allowed' versions of 'Sternhold and Hopkins' and 'Tate and Brady', to be discussed later.[19] This case has been documented by Thomas McCart who notes that following the ruling of the court in Cotterill's favour, the hymnody of the Church of England flourished.[20] The belief in the authority of 'Sternhold and Hopkins' during the long eighteenth century persisted until the ruling of this case. This authority was declared on the title-page of each edition of the text which stated that it was:

set forth and allowed to be sung in all Churches, of all the People together, before and after Morning and evening Prayer; and also before and after sermons; and moreover in private houses, for their godly solace and comfort: laying apart all ungodly songs and ballads, which tend only the nourishing of vice and corrupting of youth.[21]

Any 'licence' that was extended to the singing of the psalms, allowing extravagant and florid tunes, or the loud, full-throated vocalization that Gammon has identified, was therefore tempered by the reputation of the text as holding this privileged status. Thomas Paine's disdainful reversal of 'Sternhold and Hopkins, Hopkins and Sternhold' was a reflection of the view of the text as an entrenched part of the natural order of English society. The print history of 'Sternhold and Hopkins' thus complicates Gammon's conception of parochial psalmody with reference to the customary culture of 'rough music' and opens up another aspect of its political meaning.

This field of enquiry locates 'Sternhold and Hopkins' within a complex debate about cultural value that encompasses the elevation of certain ballads from mere songs of 'the people' to important literary artifacts of the English nation. As discussed later, John Dennis's belated response to Joseph Addison's famous *Spectator* 'ballad papers' drew upon 'Sternhold and Hopkins' as exemplars of doggerel. This idea was repeated in religious commentary on psalmody by those situated outside and on the margins of the Church of England, including Isaac Watts and John Wesley, and in Thomas Warton's important multi-volume *History of English Poetry* (1774–81), the first such history of its kind. The disciplinary divide between religious literature and secular literature had yet to be consolidated and 'Sternhold and Hopkins' played an important role in literary culture as signifiers of 'bad' poetry. Warton's commentary demonstrates that the politicization of the psalms of 'Sternhold and Hopkins' as war songs during the English civil war of the previous century continued to affect how they were viewed in the eighteenth century. Yet despite this poor reputation, the one hundredth psalm emerged from 'Sternhold and Hopkins' to attain a different status. Known as the 'Old Hundredth' because it was from the 'old version', the tune and text of this psalm would come to function as a proto-national anthem. In order to understand the way that 'Sternhold and Hopkins' became entrenched in the literary and religious culture of England in the eighteenth century, the next section will outline a history of the 'Old Hundredth' in relation to the print history of the text as a whole.

'Sternhold and Hopkins' and the 'Old Hundredth'

The 'Old Hundredth' referred to both the tune of the psalm and the following text to which it was sung:

All people that on earth doth dwell,
sing to the Lord with cheerful voice;
Serve him with fear, his praise forth tell,
come ye before him and rejoice.
The Lord ye know is God indeed,
without our aid he did us make;
We are his stock he doth us feed,
and for his sheep he doth us take.
O enter then his gates with praise,
Approach with joy his courts unto;
Praise laud, and bless his Name always
For it is seemly so to do.
For why? The Lord our God is good,
His mercy is for ever sure;
His truth at all times firmly stood,
And shall from age to age endure.[22]

The psalm, paraphrased into the eight syllable ABAB rhyming pattern known as long metre, is an invocation to praise God through 'cheerful song'. To this extent it is paradigmatic of the psalms as songs of worship. God, or 'the Lord', is the creator of man and is figured as a King at court, while the psalmists are depicted with familiar Christian pastoral imagery, as God's 'flock' who enter his court to praise him. The psalm provides a disciplinary logic for the psalmists' songs by referring not only to God as 'good', but as 'merciful', ending with an affirmation of Christian belief as God's enduring 'truth'. The psalm is thought to have emerged during Israel's post-exilic period when Judaism began to be seen as not only the religion of the Israelites but as a religion for 'all the people that on earth do dwell', the summons of the first line.[23] James Luther Mays notes that

> Of course, the psalm was written with a specific congregation in mind, and shows that in its language. But it was composed as though it was meant to be open to future times and places, and lays only the lightest foundation to its historical time and place.[24]

One foundation that acts as an important marker of time and place was the categorization of the psalm as the 'Old' at the end of the seventeenth and beginning of the eighteenth centuries. To understand how it came to be known in this way it is necessary to briefly recount the emergence of the hundredth psalm within 'Sternhold and Hopkins'.

Thomas Sternhold was groom of the robes for King Henry VIII (1491–1547) and the young King Edward VI (1537–53) who was only nine when he acceded to the throne in 1547. Sternhold produced a volume of nineteen psalms that he paraphrased into metre and dedicated to the young King titled *Certayne Psalms Chosen out of the Psalter of David, & Drawen into English Metre*.[25] The earliest edition is undated, but is thought to have been printed sometime between late 1547 and mid-1548.[26] It contained nineteen of the Psalms of David that, as Beth Quitslund has shown, were paraphrased from the vernacular biblical translations of the 1530s, including Miles Coverdale's 1535 Bible and his 'Great Bible' of 1539.[27] These bible translations were part of the Reformation project of 'sola scriptura', designed to bring the word of God to the people through scripture in their own vernacular language rather than in the Catholic Latin.[28] Metrical psalmody, or the process of paraphrasing the prose psalms into verse so that they could be sung to music, has been described by Robin Leaver as the 'natural outgrowth' of this movement, and one which found enthusiastic exponents in Martin Luther and John Calvin, the leaders of the Reformation in the early sixteenth century.[29]

Luther had produced a hymn collection of metrical psalms published in 1524 that contained tunes drawn from existing folk hymns and secular folk songs.[30] This combining of metrical psalmody with secular song traditions was a foundational moment, demonstrating the inter-relationship of the psalms and the ballad through their shared tunes. The aim in setting the psalms to popular song tunes was as an aid to memory. By 1537 Calvin had also adopted the metrical psalm as the most effective way of reaching the people, despite its deviation from literal translation.[31]

Thomas Sternhold's psalms were thus produced in the context of this European-wide adoption of metrical psalmody as part of the Reformation.[32] Seventeen of Sternhold's psalms used the rhythmical structure that would come to be known as 'Sternhold's metre' and later 'common metre', but more significantly for our purposes, 'ballad metre'.[33] This consisted of alternate lines of four and three beats, which was a commonly used rhythmic pattern for ballads. Hallett Smith notes that 179 of the 305 ballads in Francis Child's collection were based on this metre which lent itself to memorization because of its 'simplicity, regularity and emphatic beat'.[34]

Sternhold died in August 1549 and in December of that same year a posthumous edition of his text was printed which contained an additional eighteen psalms and a further seven psalms that had been translated by John Hopkins.[35] Hopkins was a Church of England clergyman and Oxford graduate who had become acquainted with Edward Whitchurch, printer of Sternhold's psalms and the *Book of Common Prayer*, which also made its first appearance in 1549 when the first Act of Uniformity made it compulsory.[36] The names 'Sternhold and Hopkins' were thus tied together through print though it is thought that these men never actually met in life.[37]

Following the premature death of Edward VII in 1553 his Catholic sister Mary (1515–58) acceded to the throne and the reforms to the Church of England that had gained pace during his reign were reversed. Those Protestants who were unwilling to turn away from the reformed faith, or who were in danger because of their position under the former reign, found exile in various European cities and towns. Beth Quitslund evocatively describes a number of copies of psalm texts travelling in baggage for the continent.[38] There the metrical psalms provided an important unifying source for the 'Marian exiles' and a way of holding onto the national church they had lost.

The original paraphrases of Sternhold and Hopkins underwent further reshaping in Europe and it was in this context that the tune and the text of the hundredth psalm emerged.[39] The tune that would come to be known as the 'Old Hundredth' in the eighteenth century originated in the French Genevan psalter of 1551, where it was set as the accompaniment of Psalm 134.[40] The text had been paraphrased by the Scottish exile William Kethe and printed in the 1560 edition of the Anglo-Genevan psalter and the 1561 version printed in London.[41] With the restoration of Protestantism in England under the rule of Elizabeth, the exiles and the printing of the psalter returned to England.[42] The hundredth psalm was then incorporated into the numerous versions of the psalter printed by John Day in the early 1560s with the attribution shifted from Kethe to 'J. H.' – John Hopkins.[43] The eighteenth century editions of 'Sternhold and Hopkins' retain the attribution of Hopkins.[44]

Elizabeth had restored Protestantism with the Act of Uniformity in April 1559. Article Forty-Nine of her injunctions from that same year, while not referring to psalm singing directly, provided for the use of music in worship for both the congregation and professional choirs, particularly

> that there be a modest and distinct song, so used in all parts of the Common Prayers in the Church, that the same may be as plainly understood, as if it were read without singing. And yet, nevertheless, for the comforting of such that delight in music, it may be permitted, that in the beginning, or in the end of Common Prayers, either at morning or evening, there may be sung an hymn, or such like song, to the praise of Almighty God, the best sort of melody and music that may be conveniently devised, having respect that the sentence of the hymn may be understood and perceived.[45]

John Day (*c.* 1522–84) was granted a Royal privilege to print psalters in October 1559 and produced a number of versions leading up to his most important version of 1562.[46] It was the 1562 version, entitled *The Whole Booke of Psalmes* and described by Ian Green as an early modern best seller, which would go on to become entrenched in the Church of England as 'Sternhold and Hopkins'.[47] In order to comply with Elizabethan printing regulations, stipulated in Injunction Fifty-One, Day stated on the title page of his text that the psalms 'were set forth and allowed in accordance with her majesties injunctions'.[48] Though the reference to Elizabeth's injunctions was dropped, all subsequent editions of the text retained the statement that they 'were set forth and allowed', including all editions printed in the eighteenth century. As Quitslund notes, this statement led to the belief that the *text* had a special status as allowed by the crown which became self-reinforcing and perpetuated with each reprinting.[49]

Following Day, the next major copyright holder of 'Sternhold and Hopkins' was the Stationers' Company. In 1603 the company raised nine thousand pounds to purchase a royal patent on 'prymers, psalters and psalms in metre or prose'.[50] The authority of 'Sternhold and Hopkins' became further entrenched through this print monopoly and a source of great profitability for the company as part of its 'English Stock'.[51] As James Doelman observes, it was consequently in the interests of the Stationers' Company to ensure that no other psalter posed a challenge to 'Sternhold and Hopkins'.[52] And despite many attempts to introduce other psalters, none were as successful.

There were nonetheless doubts expressed about the authorized status of 'Sternhold and Hopkins' and the quality of the text as literature. In *Ecclesia Restuarata* (1670), the ecclesiastical historian Peter Heylyn wrote of the rhymes of 'Sternhold and Hopkins' as being 'botching and barbaric' before noting that:

> notwithstanding being first allowed for private Devotion, they were by little and little, brought into the use of the Church: permitted rather, than Allowed to be sung, before and after Sermons; afterwards Printed, and bound up with the Common-prayer Book, and at last added by the Stationers at the end of the Bible. For though it be expressed in the Title of those singing Psalms, that they were set forth and allowed to be sung in all Churches, before, and after Morning, and evening prayer: and also before and after sermons; yet, this Allowance seems rather to have been a Connivance, than an approbation: No such allowance being anywhere found, by such as have been most industrious, and concerned in the search thereof.[53]

Heylyn reads the incorporation of 'Sternhold and Hopkins' from the margins of 'private devotion' into the centre of Church worship as a 'connivance' that was never directly decided upon but which was achieved through the decisions of the Stationers. He makes no mention of either Injunction Forty-Nine which allowed for the continuation of songs, or Fifty-One which required printers to seek a licence for each of their works.

Heylyn's position reflects the context of the English Civil War (1642–51) and its aftermath when the reputation of 'Sternhold and Hopkins' began to decline. The origin of the text at the court of Edward VI was effaced and the psalms began to be referred to pejoratively as 'Geneva jigs', reflecting the European composition of the text.[54] Most significantly, the singing of psalms began be a signifier of Puritanism. Ian Gentles records that at the battle of Dunbar at which the Scots, in support of the King, were routed by the English army, Oliver Cromwell was said to have led his troops with the first verse of Psalm Sixty-Eight, 'Let God arise and his enemies will be scattered'.[55] Consequently, as Quitslund has noted, the English Civil War transformed the meaning of psalm singing: 'Sternhold and Hopkins' became aligned with 'anti-aestheticism, sectarianism, and popular insurrection' because of their association with Puritanism and the alliance of Puritanism with radicalism.[56]

THE WHOLE BOOK OF PSALMS,

Collected into

English Metre,

BY

Thomas Sternhold, John Hopkins,
And Others:

Conferred with the HEBREW.

Set forth and allowed to be Sung in all Churches, of all the People together, before and after Morning and Evening Prayer, and also before and after Sermons; and moreover in Private Houses, for their godly Solace and Comfort: Laying apart all ungodly Songs and Ballads, which tend only to the nourishing of Vice, and corrupting of Youth.

James v. 13.
If any be afflicted, let him pray; and if any be merry, let him sing Psalms.
Colossians iii. 16.
Let the Word of God dwell plenteously in you, in all Wisdom, teaching and exhorting one another in Psalms, Hymns, and spiritual Songs, singing unto the Lord with Grace in your Hearts.

LONDON:
Printed by J. ROBERTS, for the COMPANY of STATIONERS. MDCCXLIX.

Figure 2.1: Title page of the 1749 edition of *The Whole Book of Psalms* – 'Sternhold and Hopkins'. Note that the Printer is J. Roberts, who also printed the *Collection* discussed in Chapter One. National Library of Australia, RB CLI 2221.

The important point to emerge from this necessarily brief history is that 'Sternhold and Hopkins' and the hundredth psalm became entrenched in the song culture of the state. This came about through a combination of factors, but the reference to the injunctions on the title page declaring that they were 'allowed' and the constant reprinting of this claim in the context of the Stationers' Company monopoly are highlighted here as key. Such was the dominance of 'Sternhold and Hopkins' that by the end of the seventeenth century, when the Stationers' Company agreed to print an alternative version of the metrical psalms by Nahum Tate and Nicholas Brady, it was 'authorized' by King William III in order to be a viable substitute.[57] This became known as the 'new version' and from this point onwards 'Sternhold and Hopkins' was referred to as the 'old version'. References to the 'Old Hundredth' from this point therefore indicate the origins of the hundredth psalm and its tune in 'Sternhold and Hopkins'. The new version of the hundredth psalm by Tate and Brady was given as:

> Be joyful all ye realms of earth
> Praise God, to whom your praise belongs:
> Serve ye the Lord with awful Mirth,
> Before his Presence come with Songs
> The Lord, ye know, is God alone,
> Who us, without our Aid, did make;
> Us for his Flock vouchsafes to own,
> And for his pasture-sheep to take
> For He's the Lord, supreamly good,
> His Mercy shall for ever last;
> His truth has always firmly stood
> And so shall stand for ever fast.
> O enter then with thanks sincere
> His Temple Gates, his courts with Praise,
> To bless his name devoutly there
> Your grateful Hearts and Voices raise[58]

Significantly, in their advertisement to the text, Tate and Brady state that they 'adapted their measures to the tunes that are best received, turning several psalms to those that are most musical, such as that of the 100, 113, 148, and others'.[59] In other words, though the words to the text had been altered, the 'Old Hundredth' of 'Sternhold and Hopkins' still lived on musically in the form of the tune of the text in Tate and Brady's *New Version*.

In his 1710 defence of 'Sternhold and Hopkins' High Churchman William Beveridge, Bishop of Asaph, objected to the modernizing tendencies of the *New Version*, claiming that it was 'brisk and lively, and flourished here and there with wit and fancy'.[60] Beveridge turned to the title page of 'Sternhold and Hopkins' to prove the legitimacy of the text as 'set forth and allowed' and argues that the 'old version' is the version of the 'common people'. To the objection that 'Sternhold and Hopkins' was full of obsolete 'old' words, Beveridge points out that 'late editions' of the 'old version' had been altered 'where the old words and phrases are taken out, and such put in their places as are now in common use'.[61] So in effect, there were two versions of 'Sternhold and Hopkins' circulating in the eighteenth century: the 'old version' as printed directly from the 1562 *Whole Book of Psalms*, and an updated 'old version'. This becomes an important point in Thomas Warton's later discussion of 'Sternhold and Hopkins' and the responses to Warton published in the *Gentleman's Magazine*. Beveridge also objected to the updated 'old version' and pointed to the 'immemorial custom and prescription' of the 1562 'old version'. Beveridge's trenchant defence of 'Sternhold and Hopkins', which was unusual for a high-churchman, represented a recognition of the extensive dissemination of the text and in this point he confirms the observations of Heylyn. Beveridge states:

> It is got into almost all the Bibles and Common Prayer-books, as well as churches in England; by which means, there are millions of them dispersed over the kingdom. There is not a family where any one can read, but there is one or more of the Psalm-books there; and in many families, more than inhabitants; so that no one thing can be so properly said to be got into all hands as this. How, then, is it possible to get it out again? Must all the Bibles and Common Prayer-books be changed, or bound up anew, that the New Version may be put into them? What a charge would that be to the nation! And when could it be effected?[62]

While Beveridge's defence of 'Sternhold and Hopkins' was inconsistent with other High Church positions on the text, such as Heylyn's, they were both in agreement on the effect of the dissemination of the text, bound up with Bibles and Common Prayer-books. Beveridge goes further, however, in implying that the text is bound into the very fabric of the nation. The widespread dissemination of 'Sternhold and Hopkins', and the contributing structural factor of the Stationers' Company monopoly, facilitated the text's move to become part of the language of criticism, discussed below.

'Despicable Doggerel' and the Ballad

In *Spectator* number 205, dated 25 October 1711, Joseph Addison published a facetious letter from a 'Country Clergyman' with the signature 'R. S.', requesting assistance dealing with 'a widow lady' from London who had been residing in his parish for the summer and 'astonishing' his Sunday congregation with her extravagant singing voice:

> But what gives us the most Offence is her Theatrical manner of Singing the Psalms. She introduces above fifty Italian Airs into the Hundredth Psalm, and whilst we begin *All People* in the solemn Tune of our Fore-fathers, she in a quite different Key runs Divisions on the Vowels, and adorns them with the Graces of *Nicolini*; if she

meets with Eke or Aye, which are frequent in the Metre of *Hopkins and Sternhold*, we are certain to hear her quavering them half a Minute after us to some sprightly Airs of the Opera.

I am very far from being an Enemy to Church Musick; but fear this Abuse of it may make my Parish Ridiculous, who already look on the Singing Psalms as an Entertainment, and not part of their Devotion; besides, I am apprehensive that the infection may spread, for Squire *Squeekum*, who by his Voice seems (If I may use the Expression) to be cut out for an *Italian* Singer, was last *Sunday* practicing the same Airs.

I know the Lady's Principles, and that she will plead the Toleration, which, (as she fancies) allows her Non-Conformity in this Particular; but I beg you to acquaint her, that Singing the Psalms, in a different Tune from the rest of the Congregation, is a sort of Schism not tolerated by that Act.[63]

The 'Widow Lady', with her 'fashionable extravagances', is quite unlike the singers of the rural parish choirs which Gammon describes as 'plebeian institutions', and while this letter is clearly intended to be ironic, its significance lies in the deployment of 'Sternhold and Hopkins' and the 'hundredth psalm' to comic effect in order to ridicule the Italian opera. The Italian opera had been introduced to the London stage in 1705 and was much criticized by Addison, Richard Steele and the critic and playwright John Dennis.[64] Gillen D'Arcy Wood observes that 'as early as 1707, Addison identified the arrival of Italian opera in England with the decline of native literature'.[65] The letter taps into this anxiety and achieves its comic affect through the juxtaposition of the florid operatic style of the widow, who imitates the famous Italian castrato Grimaldi Nicolini, and the unsophisticated solemnity of the 'Sternhold and Hopkins', characterized by the outmoded language of 'Eke' and 'Aye'.[66] The pun on 'the Toleration' refers to the Toleration Act of 1689, which had given the right to worship to those dissenting groups that accepted the doctrine of the Holy Trinity.[67] Using 'Sternhold and Hopkins' as a criterion of value, the letter points to the important differences between the Church of England and the Dissenters, in relation to the performance of psalms.

Arthur Bedford, who had written a pamphlet on *The Great Abuse of Musick*, clearly informed the humour behind the letter from the 'Country Clergyman', who himself refers to the 'abuse' of Church music and described his parishioners as looking 'on the singing of psalms as an entertainment, and not part of their devotion'.[68] Indeed, Bedford's pamphlet *The Great Abuse of Musick* had been advertised as 'Just published' in the *Spectator* numbers for Friday 31 August 1711 and Monday 3 September 1711.[69] Bedford had fulminated against the dangerous influence of the theatre upon church music, situating himself as a supporter of Jeremy Collier, who had written extensively about the dangerous effect of the theatre on society.[70] As part of the Society for Promoting Christian Knowledge, and the Reformation of Manners movement, Bedford advocated the formation of groups in parochial churches in order to learn to sing the psalms properly, which he believed would have the flow-on effect of reforming manners. Bedford is the nexus between Addison's deployment of 'Sternhold and Hopkins' and the hundredth psalm, and John Dennis (1658–1734), who also drew upon 'Sternhold and Hopkins' as a tool of cultural evaluation in relation to the literary canon.

This began in 1704 when Dennis published his *Grounds of Criticism in Poetry*, which was to be the preliminary to a larger work that was never completed. The context for this work was Dennis's opposition to the anti-theatrical movement exemplified in the sentiments of Collier, and followed by Bedford. In the preface, Dennis argues that religion was necessary in poetry in order to 'raise it to the greatest exaltation' and that conversely, poetry was necessary in religion in order to make 'more forcible impressions upon the minds of men'.[71] Thus a 'regulated stage' as the main 'encouragement' of poets, could function to further the cause of religion.[72] Dennis points out that much of the Old Testament was 'deliver'd in Poetry', including of course, the Book of Psalms. He reverses the terms of anti-theatrical criticism pointing to the poor quality of 'Sternhold and Hopkins' as a burlesque within the church:

> But I leave it to our Prelates and Pastors to consider, whether, since they are satisfy'd that there is a necessity, for an harmonious and a numerous style, in some parts of our public worship, they ought so long to have remain'd contented with the vile Metre of Hopkins, and by that proceeding to suffer the most lofty and most pathetick divine poetry to be burlesqu'd and ridicul'd in our churches, which is all one as if each Sunday they should dress up a Bishop in some antick habit, and expose him in that merry garb in order to raise the veneration of the people.[73]

The dressing up of a Bishop in some 'antick habit' which is 'merry garb' points to a carnival or grotesque overturning of the solemnity expected in the Church. Samuel Johnson's *Dictionary* defined 'antick' as 'Odd; ridiculously wild; buffoon in gesticulation', deriving from antique and ancient.[74] Dennis may also have been making a more specific allusion here to a satirical religious epigram by the seventeenth-century poet Francis Quarles. The epigram, which appeared in Quarles's 1632 publication *Divine Fancies*, satirized a puritan dubbed 'Zelustus' for holding a secret pride in Puritan clothing. This included his 'Geneva ruff', his steeple Hat and an 'antick habit of the old translation', a pun on 'habit' as clothing and 'habit' as a customary behaviour.[75] Despite being one of the most popular poets of the seventeenth century, Quarles's reputation in the eighteenth century was also the subject of much derision.

In his response to Addison's *Spectator* essays on the ballad, Dennis once again uses 'Sternhold and Hopkins' to consider the question of literary value. As previously discussed, Addison's essays have been read as the starting point of the 'ballad revival', or the process of re-evaluation of the ballad that was further developed with Percy's *Reliques* and the many ballad collections published throughout the century. While it has become a critical commonplace to read these essays as inaugurating a new stage in the development of English literature, less attention has been paid to the polemical nature of Addison's essays within their own context. John Dennis's essay 'Of Simplicity in Poetical Composition' offers a detailed rebuttal of Addison's claims for 'Chevy Chase' and deploys 'Sternhold and Hopkins' as part of his critique.[76] His response took the form of a letter to the translator and poet Henry Cromwell who had questioned whether Addison had been writing about 'Chevy Chase' in jest or in earnest. The substance of Dennis's answer is that Addison had been writing neither in jest nor in earnest because his premises were nonsensical. Dennis demonstrates this by showing that Addison's praise of the similarities between 'Chevy Chase' and Virgil's *Aeneid* was akin to comparing the metrical translation of Psalm 148 from 'Sternhold and Hopkins' with the hymn in the fifth book of John Milton's *Paradise Lost*.

Noting that the psalm of David had provided the 'groundwork' for both 'Sternhold and Hopkins' and Milton, Dennis 'transcribes' passages from both, beginning with the 'Sternhold and Hopkins' metrical paraphrase of Psalm 148:

> Give laud unto the Lord
> from heav'n that is so high;
> Praise him in deed and word
> above the starry sky;
> And also ye his angels all,
> Armies royal, praise joyfully.
> Praise him both moon and sun
> which are so clear and bright
> The same of you be done
> ye glittering stars of light.
> And ye no less, ye heavens fair
> Clouds of the air his praise express[77]

Dennis describes this passage as the 'contemptible dogrel of Hopkins' which is also 'despicable dogrel in spight of its being figurative'.[78] The problem is partly in the translation – the phrases here are repeated, says Dennis, 'like a parrot without understanding them and without being moved by them'.[79]

Following this damning assessment of Psalm 148, Dennis reproduces the lengthy excerpt from Book Five of Milton's *Paradise Lost* as a point of comparison. This part of the text describes Adam and Eve exiting their bower in the morning and beginning to praise God with a song:

> These are thy glorious Works, parent of Good,
> Almighty, This universal Frame,
> Thus wondrous Fair, They self how wondrous then!
> Unspeakable, who sit'st above these Heavens
> To us invincible or dimly seen
> In these thy lowest works, yet these declare
> Thy Goodness beyond thought and pow'r divine

> Speak, ye who best can tell, ye Sons of Light
> Angels, for ye behold him, and with Songs
> And Choral Symphonies, day without night
> Circle his throne Rejoycing, ye in Heav'n;
> On Earth join all ye Creatures to extol
> Him first, Him last, Him midst, and without End.[80]

Dennis concludes that by placing these passages together, the reader can be convinced that 'the one is bald and vile and wretched, and the other great and exalted Poetry'.[81] Both Dennis and Addison had been involved in the canonization of Milton as a literary genius, overlooking his political radicalism.[82] Dennis was also involved in a complex personal dispute with Addison and Steele, which Edward Niles Hooker points out may have been a motivating factor in his response to the ballad papers.[83] The emphasis here, however, is upon Dennis's act of 'laying apart', quite literally on the page, in order to establish a hierarchy in which 'Sternhold and Hopkins' are doggerel and Virgil and Milton are great and exalted poets. In Dennis's critique, there is no basis for the comparison that Addison seeks to make between 'Chevy Chase' and Virgil. However, in setting up this distinction, or hierarchy, Dennis also demonstrates the way in which 'Chevy Chase', as representative of the ballad, and the psalms of 'Sternhold and Hopkins' were indeed *similar*. In Dennis's estimation the psalms of 'Sternhold and Hopkins' and the ballad were analogous in terms of their simplicity and aesthetic crudity (and implicitly their identification as songs of the common people). Rather than 'laying apart' the psalm and the secular song, Dennis's use of 'Sternhold and Hopkins' to establish criteria of literary value actually works to bring them together: it is 'poetry' which is being laid apart as fundamentally different from the songs, both religious and secular, of the people.

Another example of the embeddedness in eighteenth-century culture of 'Sternhold and Hopkins' and the way that the psalm, the ballad and the song can be reconnected, occurs in John Gay's 1714 poem *The Shepherd's Week*, a series of mock Virgilian eclogues corresponding to days of the week. The final poem ('Saturday') opens with a summons to the 'rustic muse' to prepare 'sublimer strains' over the drunken and snoring Bowzybeus. This lofty pretence is soon undercut, however, when the sleeping Bowzybeus is discovered by Susan, who has left her companions harvesting in the field to step behind a hedge to 'relieve' herself. Hearing her screams, her companions run to her aid and the awoken Bowzybeus begins to sing to his audience.

> No sooner 'gan he raise his tuneful song,
> But lads and lasses round about him throng.
> Not ballad-singer plac'd above the croud
> Sings with a note so shrilling sweet and loud,
> Nor parish clerk who calls the psalm so clear,
> Like Bowzybeus sooths th' attentive ear.[84]

By comparing Bowzybeus's singing to the recognizable types of the 'ballad-singer' *and* the 'parish clerk', Gay undercuts the authority of the parish clerk who was charged with leading the congregation in singing psalms in parochial churches.[85] While Dennis conscripts 'Sternhold and Hopkins' into his ridicule of Addison's praise of the simple ballad of 'Chevy Chase', Gay draws upon the 'parish clerk' – transmitter of 'Sternhold and Hopkins' – and the 'ballad-singer' as a way of contextualizing the performance of Bowzybeus's songs. Both connect the ballad with the psalm in order to make an instantly recognizable point for their readers.

Nicholas Temperley has documented the role of the parish clerk in 'lining out' each line of the chosen metrical psalm of 'Sternhold and Hopkins' so that the congregation could then sing the line back.[86] This led to a dramatic slowing down in the tempo of the psalms which became the subject of much ridicule. John Wilmot, Earl of Rochester addressed the following verse to a 'psalm-singing clerk' which was reprinted as part of the *Rochester's Jests* series in the eighteenth century:

> Sternhold and Hopkins had great Qualms,
> When they translated David's Psalms
> To make the Heart full glad;
> But had it been poor David's fate,
> To hear thee sing and them translate,
> By G-d 't had made him mad.[87]

In Volume Two of his *General History of Music*, Charles Burney used an analogy from nature to explain the similar roles of the ballad singer and the parish clerk:

> It is the fanciful opinion of some naturalist that the blackbird, the thrush, the robin, or the bull-finch, that so often repeats his peculiar melody during summer, is but performing the part of a singing-master to the young birds of his own species: the nurse, the ballad singer in the street, and the parish clerk, exercise the same function in our towns and villages: and the traditional tunes of every country seem as natural to the common people as warbling is to birds, in a state of nature.[88]

The 'ballad singer' in the street and the 'parish clerk' leading the singing of the psalms both form part of the soundscape of the everyday that is naturalized. Like Burney, Ann Wierda Rowland has identified the importance of nurses and women as the 'most common ballad singers of the eighteenth century and the most significant sources of traditional ballads for antiquarian collectors'.[89] Women ballad singers were also part of the streetscape; Connell highlights their presence at markets and fairs, whilst Hogarth depicted female ballad singers in his 'March of the Guards to Finchley'.[90] By comparison, the parish-clerk had gone unnoticed, tainted as he was by the reputation of 'Sternhold and Hopkins'. However as Burney's observation demonstrates, he played an equally significant and visible role as a recognizable cultural type and a transmitter of song.

It is not only Bowzybeus's style of singing, but his choice of songs that demonstrates the inter-relationship between the metrical psalm and the ballad. Bowzybeus's song has been characterized as an assemblage of references to traditional lore, ballads, and customs which Dianne Dugaw describes as 'the genuine stuff of popular discourse'.[91] The song includes a description of a country fair and a raree-show before moving onto balladry: 'Of raree-shows he sung, and Punch's feats, / Of pockets pick'd in crowds, and various cheats; / then sad he sung the Children in the wood'.[92] 'Sternhold and Hopkins' also features in Bowzybeus's performance following his rendition of an infamous song by the seventeenth-century poet John Denham (c. 1614–69) about a Quaker having intimate relations with a horse titled 'News from Colchester', a song to which Gay provides a footnote.[93] After singing this, Bowzybeus is stricken with a 'religious qualm' and decides to sing the 'hundredth psalm':

> All in the land of Essex next he chaunts,
> How to sleek mares starch Quakers turn gallants;
> How the grave brother stood on bank so green.
> Happy for him if mares had never been!
> Then he was seiz'd with a religious qualm,
> And on a sudden, sung the hundredth psalm,
> He sang of Taffy Welch, and Sawney Scot,
> Lylly bullero and the Irish Trot.[94]

The hundredth psalm is inserted amidst songs associated with the nation state – 'Lylly bullero', which was said to have 'rhymed King James out of the England', and the figures of 'Taffy Welch' and 'Sawney Scot' representing Wales and Scotland, part of the union of Great Britain, as well as the 'Irish Trot'. Gay's Bowzybeus thus exemplifies the increasing identification of 'Sternhold and Hopkins' with secular songs – both non-political and topical – vindicating Bedford's view that psalms were becoming a form of entertainment. However, Dennis was not alone in his belief in the outmoded style of 'Sternhold and Hopkins'. Opposition also came from outside the Church of England, demonstrating that the question of the legality of 'Sternhold and Hopkins' was an important one and had begun to inform the criticism and response to the text.

Modernization and the Law

Isaac Watts (1674–1748) shared the negative views about 'Sternhold and Hopkins', but wrote not from within the Church of England but as a Dissenting member of the Church of Congregationalists. Watts had articulated his views on psalmody in 1707 in 'A Short Essay Toward the Improvement of Psalmody' which appeared in his collection of *Hymns and Spiritual Songs*.[95] Watts emphasized the need for the people to understand what they sang, not through the familiarity of repetition and custom, but through genuine comprehension. Because many of the psalms referred to the specific pre-Christian context of David and the Jewish state, Watts argued that true comprehension was impossible and moreover, that many of the psalms were irrelevant for the purposes of the contemporary Christian Church:

> There are other divine songs which cannot properly be accommodated to our use, and much less be assum'd as our own without very great alterations, (viz) such as are filled with some very particular Troubles or Enemies of a Person, some Places of Journeying or residence, some uncommon Circumstances of a Society, to which there is scarce any thin parallel in our day or case: such are many of the songs of *David*, whose Persecutions and Deliverances were very extraordinary. Again such as express the worship paid to God by carnal Ordinances and Utensils of the Tabernacle and temple. Now if these be converted into Christian Songs in our Nation, I think the Names of Ammon and Moab may be as properly chang'd into the Names of the chief enemies of the Gospel, so far as may be without publick Offence: *Judah* and *Israel* may be called *England* and *Scotland*, and the Land of *Canaan* may be translated into Great Britain.[96]

Watts clearly envisioned the psalms as songs of the nation in the *present* where the 1707 union of England and Scotland had created 'Great Britain'. With Watts therefore, we see how the psalms attain political meanings because they are tied to the political construction of Great Britain.

Watts provided a series of answers to the possible objections to this conception of the psalms. To the objection that the psalms were the direct word of God, and therefore should not be altered, he replied that the translation of the psalms from Hebrew and then into metre, rendered them 'so far different from the inspired words in the original languages, that it is very hard for any man to say that the version of *Hopkins and Sternhold*, the *New England* or the *Scots* Psalms are in a strict sense the Word of God'.[97] Having established that David's language is 'adapted to his own Devotion and the worship of the *Jewish* Church', Watts ingeniously established a precedent for the singing of the psalms in the language of the New Testament: 'Should the sweet-singer of Israel return from the Dead into our age, he would not sing the words of his own psalms without considerable alteration'.[98] By extension, Watts saw no authority in the version of 'Sternhold and Hopkins' and committed himself to the alteration and modernization of the psalms. He addressed the issue of the lawfulness and authority of 'Sternhold and Hopkins' obliquely by posing the rhetorical question:

> Why should every part of Divine Worship under the Gospel be express'd in language suited to that Gospel (viz) Praying, Preaching, Baptism and the Lord's Supper; and yet when we perform that part of worship which brings us nearest to the heavenly State, we must run back to the Law to borrow Materials for this Service?[99]

Rather than 'running back to the law', or the authority proclaimed on the title page of 'Sternhold and Hopkins', Watts produced his own corpus of psalms in 1719 titled *Psalms of David Imitated in the Language of the New Testament, And apply'd to the Christian State and Worship*. The reference to the 'Christian State' reflected his belief that the psalms be songs of the modern Christian state of Great Britain, rather than the state of Israel of the Old Testament. 'Worship' included the Dissenting groups that belonged to this broader Christian State as opposed to the Church of England as the state Church. Earlier, in 1712, Watts had published his imitation of 'Psalm CXIV' in the *Spectator* for August of that year, a psalm which would later form part of the 1720 collection.[100] Writing anonymously in a letter introducing the psalm, he appealed to 'Mr Spectator's taste' as overriding religious and party divisions: 'whilst we are distinguish'd by so many thousand humours, and split into so many different Sects and Parties, yet Persons of every Party, Sect, and Humour are fond of conforming their Taste to yours'.[101] Thus despite Watts's position as a Dissenter, Addison's – 'Mr Spectator's' – 'taste' cuts across this religious division. The application of taste and a criteria of literariness would be applied to the judgement of 'Sternhold and Hopkins' and the psalms.

Watts was joined by John Wesley, who also criticized 'Sternhold and Hopkins' from a different position, as a Methodist: still within the established Church of England, but on its margins. In a letter dated 20 September 1757 and published in Volume Three of the *Arminian Magazine* in February 1780 he writes,

> The longer I am absent from London, and the more I attend the service of the Church in other places, the more I am convinced of the unspeakable advantage which the people called Methodists enjoy. I mean, even with regard to Publick Worship, particularly on the Lord's Day ... Nor is their solemn address to God interrupted either by the formal drawl of a parish clerk, the screaming boys, who bawl out what they neither feel nor understand, or the unseasonable and unmeaning impertinence of a voluntary on the organ. When it is seasonable to sing praise to God, they do it with spirit, and with the understanding also: not in the *miserable scandalous doggerel of Hopkins and Sternhold*, but in psalms and hymns which are both sense and poetry; such as would sooner prove a Critic to turn Christian, than a Christian to turn Critic. What they sing is therefore a proper continuation of the spiritual and reasonable service; being selected for that end (not by a poor hum-drum wretch who can scarce read what he drones out with such an air of importance, but) by one who knows what he is about, and how to connect the preceding with the following part of the service. Nor does he take just 'two-staves', but more or less, as may best raise the soul to God: especially when sung in well composed and well adapted tunes, not by a handful of wild unawakened striplings, but by a whole congregation: and then not lolling at ease in the indecent posture of sitting, drawling out one word after another, but all standing before God, and praising him lustily and with a good courage.[102]

Wesley depicts the many aspects of the soundscape of psalmody in his description – the droning, near illiterate parish clerk, the 'bawling' screaming boys, presumably charity children, which he later describes as 'wild unawakened striplings', and most importantly 'the miserable scandalous doggerel of Hopkins and Sternhold'. Wesley's account shows how inextricably linked 'Sternhold and Hopkins' were to the performance practice of parochial psalmody, yet, as previously mentioned, the role and reputation of the text has not featured in scholarship on this topic. It is by acknowledging the cultural significance of the text that a more nuanced account of the politics of songs at this period can be given, one that takes into account the different approaches to psalmody by the Dissenting churches and connects this to a language of criticism and evaluation as seen in the work of Dennis. Wesley himself explicitly links the language of criticism to the practice of Christianity when he states that the music of the Methodists could 'prove a critic to turn Christian, than a Christian to turn Critic'.

And once again, the point needs to be made that Wesley's Methodists existed as distinct from the Church of England and were not subject to the belief that 'Sternhold and Hopkins' was authorized.[103] They produced their first hymnal in 1737 titled *A Collection of Psalms and Hymns* and, over the course of his life, Wesley's brother, Charles, was to write approximately 9,000 hymns. A massive compendium of hymns was published in 1780 titled *A Collection of Hymns for the use of People Called Methodists*, with the aim of bringing various hymn books together. In the Preface, Wesley addresses the 'judges of poetry' stating that the hymns contain:

> No doggerel, not botches, nothing put in to patch up the rhyme, no feeble expletives. Here is nothing turgid or bombast on the one hand, nor low and creeping on the other ... We talk common sense (whether they understand it or not) both in verse and prose, and use no word, but in a fixt and determinate sense. Here are (allow me to say) both purity, the strength and elegance of the ENGLISH language: and at the same time the utmost simplicity and plainness, suited to every capacity. Lastly, I desire men of taste to judge (these are the only competent judges;) whether there is not in some of the following verses, the true Spirit of Poetry: such as cannot be acquired by art and labour; but must be the gift of nature.[104]

Given his earlier reference to the 'scandalous doggerel' of 'Sternhold and Hopkins' and the form of this work as a collection, it is clear that Wesley's preface, with its assurance of 'no doggerel', obliquely situates the Methodist collection *against* 'Sternhold and Hopkins', a point which is then reinforced when he points out the literary qualities of the text. These literary qualities are rendered in 'the purity, the strength and the elegance of the ENGLISH language', which is another oblique reference to the problems with 'Sternhold and Hopkins' as a result of their paraphrasing the psalms from Hebrew into English metre to 'patch up the rhyme'. This recalls Watts's point that 'Sternhold and Hopkins' were mediators of the psalms and that the notion that their text was the 'word of God' was therefore false. Despite his deviation from the reformation text of 'Sternhold and Hopkins', Wesley is careful to point out that the reformation principles of 'simplicity and plainness, suited to every capacity' are still evident in the Methodist hymns. Critical taste once again emerges as a factor in the sanction of an alternative set of songs and the word of God is defined as the 'true spirit of poetry'. 'Sternhold and Hopkins' was thus clearly deployed by Wesley as a tool of cultural evaluation in his characterization of Methodist song.[105]

Warton's *History of English Poetry*

The literary value of 'Sternhold and Hopkins' was further questioned by Thomas Warton, Oxford scholar and later Poet Laureate, in his sprawling narrative of the history of English literature, the *History of English Poetry,* published in three volumes in 1774, 1778 and 1781. David Fairer notes that literary history had been previously conceived of in terms of catalogues, chronologies and dictionaries and that Warton's narrative was the first of its kind.[106] In Volume Three of the *History*, Warton reluctantly conceded that of all the metrical translations of the scripture, the versification of the psalms by 'Sternhold and Hopkins' had 'acquired an importance' and was included in his series, though 'not so much from any merit of its own, as from the circumstances with which it is connected'.[107] Those circumstances were the wider context of the Reformation. Warton faced the problem of how to reconcile the 'circumstances' of this history with the aesthetics of the text. He believed 'Sternhold and Hopkins' had been unqualified to produce poetry and that their versifications elicited disgust:

> Allowing for the state of our language in the middle of the sixteenth century, they [Sternhold and Hopkins] appear to have been but little qualified either by genius or accomplishments for poetical composition. It is for this reason that they produced a translation entirely destitute of elegance, spirit, and propriety. The truth is, that they undertook this work, not so much from an ambition of literary fame, or the consciousness of abilities, as from motives of piety, and in compliance with the cast of the times. I presume I am communicating no very new criticism when I observe, that in every part of this translation we are disgusted with a languor of versification, and a want of common prosody. The most exulted effusions of thanksgiving, and the most sublime imageries of the divine majesty, are lowered by a coldness of conception, weakened by frigid interpolations and disfigured by a poverty of phraseology.[108]

Once again the idea of the 'old' as being outmoded emerges in this passage. 'Sternhold and Hopkins' were motivated by 'piety', rather than literary ambition and ability and produced a psalter 'in compliance' with 'the cast' of their own times which in Warton's account, has not stood the test of time and the standards of his present. In 'communicating no very new criticism' of this point,

Warton signals the entrenched role of 'Sternhold and Hopkins' as both the focus, and tool, of criticism.

To prove his point, Warton provides an example from Psalm Seventy-Four, a psalm in which God is implored to come to the aid of the Jewish people, held captive by the Babylonians who had destroyed their temples. The psalmist asks God why he has allowed the destruction to continue and why no retribution is forthcoming:

> Why doost withdrawe thy hand aback,
> And hide it in thy lappe?
> O plucke it out, and be not slack
> To Give thy foes a rappe![109]

Warton describes this verse as 'ludicrous' and exhibiting 'trivial expressions'.[110] The plea to God to give the Babylonians a 'rappe' evokes the idiomatic phrase to 'rap across the knuckles', which is a comically inadequate response to the Jewish plight. Warton notes the 'burlesque' effect of this, echoing Dennis's use of the term.[111] The *Parish Clerk's Guide* to the use of the psalms for 'various subjects and occasions' noted that this psalm was to function as 'a prayer against enemies in general that rouse tumults and uproars in the Church and State' and as 'a prayer for aid and help implored'.[112] By contrast, the new version of 'Tate and Brady', published in 1782, paraphrased this passage in a much more forceful way:

> Why hold'st Though back thy strong Right-hand,
> and on thy patient breast,
> When vengeance calls to stretch it forth,
> So calmly let'st it rest?[113]

Even more egregious was an example of 'vulgar phraseology' from Psalm Seventy-Eight. Categorized as a 'historical psalm', Psalm Seventy-Eight details the history of Israel and describes the periods when the people were disobedient and failed to uphold the covenant with God and to worship him. The fourth part of the psalm, quoted by Warton, states: 'for why, their hearts were nothing bent/to him, nor to his trade'.[114] God's work is here depicted as a trade, which, for Warton, had the effect of 'degrading' the practice of religion.[115]

After providing numerous other examples, Warton makes the case for the eradication of 'Sternhold and Hopkins' from the liturgy and public worship:

> To the disgrace of sacred music, sacred poetry, and our established worship, these psalms still continue to by sung in the church of England. It is certain, had they been more poetically translated, they would not have been acceptable to the common people. Yet however they may be allowed to serve the purposes of private edification, in administering spiritual consolation to the manufacturer and mechanic, as they are extrinsic to the frame of our liturgy, and incompatible with the genius of our service, there is perhaps no impropriety in wishing, that they were remitted and restrained

to that church in which they sprung, and with whose character and constitution they seem so aptly to correspond. Whatever estimation in point of composition they might have attracted at their first appearance in a ruder age, and however instrumental they might have been at the infancy of the reformation in weaning the minds of men from papistic ritual, all these considerations can now no longer support even a specious argument for their being retained.[116]

While acknowledging the important political function of 'Sternhold and Hopkins' as Protestant songs of the Reformation, Warton views their ongoing place in the liturgy as a disgrace. Their religio-political function was to make the psalms more accessible to the 'common people', but with the passage of time and the progress of literature this role had ceased to be valid. Unlike Wesley's appeal to the 'judges of criticism', the understanding of the common people is placed at odds here with the idea of a 'poetic translation'. Finally, Warton echoes Heylyn's position by noting that 'Sternhold and Hopkins' were 'first introduced by the puritans, afterwards by connivance they never received any royal approbation or parliamentary sanction, notwithstanding it is said in their title page, that they are 'set forth and allowed'.[117] In disputing the claim that 'Sternhold and Hopkins' was allowed, and emphasizing the poor quality of the text, Warton shared much in common with Watts and Wesley. Yet the position from which he spoke was as a High Churchman, demonstrating that the politics of this text engendered complex alignments.

The reaction to Warton's treatment of 'Sternhold and Hopkins' in the *Gentleman's Magazine* is an example of this complicated response. In a letter dated 19 May and published in the June 1781 issue, the correspondent 'N. Y.' observed that:

> there is something unbecoming in Mr W. wishing them [Sternhold and Hopkins] to be restrained to any society of Christians (whether confined to manufacturers and mechanics, or otherwise), while he is conscious that many versions exist at this day which would far more elevate the minds of the people to the God whom they profess to worship.[118]

In addition to pointing out the errors in Warton's text, 'N. Y.' points out his sleight of hand in quoting from the 1562 *Whole Book of Psalms* rather than the updated 'old' versions circulating. This recalls the point made earlier that there were actually two versions of 'Sternhold and Hopkins' available in the eighteenth century: the version drawn from the 1562 *Whole Books* and an updated 'old version' that Bishop Beveridge had alluded to.[119] While 'N.Y.' suggests that Warton's use of the 1562 old version is strategic, the comments of the musician Edward Miller indicate that the 1562 version was still widely used, and as Bishop Beveridge had predicted, it had been difficult to replace. Writing in 1791, Miller quotes a list of ridiculous examples drawn from the older editions including the same example used by Warton from Psalm Seventy-Four. He observes:

> It would scarcely be supposed, that most of these passages are to be found in editions of the *old version*, printed so lately as the year 1781. Many may say, that the *stanzas* here selected from the *older*, have been altered in the *newer* editions, so as to make them more tolerable. This is true; but poor people in the country are seldom in possession of these new editions. Their family bibles and prayer-books are, to many, almost the only legacy left them by their forefathers. It is a custom with me, when I go into a *village cottage*, to look into their bibles and prayer-books; and I aver, that for *one* in which the above passages are not contained, I have met at least with *four* in which they are to be found; even in those printed about the beginning of the present century; and it is no uncommon thing, to hear even these *cottagers* remark, '*That there are strange verses in some of their singing psalms!*' Should then an enlightened people suffer their poor brethren to be still enveloped in the dark night of ignorance? Should the miserable rhymes, and obsolete language of a groom of the chamber to *King Edward* VI. Be still imposed upon us? Surely No.[120]

Miller's 'custom' of looking in the bibles and prayer-books when entering a village cottage recalls Addison's confession that upon entering 'any house in the country' he was unable to leave a room before studying the walls for broadsides.[121] As previously discussed, one such encounter with a broadside of 'Two Children in the Wood' gives rise to his description of the ballad as 'one of the darling songs of the common people'. While Miller's encounters result in a far less enthusiastic appraisal, they are nonetheless an important reminder of the way that 'Two Children in the Wood' and 'Chevy Chase'– the subject of Addison's other meditation – are connected with 'Sternhold and Hopkins' in time, space and criticism.

In the August edition, of the *Gentleman's Magazine* the correspondence continues with a sarcastic letter from the correspondent, 'No Psalm-Singer':

> I have examined the controverted sections in the third volume of Mr. Warton's *History of English Poetry*, the purport of which seems to be this: A congregation of Calvinists, under whom we may also include Methodists, Anabaptists, and Independents, usually consists of *manufacturers* and *mechanics*; and to the meanness of such a congregations Mr. Warton seems to think the miserable stanzas of Sternhold perfectly well adapted. He therefore wishes this mode of psalmody was sent back and restrained to that church in which it first originated at Geneva, and to which it seems so properly to belong. It is certainly better calculated for the spiritual consolation of tallow-chandlers and taylors, than for the pious uses of the liberal and intelligent. Psalm-singing and Republicanism naturally go together. They seem both founded on the same leveling principle. The republican Calvin appears to have been of opinion that all people should sing in the church, as well as *act* in the state, without distinction or inequality. Hence his necessity of *vulgar* and *popular* psalmody.[122]

As previously discussed, Wesley as leader of the Methodists and Watts as an independent Congregationalist, responded to the unsuitability of 'Sternhold and Hopkins' by developing their own psalm paraphrases and hymns. 'No Psalm-

Singer' thus drew attention to Warton's simplistic characterization of these Dissenters as 'manufacturers and mechanics' to whom 'Sternhold and Hopkins' were 'well adapted'. He further mocks Warton's High Church position by conflating psalm singing with republicanism, levelling, and Calvinism. Imbued in this sarcasm was the recognition that 'Sternhold and Hopkins' had a polemical political meaning that tapped into key associations of Puritanism, fanaticism and levelling. Nicholas Temperley has read this letter as the straight response of a genteel parishioner wanting to 'curb the excesses of country choirs'.[123] His reading, like Gammon's, misses the politics of the text of 'Sternhold and Hopkins'. By contrast, the approach taken here foregrounds the text of 'Sternhold and Hopkins' as a key to understanding the broader politics at work in 'parochial psalmody'. From Addison's opera singer, to the tallow-chandlers and taylors described by 'No Psalm-Singer', 'Sternhold and Hopkins' was not only at the centre of debates about singing, but an important part of the critical lexicon in the eighteenth century.

'God Save the King' and the Psalmic Context

It was as a tool of criticism that 'Sternhold and Hopkins' formed another important framework from which to examine the category of the national song in the eighteenth century. The 'Old Hundredth' emerged from 'Sternhold and Hopkins', thus becoming implicated in debates about cultural and literary value at a time when the songs of the 'common people' started to be re-evaluated by figures such as Addison and Percy. Bowzybeus's performances of the hundredth psalm as part of his repertoire of secular, national songs seen as emblematic of popular culture and folklore, thus presents 'Sternhold and Hopkins' as another context in which to consider the idea of national song in this period, with a particular focus on what is arguably the most important song of the nation to emerge in England – 'God Save the King'.

The emergence of 'God Save the King' in response to the threat of Jacobite invasion in 1745 has been thoroughly documented by Percy Scholes.[124] The song was first performed in September 1745 at the Drury Lane theatre in response to the encroaching threat of 'the young pretender' who had landed with his forces on the west coast of Scotland in mid-July and was marching toward England.[125] Scholes presents evidence that prior to this date 'God Save the King' was a Stuart song. He records that Benjamin Victor wrote to David Garrick in 1745 describing the performance of 'an old anthem tune' in London theatres that had originally been sung for King James II upon the landing of William of Orange.[126] The song was altered by Thomas Arne for the Drury Lane performance with the insertion of the name 'George', so that no doubt could arise about to which King loyalty was being pledged. By this time, the song was already in circulation in print, appearing in a song collection from the previous year, *Thesaurus Musicus* (1744). Numerous publications followed, including that of the *Gentleman's Magazine*, in October 1745, which introduced it as 'A Song for two Voices. As sung at Both Playhouses' – making it clear that the expression of loyalty was also performed by the other royal theatre, Covent Garden, and suggesting national unanimity. The words of the song were given as:

> God save great George our King,
> Long live our noble king
> God save the king.
> Send him victorious,
> Happy and glorious,
> God save the king.
> Long to reign over us
> God save the king.
>
> O Lord our God arise,
> Scatter his enemies,
> And make them fall;
> Confound their politics,
> Frustrate their knavish tricks,
> On him our hopes we fix,
> O save us all.
>
> Thy choicest gifts in store
> On George be pleas'd to pour,
> Long may he reign;
> May he defend our laws,
> And ever given us cause,
> To say with heart and voice
> God save the king.[127]

In her influential account of the formation of British national identity, Linda Colley reads the emergence of 'God Save the King' as part of her broader thesis that national identity was closely 'yoked to religion' with Protestantism being 'the foundation that made Great Britain possible'.[128] The song was a 'blessedly familiar lifeline' in a time of uncertainty and invasion, reflecting the reassurance 'demanded' by Protestant culture that the people 'were in God's particular care'.[129] Following Scholes, she notes that it was not until the 1800s that the term 'national anthem' was used to describe the song, though it had been referred to as an 'anthem tune' before this.[130] This in itself was perhaps an indication of the song's origins at the chapel of St James and its straddling of secular and religious spaces. The term 'anthem' had yet to be secularized. Dr Johnson defines 'anthem' in religious terms as 'a holy song; a song performed as part of divine service'.[131] Musicologists such as Nicholas Temperley have also pointed to the religious

552   *A Song for two Voices.   As sung at both Playhouses.*

God save great GEORGE our king, Long live our noble king.
God save great GEORGE our king, Long live our noble king.
God save the king. Send him vic-to-ri-ous, Happy and glo-ri-ous,
God save the king. Send him vic-to-ri-ous, Happy and glo-ri-ous,
Long to reign o-ver us, God save the king.
Long to reign o-ver us, God save the king.

2.
O Lord our God arise,
Scatter his enemies,
And make them fall;
Confound their politics,
Frustrate their knavish tricks,
On him our hopes we fix,
O save us all.

3.
Thy choicest gifts in store
On *George* be pleas'd to pour,
Long may he reign;
May he defend our laws,
And ever give us cause,
To say with heart and voice
God save the king.

Figure 2.2: 'God Save the King', as printed in the *Gentleman's Magazine* in October 1745. From the collection of the State Library of New South Wales, Australia.

meaning of the 'anthem' in the eighteenth century as a musical setting of biblical text, usually psalms.[132]

Notwithstanding the important divisions within the 'Protestantism' of Great Britain, reflected in the different version of the psalms used in Scotland, and the entrenched place of 'Sternhold and Hopkins' in the Church of England, Colley's observations about 'God Save the King' hint at the importance of the psalms as a *specific* context in which to understand the song. And while Scholes employs the term 'metrical hymn' to describe 'God Save the King', it is with specific reference to 'Sternhold and Hopkins' that the song is situated here. As Scholes has suggested, one of the most interesting aspects of the song was its historical malleability, originating as a Stuart song and then adapted to demonstrate loyalty to the Hanoverian dynasty. In Platonic terms this reflects the changing of song styles and the implications of this alteration for change of the law. In terms of the psalms, the song performs another reversal: specifically, the recuperation of Psalm Sixty-Eight. As discussed earlier, this psalm was sung by Cromwell's army and still retained an association with puritanism and levelling; associations that were still very apparent for critics such as Warton. Psalm Sixty-Eight depicts God as a marching warrior and a destroyer of enemies, opening with the lines: 'Let God arise, and then his foes / will turn themselves to flight: / His enemies for fear shall run, and scatter out of sight'.[133] Verse two of 'God Save the King' employs this same language calling on God to 'arise' and to 'scatter' King George's enemies: 'Oh Lord our God arise, / scatter his enemies / and make them fall'. The *Parish-Clerk's Guide* lists Psalm Sixty-Eight to be sung 'against enemies in general, that raise tumults and uproars in the Church and State'.[134] During the threat of Jacobite invasion therefore, performances of the anthem which took place at the theatre would have more than likely been complemented by the singing of the psalm in church. The psalm and the anthem were thus made to repudiate the threat of two political extremes – the immediate threat of the Jacobites and the doctrine of the divine right of Kings and, stretching back into historical memory, the threat of Cromwell's army of saints.

'God Save the King' also played a prominent role and consolidated its popularity during the illness of King George III in 1789 and following his recovery. Frances Burney, daughter of Charles Burney, who as second keeper to the robes of Queen Charlotte travelled with the royal family to Weymouth in June 1789 for the King's convalescence, noted the many performances of the song in her diary. The most significant, in terms of the argument of this chapter, was the performance of the song in the Sunday service Burney attended:

> On the Sunday we all went to the parish church; and after the service, instead of a psalm, imagine our surprise to hear the whole congregation join in 'God save the King!' Misplaced as this was in a church its intent was so kind, loyal, and affectionate,

that I believe there was not a dry eye amongst either singers or hearers. The King's late dreadful illness has rendered this song quite melting to me.[135]

Here quite literally 'God Save the King' becomes a psalm and the authority of 'Sternhold and Hopkins' is overturned by a congregation intent on demonstrating loyalty to the royal family, though Burney notes that its singing in this context was 'misplaced'.

This followed another church performance celebrating George's recovery on 24 April 1789, though in the cathedral setting of St Paul's Cathedral. The day had been appointed by the King's Royal Proclamation as a day of 'General Thanksgiving' to 'his divine majesty' for his 'signal interposition' in removing the illness afflicting the King.[136] The acknowledgement of 'divine interposition' in the restoration of the King's health was restated in the many addresses published in the issues of the *London Gazette* leading up to the day, which accords with Colley's description of the 'Protestant elect'. The procession was reported extensively in newspapers. The *Times* enthused that the event would surpass the greatest spectacles of pagan civilizations past:

> the ceremonies of Pagan adoration, the Games of polished Greece, and the triumphs of imperial Rome, formed no such Spectacle as that which this day honours and delights the metropolis of the British Empire: – The Sovereign adoring the world's creator for mercies showered down upon him, and his people overflowing with grateful praise to the same almighty power, on the reflection that the mercies granted to their monarch, are mercies granted to themselves.[137]

Even those papers which had supported the Prince of Wales during the Regency crisis could not help but be captivated by the display of awe and majesty on Thursday 23 April 1789. The *World* notes 'whether this paper has or has not spoken truth – was yesterday seen by *all London*, and perhaps *half the country*. Did WE *not say* – THE KING WAS WELL?'[138]

All sections of the press gave detailed accounts of the order of procession for 23 April creating a virtual experience for readers. A procession through the streets of London began at eight o'clock in the morning from the Palace Yard, beginning with the coaches of the House of Commons and followed by the House of Peers with accompanying dignitaries. The *London Gazette* described the royal family setting out soon after ten o'clock and travelling along Pall Mall and the Strand, 'amidst a prodigious concourse of people'.[139] Many of the onlookers were spectating from decorated scaffolding that, as reported by the *Gentleman's Magazine*, had been erected against houses and churches along the route.[140] The procession was then met at the Temple Bar by the Lord Mayor and officials of the city who, on the approach of the King, are described as mounting their 'beautiful white palfreys' which were 'richly caparisoned' in blue and gold silk, the front of their bridles embroidered with the words 'God Save the King'.[141] The King and royal family were met by the peers and clergy at the West doors of St. Paul's shortly before twelve o'clock and as the grand procession entered, approximately 6,000 'charity children' from the charity schools of the London parishes sang the hundredth psalm. The children had been seated in specially built semi-circular galleries under the dome at the north and south doors so that they could be seen by the procession.[142] The *Times* specifies that the song was sung to the 'old tune' and it is clear that the version used was the 'Old Hundredth' from 'Sternhold and Hopkins' as the first line is given as 'All people that on earth do dwell'.[143]

The role of the charity children as singers of the 'Old Hundredth' in the thanksgiving ceremony was significant because it re-staged, for the King's recovery, the annual anniversary meeting of the charity children, a major event on the London charitable and social calendar. The *Gentleman's Magazine* reports that 'they had a place appropriated for their appearance, much in the same manner as at their anniversary meeting – this was at the particular desire of her Majesty'.[144] The 'charity children' were those children who attended day schools which were funded by charitable subscription under the auspices of the Society for Promoting Christian Knowledge. Since 1704 the children of the charity schools from the different parishes of London had joined together to walk in procession to a church to hear a sermon and attend Divine Service.[145] This annual event grew in size and significance; in 1782 it began to be staged in St. Paul's Cathedral and drew large crowds of spectators. Sarah Lloyd has identified the significance of this annual meeting, in the context of conspicuous displays of charity as spectacle, 'blurring distinctions between resorts, theatres, livery halls and churches'.[146]

The blurring of boundaries between theatre and the church in the spectacle of the National Thanksgiving ceremony was evident in the account of the Whig politician Sir Gilbert Elliot, given in a letter to his wife. Elliot had travelled to St. Paul's as part of the procession of the House of Commons in Lord Palmerston's coach, which took two hours. He reflected that the day 'answered extremely well as a show, and was affecting in some moments of it'.[147] The language of exhibition and spectacle continues in his description of the charity children as 'piled up to a great height all around ... by far the most interesting part of the show'.[148] He also advises his wife of the annual anniversary performance – 'you may see this any year, for they are brought to St. Paul's, and placed in the same order one day every year, and I think it will be worth your while if you ever come within sight of St. Paul's again'.[149] The most memorable part of the 'show', however, was the performance of the hundredth psalm as the King processed through the cathedral:

> As soon as they began to move up the church, the drums stopped, and the organ began; and when the King approached the center all the 6,000 children set up their little voices and sang part of the hundredth psalm. This was the moment that I found

most affecting; and without knowing exactly why, I found my eyes running over, and the bone in my throat, which was the case with many other people.[150]

The power of the charity children's performance was that their multitudinous number meant that they could be heard by all present. Elliot could not hear the Bishop of London's sermon from his seat, which he is told later was 'dull' and 'courtly', so the singing was the most striking and memorable aspect of the day.[151] The King and Queen were greatly affected by the singing as they entered and Elliot observes that during the mass the King 'looked about with his opera-glass and spoke to the Queen during the greatest part of the service, very much as if he had been at a play', once again reinforcing the blurring of boundaries between the theatre and the church.[152]

David Fairer has drawn attention to the presence of the charity children on the day of thanksgiving for George's return to health as an exploitation of the positive associations which were attached to their own annual thanksgiving day at St. Paul's.[153] They became 'entangled in the nation's power politics' because the celebration of the King's regeneration meant that the hopes of a Regency and Whig government were foiled.[154] Fairer uses Elliot's account to highlight the ability of the children to neutralize the politics of the occasion and to evoke a response of sympathy from a member of the opposition. The important point here, however, which also emerges in Elliot's description, is that in eliciting this response the children were singing the hundredth psalm. As Fairer also notes, the psalm was sung yearly at the anniversary meeting and, as such, had become a tradition of the charity children's performance.[155] For the 1785 anniversary meeting, for example, a broadside was printed of the 'Psalms and anthem to be sung at the anniversary meeting' in which all four verses of the 'old version' were printed.[156] By the late eighteenth-century therefore, the 'Old Hundredth' was increasingly detached from the contexts of 'Sternhold and Hopkins', to assume a definitive place in the nation's consciousness as an anthem of the nation-state. In his essay on 'Music as Amusement', Vicesimius Knox described the one hundredth and the one hundred and fourth psalms as 'the most popular music in England'. 'Popular' in this case meaning not the 'vulgar' parish clerk leading the common people in full-throated singing of 'Sternhold and Hopkins', but the psalm as exemplary of the national order – the idealized 'people' of Britain – with the monarchy at its apex.[157] As the royal family exited St. Paul's following the thanksgiving mass, the children sang the one hundred and fourth psalm. These performances were part of a politics of song that stretched beyond the issues raised by the Regency crisis in 1788–9 to encompass the cultural politics of 'Sternhold and Hopkins', demonstrating the interconnected nature of songs at this period, where a psalm could be a national song, and a 'secular song' such as 'God Save the King', could draw so heavily from the psalms.

This chapter began with Thomas Paine's disparaging reference to 'Sternhold and Hopkins, Hopkins and Sternhold' from *Rights of Man*. In concluding then, it is perhaps appropriate to draw upon Paine's observation about the Psalms in the second part of the *Age of Reason*, in which he dismantles the religious aura surrounding the Psalms as songs. Much like Watts, Paine writes that the Psalms relate to the 'local circumstances' of the Jewish nation, and as such have nothing to do with his own times.[158] For Paine, the 'Psalms of *David*' is a misnomer because 'they are a collection, as song-books are now-a-days, from different song writers'.[159] Psalm 137, written hundreds of years after David's death, describes the captivity of the Jews in Babylon where they were taunted by their captors to sing 'Hebrew songs'. This is the same, writes Paine, 'as a man would say to an American, or to a Frenchman, or to an Englishman, sing us one of your American songs, or your French songs, or your English songs'.[160] And here Paine gets at the central point of this chapter: that, in the eighteenth century, psalms *were* national songs. The post-enlightenment focus of literary criticism on the category of the 'ballad' in relation to the formation of the canon of national literature as 'English literature' has obscured this point. 'Sternhold and Hopkins', a text deeply embedded in the practice of worship and singing as the 'allowed', 'old version', was an important part of criticism as a measure of what good poetry should be defined *against*. Such was the complexity of the text, however, that 'Sternhold and Hopkins' also produced one of the most important songs of the eighteenth century, the 'Old Hundredth'. The 'Old Hundredth' took its place with 'God Save the King' as a national song before the term 'national anthem' entered language and the divisions between religious songs and secular songs were consolidated. Far from 'laying apart' songs and ballads as the title page proclaimed, 'Sternhold and Hopkins' and the 'Old Hundredth' reveal the way in which these categories were interconnected.

3 SONGS AS PHILIPPICS: THE 'HARMONDIUM MELOS' AND THE 'IO PAEAN' OF REVOLUTION

On 7 October 1761, a Royal Proclamation was made requiring that the four 'forms of prayer with thanksgiving', commemorating significant dates from the nation's history, 'be forthwith printed, and published, and annexed to the Book of Common Prayer'.[1] The form of prayer for 5 November commemorated the thwarting of the Gunpowder Plot of 1605 and the arrival of William III at Torbay in South West England in 1688. Drawing upon Psalm Forty, the prayer giving thanks for William begins:

> Accept also, most gracious God, of our unfeigned thanks, for filling our hearts again with joy and gladness after the time that thou hadst afflicted us, and putting a new song into our mouths, by bringing his majesty King *William* upon this day, for the deliverance of our Church and Nation from popish tyranny and arbitrary power.[2]

Having examined in the previous chapter the psalmic imagery of God putting songs in mouths and the hundredth psalm's movement into political and nationalist consciousness, the politics of song can equally be explored through the context of the French Revolution, with particular discussion of the political song tradition of the 'Harmodium Melos', and the ways in which political actors of the period either 'put songs into mouths' or were concerned with those who did.

This chapter examines the role of songs in the commemoration of revolutions in the long eighteenth century, beginning with the commemoration of the Glorious Revolution of 1688 and ending with the French Revolution of 1789. Part One examines the role of songs in the commemorative celebrations of the Revolution Society, and the attempt of the society to inaugurate a new state anniversary for the celebration of the 1688 Revolution, one that would emphasize the rights of the people in the form of a 'new song' in addition to those sung on 5 November. Attempts to shift the interpretation of the 1688 Revolution were strenuously denounced by Edmund Burke in his *Reflections on the Revolution in France* (1790). Part Two examines Burke's response in the *Reflections* and his depiction of Dr Richard Price, a prominent member of the Revolution Society, as a 'philippizing', 'chaunting' singer. Burke's use of the verb 'philippizing' is key here in uncovering the importance of the 'Harmodium Melos', a political song from Classical Greece that commemorated the deliverance of Athens from tyranny in 415 BC. Part Three turns to work of Bishop Robert Lowth, who regarded the 'Harmodium Melos' as having more power than a philippic. The 'Harmodium Melos' was recorded by the writer Athenaeus (fl. AD 200) in his text *The Learned Banqueters*, thought to have been written in AD 192. The song originated in the performance context of the classical symposion, that part of the evening, following a banquet, where toasts were made and convivial 'skolion', or songs, were sung.[3] This chapter reveals the continuity of the 'Harmodium Melos' in the eighteenth-century equivalent of the symposion – the celebrations and sociability of the extra-parliamentary associations, the Revolution Society and the Society for Constitutional Information. Burke's denunciation of Price using metaphors of classical song is also apparent in his reference to the 'Io Paean', the song of triumph, which is alluded to in his *Appeal from the New Whigs to the Old Whigs* (1791), and is the subject of Part Four of this chapter. The final section of the chapter explores the radicalization of the 'Harmodium Melos' and the songs sung at the anniversary celebrations of 1792, charting their circulation through the different print media of the songster, the newspaper, and as slip songs. This chapter argues that this classical song tradition was fundamental to the language of revolution commemoration and that it was deployed in all kinds of political songs in the eighteenth century. This dimension of political and song culture has remained unexplored in ballad studies and in political and social histories of the period. Whereas the political character of songs has often been identified in terms of topicality – of how they relate to a specific event or person – this chapter will show that this topicality was fused with classicism. The political song culture of the eighteenth century needs to be conceived in terms of this long *durée*, which, after 1789, gained more potency as the traditions of elite political life became popularized through print.

Anniversary Songs

In 1979 Albert Goodwin stated that historians have not paid 'sufficient attention to the political effects of the nation-wide celebrations of the centenary of the English revolution of 1688'.[4] Far from being merely an interesting backdrop, Goodwin argues that the centenary worked to counter the effects of public apathy toward parliamentary reform following the defeat of William Pitt's reform proposals of 1785, re-energizing the reform cause.[5] Since Goodwin's observation, further elaboration of the importance of the centenary of the revolution has been provided by Kathleen Wilson. Her exhaustive account, which spans across the eighteenth century, argues that the Revolution had a profound impact on popular political consciousness and discourse during the eighteenth century.

While Wilson notes that commemoration of the Revolution could be made to serve the purposes of both the establishment and the opposition, she places a special emphasis upon the mobilization of the commemoration by reformist and radical groups who wished to see greater popular representation in Parliament.[6]

The Revolution Society was comprised of Dissenters who commemorated the Glorious Revolution by celebrating the birthday of William III on 4 November each year with a religious service, a meeting of the society and a dinner.[7] The celebration of the centenary in 1788 presented the Revolution Society with another opportunity to put forward an agenda for parliamentary and civil reform. The first section of this chapter examines the celebrations of the Society with a particular attention to song as a codified part of this anniversary culture. Songs were an important part of the dinner ritual of the society and presented a way of incorporating celebrity stage performers into these rituals. Chapter One has already shown how Rapin's account of the Revolution of 1688 affected the interpretation of certain songs. This section will focus upon how the Revolution Society's song culture, an important part of its convivial sociability, functioned as part of its broader aim to reinterpret 1688.

The work of Gillian Russell and Clara Tuite on sociability provides an important framework for this consideration of song. Their ground-breaking collection, *Romantic Sociability* (2002), aimed to recover the significance of sociability as a text 'in its own right', challenging the conventional narrative of the Romantic paradigm in its stress on individualism and isolation.[8] Russell and Tuite note that earlier Hanoverian ideals of sociability, in which the club is a space which excludes the 'spirit of faction', do not hold true later in the century. Moving into the 1790s, they point to 'highly charged combinations of politics and sociability'.[9]

The meetings of the Revolution Society in the 1780s can be seen as one such highly charged combination of politics and sociability. The surviving minute book of the Society records the proceedings of the day for the centenary meeting of 1788:

> after a sermon preach'd by the Rev Dr Kippis at the old Jewry meeting house a numerous & respectable meeting of about 300 Gentlemen dined at the London Tavern, to celebrate that important aera where universal harmony and good order prevailed and the generous spirit of Freedom glowed in every breast. An Oration was delivered by the Rev Dr Towers, the Character of King William was read by the Rev. Dr Rees; an Ode written by Mr Hayley was recited by Mr Jenkins & Messrs Arrowsmith, Sedgewich, Dignum, Deeble, Tilley & others crown'd the day with songs of conviviality suited to the occasion.[10]

The anniversary combined religious ritual at a morning service with secular conviviality during the evening dinner at the tavern, which included an anniversary meeting. Of particular interest here, however, are the 'songs of conviviality suited to the occasion' by five named singers. 'Arrowsmith, Sedgewich, Dignum, Deeble and Tilley' were all professional singers and actors who were engaged especially for this occasion. The most famous were Arrowsmith and Dignum. A well-known oratorio singer, Daniel Arrowsmith had performed at the Handel memorial concerts in 1784 and at the Vauxhall Pleasure Gardens throughout the 1780s, whilst Charles Dignum was a singer and actor at Drury Lane (he had played the part of 'Sir Owen' in the 1786 production of *Richard Coeur de Lion*).[11] Dignum, who was well-known for his corpulent figure, was also a singer at Vauxhall Gardens during the summer, in addition to performing for the Anacreontic Society, at Freemason's Hall, at Willis's Rooms and in taverns.[12] John Roach's *Authentic Memoirs of the Green Room* notes that Dignum was employed on 'occasions of public festivity, and convivial meetings, to enhance the charm of good fellowship and good cheer, by the attraction of a good song'.[13] Tickets to this meeting were advertised in the *Morning Post* for the comparatively expensive amount of 10s 6d, so evidently the meeting brought together an audience drawn from the wealthy who were paying to be entertained.[14]

The song sung on this occasion 'by Arrowsmith' was printed in the *Public Advertiser* on 6 November 1788 and was entitled 'A Song on the Revolution':

> Britannia's sons attend, while I attempt to sing,
> Of noblest deeds that ever grac'd the British Crown,
> The Glorious Revolution by England's Royal King,
> Great William the Third of ancient fame and renown
> He calm'd his people's frights,
> And pass'd the Bill of Rights,
> Fix'd freedom – settled Brunswick's time
> Then let us sing
> God Bless the King!
> And may Brunswick's name for ever shine.
>
> James aided by the French, on Erin's famed isle,
> Pretending royal William had usurp'd the British throne,
> Put Protestants to death in cold blood, meanwhile,
> Proclaim'd the clergy traitors to his Crown.
> This Jacobite, we're told,
> Com'd brass for sterling gold.
> And papists to his standard drew,
> But his hard fate,
> It was so great,
> To the Continent he quickly flew.
>
> Great William stem'd the tide to plots and Popish liars
> Establish'd England's church, and reform'd the British coin;
> Victorious were his arms, in all his foreign wars,
> When Russel, Rooke, and Marlbro did with him join.
> They bore the chief command,
> By sea as well as land

His enemies they put to flight.
While here we sing
Their fame shall ring,
For to whom we owe this happy night.

Had not these brave men fought, where should we
Have been?
Perhaps some abject slaves, under dread tyrannick
Sway;
But free-born Britain's sons, under laws serene
We live to welcome this auspicious happy day!
Then Briton's all unite;
In peace, in war, in fight.
Let fury on our foes be hurl'd ;
For British fame,
With George's name
Shall bid defiance to the world.[15]

The song presents the Whig account of the Glorious Revolution of 1688, when the Protestant King William III of Orange rescued the English people from the Catholic King James II, putting an end to their 'frights' with 'the Bill of rights', limiting the power of the crown and ending the threat of Catholic absolutism. James's attempt to regain his Kingdom from the Catholic stronghold of Ireland – 'Erin's' famed isle' – with the aid of France was ultimately defeated. 'Great William' not only 'stem'd the tide of Popish liars' but 'establish'd England's church', a reference to the 1689 Act of Toleration which allowed Dissenters the right to worship, and 'reform'd the British coin', an acknowledgement of the creation of the Bank of England in 1694, celebrated here as another achievement of the new state.[16] The song also commemorates the leaders of William's armed forces – 'Russel, Rooke, and Marlbro'– who are called into the time and space of the Revolution Society Meeting in 1788: 'While here we sing, / their fame shall ring, / for to whom we owe this happy night'.[17] Finally, the concluding stanza imagines the tyranny that might have been were it not for the struggles of these 'brave men' and with bellicose pride declares that united 'free-born' Britons, now under Hanoverian rule in the eighteenth century, will defy the world.

The performance of such songs was interspersed with the giving of toasts at convivial gatherings, a convention discussed in *Pocock's Everlasting Songster* which also offers 'rules for behaviour'. The introduction to this text notes that the authority of a good Chairman, sometimes of a superior rank, was necessary to 'regulate' the order of proceedings as the sole giver of the toasts and who 'commands the Songs alternately with the toasts and sentiments'.[18] Where other toast books provided copious lists of toasts in order to ensure that no man would ever be caught in the embarrassing situation of being toast-less at a convivial gathering, Pocock's introduction is notable for its emphasis on proper conduct.[19] The introduction explains that the

> chief design in the little book was to collect and present a selection of songs, toasts, and sentiments, avoiding those of a political, wicked or vulgar tendency, which have so long been suffered by Chairmen of different Societies to reign predominant: and at this place it will not be amiss to say, that a popular toast which has been the too general rule to give first ('To the Exclusion of every Female', whose company we ought rather to court than discourage) has been a disgrace.[20]

The exclusionary toast demonstrates the homo-social nature of these convivial gatherings and is a reminder that the Revolution Society at the tavern was exclusively the domain of men. Pocock further advises that in situations where the chairman gives the first three toasts, the first should be 'The King', the second 'The Queen', and the third 'The Royal family'.[21]

The first toast of the Revolution Society at the centenary celebration was 'to the majesty of the people', contravening this accepted order. There were forty-one toasts made in total, which were printed at the back of an edition of the Society's *Abstract*.[22] Kathleen Wilson points out that this number was significant, forty-one being a provocative allusion to the first English Revolution of 1641.[23] The toast to 'The Majesty of the People' was followed by 'The Glorious Revolution, and the immortal memory of our great deliverer, King William the Third', and then 'The King and Royal Family'.

James Epstein has noted a pattern of political convivial activities from the late seventeenth century which were particularly evident during the Wilkite campaigns and in response to the War with America.[24] His work on the importance of dining and toasting in the radical political culture of the nineteenth century establishes 'the importance of meanings that were expressed in terms of a highly ritualized field of political and symbolic practice rather than in terms of more formally articulated ideology, whether written or spoken'.[25] Epstein's insights equally pertain to the context of the centenary celebrations in the late eighteenth century under analysis here.

A figure at the centre of this late eighteenth-century culture of convivial dining, singing and toasting was Charles Morris (1745–1838) known as 'Captain Morris' after he achieved this rank in the war against America.[26] The nineteenth-century historian of song and satire, Thomas Wright, described Captain Morris as 'the best song-writer of his day, and many of his effusions have been thrown into unmerited oblivion'.[27] Morris wrote the songs 'Billy's Too Young to Drive Us' and 'Baby and Nurse' which featured prominently in the Westminster election of 1784, both ridiculing the youth of William Pitt who had assumed the office of Prime Minister at just 24 years of age following the failure of the Fox-North coalition.[28] Morris attached himself to Charles James Fox, the Whig candidate for Westminster who stood against Lord Hood and Sir Cecil Wray. He was a fixture at the political meetings where his singing, interspersed with toasting, was an important aid to conviviality.[29] The account of the meeting of the electors of Westminster, held on 12 March 1784 at The Shakespeare Tavern, reports that

> between the several toasts, the company were highly entertained by Captain Morris, and Mr. Johnstone, of Covent Garden Theatre, who alternately sung... Perhaps in the annals of song-writing there cannot be found a more pointed or a more humourous composition than that sung by the Captain.[30]

In 1785, Captain Morris was admitted to the Sublime Society of Beef Steaks, an elite group of twenty-four men who met each Saturday to dine on roast beef and who performed an elaborate series of rituals at their meetings.[31] Singing was central to the society with Morris known as 'the bard of the beefsteaks' and described as the 'life and soul of the Society'.[32] His song 'The Toper's Apology', in which he explains why he calls for his glass to be filled again and again, was a testament to the powers of alcohol and was paradigmatic of Morris's other drinking songs sung at society meetings.[33] Morris's drinking and political songs achieved much popularity and were published in songster compilations.[34] The first compilation of his own songs appeared in 1786 which ran to many editions in the last decade of the eighteenth century.[35]

In the picture following, Captain Morris holds up a slip-song 'to the tune of plenipoy' (a reference to his bawdy song 'The Plenipotentiary') at a convivial gathering of the Whigs. The figure to his right is Charles James Fox, and to his left is Richard Sheridan. Protruding from his pocket is a copy of 'Captain Morris's Songs by subscription'. Mary Dorothy George points out that Fox says 'come sing me a Boosey-song' which is a misquotation of Falstaff from Shakespeare's Henry IV, part I, who says 'come, sing me a bawdy song; make me merry'.[36]

Captain Morris wrote the song for the Whig Club's celebration of the 1688 centenary, held at the Crown and Anchor Tavern on 5 November 1788. The club had an illustrious membership of the leading Whig politicians of the time, including Charles Fox, Edmund Burke and Richard Sheridan, with Fox and Sheridan depicted in Gillray's print of the Captain as Homer 'singing his verses to the Greeks'. The *General Evening Post* printed the chorus lines of the Captain's song: 'And oh! To no spot be the true Whigs confin'd, / But wide spread the spirit that breathes for mankind'.[37] The papers were possibly precluded from printing the song in its entirety because the Captain's songs were so popular that they were being printed as part of songster compilations at this time. The Whig Club gave its first toast on this occasion to the 'glorious and immortal memory of King William the Third', which was in line with the convention of toasting the King first.[38]

The Revolution Society and the Whig Club maintained close links at this time. At their anniversary meeting in 1788, the Revolution Society resolved to seek

Figure 3.1: 'Homer singing his verses to the Greeks'. Print by James Gillray, published by Hannah Humphrey, 1797. © Trustees of the British Museum

the support of the Whig Club for their proposal to bring a bill forward in parliament which proposed a new date on the commemorative calendar. This was the subject of their eighth toast on the evening of 4 November: 'to the Revolution Commemoration Bill' which proposed a significant addition to the commemorative focus of the Glorious Revolution. The Bill proposed a new anniversary in which 'the true and genuine principles of our free constitution, be hereby propagated throughout the kingdom'. It was resolved

> that a perpetual Anniversary Thanksgiving to Almighty God, ought to be established by Act of Parliament, in order to commemorate the Revolution, and the confirmation of the people's rights and to perpetuate the happy memory thereof. And that it is also the opinion of this Meeting, that in order to celebrate those illustrious events, in a manner suitable to their supreme importance, the said perpetual Anniversary ought to be kept on the 16th day of December, namely, on that memorable day when the Bill of Rights passed into a law; by which solemn Act of Parliament the Throne

was declared to have become vacant, the true and ancient liberties of the subject were recognized, ratified, and confirmed, and the Glorious revolution completed.[39]

The Whig politician Henry Beaufoy, present at this meeting, agreed to introduce the Bill in the House of Commons. He did so on 24 March 1789, arguing that while the fifth of November was the day set aside to celebrate the thwarting of the Gunpowder Plot and for the arrival of King William, there was no designated day to celebrate the Bill of Rights.[40] This was a significant omission, Beaufoy argued, because the people had been 'too much disposed' to rely upon the Magna Carta, the elective branch of the legislature and the right of trial by jury 'for the maintenance of their freedom'.[41] The reign of Henry VIII and Cromwell's Commonwealth had proved that these 'securities' could fail.[42] The remedy to this was that 'a brief but comprehensive abstract of the rights and privileges of the people ... should be annually read in our churches as part of the service of the day. Thus ... the people would be instructed in the nature of their rights'.[43] With this Bill the emphasis of the 'Glorious Revolution' upon the dynastic change from the Stuarts to the Hanoverians would be matched by a thanksgiving ceremony which emphasized the rights of 'the people'.

The Bill was defeated in the House of Lords by thirteen votes to six.[44] The Bishop of Bangor, John Warren, argued that 'the great event of the revolution was in a very particular manner taken notice of every year in the service of our church, for the fifth of November'.[45] Warren went on to state that he thought it highly improper that the Bill of Rights be read out in Church every year, though Hansard does not record the reasons he gives.[46] Lord Stanhope, who had chaired the meeting of the Revolution Society at the London Tavern at which the resolution was made, replied that thanks to God were not returned for the restoration of liberties, 'but only because he made an opposition fall before the king – a foreign king, with a foreign army'.[47]

The importance of the Revolution Commemoration Bill here is that it sought to change the emphasis of the established ceremony of the state, a foundation moment which gave thanks to God for putting a new song into the people's mouths. With the constitutional crisis that beset the country, the Revolution Commemoration Bill has largely remained a footnote for historians of this period.[48] Beaufoy's involvement in this bill has been overshadowed by the fact that during this same session, on May 8 of 1789, he introduced another motion to repeal the Test and Corporations Acts, which was rejected in the Commons by 122 votes to 102.[49] That the Revolution Commemoration Bill was largely symbolic, however, does not lessen its significance in terms of the anniversary culture that was so important in the celebrations of the Revolution Society and the state. The Bill foreshadowed Richard Price's *Discourse* given in November of the same year, which gave thanks for the Glorious Revolution but at the same time pointed to its incompleteness by looking externally, to France. The implications of this were profound for Burke who, reading the *Discourse* in January 1790, was compelled to write his *Reflections*, invoking the resonances of classical song in his attack upon Price.

Songs as Philippics

Price's infamous sermon entitled *A Discourse on the Love of Our Country* was delivered at the Meeting-House in the Old Jewry on 4 November 1789 as part of the Revolution Society's annual celebration of King William III's birthday. *Discourse* was a celebration of the revolution of 1688 in light of the recent events in France. Reverence and veneration for the memory of the 'Glorious revolution' are coupled in Price's discourse with the belief that it was yet incomplete:

> We have, therefore, on this occasion, peculiar reasons for thanksgiving – But let us remember that we ought not to satisfy ourselves with thanksgivings ... I would farther direct you to remember that though the Revolution was a great work, it was by no means a perfect work.[50]

While the Bill of Rights had granted Protestant Dissenters the right to worship and to open their meeting houses under the protection of the Toleration Act, Dissenters were still subject to the operation of the Test and Corporation Acts, which prevented them from holding civil and military office. The two most recent attempts to repeal the Test Acts, in 1787 and in May 1789, as previously mentioned, had failed.[51] The other great imperfection Price declaimed was the 'inequality of representation'.[52] Significantly, he links the act of remembrance with parliamentary reform:

> The inadequateness of our representation has been long a subject of complaint. This is in truth our fundamental grievance; and I do not think that anything is much more our duty, as men who love their country, and are grateful for the revolution, than to unite our zeal in endeavouring to get it redressed.[53]

France had recently solved both problems with the 'Declaration of the Rights of Man and of the Citizen', which was approved by the National Constituent Assembly on 26 August 1789.[54] The 'Declaration' was printed as part of Paine's answer to Burke in Part One of *Rights of Man* (1791).[55] Article Six provided that the ability to participate in the formation of the law was open to all citizens: 'all being equal in its sight, are equally eligible to all honours, places, and employments, according to their different abilities, without any other distinction than that created by their virtues and talents'.[56] Article Ten specified that 'No man ought to be molested on account of his opinions, not even on account of his irreligious opinions'.[57]

Though Burke had offered tentative support to the Dissenters' cause the previous year, as well as at other points in his career, the alignment of the cause to repeal the Tests and Corporation Act with parliamentary reform was something he could not countenance following the tumult of the French Revolution. Richard Bright, the prominent Bristol merchant and Dissenter, had written to Burke seeking support for the cause of repeal in May 1789. Burke's reply of 18 February 1790, following the fall of the Bastille, demonstrates his surprise at the contamination of religion and politics in the wake of the revolution:

> Extraordinary things have happened in France; extraordinary things have been said and done there, and published with great ostentation ... I was much surprised to find religious assemblies turned into sorts of places of exercise and discipline for politicks; and for the nourishment of a party which seems to have contention and power much more than Piety for its Object.[58]

As Alfred Cobban notes, the 'extraordinary things' were the congratulatory addresses to the National Assembly sent by the Revolution Society at the suggestion of Dr Price.[59] Burke writes:

> On my coming to town, I sent for an account of their proceedings, which had been published by their authority, containing a sermon of Dr Price, with the Duke de Rochefaucault's and the Archbishop of Aix's letter and several other documents annexed.[60]

The third edition of the Price's *Discourse* contained the Congratulatory addresses sent by the Revolution Society to the National Assembly of France and the replies of the National Assembly as appendices.[61]

Burke's particular concern at the beginning of *Reflections* is with the communications of the Revolution Society, and the lack of authority from which they speak. Though he initially includes the Society for Constitutional Information in his aim, the Revolution Society emerges as his main concern, since, 'the National Assembly of France has given importance to these gentlemen by adopting them; and they return the favour, by acting as a sort of sub-committee in England for extending the principles of the National Assembly'.[62] Burke questions the legitimacy of the Revolution Society by casting doubt on the Society's claim that it had been formed soon after the 1688 Revolution for the purpose of commemoration. He, who belonged 'to more clubs than one' could not recollect 'until very lately' of hearing of them.[63]

> I find, upon enquiry, that on the anniversary of the revolution in 1688, a club of dissenters, but of what denomination I know not, have long had the custom of hearing a sermon in one of their churches; and that afterwards they spent the day cheerfully, as other clubs do, at the tavern.[64]

In addressing the National Assembly, the Revolution Society have intruded into the role of government in matters of diplomacy and Burke observes sarcastically that 'Henceforth we must consider them as a kind of privileged persons as no inconsiderable members in the diplomatic body'.[65]

After describing the circumstances in which Price's *Discourse* was delivered and acknowledging it 'a very miscellaneous sermon, in which there are some good moral and religious sentiments and not ill expressed', Burke delivers his judgement of Dr Price:

> For my part, I looked on that sermon as the public declaration of a man much connected with literary caballers, and intriguing philosophers; with political theologians, and theological politicians, both at home and abroad. I know they set him up as a sort of oracle; because, with the best intentions in the world, he naturally philippizes, and chaunts his prophetic song in exact unison with their designs.[66]

Goodwin observes that Burke's reference to 'literary caballers' and 'intriguing philosophers' was a 'clear allusion' to Price's link with the First Marquess of Lansdowne, who had been a patron of ecclesiastical, legal and administrative reform.[67] The 'political theologians' and 'theological politicians' prefigures Burke's linking of Price with the seventeenth century regicide preacher Hugh Peters 'at home' and refers to the replies from the Archbishop of Aix, President of the National Assembly, to the congratulatory addresses sent 'abroad' by the Society to the National Assembly. A letter from the Archbishop to the Revolution Society reiterated the cosmopolitan ideal preached by Price, where ingrained enmity would dissolve, and repeated the central motif of *Discourse*, the love of country:

> It undoubtedly belongs to our age, in which reason and liberty are extending themselves together, to extinguish for ever national hatred and rivalship ... the two most enlightened people of Europe ought to shew, by their example that the love of their country is perfectly compatible with every sentiment of humanity.[68]

This allows Burke to claim that Price, 'with the best intentions in the world', has been set up as a dupe to appear as a sort of oracle, but in reality is a sham.

The image of Price philippizing and chaunting in unison with the designs of the French and their sympathizers combines the classical oratorical notion of philippizing with the metaphor of song. In his annotation to this passage, J. C. D. Clarke cites the *Oxford English Dictionary* definition of 'philippize': 'to favour or take the side of, Philip of Macedon ... to speak or write as one is corruptly "inspired" or "influenced"'.[69] Conor Cruise O'Brien writes that Burke invokes the *Philippics* of the Greek orator and politician Demosthenes who had claimed that the Delphic Oracle was *philippizing* – meaning that the prophecies served the secular interests of Philip of Macedon.[70] The surviving speeches of

Demosthenes (384 BC–322 BC) from the fourth century, in which he attempted to warn the citizenry of Athens about the Persian King Philip II's ambitions to conquer the city, are known as the Philippics.[71] The oracle of Apollo, located at Delphi, was frequently consulted for guidance concerning military campaigns and during times of war. The oracles were delivered by a priestess known as the 'Pythia', who sat upon a tall bronze tripod in a sunken room in the temple of Apollo.[72] Peter Hunt observes that though it is unknown exactly how Philip would have been able to influence the responses of the Pythia, earlier accounts of the corruption of the oracle lend credibility to Demosthenes' suspicions.[73] We know of Demosthenes's suspicion of the predictions of the Delphic oracle of Apollo from the fourth century orator Aeschines (390 BC–314 BC), and later, in the first century, from Plutarch (AD 46–120). In the oration 'The Speech Against Ctesiphon', Aeschines claimed that Demosthenes had accused the oracle of prophesying in favour of Philip: 'And did not Demosthenes oppose, and say that the Pythia had gone over to Philip?'[74] Plutarch repeated this account in his biography of Demosthenes: 'in consequence he [Demosthenes] would not allow his countrymen to pay attention to the oracles or listen to the prophecies. Indeed he even suspected that the Pythian priestess was on the side of Philip'.[75]

Demosthenes thus inaugurated the tradition of the 'philippic' and in AD 44 the Roman orator Cicero also became famous for his fourteen philippics against Mark Antony who had come to power following the assassination of Julius Caesar.[76] In the eighteenth century, Dr Johnson's dictionary gives a more general meaning of the term 'Philippick' as '[from the invectives of Demosthenes against Philip of Macedon] any invective declamation'.[77] According to the prominent man of letters, Hugh Blair, Demosthenes's orations embodied the ideals of eloquence because they were 'founded upon good sense and solid thought ... in order to persuade, or to work on the principles of action'.[78] While the associations of the term with Demosthenes are clear, the role of the Delphic oracle as evident in Aeschines, raises a complexity in the origin of the term. Whereas Demosthenes in his philippics was speaking *against* Philip of Macedon, the Delphic oracle as described by Aeschines was accused of 'philippizing' in *favour* of Philip.

The latter is evident in Jonathan Swift's *A Discourse of the Contests and Dissentions between the Nobles and Commons in Athens and Rome*, first published in 1701:

> Philip, Alexander's father (the most Christian King of that age) had indeed some time before begun to break in upon the republic of Greece by conquest or bribery; particularly dealing large money among some popular orators, by which he brought many of them, as the term of art was, then to Philippize.[79]

Swift's text is also relevant because it is part of a broader tradition, in which Burke situates himself, of drawing upon Demosthenes in order to make a comment on the current situation between Britain and France. In *Several Orations of Demosthenes*, published in 1744, the advertisement to the reader makes the connections explicit:

> This work was first undertaken in the year 1702, when the last war against France was proclaim'd. The Danger, to which our country was then exposed, from the growing power, and ambitious designs, of Lewis the Fourteenth of France, was thought to bear a near resemblance to that, which threatened the state of Athens, from the like power and designs of Philip King of Macedon ... A Return of the like conjecture of time, when the same causes have again involved this nation in a war with France, has occasione'd the present republication of this work, with the addition of some other philippic orations, now first translated, to complete the subject.[80]

The war of the Spanish Succession (1702–13) and the War of the Austrian Succession (1739–48) raised Britain's fear of invasion by the French, aided by the Jacobites from within, and the Stuart claim to the throne under the exiled James II, who was recognized by Louis XIV as the rightful heir. Burke's *Reflections* is thus part of the tradition of the philippic as a declamation against the danger of a foreign power, but his descriptions of Dr Price as oracular also draw upon the classical history of the Delphic oracle as a corrupt philippizer with the implicit suggestion that he has been suborned by the enemy France.

Burke's description of Price as 'philippizing' becomes musical when he says Price 'chaunts his prophetic song'. The manner in which the Pythia delivered her oracles has been a matter of uncertainty for scholarship, with some accounts claiming that she spoke in verse, others in prose. Plutarch explored this question in his dialogue 'the Oracles at Delphi no Longer given in Verse', concluding that both options were likely.[81] He observed that the oracle existed in an era when 'personal temperaments and natures which had an easy fluency and a bent towards composing poetry' and 'when men came under the influence of abundant wine of emotion, as some note of sadness crept in or some joy befell, a poet would slip into a "tuneful utterance"'.[82] Burke's depiction of Price's 'prophetic song' also draws upon the idea of chaunting which was in his own time commonly associated with the psalms of 'Sternhold and Hopkins', referring to a method of singing psalms. In *The Art of Speaking*, James Burgh lamented that the chaunting of psalms could be ill-matched to their subject matter:

> Whereas chaunting in Cathedrals, psalmody in parish-churches, ballad music put to a number of verses, differing in thoughts and images, and cant, or monotony, in expressing the various matter of a discourse, do not in the least *humour* the *matters* they are applied to; but on the contrary, confound it.[83]

Burke suggests that Price does not understand the implications of his chaunt as he applies it to the matters of the English constitution, because it is in 'exact unison' with French designs. 'Unison' further develops the musical focus of this passage. Johnson's definition of unison encompasses the musical and national:

> 1. A string that has the same sound with another', and quoting from Book IV of Pope's *Dunciad* to describe a unity of sense and opinion 2. A single unvaried note. 'Lost was the nation's sense, nor could be found/ While a long, solemn unison went round.'[84]

Burke's use of the term 'philippizing' is therefore complexly resonant.

The 'Harmodium Melos'

The 'Harmodium Melos' was discussed in the work of Bishop Robert Lowth (1710–87) in the context of his lectures on Hebrew poetry, delivered in Latin at the University of Oxford in 1741.[85] The lectures were published in Latin in 1753 as *De sacra poesi Hebraeorum*, and in an English translation by G. Gregory in 1787. While Lowth's central claim was that 'the original office and destination of poetry was the observance of religion', he also examines the other functions of poetry. Anna Cullhed has pointed out that the lectures can, therefore, be situated in the tradition of Aristotle's *Poetics* and Horace's *Ars Poetica*.[86] In the first lecture, 'Of the Uses and Design of Poetry', Lowth asserts the superiority of poetry in comparison to the other liberal arts of philosophy and history because the poet's works are more 'agreeable' and the 'poet teaches not by maxims and precepts, and in the dull, sententious form'.[87] In making his case for the value of poetry, Lowth catalogues different forms of poetry through the ages, including the canon of classical authors and genres of the epic, tragedy, the ode or lyric, and the elegy. He points to the great classical poet Alcaeus, who wrote convivial songs known as skolion, as an exemplar of the power of poetry in relation to politics: 'As a man, indeed, how great! As a citizen how strenuous! What a spirited defender of the laws and constitution of his country!'[88] It is in the context of this discussion of Alcaeus and 'the amazing power of lyric poetry in directing the passions' that Lowth points to the power of another skolion, the 'Harmodium Melos'.[89]

According to Lowth, the 'Harmodium Melos', attributed to Callistratus, presents an example of the political power of the lyric because the song maintained the civil life of the state by keeping the populace aware of their liberties. The song prevented the re-emergence of tyranny as experienced under 'Pisistratus':

> Could an apprehension arise, that another Pisistratus would meditate the enslaving of that city, where at every banquet, nay in the streets and in the meanest assemblies of the common people, that convivial ode was daily sung, which bears the name of Callistratus?[90]

Lowth describes a song that creates a polity and engenders national spirit by crossing the social divides between the banquets of the elite and the common people of the streets and 'meanest assemblies'.

Reinforcing the power of the 'Harmodium Melos' to the Greeks, Lowth points to the counter-example of Rome.

Lowth asserts that it was for want of a political song such as the 'Harmodium Melos' that, following the assassination of Caesar on the Ides of March, Rome fell under the rule of Marc Antony:

> If after the memorable *Ides of March,* any one of the Tyrannicides had delivered to the populace such a poem as this [the Harmodium Melos], had introduced it to the Suburra, to the assemblies of the Forum, or had put it into the mouths of the common people, the dominion of the Caesars and its adherents would have been totally extinguished: and I am firmly persuaded, that one stanza of this simple ballad of Harmodius would have been more effectual than all the Philippics of Cicero.[91]

Lowth echoes the imagery of Psalm Forty, used to commemorate the 'Glorious Revolution', with his evocation of 'songs being put into the mouths of the common people'.

Callistratus's 'Harmodium Melos' has been transmitted to us in the text of the *Deipnosophistae,* or *The Learned Banqueters,* by the Greek writer, Athenaeus of Naucratis (fl. AD 200). The text unfolds over fifteen books which detail the conversations of a group of learned men (*sophistae*) at the different phases of a grand dinner (*deipnon*).[92] The text has been viewed as part of the *sympotic* tradition in which dialogue and philosophical discussion occurs amidst the consumption of food and alcohol.[93]

The 'Harmodium Melos' is quoted in Book Fifteen, following an extensive discussion on wreaths, and in the context of a discussion about the genre of the *skolia*. Athenaeus, the narrator at this point, describes the scene of the banquet to Timocrates:

> Many of the guests also referred to the well-known Attic skolia; these deserve to be cited for you, both because of their antiquity and because of the simplicity of the men who composed them.[94]

Athenaeus observes that Alcaeus, Artemon and Praxilla of Sicyon won high praise for their skolion before offering further explanation of the different types:

> according to Artemon of Cassandreia in Book II of *On the Use of Books,* the various songs performed at parties belong to three categories. The first was the type that everyone customarily sang; the second was the type that everyone sang, not (in a group), however, but in rotation, one after another; and the third type came after all the others, and not everyone participated at this point, but only those regarded as intelligent, regardless of where they happened to be sitting ... Individual members of the group

of learned banqueters recited different skolia; what follows is a complete collection of all those that were sung.⁹⁵

The 'Harmodium Melos' is then recited as part of the conversation of the banqueters. It is not introduced as a discrete text but appears as verses mixed together with other skolia:

> I will bear my sword in a myrtle branch,
> Like Harmodius and Aristogiton
> When the two of them killed the tyrant
> And made Athens a place of political equality
> Beloved Harmodius, you are not dead at all;
> Instead, they say your are in the Isles of the Blessed,
> Where swift-footed Achilleus is,
> And Tydeus's son they say the noble Diomedes.
> I will bear my sword in a myrtle branch,
> Like Harmodius and Aristogiton
> When at the sacrifice in honour of Athena
> The two of them killed the tyrant Hipparchus
> The story of you two will always survive in our land,
> Beloved Harmodius and Aristogiton,
> How the two of you killed the tyrant
> And made Athens a place of political equality.⁹⁶

In Volume One of his *General History of Music*, Charles Burney devoted a chapter to the 'scolia' of the Ancient Greeks, noting that those which remain were chiefly 'sung at table, during the time of banquets, or repasts'.⁹⁷ Drawing from Plutarch, Athenaeus and Lucian, Burney reiterated the three performance methods: the first where songs were sung by the whole group; the second where songs were sung individually as a branch of myrtle was passed to each singer; and the third where songs were sung by 'professed musicians'.⁹⁸ Burney also identified distinct genres of skolia – moral, mythological, historical and patriotic, as well as 'common songs' on wine and love.⁹⁹ He asserted that the fragments from *The Learned Banqueters* were from several 'patriot' songs which honoured Harmodius.¹⁰⁰ Bishop Lowth also noted that the tradition that 'whoever sung any convivial song in company, always held a branch of myrtle in his hand' perhaps arose from Harmodius and Aristogeiton drawing their swords from their myrtle boughs.¹⁰¹ The imagery of the myrtle is employed time and again in eighteenth-century songsters, most famously in the series *The Myrtle and Vine; or A Complete Vocal Library*.¹⁰² Unlike Lowth, however, Burney was less impressed by the skolia recorded by Athenaeus, finding most of them to be 'unmeaning and insipid', and the songs on love and drinking to be inferior to those of Anacreon.¹⁰³

So what were the events commemorated by the 'Harmodium Melos'? The song describes the slaying of Hipparchus at the feast of Athena. Hipparchus was the son of Peisistratus (c. 600 BC–527 BC), whom Lowth had described as the tyrant. Peisistratus had seized power in Athens three times: first in about 560 BC then in the 550s BC and finally in 546 BC.[104] This period of tyranny in the sixth century quashed the earlier reforms of the Athenian constitution founded by Solon in 594 BC which are regarded as a significant moment in the development of democracy.[105] When Peisistratus died in 527 BC, his three sons Hipparchus, Hippias and Thessalus shared power and continued the tyrannical dynasty until Hipparchus was slain by Harmodius and Aristogeiton in 514 BC. Harmodius and Aristogeiton were killed for their crime and Hippias ruled for a further four years. He was finally driven out of Athens with aid of the Spartans in 510 BC.[106]

The Greek historian Thucydides, in the opening book of his *History of the Peloponnesian War* (431 BC–404 BC), uses the example of Aristogeiton and Harmodius to make a point about the unreliability of oral history and to establish his own credibility as an historian.

> People, you see, unquestioningly accept the legends handed down by their forebears even when those legends relate to their own native history. Why, most Athenians even believe that Hipparchus was the tyrant in Athens when he was assassinated by Harmodius and Aristogeiton.[107]

Thucydides, by contrast, maintains that Hippias, who was one of the three brothers sharing power, was the elder and therefore held the most power in the tyranny, one of a number of complex inconsistencies he points out.[108] Rather than the political motive ascribed by the skolion, Thucydides outlines in book six of his history a complex series of personal motivations that led to the murder.[109] Central to this was the sexual relationship between the young Harmodius, 'in the first bloom of youth' and the older Aristogeiton.[110] Hipparchus had attempted to seduce Harmodius but was twice rejected. The spurned Hipparchus then insulted Harmodius's sister in retaliation, an act which further provoked Harmodius and Aristogeiton who formed the conspiracy to overthrow the tyranny, leading to the murder of Hipparchus. Not unlike the editor of the *Collection*, discussed in Chapter One, Thucydides aims to correct the inaccuracy of the song through recourse to further historical detail than it is possible to give within the confines of a song. In contrast to the 'Harmodium Melos', where the murder plot leads to the freedom of Athens, Thucydides's narrative concludes with a profoundly different version of events: 'The plot, then, resulted from the pangs of love, and the pointless murder from the sudden panic of Harmodius and Aristogeiton. Afterward, the tyranny was harder on the Athenian people'.[111]

In the eighteenth century, however, the song continued to be understood as a commemoration of the freedom of the people from tyranny. Neither Lowth nor Burney mention the intricacies of the Thucydides account, nor his questioning of the accuracy of its message. Burney simply writes, 'Hipparchus having publicly insulted the sister of Harmodius, he, in conjunction with his friend Aristogeiton, slew him at the Panathenaean Games, which event was the signal to the natives of Athens for recovering their liberty'.[112] The song had transcended the details of its own topicality and become a symbol of the commemoration of national political freedom. As such, in the eighteenth century it was viewed as part of a long history of song and became implicated in discussions of national songs. In 1783, Joseph Ritson discussed the 'historical scolia' and the song of Harmodium and Aristogeiton in his 'Essay on the Origin and Progress of National Song' which introduced his *Select Collection of English Songs*. This essay has previously been discussed in terms of Ritson's opposition to Thomas Percy's 1765 essay on the English minstrels.[113] Whereas Percy was intent on establishing a genealogy of English minstrelsy, and was much criticized for his mythologizing, Ritson approached the subject of national song less parochially, from the perspective of its history amongst the European nations. He drew upon the scholarship of Burney in his discussion of Harmodius and Aristogeiton, noting that they killed Hipparchus following the insult to Harmodius's sister. However, Ritson also went beyond Burney by returning to the words of Robert Lowth in *de Sacra poesi*: 'The author is supposed to be one Callistratus, whom the present Bishop of London has pronounced an ingenious poet and excellent citizen'.[114] Lowth had become Bishop of London earlier in 1777.[115]

Ritson's reference to Lowth's discussion of the 'Harmodium Melos' is especially meaningful in this context. Lowth had been involved in a controversy with Price in 1779 concerning the war with America. On preaching his sermon to the Chapel Royal of St James's Palace for Ash Wednesday in 1779, which was subsequently printed, Lowth made a pointed reference to Dr Price which criticized his stance on the American war. Lowth asked his congregation:

> Are there not many, whose study it has long been to introduce disorder and confusion, to encourage tumults and seditions; to destroy all rule and all authority, by traducing government, despising dominion, and speaking evil of dignities? By assuming visionary and impracticable principles, as the only true foundations of a free government, which tend to raise discontent in the people.[116]

A note to this passage quoted excerpts from Price's *Observations on Civil Liberty*, including the passage, ' ... a vast majority of the people of England, all that have no vote for Representative in Parliament, are slaves'.[117] Price, of course, retaliated with a postscript to his own published Ash Wednesday sermon addressed to 'the Bishop of London', in which he framed his position as consistent with a defence of the 'sentiments of civil liberty which were once the boast of the kingdom, and to which we owe our excellent constitution, the Glorious Revolution, the accession, and all our dignity and happiness'.[118] Ash Wednesday was a day replete with religious and political significance: the day that King William and Queen Mary had accepted the throne at Whitehall, 13 February 1689, as Ritson's broadside had noted. By reprinting the skolion of Harmodius and Aristogeiton, and Robert Lowth's earlier praise of the song, the politics of the song becomes reanimated in the topical context of his Ash Wednesday disagreement with Price.

At the same time, the 'Harmodium Melos' also functioned topically when it was used in the celebrations of the Society for Constitutional Information (SCI), an extra-parliamentary association comprised of gentlemen. At the anniversary of the founding of the Society, held at the Shakespeare Tavern on 14 May 1782, 'Mr Webb' sang an *Ode in Imitation of Callistratus* which was printed for the occasion.

> Verdant myrtle's branchy pride
> Shall my biting falchion wreathe:
> Soon shall grace each manly side,
> Tubes that speak, and points that breathe.
>
> Thus *Harmodius,* shone thy blade!
> Thus Aristogiton, thine!
> Whose, when Britain sighs for aid,
> whose shall now delay to shine?
>
> Dearest youths, in islands blest,
> Not, like recreant idlers, dead;
> You with fleet Pelides rest,
> And with godlike 'Diomen'
>
> Verdant myrtle's branchy pride
> Shall my thirsty blade entwine:
> Such, *Harmodius,* deck'd thy side!
> Such, *Aristogiton*, thine!
>
> They the base *Hipparchus* slew,
> At the feast for *Pallas* crown'd;
> Gods! How swift their poniard flew!
> How the monster ring'd the ground!
>
> Then, in *Athens*, all was Peace,
> equal Laws and Liberty:
> Nurse of Arts, and eye of *Greece!*
> People valiant, firm and free!
>
> Not less glorious was thy deed,
> *Wentworth,* fix'd in Virtue's cause;
>
> Nor less brilliant be thy meed,
> *Lenox,* friend to Equal Laws!
>
> High in freedom's temple rais'd,
> See *Fitz-Maurice* beaming stand,
> For collected Virtues prais'd,
> Wisdom's voice, and Valour's hand!
>
> Ne'er shall Fate their eyelids close;
> They, in blooming regions blest,

With *Harmodius* shall repose,
With *Aristogiton* rest

Noblest Chiefs, a hero's crown
Let the Athenian patriots claim:
You less fiercely won renown;
You assum'd milder name.

They through blood for glory strive,
You more blissful tidings bring;
They to death a *Tyrant* drove,
You to fame *restor'd* a KING

Rise BRITANNIA, dauntless rise!
Cheer'd with triple harmony,
Monarch good, and *Nobles* wise,
People valiant, firm and FREE!![119]

The ode is striking because it shows the political relevance of Harmodius and Aristogeiton to Britain's present, with the central question being whose blade will come to 'shine' for Britain when she 'sighs for aid'? The text pays homage to other notable statesmen: *Wentworth* being the second Marquess of Rockingham, Whig grandee and prime-minister who had been Burke's patron; *Lenox* being Charles Lennox, the third Duke of Richmond, who had advocated parliamentary reform for Ireland in his letter to Colonel Sharman of the Irish Volunteers, a text that would become deeply significant to the radical movement moving into the 1790s; and *Fitz-Maurice* being William Petty-Fitzmaurice, the second Earl of Shelburne and first Marquess of Lansdowne, who as Prime Minister had been responsible for ending the war with America and publicly supported legislative independence for Ireland.[120] As defenders of liberty, they have earned their repose with Harmodius and Aristogeiton, though the ode makes it clear that they have 'less fiercely won renown'. Whereas Harmodius and Aristogeiton had killed Hipparchus the tyrant of Athens, Shelburne had 'restor'd' the fame of George III with the ending of the dispute over America. The last stanza refers to the 'triple harmony' of the three individuals mentioned, and the harmony of England, Scotland and Ireland, despite the loss of the American colonies.

The ode was sung at the anniversary of the formation of the Society for Constitution Information, which Burke would describe in the *Reflections* as 'charitable, and so far of a laudable, nature: it was intended for the circulation, at the expence of the members, of many books, which few others would be at the expence of buying'.[121] The Society had been formed in April 1780 with the aim of disseminating to every Briton – including the humble cottager – the knowledge that under the constitution 'handed down' from their Saxon ancestors, 'the law must be assented to by all', and that this assent came from a 'freely chosen, a full and equal representation'.[122] 'Ode in Imitation of Callistratus' was written by Sir William Jones, an orientalist scholar and linguist who was elected to the society in 1782.[123] The version that was published in Jones's collected *Works* is preceded by a stanza from 'Callistratus's song', printed in Ancient Greek, and a quote in Latin from Bishop Lowth's Lecture. The quote reads 'one song of Harmodius, by the Lord, is worth more than all of Cicero's Philippics'.[124] Jones's other works included the 'Ode in Imitation of Alcaeus' and 'The Principles of Government, in a Dialogue between a Scholar and a Peasant' which were printed and distributed *gratis* by the Society.[125] The 'Ode in Imitation of Alcaeus' begins by asking 'What Constitutes a State?' and answers: 'Men, who their duties know/But know their rights and knowing, dare maintain,/ Prevent the long-aim'd blow/ And crush the tyrant while they rent the chain:/ These constitute a State'.[126] In the dialogue, the scholar's questioning of the peasant about the workings of the village club he belongs to reveals that the club is not only an association of merriment. It is a benefit society where small financial contributions are made by members to prevent their sole reliance upon the parish for relief should the need arise. The peasant already understands the principles of government, as these are all evident in the workings of the club and include: equal voting rights, accountability for taxation and the right to overturn the violation of these principles with arms. The dialogue ends with the Scholar giving the peasant a musket with a bayonet. Jones clearly understood the relationship between merriment, remembering that Callistratus's song was sung at the convivial symposia, and political consciousness evident in his ode and dialogue. When men like the peasant did begin to associate for avowedly political purposes, such as those espoused by the London Corresponding Society, radicals such as Thomas Spence capitalized upon the intellectual status of men such as Jones by reprinting their works. Drawing its name from Burke's reference to a 'swinish multitude', Spence's radical journal *Pigs' Meat,* printed 'The Ode in imitation of Alcaeus By Sir William Jones Kt, One of the Judges of the Supreme Court of Judicature at Calcutta' in the early 1790s.[127]

Bishop Lowth's observations about the power of the 'Harmodium Melos' were once again recapitulated by Vicesimus Knox in his essay on 'The Effects of Songs' which was part of his *Winter Evenings* collection published in 1788:

> Every scholar knows that Bishop Lowth, in a solemn introduction to his lectures on sacred poetry, has inserted, in the very first place, and as one of the most striking instances of the power of poetry, a Greek political ballad, which used to be sung by the Athenian liberty-boys, at all their jolly drinking bouts, and by the mob and the ballad singers, in the streets and the alleys of the city.[128]

The point of Knox's essay was not to discuss the power of 'political ballads', but rather the 'influence' of 'Bachanalian and amorous songs'. Thanks to Lowth, the 'power' and the influence of the 'Harmodium Melos' was self-evident in the eighteenth century and it continued to operate as a paradigm for discussions of the influence of songs more broadly.

The 'Io Paean' of the Revolution

Burke employs another song metaphor, that of the 'Io Paean', in his discussion of the peroration of Price's *Discourse*. John Bell's *Historical Dictionary of the Gods*, printed in 1790, defines the 'Io Paean' as 'a song of triumph derived from Apollo's encounter with Python'.[129] In his history of music, Burney elaborates that the serpent Python, who had been terrorizing the country around Delphos, was killed with darts by the God Apollo.[130] He quotes Callimachus's 'Hymn to Apollo' which describes the way in which the "Io Paean" came to be used as a triumphal cry in commemoration of this:

> The mon'strous Python
> Durst tempt thy wrath in vain; for dead he fell
> To thy great strength, and golden arms unequal.
> *Io!* While thy unerring hand elanc'd
> Another and another dart, the people
> Joyful repeated *Io! Io Paean!*
> Elance the dart, Apollo: for the safety
> And health of man, gracious thy mother bore thee![131]

Like the philippic, the term comes to have a general usage in the eighteenth century to describe a song of triumph in the context of battle. The translator of the Marquis de Chastellux's *Travels in North America* describes the song *Yankee Doodle*, for example, as 'the 'Io Paean' of America', the song having been adopted by American soldiers during the revolutionary war.[132] Burke's deployment of the 'Io Paean' is significant because it occurs when he discusses the climax of Price's *Discourse*.

Price concluded his Discourse by expressing his gratitude at having lived through an age of revolutions, drawing upon a well-known passage from the Gospel of Luke, the *nunc dimittis*, to imply that his life was, therefore, complete:

> What an eventful period is this! I am thankful that I have lived to it; and I could almost say *Lord, now lettest thou thy servant depart in peace, for mine eyes have seen thy salvation*. I have lived to see a diffusion of knowledge, which has undermined superstition and error – I have lived to see the rights of men better understood than ever; and nations panting for liberty, which seemed to have lost the idea of it. – I have lived to see thirty millions of people, indignant and resolute, spurning of slavery, and demanding liberty with an irresistible voice; their king led in triumph, and an arbitrary monarch surrendering himself to his subjects. – After sharing in the benefits of one Revolution, I have been spared to be a witness to two other Revolutions, both glorious. – And now methinks I see the ardour of liberty catching and spreading.[133]

This passage vividly depicts the progress of political enlightenment: from 'superstition and error' to the universal language of the 'rights of men' demanded through the 'irresistible voice' of the people'. Past, present and future coalesce for Price in his linking of the three revolutions – the Revolution of 1688, the

American Revolution and the French Revolution. He prophetically 'sees' liberty 'catching and spreading' with the implication being that further revolutions, and another British one, will follow.

It is in responding to this passage that Burke invokes the 'Io Paean'. He interpreted Price's description of 'the king led in triumph' as referring to the capture of King Louis on 6 October 1789 by 'a band of cruel ruffians and assassins', who marched him back to Paris from Versailles in a gruesome procession led by the heads of the King's body guards mounted upon spears:

> Is this a triumph to be consecrated at altars? To be commemorated with grateful thanksgiving? To be offered to the divine humanity with fervent prayer and enthusiastic ejaculation? ... At first I was at a loss to account for this fit of unguarded transport. I knew, indeed, that the sufferings of monarchs made a delicious repast to some sort of palates. There were reflexions which might serve to keep this appetite within some bounds of temperance. But when I took one circumstance into my consideration, I was obliged to confess, that much allowance ought to be made for the Society, and that the temptation was too strong for common discretion; I mean, the circumstance of the 'Io Paean' of the triumph, that animating cry which called 'for all the BISHOPS to be hanged on the lamp-posts', might well have brought forth a burst of enthusiasm on the forseen consequences of this happy day. I allow this prophet to break forth into hymns of joy and thanksgiving on an event which appears like the precursor of the Millenium, and the projected fifth Monarchy, in the destruction of all church establishments.[134]

Burke quotes M. Lally Tollendal, a former member of the French National Assembly, as the 'eyewitness' to the 'pious triumph' of the cry 'for all the bishops [to] be hanged from the lamp-posts', as the procession entered Paris.[135] Here the sufferings of the monarch are consumed like food in 'a delicious repast', a significant metaphor, given the convivial and prandial celebrations of the Revolution Society at the London Tavern on 4 November, following Price's sermon. Burke acknowledges that some parts of the sermon were not dangerous, conceding that 'there were reflexions which might serve to keep this appetite within some bounds of temperance'. However, he is overcome by sarcasm when he mockingly confesses that it was too much to have expected discretion and temperance from the members of the Revolution Society given the circumstances of the "Io Paean' of triumph' – the cry that that the Bishops be hanged. This "Io Paean' of triumph' caused the gentlemen of the Revolution Society to lose control of discretion with a 'burst of enthusiasm', once again invoking the religious fanaticism of the seventeenth century and the Civil War. Reprising his role as a philippizer, Price, the 'prophet', breaks forth into hymns of joy which foretell the destruction of the church. Burke's implicit attack on the forms of sociability enacted by the Revolution Society is an important element to emphasise. The complex passage repudiates Price's sermon by also attending to the circumstances that surrounded it – the meeting at the London Tavern in the evening, the songs, the toasts and the atmosphere of a dinner that could lead to 'unguarded transport'.[136] Burke develops a prophetic musical logic here, highlighting the multivalent power of song in its classical, religious, secular and topical forms.

Price denied that he was talking about the events of 6 October 1789 in this passage. In the preface to the fourth edition of *Discourse*, which was published in November 1790 in response to the *Reflections*, he explains that he was referring to the fall of the Bastille in the preceding July:

> I assure the Public that the events to which I referred in these words were not those of the 6th of October, but those only of the 14th July and the subsequent days; when, after the conquest of the Bastille, the King of France sought the protection of the National Assembly, and, by his own desire, was conducted, amidst acclamations never before heard in France, to Paris, there to shew himself to his people as the restorer of their liberty.[137]

F. P. Lock rightly describes Price's denial as 'scarcely credible'.[138] As a man who participated in politics for much of his life, it is unlikely that Price could have been unaware of the potential association between the "Io Paean" of his sermon and the events of the October Days. Even though Burke's text was not published until November 1790, his position in relation to Price was evident when he referred in parliament to the *Discourse*, and a number of other publications by Dissenters, in his response to a motion to repeal the Test and Corporations Act, put forward by Fox on 2 March 1790.[139] Burke deduced from these writings that 'the leading preachers among the Dissenters were avowed enemies to the church of England' which was, he argued, in more serious danger than the church of France had been the year before.[140] This speech was significant as it marked the beginning of the bitter split between Burke and Fox. The motion was defeated by 189 votes.[141]

Price continued to make provocative and deliberately ambiguous toasts. In July 1790 when he attended a dinner to celebrate the first anniversary of the fall of the Bastille wearing a tricolour cockade he proposed: 'An Alliance between France and Great Britain, for perpetuating peace, and making the world happy'.[142] Hearing of the dinner, Joseph Priestley wrote to congratulate him on this 'glorious effulgence' and observed of the toast that 'little things have sometimes great effects'.[143] The *Times* and the *Gazetteer and New Daily Advertiser* both carried reports of this dinner and Price's toast.[144] The report of the former, a ministerial paper, stated upfront its disagreement with the opinion of the gentlemen at the dinner while the *Gazetteer* printed an account together with the song that was sung – another re-working of Callistratus's 'Ode to Harmodion and Aristogeiton':

I.
Gallant Nation, foes no More!
Gen'rous Britons hail the day,
That from Gallia's cultur'd shore
Chac'd tyrannic pow'r away

II.
Late a band of Patriots rose,
Firm in Freedom's glorious cause;
Feeble slaves in vain oppose
Rights secur'd by equal laws.

III.
Myrtle wreaths entwine their brows,
Branchy myrtle decks the blade,
While, like us, they pay their vows
To each Patriot Hero's shade.

IV.
Hampden, Sydney, names rever'd!
Boast of Albion's sea girt isle,
Martyr'd Russell, shade endear'd
On this day propitious smile.

V.
Transatlantic spirits bend,
Pleas'd our festive rites to see,
Franklin, Freedom's ablest friend!
Warren and Montgomery!

VI.
Martial youths, in Britain bred,
Kindle with congenial zeal,
Freedom's path resolv'd to tread,
Jealous of the public weal.

VII.
Should tyrannic force again
Raise her Hydra heads on high,
Welcome, then, the hostile plain,
Freeman dauntless dare to die.

VIII.
Verdant Myrtle's branchy pride
Shall my thirsty blade entwine,
Such Harmodius, deck'd thy side!
Such Aristogeiton thine![145]

The song fuses the symbols of revolution across time and space. The myrtle decking the 'brows' and 'blades' of the French revolutionaries is the iconography of Harmodius and Aristogeiton. Recapitulating Price's toast, the end of 'tyranny' in France has resulted in the end of the long-held enmity in Britain and France as both countries are joined in the 'glorious' cause of freedom. Like the climax of Price's sermon, previously discussed, the song invests heavily in a sense of destiny, with the renowned dead patriots each giving their blessing to the French Revolution and the celebration of the fall of the Bastille. The Whig patriot heroes of the seventeenth century, John Hampden (d. 1696), Algernon Sydney (1628–83) and the martyred William, Lord Russell (1639–83) smile on the 'propitious day'; and the dead heroes of the American Revolution, Benjamin Franklin (1706–90), Joseph Warren (1741–75) and Richard Montgomery (1738–75) are 'pleas'd' with the 'festive rites' of the occasion in which the song was performed, including Price's controversial toast. The last three verses warn that the martial youths of Britain would be prepared to die for freedom in the face of 'tyrannic force' and ultimately return to the 'myrtle' and 'blade' of Harmodius and Aristogeiton. This verse was evidently taken directly from the version by William Jones sung at the SCI anniversary celebrations in 1782. Whereas Jones's song had reinforced the 'fame of King George', in this version, by contrast, the blade and myrtle have become radicalized, hinting at the potential overthrow of monarchy in the wake of the fall of the Bastille.

Price's biographer, D. O. Thomas, and, more recently, the historian H.T. Dickinson have viewed Price as a figure in need of rescue from Burke's depiction of him as an enthusiastic incendiary.[146] It is the contention here, however, that locating Price in relation to the political song culture in the early 1790s reveals him to be a skilful rhetorician and political actor. Burke, who was equally immersed in the contexts of song and sociability, knew what Price was doing here. Accounts of Price have perhaps underestimated his ability as a knowing political actor to exploit language, an ability which worked in conjunction with his image as an 'honest' straightforward and moderate reformer. The two are not necessarily mutually exclusive.

While Burke accuses Price of philippizing and chaunting a prophetic song, he is, of course, philippizing himself. In the tradition of Demosthenes, Burke's *Reflections* was a warning of the dangers of the spread of French ideas and the false prophecy of the 'Io Paean' of triumph. The observation that Burke became, in effect, what he denounced was used strategically by his opponents. During the Regency crisis, as Christopher Reid outlines, Burke's extensive investigations into madness and his willingness to speak indelicately about the King's condition led to Burke himself being caricatured as mad.[147] John Barrell writes that Burke's speech at the tail end of the Regency crisis, in which he had quoted Milton's *Paradise Lost* that 'the almighty had hurle'd the king from the throne', would come to be used against him as evidence of his own regicidal imaginings.[148] In relation to a later episode, Gillian Russell discusses Burke's theatrical behaviour during his speech on the Alien Bill in 1792, when he produced a dagger from his pocket and threw it on the floor, as evidence of the 'histrionic excess' that he condemned in the revolutionaries.[149] Burke's role as a 'philippizer' contributed to his irrevocable and traumatic break with Fox and his fellow Whigs.

When Burke forwarded the draft of *Reflections* to his fellow Whig Philip Francis, the latter's reply of 19 February 1790, revealed him to be an increasingly alienated figure amongst his colleagues:

> I know with certainty that I am the only friend, and many there are, who ever ventures to contradict or oppose you, face to face, on Subjects of this nature. They either care too little for *you*, or too much for *themselves*, to run the risk of giving you immediate offence, for the sake of any subsequent or remote advantage you might derive from it.[150]

In this letter, Francis critiques the *Reflections* for being 'very loosely put together' and describes Burke's description of Marie Antoinette as 'pure foppery': he beseeches Burke to 'deliberate a little' before publishing.[151] Francis delivers a philippic of his own, as the only Whig who would dare to contradict Burke. The other Whigs merely humour him out of 'self interest', like the oracles paid by Philip to philippize in his favour. When Francis did obtain a copy of the *Reflections* after it was published in November, he wrote again to Burke over two days on the third and fourth. Likening the text to wine, he explained that he must taste it deliberately because 'the flavour is too high; the wine is too rich; I cannot take a draught of it'.[152] Not unaware of the resonances of his Christian name, Francis ends his second letter by quoting from the ghost of Julius Caesar to Brutus, when he tells Burke 'you shall see me again at Philippi'.[153]

Burke's differences with Fox on the subject of the French Revolution were apparent in the debate to repeal the Test and Corporations Act on 2 March 1790. The rupture was completed in a debate on the Quebec Government Bill of 6 May 1791, when Burke dramatically renounced Fox's friendship and described himself as separated from his fellow Whigs.[154] Burke's statement to his former party in defence of the *Reflections*, took the form of the *Appeal from the New to the Old Whigs*, published in August 1791. Writing as a third party, and referring to himself as 'Mr Burke', the text seeks to take the party back to the principles as laid down following the settlement of 1688 and embodied by the 'antient Whigs' as opposed to the 'new Whigs' who support the French Revolution.[155] The author imagines himself as perhaps the last of the 'antient Whigs' and the appeal is actually that the new Whigs will make the choice to act on the example of their constitutional ancestors.[156] The new Whigs had deviated from these principles by aligning themselves with French ideas of liberty. Burke reiterated his warning about the danger of abstracting political principles from the circumstances of particular situations by returning to the imagery of the 'Io Paean' and song:

> I allow, as I ought to do, for the effusions which come from a general zeal for liberty. This is to be indulged, and even to be encouraged, as long as the *question is general*. An orator, above all men, ought to be allowed the full and free use of the praise of liberty. A common-place in favour of slavery and tyranny delivered to a popular assembly, would indeed be a bold defiance to all the principles of rhetoric. But in a question whether any particular constitution is or is not a plan of rational liberty, this kind of rhetorical flourish in favour of freedom in general, is surely a little out of its place. It is virtually a begging of the question. It is a song of triumph, before the battle.[157]

Burke refers to the danger of general praise for the French constitution here, arguing that the nuance of particular circumstances must be taken into account in considering the question of the French constitution. This is clearly a criticism of Fox's 'panygerics' in praise of the Revolution in his parliamentary speeches; however, the relevance of this passage in terms of this chapter's focus on song is its invocation of the 'Io Paean'. The song of triumph in praise of the Revolution evades the complexity of circumstances and 'particular' constitutions by endorsing and legitimating events before they are properly understood. In this sense Burke's concerns resonate with those of Thucydides in his discussion of the historiographic problems of the 'Harmodium Melos'.

It is the role of the *natural* aristocracy, Burke argues, to exercise their influence on 'the people', as a kind of grand chorus: 'In all things the voice of this grand chorus of national harmony ought to have a mighty and decisive influence'.[158] When the aristocracy do not direct the 'grand chorus', when they join in the singing and disseminating of revolutionary songs, which elide the constitutional and circumstantial complexities that Burke expounds, the result is the same as if they had preached sedition to the lower orders.[159] The first part of Thomas Paine's *Rights of Man* had been published in February 1791 and Burke quoted extensively from it as 'the notions' of the 'new Whigs'. Those Whigs that continued to favour the cause of parliamentary reform regardless of the situation in France, including Richard Sheridan and Charles Grey, broke away from Fox to form an association called the Friends of the People in April 1792.[160] They attempted to steer a middle path between Burke's conservatism and Paine's radicalism, proving unsuccessful as, by this point, the lower orders were able to access Paine's work in cheap six pence editions.[161] As the revolution debate developed, the 'chorus' of the Revolution Society moved from the confines of the symposion of gentlemen to the lower orders with print playing a major role in the radicalization of political song.

The Streets and the Meanest Assemblies of the Common People

A song 'sung by Mr Dignum at the Revolution Society' found its way into a sixpence songster called *The Muses Banquet or Vocal Repository for the Year 1791*:

> Behold Gauls free enlighten'd land
> The rights of man declare,
> and other realms those rights demand,
> which all mankind should share:
> This flame which ev'ry breast should know,
> In Britons bosoms learn'd to glow
> Fair freedom shot its transient light,
> On ancient Greece and Rome,
> Then sudden sunk in erring night,
> Nor could she fix her home;
> Thus Albion's happy shore she found,
> Whose radiance lights the nations round
> Should Franks and Britons nobly join
> As arbiters of right,
> And each emancipated clime,
> Oppression put to flight;
> Then might we hope one day to see
> All nations, happy, great and free.[162]

This same song was sent by Benjamin Cooper, the secretary of the Society in London, to the Revolution Society at Norwich together with a pamphlet in a gesture to solicit further correspondence.[163] Through the printed songster, the 'festivities' of the Revolution Society could be disseminated to a much broader audience. Echoing the cosmopolitan optimism of Price who had lived to hear the demands for liberty from an 'irresistible voice', the song *demands* the 'rights of man' in other realms, for all mankind. The second stanza alludes to the pre-Norman past of the Anglo Saxons, when freedom found a home in Albion. In line with Price's toasts, the climactic stanza poses the breaking down of the traditional enmity of France and Britain, an enmity that, as previously discussed, had prompted the reprinting of Demosthenes' philippics in the eighteenth century and, as Linda Colley has argued, had been fundamental in the invention of a British national identity as one defined against France and through war with France.[164] That Britain and France might 'nobly join' so that as 'arbiters of right' they might help all nations be 'happy, great and free' thus posed a challenge to the very idea of the British nation.

The printing of this song in a cheap songster is another important point in the context of Burke's address to the Whigs and his distrust of the 'Io Paean'. The selling points of the songster were that it contained new songs and was cheap:

> The printer returns his sincere thanks to a generous Public, for their liberal Support, in so speedily purchasing his first Collection of songs; and begs leave to assure them, that nothing shall be wanting in him, to get the newest and most admirable Songs

which are sung at all the Public Places during this Season, together with the Addition of many wrote on Purpose for this Selection. He will not (like some Pretenders) boast of the Beauty and Elegance of the Type and Printing, but leave it to that Public whose favour and support he has experienced, and who always can discover real merit. He further begs leave to inform them, that being the Printer, he is enabled to sell for sixpence nearly as much in Quantity, as that for which some Persons charge One Shilling.[165]

Within the bounds of the songster, this address can be read as analogous to the breakdown of order at a societal level that Burke so feared with the overturning of authority and manners that had resulted in the French Revolution. The 'public' drives the production of this songster by a *printer*, overturning authorial authority. The beauty and elegance of the type, the equivalent of manners for Burke, have no role to play in its production. The printer, unlike other 'pretenders', openly declares that he has no concern with the type, the natural aristocracy of printing, and the haste to print is evident in the many dropped apostrophes in the text. The discovery of merit is left to the public who have supported him in the consumption of new songs, rather than through a system of patronage.

The songster also reprinted the re-worked song of Harmodius and Aristogeiton which was sung at the first anniversary of the fall of the Bastille – the celebration at which Richard Price had proposed his controversial toast and which, as previously discussed, had been printed in the *Gazetteer and New Daily Advertiser*. The songster version included an additional chorus:

Hail, sacred freedom!
Let Britons hail the day
That rescued France
From Lawless sway.[166]

This song was part of a compilation that proclaimed it offered 'the newest and most modern' songs gathered at 'convivial and polite assemblies', including the Anacreontic Society, the Beef Steak Club and the theatres. The political implications of the song, in this context, are secondary to its status as the 'newest and most modern', as the title proclaims. Thus it appears along with many songs by Charles Dibdin from the theatres, some of which are overtly loyalist.

In re-printing the song sung 'by Mr Dignum at the Revolution Society', the experience of the exclusivity of the club, and the performance of the third kind of skolion at the symposion by a performer especially skilled, are reproduced for the reader. Dignum had been engaged by the Revolution Society for the 5 November celebration in 1788 and 1790 as shown by the minutes of the society, and in 1791 as the *Muses Banquet* indicates. Two slip-song versions of the songs he sang in 1792 were published by 'R. Hawes' of the Constitutional Liberty Press, the first to the tune 'How imperfect is expression' and the second to the tune 'The tear that bedews sensibility's shrine'.[167] The 'slip-song' was a song printed on a single sheet or 'slip' of paper.

A SONG

SUNG AT THE

Anniversary of the Revolution of 1688,

Held at the LONDON TAVERN, Nov. 5, 1792.

Tune, "*How imperfect is expression.*"

I.

SEE! bright LIBERTY descending,
   O'er the verdant hills and plains:
And bold GALLIA, nobly sending,
   FREEDOM and relief from CHAINS.

II.

See! fell TYRANNY defeated;
   By each bold and PATRIOT band:
May their triumphs be repeated,
   O'er OPPRESSION's iron HAND.

III.

Oh! may we partake the rapture,
   Which triumphant PATRIOTS feel:
May they ev'ry TYRANT capture,
   Who attacks the COMMONWEAL.

IV.

May the CAUSE which they're protecting,
   Spread thro' ev'ry STATE and CLIME:
That MEN on their RIGHTS reflecting,
   REVOLUTIONS well may time.

V.

Let not MEN of any NATION,
   By false arguments deceiv'd
Startle at a REFORMATION,
   When their COUNTRY is aggriev'd.

VI.

But as human INSTITUTIONS,
   Are by nature prone to change:
Let succeeding REVOLUTIONS,
   Wise and equal LAWS arrange.

VII.

May each future REVOLUTION,
   Serve to make MANKIND more just.
Give each STATE a CONSTITUTION,
   And secure each PUBLIC TRUST.

VIII.

Thus secur'd, shall future AGES,
   Who may celebrate this DAY:
Say "No more wild DISCORD rages,
   REASON only bears the SWAY.

Printed and sold by R. Hawes, No. 107, Whitechapel-Road. Where may be had, The STAR of LIBERTY; Price 6d, Gilt, or 3d Plain; also variety of Constitutional Songs, at 1s per 100, or six a penny.

Figure 3.2: A Song Sung at the Anniversary of the Revolution of 1688. © The British Library Board, shelfmark: General Reference Collection 648.c.26.(6)

A NEW SONG.

Sung by Mr. DIGNUM.

At the Anniversary of the Revolution of 1688,

Held at the LONDON TAVERN, *Nov.* 1792.

Tune, "*The tear that bedews Sensibility's Shrine.*"

I.

UNFOLD, Father Time, thy long records unfold,
Of noble atchievements accomplish'd of old;
When men by the Standard of Liberty led,
Undauntedly conquer'd or chearfully bled:
But now 'midst the triumphs these moments reveal,
Their glories all fade, and their lustre turns pale;
While France rises up and proclaims the decree,
That tears off their chains, and bids millions be free.

II.

As spring to the fields, or as dew to the flowers,
To the earth parch'd with heat, as the soft dropping
 showers,
As health to the wretch that lies languid and wan,
Or rest to the weary,—is Freedom to man:
Where Freedom the light of her countenance gives,
There only He triumphs, there only he lives;
Then seize the glad moment and hail the decree,
That tears off their chains, and bids millions be free.

III.

Too long had oppression and terror entwin'd,
Those tyrant form'd chains that enslav'd the free
 mind;
While dark Superstition with nature at strife,
For ages had lock'd up the fountains of life:
But the Dæmon is fled, the delusion is past,
And reason and virtue have triumph'd at last;
Then seize the glad moment, and hail the decree,
That tears off their chains, and bids millions be free.

IV.

France, we share in the rapture thy bosom that fills,
While the Genius of Liberty bounds o'er thine hills;
Redundant henceforth may thy purple juice flow,
Prouder wave thy green woods, and thine olive trees
 grow!
While the hand of philosophy long shall entwine,
Blest emblem, the laurel, the myrtle and vine;
And Heav'n thro' all ages confirms the decree,
That tears off their chains, and bids millions be free.

Printed and sold by R. Hawes, No. 107, Whitechapel-Road.
Where may be had, The STAR of LIBERTY; Price 6d, Gilt,
or 3d Plain; also variety of Constitutional Songs, at 1s per 100,
or six a penny.

Figure 3.3: A New Song, Sung by Mr Dignum at the Anniversary of the Revolution of 1688. ©The British Library Board, shelfmark: General Reference Collection 648.c.26.(7)

The singing of these songs at the November Anniversary demonstrates the extent to which the Revolution Society had become radicalized by 1792, forcing Whigs such as Sheridan and Lord Stanhope, who had associated themselves with the cause of the Revolution Commemoration Bill of 1789, to sever ties with it.[168] The movement for reform gained much momentum in 1792 with the spread of Paineite radicalism and the emergence of clubs and societies throughout the country, spearheaded by the formation of the Sheffield Society for Constitutional Information (SSCI) on 24 October 1791. The SSCI drew heavily on the model of organization offered by the Society for Constitutional Information, formed in 1781. The salient different between the two organizations, however, was that whereas the SCI was comprised of gentlemen of property, such as William Jones whose 'Ode to Callistratus' has previously been discussed, the SSCI was comprised of artisans, or men of the 'lower orders'.[169] The SSCI was also instrumental in providing assistance and advice to Thomas Hardy as the driving force behind the formation of the London Corresponding Society in the early months of 1792.[170] Paine's blueprint for the reformation of government in the second part of the *Rights of Man*, published on 16 February 1792, galvanized the societies, leading them to sponsor the printing and distribution of hundreds of copies.[171] The government responded to these developments with a Proclamation on 21 May against 'wicked and seditious publications', asking loyal subjects and magistrates for assistance in discovering the authors and printers of such publications.[172]

The sentiments expressed in Hawes's songs reflect a realignment of the anniversary culture of 5 November with the revolutionary events in France. The 'August Revolution' of 1792 had seen the massacre of the Swiss guards, the French monarchy overturned and the Royal family imprisoned.[173] On 21 September the first French Republic was proclaimed following the outbreak of shocking violence in the 'September massacres'.[174] By this time France was also at war with Austria and Prussia after they had unsuccessfully attempted to come to the aid of the French monarchy.[175] The song to the tune, 'How imperfect is expression', which had been popularized in stage versions of Shakespeare's *Twelfth Night*, imagines 'bold Gallia, nobly sending, / freedom and relief from chains'.[176] The song urges the international spread of revolution:

> May the CAUSE which they're protecting
> Spread thro' ev'ry STATE and CLIME:
> that men on their RIGHTS reflecting,
> REVOLUTIONS well may time

The final stanza, imagines a future celebration of the day:

> Thus secur'd, shall future AGES,
> Who may celebrate this DAY;
> Say "no more wild discord rages,
> REASON only bears the SWAY.

This goes one step further than the attempt of Beaufoy to add a commemorative date to the state's religious calendar: in the context of the song the 'future' day will be to commemorate 'succeeding revolutions'.

The second 'New Song' sung by Dignum and printed by Hawes continues this idea of reimagining 1788 against a projected future revolution inspired by the events in France:

> Unfold, Father Time, thy long records unfold,
> Of noble achievements accomplish'd of old;
> When men by the standard of Liberty led,
> Undauntedly conquer'd or cheerfully bled:
> But now 'midst the triumphs these moments reveal,
> their glories all fade, and their lustre turns pale;
> While France rises up and proclaims the decree
> that tears off their chain, and bids millions be free.

The reference to 'the decree' is repeated in each stanza in the chorus: 'Then seize the glad moment and hail the decree,/that tears off their chains, and bids millions be free'. On 5 November this could be taken to refer to the proclamation of the French Republic in September; by 19 November 1792, however, it would have taken on a more direct meaning for British radicals, as it was on this date that the French Convention issued a decree 'offering fraternal aid to promote revolutions abroad'.[177] The tune to the song is given as 'The tear that bedews sensibility's shrine' which was a song by Captain Morris, appearing in his 1786 *Complete Collection* and in many songsters at this period.[178] The mixing of these song lyrics with well-known and popular tunes ensured their ability to reach a wider, even non-literate audience. This was exactly what Plato had cautioned against in his warning about the power of songs to affect the state.

Hawes was a radical printer for a society calling themselves 'the Constitutional Whigs', whose radical acrostical songs found their way into the Treasury Solicitor's papers for 1792, together with three sheepshearing songs of John Thelwall.[179] At the bottom of each song Hawes advertised songs at '1s per 100 or six a penny'. Their low price clearly also facilitated their spread. An anonymous correspondent to John Reeves's Association for Preserving Liberty and Property wrote on 3 Dec 1792:

> A very sincere well wisher to the principles & purposes of your very laudable Association, begs leave to acquaint you that he has lately seen some very improper ballads, which have been circulated among the lower classes with much industry, & from a memorandum taken from one of them these were,
> "Printed & Sold by R. Hawes "Printer to the Constitutional Whigs" At the Constitutional Liberty Press "No. 107 Whitechapel Road."
> If this communication is in the least useful to you it will very much rejoice,
>   A loyal Subject.[180]

The circulation of songs through the anniversary celebrations of the Revolution Society, the *Muses Banquet,* and the radical press of Robert Hawes illustrates the escalating consequences of the 'loose expressions' and abstractions that Burke railed against in *Reflections* and *An Appeal from the New to the Old Whigs.*

This chapter has explored the complexity of political song culture in relation to the developing crisis created by the response to the French Revolution. This was not a matter of simple topicality but was a complex interwoven pattern that combined the sacral potency of anniversary songs – 'putting songs into mouths' – with the classical traditions of 'Harmodium Melos' and the 'Io Paean'. It is difficult to disentangle these elements. Burke and Price knew how deeply inter-implicated they were and this underpins their performances, in the meeting hall, the tavern dining room and House of Commons, and in their printed texts. The fundamental importance of song in male homosocial culture in its widest sense made their arguments resonate in powerful ways. After 1792 the radical societies and printers adopted and transformed this politics of song. The next, and final, chapter examines a particular place in which this was done – Sheffield.

4 SONGS AND PIKES IN SHEFFIELD: THE TRIAL OF JAMES MONTGOMERY

> No wretched captive of his prison speaks,
> Unless with pain, and bitterness of soul;
> Yet consolation from the Muse he seeks,
> Whose voice alone misfortune can control.
> Where now is each ally, each baron, friend,
> Whose face I Ne'er beheld without a smile,
> Will none, his sov'reign to redeem, expend
> The smallest portion of his treasures vile?[1]

This opening stanza of Richard Coeur De Lion's 'Song of Complaint' was first translated and published in English in Charles Burney's History of Music in 1787. The song had previously appeared in the Provençal language in Horace Walpole's *Catalogue of Royal and Noble Authors* in 1759, and was said to have been written during Richard's imprisonment in the castle from which Blondel would rescue him. The source of Richard's 'complaint' is not only his imprisonment, but his abandonment by the 'barons' and 'friends' who had failed to raise a ransom while, as a later stanza records, his lands are 'ravag'd by the Gallic chief', King Philip. This final chapter turns to James Montgomery (1771–1854), another prisoner who sought the 'consolation from the muse' in his castle prison in York in 1795. Montgomery's *Prison Amusements* was first published in 1797 under his pseudonym 'Paul Positive' and can be located within the corpus of 'prison literature' emerging in the context of the treason trials of 1795, including John Thelwall's *Poems Written in Close Confinement* (1795).[2] In an introduction to the text penned in 1840, Montgomery narrated the incidents that led to his incarceration, revealing that his prosecution for seditious libel for the publication of 'A Patriotic Song by a Clergyman of Belfast' was a 'state prosecution'.[3] Insight can be gained in revisiting Montgomery's prosecution as part of an exploration of the wider context of song in 1790s Sheffield. This includes the songs of the local song writer and song seller Joseph Mather, as they come to embrace Joseph Gales, Montgomery's employer and printer of the *Sheffield Register*, who was heavily involved in the movement for political reform. Through song Montgomery became implicated in the London Treason trial of Thomas Hardy in 1794, and in the network of reform societies that the state attempted to quash, including the Scottish and Irish societies. The chapter brings song into the centre of the analysis of the trial literature: the use of the song 'Ça Ira' in the trial of Thomas Muir in Scotland, and the response of the United Irishmen in their satires, *The Lion of Old England* (1794) and the *Trial of Hurdy Gurdy* (1794) are read as precursors of Montgomery's fate, which was sealed following the failure of the treason prosecutions. Indeed, the United Irishmen are shown to be the source of the song used to prosecute Montgomery in a series of connections which reveal the intensely local as well as national dimensions of the songs discussed. Song is thus foregrounded as the central mode of protest *and* policing, recalling Plato's caution about the malleability of songs and the potential for changes in song styles to alter the constitution of the state. All of the 'song styles' explored in the book emerge in the narrative of this chapter – the chivalric songs of Richard the Lionheart, the political song, and the psalm – revealing the value of a more expansive approach to song scholarship that reaches beyond the confines of the literary ballad. Ultimately, this chapter makes the final argument of the book by demonstrating the importance of the forgotten songs of this period, which are shown to be a central means of political expression.

Intrude our Songs

On 2 March 1792, Joseph Gales, printer and part owner of the *Sheffield Register*, placed an advertisement in the newspaper for a clerk.[4] It was answered by James Montgomery, a twenty year old orphaned Moravian with literary ambitions who was then residing in Wath. John Holland and James Everett, Montgomery's nineteenth-century biographers, record that he ended his letter of application to Gales with the words 'God Save the King' in 'long flourishing characters', which was an expression of youthful loyalty and an 'odd prelude' to the fact that within three short years both he and Gales would be charged with sedition.[5] The relationship between Montgomery and Gales initiated by this letter establishes a new context for 'God Save the King', amidst the threat of French invasion during the revolutionary war. To understand the way in which song is the catalyst of his fate it is necessary to outline the broader context of Sheffield's reform movement and Gales's role at the centre of town meetings surrounded by political singing.

The *Sheffield Register* was an innovative paper for its time. Donald Read notes that it was the first newspaper in the north of England to offer substantial editorial opinion and reports of local meetings, rather than simply reprinting excerpts from the London Papers as was customary.[6] In early April 1792, when twenty year old Montgomery arrived at the printing office of the *Register* in 'the Hartshead', at that time a busy thoroughfare of Sheffield, Gales's press was at work printing the first edition of a periodical entitled the *Patriot*.[7] Edited anonymously by the reformer Matthew Campbell Brown, who had attended the Edinburgh Convention on parliamentary reform the year previously, the 'editors' address' of the first issue declared that 'a reform of abuses, and *an equal Representation of the People*, are the first objects of our paper'.[8] This would be achieved through the dissemination of information on 'the grand and important science of politics, and the various branches of philosophy connected with it, at a price so very moderate as to come within the compass of almost everyone's purchase'.[9] The title page of the *Patriot* carried an image of a cupid holding a Phrygian cap atop a pole with one hand, and with the other hand holding a roll of the 'Magna Charta'. In the background sits a lion. This image would be an important detail in Montgomery's later encounter with the song seller, Joseph Jordan, to be discussed later.

The *Patriot* appeared just a few weeks after the publication of Part Two of Thomas Paine's *Rights of Man* on 16 February 1792.[10] Part One of the *Rights of Man* had been published eleven months before this on 16 March 1791.[11] Whereas the first part had been framed as a response to Edmund Burke's *Reflections* and a defence of the French Revolution, the second part referred to the example of America as a blueprint for representative republican government and outlined the 'ways and means' of achieving this – through taxation reform, the eradication of the extravagance of court, and the establishment of a range of welfare measures for the poor.[12] In the preface to Part Two, Paine declared that 'it is time to dismiss all those songs and toasts which are calculated to enslave and operate to suffocate reflection', an acknowledgement of the important role of songs and toasts in political culture at this time.[13] In Paine's view, songs operated outside of the sphere of rational enlightenment that was necessary to achieve the rights of man and they were designed with forethought, or 'calculated' to oppress the people by keeping them 'enslaved'.

E. P. Thompson observed that the success of the second part of *Rights of Man* was 'phenomenal' and that it 'effected a bridge between the older tradition of the Whig "commonwealthsman" and the radicalism of the Sheffield cutlers, Norwich weavers and London artisans'.[14] As discussed in the previous chapter, the London-based Society for Constitutional Information (SCI), which had been formed in April 1780, proved to be the organizational model for the Sheffield Society for Constitutional Information (SSCI), formed on 24 October 1791, and its more well-known and studied counterpart in the capital, the London Corresponding Society (LCS), which followed in January 1792.[15] The SCI had published short tracts on the need for constitutional reform and distributed them gratis during the 1780s. Unlike the membership of the SCI which comprised of gentlemen reformers, the SSCI was an association of mechanics, cutlers and men who had previously been excluded from political groups. Their meet-

THE PATRIOT:

OR,
POLITICAL, MORAL, AND PHILOSOPHICAL REPOSITORY.

CONSISTING OF

ORIGINAL PIECES,

AND

SELECTIONS FROM WRITERS OF MERIT,

A Work calculated to diffeminate thefe Branches of Knowledge among all Ranks of People, at a fmall Expence.

BY

A SOCIETY OF GENTLEMEN.

PRO PATRIA.

VOL. I.

POPULUS, LIBERTAS, LEX, ET REX.
THE PEOPLE, LIBERTY, THE LAW, AND THE KING.

LONDON:

Printed for G. G. J. and J. Robinfon, and fold by all the Bookfellers in the Country.

Figure 4.1: Title page of the *Patriot*, 1792. State Library of Victoria, Australia, Rare Books, 320.5

ings and activities were reported upon to the second Earl Fitzwilliam, William Wentworth Fitzwilliam (1748–1833), the Lord Lieutenant of the West Riding who was responsible for law and order in the district.[16] Fitzwilliam had been deeply concerned about the movement for parliamentary reform and was active in seeking out information on the SSCI. A correspondent reported to him on 28 December 1791:

> As to your question 'who the persons are who stand forward therein' – I can only say that they are strangers to me but I understand they are of the lower classes of manufacturers and amount to several hundreds, and that they profess to be admirers of the dangerous doctrine of Mr Payne, whose pamphlet they distribute with industry and support the dogmas with zeal, and those new doctrines (with much declamation against the supposed abuses of Government) constitute great part of their weekly debates.[17]

Henry Zouch, magistrate for the West Riding of Yorkshire and an assiduous correspondent to Fitzwilliam, provided an update on the SSCI on 3 March 1792, noting that subscribing numbers now amounted to 1500, '80 or 90 of which' assembled at 'the Lodge' and paid 6 pence each for admission.[18]

Jenny Graham has sought to emphasize the continuity between the gentlemen reformers of the 1780s and the radicals of the 1790s. In this respect, she aims to fill a gap left by historians such as Thompson whom, she argues, acknowledges the role of intellectuals and the middle-class upon the radical movement in *The Making of the English Working Class* (1963), but does not offer a detailed examination.[19] In the case of Sheffield, for example, Graham observes that historians have tended to 'excise' the role of 'middle-class' reformers in the community.[20] She points to Gales in support of her thesis that 'middle class' radicals played an important and under-acknowledged role in the reform movement of the period, noting 'the dependence of the Sheffield reformers' upon Gales's 'organizing, literary and oratorical abilities'.[21] In this assessment Graham follows the earlier work of W. H. Armytage and F. K. Donnelly.[22] Donnelly described Gales as one of the few 'men of substance' involved in the SSCI, noting that a 1787 insurance policy revealed assets worth £500, including his half share of the *Sheffield Register*.[23] However, Donnelly also contends that 'Gales did not play a leading public role in SSCI affairs' because his name did not appear on SSCI public notices, even though these notices were printed in the *Register*.[24] The exact role of Gales in the SSCI has never been satisfactorily established, but it is the contention here that the song culture of Sheffield offers the most valuable insight into the way Gales negotiated his status as a respectable 'man of substance' and his political involvement in the SSCI. As will emerge, this song evidence is also central to understanding Montgomery's fate. Categories such as 'middle-class' fail to capture the complexity and fluidity of Gales's involvement and the clandestine ways in which his print workshop had to operate in support of the movement for reform. By bringing song into the centre of the analysis, a more nuanced assessment of his role becomes possible.

This history begins with the two town meetings that followed the King's Proclamation against Seditious Writings made on 21 May 1792. Samuel Ashton, then secretary of the SSCI, described the first meeting which took place on 11 June 1792 at the town hall, in a letter dated 5 July 1792 to Thomas Hardy, secretary of the LCS.[25] Ashton recounts that the meeting was convened 'on the subject of an address of thanks for the late publication called a proclamation'.[26] However, the SSCI had organized a contingent to attend the meeting in opposition to this measure and for a speech to be read to this effect.[27] The impact of this speech upon a local loyalist 'Russell from Dronfield' is described by Ashton:

> The business was opened by Doctor Browne in the chair, when the speech [against the vote of thanks] was delivered a certain curate (Russell from Dronfield a village 6 miles from Sheffield) immediately stood up but so inflamed with anger that he very little resembled a rational being his language was certainly diabolical alluding to the speech he said 'it was the language of Paine & that was the language of Hell, Paine is an incendiary a fiend from the infernal Regions of Hell, he was spued out of America, has poisoned the minds of thousands of good people of England, these societies are a deluded discontented set of People & are in the high road to destruction &c &c'. Mr Paine's principles & our cause was ably defended & the mock minister very much foiled & cut down without any apparent comfort left for not a single person stood up nor one word spoke on his side the question some 8 or 10 for the address.[28]

Ashton's account of the histrionics of 'Russell from Dronfield' is confirmed by a song about this meeting titled 'Britons Awake' by the local song-writer and song-seller, Joseph Mather, which was published as part of an annotated collection of Mather's songs by John Wilson in 1862.[29] The song opens with an urgent call for Britons to wake up to the emerging powers of darkness:

> Awake from your lethargy, Britons, awake,
> Your lives and your liberties all are at stake;
> Why should you repose in security's arms,
> When every moment's expos'd to alarms;
> The powers of darkness afresh are enrag'd,
> To work out your ruin they all are engaged.
> See liberty banish'd! the clergy deprav'd!
> Religion in sackcloth ! the people enslaved![30]

In the remainder of the song Mather turns the 'diabolical language' of Russell against him. Russell and his supporters at the meeting are depicted as agents of the devil through Mather's extended use of the imagery of hell.

Last Monday, if Beelzebub had not been chained
A most diabolical point he had gained,
He stretched the last link to collect a vile crew,
To render thanksgiving where stripes were most due.
He rallied his forces his cause to maintain,
At Bang-beggar Hall he assembled his train,
With teeth and nails sharpen'd soliciting power,
Like ferocious hell-hound the poor to devour.

A fire engine pan when discharging the stream,
Those fiends represented when backing their scheme;
Their breath was so hot, made me stand in amaze,
Expecting to see it break forth in a blaze;
Such infernal sulphur and sparks flew about,
Some coughing, some sneezing, some f — came out,
Declaring when they had recover'd their breath,
That Bang-beggar Hall was a hell upon earth.

Like Jericho's walls, the address tumbled down,
Which gave satisfaction to thousands in town,
But gave the vile crew both the cholic and gripes,
They all stood in need of old B—n's glister pipes.
When R— discovered his scheme was made void,
Altho' a black hell-hound some thought he'd have dy'd,
An ague fit seized him, convulsions ensued.
And all the way home fire and brimstone he spued.

Old Br—n with two faces, a popular tool,
That day filled the chair to keep order and rule;
His gilded deception threw dust in some eyes,
All could not descern him a fiend in disguise.
A vile proclamation pick'd up at hell's mouth,
That means to make libels or treason of truth –
They met to give sanction, but I must confess
I've seen a more excellent speech by an ass.[31]

The loyalist body politic is depicted in scatological terms as coughing, sneezing and farting, and suffering from 'cholic and gripes' following the failure of the address of thanks for the 'vile proclamation pick'd up at hell's mouth'. The topicality of the song is evident in the reference to the meeting having taken place 'last Monday' and in the local personalities described, including fiery 'Russell' and 'Dr Browne' and his 'glister pipes' – a device to administer enemas. It has been suggested by Charles Hobday that 'Beelzebub' was George Wood, the Master Cutler from 1791–2, who had convened the meeting.[32] Mather's reference to the proclamation 'as a means to make libels or treason of truth' referred to the call upon magistrates to prosecute. A warrant for the prosecution of Thomas Paine had been issued alongside the proclamation of 21 May. In Paine's response to the Proclamation in *Address to the Addressers*, he attributed this to the success of the cheap edition of his text, revealing that the printer J. S. Jordan had been indicted earlier on 14 May for printing the text.[33]

In locating Mather's role as the author of this song, it is worthwhile to recall Joseph Ritson's remarks on minstrels. As previously discussed in Chapter One, these were written in response to Thomas Percy's construction of the ancient English minstrel as part of an aristocratic tradition. Ritson countered 'that there were men in those times, as there are in the present, who gained a livelihood by going about from place to place, singing and playing to the illiterate vulgar is doubtless true'.[34] Ritson could have been writing about Mather here. In his 'Memoir of Mather', John Wilson notes that Mather, a file hewer by trade, would sing his songs in the public houses and at recruiting parties and sell them in the streets on a grinder's donkey and at the local races and fares.[35] John Wilson leaves no further details concerning the publication or circulation of this song. In the preface to his collection of Mather's songs Wilson notes that 'some of the songs have never before been printed and in obtaining such from the oral tradition some defects may have occurred'.[36] He refers to a 'manuscript copy of songs which I collected' though does not name the original complier of this collection nor how he acquired it.

Wilson is keen to emphasize that Mather exercised considerable influence over his fellow workmen at Sheffield by acting as a 'champion of labour'. His annotations of one of Mather's most well-known songs – 'Watkinson and his Thirteens' – provides a striking example of the power of music. Mather wrote this song in response to a dispute that had arisen in 1787 between the cutlers of Sheffield and the master cutler, James Watkinson. The production of cutlery and tools was Sheffield's main industry at this time and rather than being integrated into a factory system, journeymen cutlers maintained a large degree of independence through their small workshops where they effectively operated as 'little masters'.[37] Peter Garlick describes the operations of such a small workshop: 'they were provided materials from the warehouse of the employer for the following week, and returned the goods they had taken the previous week, their stage of the work complete, for which they received payment, or cash on account ("sours")'.[38] After they had made their dozen implements, it had been customary for journeyman cutlers to be able to keep any surplus material. Watkinson caused outrage by instituting a measure whereby the journeyman would make thirteen knives and be paid for a dozen.[39] In response Mather produced 'Watkins and his Thirteens', which imagined the extra knife eviscerating Watkinson:

> And may the odd knife his great carcase dissect,
> Lay open his vitals for men to inspect,
> A heart full as black as the infernal gulph
> In that greedy, blood-sucking, bone-scraping wolf.[40]

Like 'Britons Awake' this song carries a similar emphasis upon the body.[41] Mather has been categorized as a local occupational song writer because his songs such as 'Britons Awake' lampooned local figures of authority. However the politics of his songs also intersected with the broader concerns of the nation in the 1790s.[42] A case in point is the use of Mather's song 'God Save Great Thomas Paine' in response to the second town meeting, called on 13 June 1792 owing to the failure of the first meeting to obtain an address of thanks. John Wilson describes the second meeting as a 'hole and corner meeting', meaning that it was stacked with those who supported the outcome of obtaining the address of thanks.[43] Those 'Jacobins' in attendance thus felt duped and called upon Joseph Gales to intercede. At this point Mather's song history reveals the important role of Gales in the community:

> on finding themselves duped, they again filled the Town Hall and called Mr. Gales to the chair ... The substance of his address was that having carried their amendment at the public meeting, they ought to allow those who differed from them in opinion to meet and express their own sentiments as they thought fit. Mr Gales reminded the meeting that those who voted for the Amendment on the 11th inst. would *not sign* the address of the 13th. It is probable that an incident that took place when the meeting broke up rendered Mr. Gales more obnoxious than before. The majority present, as if to assert their principles, accompanied the chairman to his office in the Hartshead, singing Mather's song, beginning – 'God Save Great Thomas Paine'.[44]

Though he makes no reference to Gales's part in diffusing the tension at the meeting, Samuel Ashton's letter to the LCS also confirms that this follow-up meeting took place on Wednesday 13 June 1792:

> But lo' on the Wednesday following the combined small minority put forth an anonymous Hand Bill inciting such as wished to sign the address to attend that Day at the Cutlers Hall, this caused a great stir in the town, the measure was reprobated almost universally, multitudes assembled & for some time would not suffer the small group to enter the hall unless all had an equal privilege of being present, several arguments were discussed in the street, the Royalists declared that if they were refused enterance there they would go to one of the Inns pleaded their Right to do as they pleased in forming an address &c at length by the persuasion of some of the Society the People retired the Thing was passed & every Day since the town bedle has been hawking it from house to house shop to shop.[45]

A correspondent to Earl Fitzwilliam also reported on this second meeting in a letter dated 13 June 1792, though in strikingly different terms:

> We had a meeting this day for the purpose of considering an address to his Majesty. The constitutional society came with a full determination to have an address of their own but we persuaded them to go to the town hall & prepare their own address whilst we prepared ours.[46]

In this account it is the loyalists who emerge as controlling the proceedings. The correspondent goes on to report that the 'gentlemen supporting the address were much hissed and hooted at by the Mobility' on the outside of the Hall but 'we do not hear their efforts'.[47]

Mather's version of 'God Save Great Thomas Paine' is printed by Wilson as:

God save great Thomas Paine,
His 'Rights of Man' to explain
To e'vry soul.

He makes the blind to see
What dupes and slaves they be,
And points out liberty
From pole to pole.

Thousands cry 'church and king'
That well deserve to swing,
All must allow
Birmingham blush for shame,
Manchester do the same,
Infamous is your name,
Patriot's vow.

Pull proud oppressors down,
Knock off each tyrant's crown,
And break his sword;
Down with aristocracy,
Set up democracy
And from hypocrisy
Save us Good Lord.

Why should despotic pride
Usurp on every side?
Let us be free;
Grant freedom's arms success,
And all her efforts bless,
Plant thro' the universe
Liberty's tree.

Facts are seditious things
When they touch courts and kings,
Armies are rais'd,
Barracks and bastiles built,
Innocence charged with guilt,
Blood most unjustly spilt,

God's stand amaz'd.
Despots may howl and yell,
Tho' they're in league with hell
They'll not rein long;
Satan may lead the van,
And do the worst he can,

Paine and his Rights of Man
Shall be my song.[48]

Whether or not this was the actual version of the song sung when Gales was carried is difficult to say. The call for Birmingham and Manchester to 'blush with shame' referred to the riots of 1791. However the reference to 'armies are raised' may have been in reference to the army of Austria which had been at war with France since April, or France's declaration of war against England in 1793. The reference to barracks being built referred to the building of a permanent barracks at Sheffield which was completed in 1793. Gillian Russell has observed that the program of building barracks began before the war with France as a way of policing radical towns such as Sheffield and was 'as much a response to the domestic political situation as it was to the demands of a foreign war'.[49] Troops had been stationed at Sheffield since a series of disturbances, but as a result of a report to the Secretary of War from Colonel De Lancey, dated 13 June 1792, a permanent barracks was built. De Lancey reported that

> the seditious doctrines of Paine & the factious people who are endeavouring to disturb the peace of the country, had extended to a degree very much beyond my conception, and indeed they seem with great judgement to have chosen this as the centre of all their seditious machinations, for the manufactures of this town is of a nature to require so little capital to carry them on, that a man with a very small sum of money can employ two, three or four men, and this being generally the case, there are not in this, as in other great towns, any number of persons of sufficient weight who could by their influence, or the number of their dependents, act with any effect in case of a disturbance[50]

Gales was a central disseminator of the 'seditious doctrines of Paine' in the community. In her memoirs of this period entitled 'Reminiscences of our Residence in Sheffield', written in 1831, his wife Winifred Gales recalled that they had sold 'hundreds' of Paine's works in the shop and printed 'thousands' by order of the Constitutional Society.[51] Gales thus came to symbolize Paine himself, as evident in the authority he exercised over the men at the meeting and in their accompanying him home to Mather's 'God Save Great Thomas Paine'.

Winifred also provided an account of the second meeting in that part of her memoirs.[52] Her overriding concern is to represent her husband as a measured man of respectability: to this end she describes his role in the second meeting, organized using the anonymous handbill.

> The next day another meeting was called of all such persons as were favourable to addressing the King. All (the friends of liberty) who thought properly, remained at home, in the number your father was of course. We were at tea very early on that evening, Lord Effingham's Land Agent with us, when an alarming shout called our attention, for what riots were we well knew, and our enquiries were answered by the appalling fact that the people had assembled in thousands, and were threatening to pull down the Cutler's Hall, the place where the meeting was to be held.[53]

Your father and his guest ran immediately without their hats (the scene of riot being now at hand) They found the report true and (the Rev'd) Mr Radford Vicar of Trinity Church haranguing the crowd. He talked to the Winds. In a moment the two new comers were discovered by someone in the outer circle who called out 'Mr Gales in the Chair' – it was repeated by a thousand voices, and without either his mental acquiescence, or personal volition, he was carried bare headed to the seat which Mr Radford had rapidly vacated. Very unpleasantly was your dear Father situated, for he knew that an exasperated mob was a dreadful monster. Someone has said and we think justly, that a mob if it were composed of philosophers would be in danger of perpetuating mischief. There was no time to hesitate, and eloquence, had your Father possessed the power of Tully himself, would have little availed at that crisis.[54] A few plain sentences appeared best to suit the occasion, and in his usual quiet and composed way, he enquired 'if the large assembly of people he saw were there in consequence of the Hand Bill that day issued'. A few voices answered yes. 'Did you intend to sign a vote of thanks ?'

Several voices moderately answered No. 'Then my friends you have certainly no business here. You expressed your sentiments yesterday, and you surely would not deprive your neighbours of the same privilege. Hitherto Sheffield has been celebrated for the orderly and peaceful conduct of the manufacturing part of the community. Do not now forfeit your claim to this honourable distinction' Several voices said 'Speak on Mr Gales you are a good man, we will mind what you say', 'If you rely upon my advice answered your father because you believe me to be your friend, I will prove it to you, by recommending that every man opposed to the object of the meeting depart peaceably home. Oblige even those who differ in opinion with you, to respect you, by shewing that you respect yourselves'. Home – Home was the general cry and in twenty minutes not one of the opposition thousands there assembled, were to be seen.

You will hardly believe it, my children, that there were men illiberal enough to be angry that your father had so easily settled what appeared, and really was a tumultuous and disorderly assembly.

'See, said an anti-reformer, what influence Gales has over the multitude – if he speaks, their wild rasings are hushed into gentle murmurs. By what means has he obtained this dangerous influence'. One of his own political party, answered. 'By pleading the poor man's cause, by advocating equal Representation; by treating them as Brethren – Gales is a good man, a friend to the oppressed, and a most exemplary man in all his domestic relations'. Thus spoke a person who though opposed to Mr Gales, was too upright himself to withhold justice from another.[55]

Details such as Gales and his guest having to leave so hurriedly without their hats, and Gales assuming the chair 'bare-headed', point to an attention to respectability in Winifred Gales's narrative. Michael Davis has pointed to the 'politics of civility', as part of the model of respectability that the LCS sought to engender through strict rules of behaviour at meetings, in opposition to its characterization as a 'mob club' by loyalists.[56] Joseph Gales emerges as the model of respectability and rationality here; his is the voice of reason in 'the chair' that convinces the mob to go home. Gales's authority as an advocate is such that he can quiet the 'wild rasings' of the people and 'Home' is the cry rather than the song 'God Save Great Thomas Paine', to which Winifred Gales does not refer. This also reflects his status as an exemplar of domestic relations. Borrowing Davis's term, a domesticated 'politics of civility' is prized here, as opposed to the very public politics of song and licence evident in Wilson's account.

Gales's own identification with Paine also emerges in his response to the effigy burnings at the end of 1792 and 1793. The *Sheffield Register* was the central means by which Gales, 'the friend to the oppressed' pleaded 'the poor man's cause'. He printed the resolutions of the SSCI meetings in the first column of the *Register* and reported events such as the victories of Republican France against the Duke of Brunswick which were celebrated in Sheffield in what John Stevenson describes as 'extraordinary scenes'.[57] The victory at Valmy was marked on 15 October with a Civic fete which included an effigy of the Duke of Brunswick.[58] A later celebration, on 27 November 1792, involved the roasting of an ox and a procession through the town as the meat was distributed to the poor. The procession, in which banners and the national cockade of France were displayed, was accompanied by cannon fire and culminated in the ringing of the bells of the parish church in support of France.[59] In the winter of 1792–3, these celebrations were countered by displays of loyalism and the burning of Thomas Paine in effigy, described by Thompson as 'the most effigy-burned man in British history' after Guy Fawkes.[60]

Frank O'Gorman has revised previous estimates of the number of such incidents to conclude that there were 'well over 500 burnings' during the winter of 1792–3.[61] However O'Gorman's analysis misses the efforts of Joseph Gales to undermine the Thomas Paine effigy burnings in the *Register*. O'Gorman writes that:

> newspapers sympathetic to reformers and the Whig opposition were disinclined to print details of the burnings, which were, of course, celebrations of popular loyalism. For example, the Foxite *Newcastle Chronicle* reported only one burning that in Dronfield in Derbyshire, ignoring the 13 burnings which the *Newcastle Courant* was able to report. Similarly, the *Sheffield Register* contained larger news sections than most other newspapers but contained not a single reference to burnings. Significantly, its editor, Joseph Gales, was a reformer.[62]

O'Gorman is incorrect to suggest that Gales chose to ignore the Paine burnings. Instead, Gales saved his thoughts for the editorial columns at the *back* of the *Register*, rather than reporting on them in the news sections at the front of the paper. Gales actually ridiculed the effigy burnings on 4 January 1793 employing the language of diablerie used by Russell of Dronfield:

> Paine has suffered universal martyrdom. At parish and corporation meetings he has been condemned by bell, book, and candle and punished with fire and faggot! ... In one parish he was burnt for being a *Presbyterian* in another for being a Jacobite – in a third for being a *Popish Jesuit* – and in a fourth for being nothing less than the Devil

himself! Though we do not altogether subscribe to so black a charge as the latter, yet we cannot help thinking he must be something more than man, who, at the close of the eighteenth century, can work such wonders simply by the magic incantation of a – goose quill![63]

In the *Register* of Friday 18 January 1793, Gales reported an example of a counter-effigy burning of Burke and reworks the notions of loyalty through reference to song:

> Yesterday fortnight, the inhabitants of Dronfield, in this neighbourhood, testified their loyalty to his Majesty, by burning the effigy of the man who exultingly exclaimed in the British senate, at the time when our beloved Sovereign was afflicted with a most dreadful and malignant disorder, 'That it had pleased heaven, in its divine vengeance to hurl the Monarch from the throne'. – A most excellent and characteristic Figure was carried through the town, mounted on an Ass, preceded by music, several Labels fixed on Poles, and a Painting exhibiting Mr. Dundas and Mr Burke attacking Britannia. After parading the principal streets, the Figure was suspended on a gibbet 20 feet high, where it hung about an hour and was afterwards burnt amidst the acclamations of the people. God Save the King was sung and received with the warmest applause. The following additional verse, suited to the occasion, produced a particular effect:

> Let us detest the man,
> Whose jesuitic Plan
> Must ruin Bring;
> Let us, the Multitude,
> Tho' Swinish, yet intrude
> Our songs, and shout aloud
> God Save the King[64]

The effigy description and verse contests Burke's loyalism by ironically claiming that the radicals were more loyal to the king. Gales draws upon Burke's notorious parliamentary speech made during the King's illness and the Regency crisis of 1788 when, using an allusion to Milton's *Paradise Lost*, he had described the King being 'hurled from the throne' by God – 'the almighty'.[65] This instance of rhetorical excess continued to dog Burke, because as John Barrell notes, and as evident in Gales's comments, his opponents accused him of blasphemy and of exulting in the king's illness.[66] The 'jesuitic plan' draws upon a stock caricature representation of Burke as an ascetic Jesuit and the 'intrusion' of the songs of the 'multitude, tho' swinish' also turns Burke's evocative language against him.[67] He used this image in *Reflections* in the context of a discussion about how the fall of the nobility and clergy in France would result in the end of learning, which would be 'trodden down under the hoofs of a swinish multitude'.[68] The phrase was appropriated by radical culture as *'the* swinish multitude', and as evidence of ruling class disdain for the people in general.[69] This extra verse to 'God Save the King' – author unknown – appropriates Mather's subversion of the anthem and, by reporting it in the paper, Gales legitimates and endorses a less respectable mode of radicalism.

The other notable dimension of this account is the role of music in the procession of the effigy. In his work on rough music, Thompson noted that many of the ritual burnings of Paine undoubtedly drew upon elements of 'rough music' and so too, in Gales's description of the effigy of Burke, it is noted that the procession went through the town with the figure mounted on an ass 'preceded by music' and 'labels' on poles depicting Burke and Henry Dundas, Secretary of State. As discussed in Chapter Two, rough music was the cacophonous sounds attached to customary rituals of discipline such as skimmington rides, and effigy burnings. In Thompson's theory of social relations between patricians and plebs, these rituals of punishment and their attendant ceremonies were tolerated because they provided the 'plebs' with a degree of expression but also self-regulation and autonomy that ultimately worked to maintain the existing hierarchy. While Thompson notes that rough music was socially conservative in that it 'defended custom and male dominative tradition', it was, however, 'always potentially subversive, with its rites of inversion, its blasphemies and obscenities'.[70] What I would like to emphasize here is how these customary elements of rough music – the effigy of Burke mounted on an ass processing through the town – aligned with the medium of print to pose a threat to customary relations, in this case, the subversive extra verse of 'God Save the King', which is transmitted by Gales through the *Sheffield Register*. Gales emerges as a complex figure at the centre of rough music as it comes to embrace political song. This is evident in another incident which he describes in a letter to his friend the Manchester journalist and playwright, Joseph Aston, on 26 September 1793.

> You were misinformed as to any riot having taken place here. In one part of the day, however, things wore rather a serious appearance. The C. and K. party (very small indeed), accompanied by a recruiting party, with a drum and fife, presented themselves before my house and gave me most loyal music, firing and shouting: and someone was heard to say, that my house should not have a whole window in it that night. This circumstance, I am firmly of opinion, had the effect of calling together a wall of defence, for, about an hour afterwards, upwards of a hundred stout democrats stood before us, singing 'God Save Great Thomas Paine!' to the loyal tune. This party increased to 500, and paraded the streets peaceably (except singing) all the day. Nor would they leave till they apprehended all danger to be past.[71]

The customary elements of rough music – the public shaming of Gales outside his house for his transgressive politics and the threat to his property – plays out militarily here, with the 'C and K' party being accompanied by a recruiting party and the performance of 'loyal' music with the martial instruments of the drum and fife accompanied by gunfire and customary raucous shouting. By September 1793, England and France were at war and a permanent barracks had been built at Sheffield. The emergence of the 'stout democrats' who defend Gales by singing 'God Save Great Thomas Paine', presumably a version by Joseph Mather, underscores the importance of political singing in Sheffield, and once again, Gales emerges as a surrogate Paine figure. This scene of rough musicking outside the Gales's house brings together all of the elements that this first section of the chapter has sought to foreground: the minstrelsy of Joseph Mather as it came to embrace the power of print harnessed by Joseph Gales in the *Sheffield Register*; the role of song in the clash of political song cultures, both loyalist and radical in Sheffield; and finally the presence of James Montgomery. Winifred Gales had recorded in her reminiscence that in 1792 'the amiable, the intellectual, the pious James Montgomery, came to live with us. Previous to this period, we had lived in domestic ease and social harmony'.[72] It is plausible to imagine that Montgomery must have been inside the house with the Gales family listening to singing in the incident described. It is necessary now to outline the way in which the arrest of the LCS reformers in 1794 came to implicate Gales and Montgomery through song.

Handbill Hymns and Lost Petitions

In London in early May 1794 the leading reformers of the movement for political reform were arrested for treason: Thomas Hardy, Secretary of the LCS, and Daniel Adams, Secretary of the SCI, had their books and papers confiscated, and were placed in custody on 12 May; followed by John Thelwall on 13 May; and John Horne Tooke on 16 May.[73] The leading members of the Sheffield Constitutional Society – William Broomhead, Robert Moody, Henry Hill, George Widdeson, and William Camage were arrested on 29 May and taken to London by military escort.[74] Their apprehension had been enabled by the suspension of Habeas Corpus on 23 May, meaning that the government had the power to hold the prisoners without bringing them to trial.[75] Joseph Gales escaped arrest in large part due to good fortune. He happened to be away from Sheffield conducting business in Derby 'on some family affairs' when rumours started to circulate that the King's messengers were on their way to the town.[76] Gales was advised to stay away for a few days and once it became apparent that there was a warrant for his arrest he escaped to Germany en route to America. Winifred was left to answer questions and to soon make her own escape with their children.[77]

A draft of Gales's indictment in the Treasury Solicitor's papers shows that he was to be charged with seditious libel for printing a handbill and a pamphlet of a 'serious lecture' that had been read at a meeting of reformers at Sheffield on 27 February 1794.[78] Both the handbill and 'a serious lecture' were forwarded to Joseph White of the Treasury Solicitor's office by John Brookfield, a Sheffield solicitor. Brookfield wrote on 1 March 1794 that in consequence of the inclosed handbill being distributed thro' this town, about 1500 persons assembled yesterday when the 'serious lecture' of which I inclose you a copy was read by one of the company. I am informed that several thousand copies have been printed, & this day they have been sold at 2d each in several private houses in different parts of the town, and great pains has been taken to inform the public where they might be had.

I have every reason to believe that both papers were printed by Mr Gales, but he has avoided selling them, or suffering any to be seen in his shop. I think however, there is great probability of finding out the fact, if you think proper to take any notice of the matter, – the man who sold the inclosed is a very despicable character, & I verily believe the fear of punishment would induce him to disclose the author & printer also. – We have a set of sad dogs here, & nothing but a little wholesome correction will I am afraid keep them quiet.[79]

The 'hand bill', dated 'February 27, 1794' which was a Thursday, artfully disguises its intentions. The 'serious lecture' is to be delivered 'on Friday next' which would suggest not the next day but rather, the next week. The next day, 28 February 1794, had been appointed by royal proclamation to be a day of General Fast, for the purpose of 'sending prayers and supplications to the divine majesty ... and imploring his blessing and assistance on our Arms'.[80] The hymn, however, which is to be sung *after* the serious lecture is 'for February 28, 1794, being the Day appointed for a general fast'. The handbill thus cleverly avoids actually stating that the meeting was to be held the next day, on the fast day, which would have drawn suspicion, but gives enough information for the reader to be able to decode this. If looked at quickly, the handbill presents nothing untoward as the hymn is *for* the fast day to be sung to the tune of the 'Old Hundredth', which as discussed in Chapter Two, had achieved the status alongside 'God Save the King' as a national anthem.

The text of the hymn, however, presents a direct challenge to the aims of the General Fast and indirectly the late eighteenth-century elaboration of the 'Old Hundredth' as the state anthem, used in celebrations such as the Thanksgiving for the King's recovery. Instead of asking for God's assistance with the war effort, the hymn asks for God's intercession for the cause of the reformers who were opposed to the war: 'our cause be thine'. The war is God's vengeance against the guilty and he is asked to tame the 'mad tyrants' and to show his might: 'make bare thine arm great King of Kings'. This imagery comes from Exodus, when God led the Israelites out of enslavement in Egypt, an event alluded to in the lines 'that wonder-working arm which broke / From Israel's Neck the Egyptian Yoke'. John Wesley draws upon the same image in the third of his hymns to be used 'in time of persecution', where God is implored 'make bare thine arm; appear, appear, and for thy people fight'.[81] The last stanza of the hymn brings the biblical imagery into the revolutionary present by conjuring up the storming of the Bastille and the new language of 'rights' harnessed by Paine: 'burst every

A Serious Lecture.

A PUBLIC MEETING of the FRIENDS of PEACE and REFORM, is intended to be held on Friday next, at one o'Clock in the Afternoon, at the Head of West-Street, Backfields, in order to attend a SERIOUS LECTURE which will be then delivered.—After the LECTURE will be sung the following HYMN prepared for the Occasion, and the Meeting will be concluded, by passing such Resolutions as the present Juncture of Affairs seems to call for.

Sheffield, February 27, 1794.

HYMN

For February 28, 1794, *being the Day appointed for*

A GENERAL FAST.

[To the Tune of the Old Hundredth Psalm.]

I.
O GOD of HOSTS, thine Ear incline,
Regard our Prayers, our Cause be thine;
When Orphans cry, when Babes complain,
When Widows weep—can'st thou refrain?

II.
Now red and terrible thine Hand,
Scourges with WAR our guilty Land;
Europe thy flaming Vengeance feels,
And from her deep Foundations reels.

III.
Her Rivers bleed like mighty Veins;
Her Towns are Ashes, Graves her Plains;
Slaughter her groaning Vallies fills,
And reeking Carnage melts her Hills.

IV.
O THOU! whose awful Word can bind
The raging Waves, the raving Wind,
Mad TYRANTS tame; break down the High
Whose haughty Foreheads beat the Sky;

V.
Make bare thine Arm, great King of Kings!
That Arm alone Salvation brings,
That Wonder-working Arm which broke
From Israel's Neck th' Egyptian Yoke.

VI.
Burst every Dungeon, every Chain;
Give injur'd Slaves their Rights again;
Let TRUTH prevail, let Discord cease;
Speak——and the World shall smile in PEACE!

Figure 4.2: Handbill of 'A Serious Lecture' and 'Hymn'. The National Archives. TS 11/1071

dungeon, every chain;/ give injur'd slaves their rights again'. The peace comes after God has interceded in the battle, so the hymn also holds the threat of the intervention of God's wrath. The tune of the 'Old Hundredth', a psalm that seeks to unite all of God's people evident in the first line ' All people that on earth do dwell', is used subversively here in a call for God to wage war on tyranny in the name of the people (echoing the role of 'Sternhold and Hopkins' in the English Civil War in the seventeenth century).

The distribution of this hymn through the handbill was a direct challenge to the sentiments of the 'official form of prayer for the general fast' which was printed and distributed as a pamphlet throughout the country, with its printer in Sheffield being John Northall.[82] The hymn was also circulated in print in the *Sheffield Register* on 7 March 1794, where it was reported that '5000 friends of peace and reform attended the meeting' where the serious lecture was delivered.[83] Further afield, the hymn appeared in the *Cambridge Intelligencer,* edited by the radical Benjamin Flower, in the issues of 15 March and 13 September 1794, and the LCS also had it printed together with the lecture.[84] Two comparatively recent collections of 'verse' and 'poetry' have also included the hymn: Jerome McGann's *New Oxford Book of Romantic Period Verse* (1993) and Betty T. Bennett's *British War Poetry in the Age of Romanticism*.[85] The important context of the hymn as a song sung to the tune of the 'Old Hundredth' has, however, been neglected in these later anthologies, which frame it primarily in literary terms. Even if we are to accept John Brookfield's more conservative report of the numbers at the reformers meeting on the Fast Day being 1,500 as opposed to Gales's reported 5,000 the sound of over one thousand voices singing in 'full chorus' in the open air would have been extraordinarily powerful and would have filled the surrounding streets of 'Backfields'. Even those not attending would have heard the hymn.

This meeting was one of a series of open air meetings held by reformers in Sheffield and London in the first months of 1794 which Goodwin says 'clinched' the decision of the government to take decisive action against the radical reformers.[86] The second major meeting at Sheffield was held on the Castle Hill on 7 April 1794 with three objectives to consider: whether to petition the King concerning those 'patriots' imprisoned in Scotland; whether to petition the House of Commons for a second time for a reform of parliament; and finally, whether to petition the King for the abolition of slavery.[87] The meeting was presided over by Henry Yorke, also known as Henry 'Redhead' Yorke (1772–1813), described by Winifred Gales as a 'new meteor' on the 'political horizon', who had come to Sheffield at the end of 1792.[88] In London the LCS followed suit when their General Meeting was held in the open air at Chalk Farm on 14 April 1794.[89] Contrary to the characterization of his wife, Gales was implicated as being at the very centre of the Castle Hill meeting by fellow SSCI member William Broomhead in his examination taken before Richard Ford on 3 July 1794. Broomhead stated that when Yorke arrived at Sheffield he 'took a very active and leading part in the society there, and soon, together with one Gales a printer there assumed the principal management of it'.[90] Broomhead further deponed that Gales and Yorke were principally responsible for the correspondence carried on with other societies and that at the Castle Hill meeting they had instructed him to make a motion that a petition should be presented to Parliament 'for the express purpose of having it negatived and rejected'.[91]

The rejection of the motion to petition signalled a new tone to the reformers' demands. The Sheffield reformers had already petitioned parliament a year earlier, in April 1793, seeking 'a plan of effectual reform in the representation of the Commons in parliament'.[92] This petition was rejected, however, on the grounds that its language was 'indecent' and 'disrespectful' to the House, with William Wilberforce and Henry Dundas suggesting that it was deliberately couched in such language to ensure its rejection.[93] Ironically, the 1793 petition rejection enabled Henry Yorke to abandon the whole idea of petitioning parliament on the question of parliamentary reform at the meeting of 1794.[94] The proceedings of the meeting report the failure of 'one single person' to second the motion for a petition, which according to Broomhead, was made by him as a kind of 'hole and corner' tactic to get the negative answer they desired.[95]

Yorke then addressed the meeting 'in an animated speech of an hour long'.[96] He described 'in detail' the ancient constitution as established by King Alfred, which had been totally lost; spoke of the further erosion of popular liberties with the Danish and Norman invasions; and asserted that the object of the Glorious Revolution of 1688 'could not be answered' without the restoration of annual parliaments and general suffrage.[97] Because the principles of the 1688 Revolution had been violated with the triennial act and the septennial acts, which had extended the terms of parliaments, the people were justified in *demanding* their right to govern themselves rather than petitioning, as consistent with the Declaration of Rights passed in 1689.[98] In the climax to his speech, the 'experience' of the past emerges as useful so that 'humanists' might prepare their 'combustile ingredients' and produce a 'grand political explosion':

> To effect this just and useful purpose, Revolution of sentiment must precede Revolution of Government and Manners. The popular energies must be excited, that the popular voice may be felt and heard.[99]

Yorke's vision of a 'popular voice' emerging from a Revolution of sentiment thus repudiates Burke's formulation of the 'grand chorus' of the 'natural aristocracy' which would lead the people. John Barrell has noted that the sentiments expressed in Yorke's speech may have meant no more than that public opinion, expressed by a fully representative convention, would operate so powerfully as to force a dissolution of the present, unrepresentative House of Commons. It would be read by the Government, however, as a declaration that the convention was intended to replace the Commons.[100]

It is the contention here that Yorke's 'revolution of sentiment' can also be understood in relation to the specific politics of song being played out in Sheffield at this time which embraced the singing of the handbill hymn – when the people's 'voice' had actual expression.

Finally, metaphors of song emerge again in 'An exposition of the motives which had determined the people of Sheffield to petition the House of Commons no more' attached to the printed proceedings of the meeting. The exposition rejected petitioning once more through metaphors of song:

> But our petition being scouted, we shall trouble them no more with our coarse and unmannerly language. It will be our duty to proceed, as we have uniformly done hitherto, in enlightening the public mind; and, when a complete revolution of sentiment shall take place (as will shortly be the case) in our country, we shall open our mouths, in that key we think most agreeable to ourselves. And our voice, together with that of our disenfranchised Countrymen, will resemble, perhaps, the thundering from Mount Sinai!'[101]

The pervasive psalmic imagery of God putting songs into mouths is overturned here, as following the complete revolution of sentiment, the people will open their mouths and sing to the King in a key of *their* choosing. This threat to the order of the church and state demonstrates the way different songs styles, such as the hymn, could be deployed as part of the language of revolution. It also underpins the emergence of songs as evidence in the trials.

Thomas Muir, The United Irishmen and 'Ça Ira'

One of the resolutions of the Castle Hill Meeting was to address the King on behalf of the 'Scottish martyrs', whose condemnation 'was an act better suited to the Maxims of a despotic than a free Government'.[102] The Edinburgh trial of Thomas Muir in August 1793, and of William Skirving, Maurice Margarot and Joseph Gerrald between January and March 1794, resulted in their sentence of transportation for 15 years.[103] Muir's arrest followed his participation at the first Convention of the Scottish Friends of the People held from 11–13 December 1792 at which numerous resolutions were passed calling for a reform of parliament.[104] Skirving, Margarot and Gerrald had all attended a later more radicalized 'convention', styled as a 'British convention', held in Edinburgh in November 1793.[105] These trials emerge as important to Barrell's explanation of the prosecution strategy used in the treason trials of the London reformers, which would take place in London later in 1794, because the arguments used in Scotland enabled the English prosecutors to formulate their interpretation of figurative treason.[106] Song evidence in the Edinburgh trial of Thomas Muir would be similarly important in foreshadowing the strategies and themes of the later trials.

Thomas Muir (1765–99) was a Glaswegian lawyer who had played a leading role in the Glasgow branch of the Scottish Society of the Friends of the People.[107] He was indicted on charges of sedition with a lengthy charge sheet listing his distribution of a range of seditious material including the *Patriot* and *Rights of Man*, and his reading out an address from the United Irishmen 'To the Delegates for Promoting a Reform in Scotland' at the Edinburgh Convention on 12 December 1792.[108]

The Society of United Irishmen was founded by a group of middle-order professional men, including Dr William Drennan and Theobald Wolfe Tone, in Belfast in October 1791 with a branch established shortly thereafter in Dublin.[109] The resolutions of the society were to counter the 'weight of English influence' through 'a complete and radical' reform of parliament which would include 'Irishmen of every religious persuasion'.[110] At this time Catholics held no voting rights, were prohibited from political and legal office and were unable to own property. The spirit of internationalism attached to the French Revolution was especially important in the Irish context where reform had been stymied by fears that enfranchisement for the majority Catholic population would result in tyranny. Kevin Whelan observes that the French Revolution showed that these fears were without foundation, as predominantly Catholic France had demonstrated that Catholics could be entrusted to pursue the path of liberty: 'if French Catholics could display such political maturity, so too could Irish Catholics'.[111] The address from the United Irishmen, which was read by Muir at the convention, emphasized the solidarity of the Irish and Scottish reform movements, asserting that 'our cause is your cause', and called for a union of reformers in England Scotland and Ireland.[112] In the most recent analysis of Muir's trial, Nigel Leask has emphasized the international and cosmopolitan nature of the Scottish radical movement on display here.[113]

This address was one of the stronger pieces of evidence presented at Muir's trial. Perhaps one of the weakest was the testimony of Anne Fisher, a former scullery maid at the Muir home in Huntershill. Her evidence for the prosecution included details of Muir's reading habits and the accusation that Muir had sent her to a 'barrel-organist' on the streets, with the request that he play the tune to the French revolutionary song, 'Ça Ira'.[114] As Leask points out, this demonstrated that she had been carefully coached by the prosecution.[115] Muir, who chose to defend himself, was incensed by Fisher's evidence, referring to her as a 'domestic and well tutored spy' and refusing to put a question to her.[116] Muir did not deny the servant's accusation but in his closing speech poured ridicule on the prosecution's use of Fisher who spoke not to his 'serious occupation, but to the amusement of an idle hour, in listening to a foreign tune'.

> What! Was a tune, unintelligible to the multitude, to light up the flames of civil discord, and to be the forerunner of the revolution? Have you read the words of that popular song? Could you discover a single allusion in them to the state of England? But supposing you did, there is a presumption from your station in life, that you are acquainted with the French language; but is it so with the multitude of our weavers in that quarter of the country?[117]

Muir makes his case by pointing to the unintelligibility of a foreign language for the 'multitude', strategically ignoring the role of the tune to cross this divide and its circulation in Britain at this time.

A version of 'Ça Ira' set to music by William Shield, from the Covent Garden pantomime of 1790 entitled *The Picture of Paris*, had been circulating for genteel audiences as sheet music published by Longman and Broderip for one shilling.[118] The song had originally emerged in France during the first anniversary of the fall of the Bastille in July 1790. Helen Maria Williams, who was in France at this time, reported that 'Ça Ira' was 'not only sung at every theatre, and in every street in Paris but in every town and village of France, by man, woman and child'.[119] As events progressed, however, the song took on a militancy as an anthem of revolution, in opposition to the song 'O Richard o Mon Roi' from the opera *Richard Coeur de Lion*, which had been adopted by the Royalists and those loyal to King Louis.[120] By the time of Muir's trial, 'Ça Ira' had also evidently been circulating in Britain beyond the confines of those who could afford Shield's sheet music. The correspondent 'Fidelia' wrote to John Reeves's *Association* in 1792 urging the society to use the medium of 'vulgar ballads' to counter the influence of 'new seditious doctrines upon the lower class of people', noting the example of 'Ça Ira' and including a ballad she had authored for the society's approval.[121] Gillian Russell has also reported incidents when 'Ça Ira' was called for in theatres in opposition to 'God Save the King', acting, therefore, as a kind of alternative national anthem.[122] A radicalized version was printed by 'R. Thompson' in the songster titled *Tribute to Liberty* in 1793, referring to the increasing levels of surveillance and censorship experienced by radicals and hinting at the imminent overthrow of this regime: "'Tis dangerous to eat / 'Tis dangerous to meet, / 'Tis dangerous to think / ça ira ira, ça ira'[123] Muir's denial of the intelligibility of 'Ça Ira' was therefore not plausible given the numerous sites in which the song circulated.

The plausibility of his defence, however, was not necessarily the point. Muir chose to defend himself at trial, turning down the offer of defence from Henry Erskine, brother of Thomas Erskine, as a deliberate tactic so that he could use the court room as another public means in which to disseminate his views on reform.[124] Christina Bewley has noted that instead of concentrating on demolishing the prosecution's case, based entirely on circumstantial evidence, Muir played into the Court's hand by 'emphasizing that he was a reformer and making political speeches'.[125] The testimony concerning 'Ça Ira' presented an opportunity to point to the increasing levels of censorship and surveillance.[126] Once again, Muir does this by making a point about the intelligibility of language in different song contexts. He refers to the classical context – previously discussed in relation to the 'Harmodium Melos' – of Aristogeiton and Harmodius, and the biblical context of the psalms:

> Britain has always cherished freedom, and shall it be deemed criminal in me, to listen to the effusions of joy, poured out by a neighbouring people, on obtaining that first of human blessings, which always constituted our peculiar distinction? But I know it well. The word Freedom is soon to be proscribed from our language; it carries alarm and sedition in the sound. If I had caused to be recited one of those noble choruses of the Grecian drama, in which, with the enthusiasm of liberty, the glories of the Republics of Athens or of Sparta were displayed, in a language more than mortal, my offence would have been deemed the same with that of amusing myself, by having the national song of France. If it had been possible for me to have cause to be sung upon the Streets of Glasgow, one of the Psalms of the Hebrews, in the original language, in which the triumphs of the people and the destruction of tyrants are recorded in a strain of highest poetical inspiration, the criminality would have been the same with that of listening to *ça ira*[127]

In the summing up, the prosecution used this information to depict Muir as irredeemably radicalized: 'We find from the evidence of the girl Fisher, that the very organist could not pass the house of this demon of mischief, without being desired to play *ça ira*'.[128] Muir was found guilty and sentenced to be transported.

In response to this evidence introduced at Muir's trial, and faced with increasing proscription of their own freedom, two members of the United Irishmen, William Sampson and Thomas Russell, retaliated with two works of satire: the *Review of The Lion of Old England* and the *Trial of Hurdy Gurdy*. Both of these texts were serialized in the Belfast newspaper, and mouthpiece of the United Irishmen, *The Northern Star*, in 1793 and 1794, and they were also published separately as pamphlets.[129] The mock *Review* of a fictional twelve canto mock-epic poem, 'The Lion of Old England', describes for the reader the action of each canto, under the pretence of 'reviewing', and also included excerpts from the poem itself. The reviewers satirize England's participation in armed conflicts as a misguided love of chivalry through the figure of a hapless lion. For example, in Canto Two a Royal Duke rides the lion while memorizing a stirring speech for the army before setting sail for 'Martinico'. The Duke arrives too late for the battle, however, and the British forces, commanded by Admiral Gardner, have been driven off the island: an allusion to Admiral Gardner's failure to take control of

Martinique for Britain in June 1793.[130] The poem nevertheless celebrates the fact that that 'England's sons, excelling in the chase; Altho' they lost the battle, won *the* race!'[131] In Canto Three when the poet momentarily questions whether Spitalfields weavers should be sent to fight in European wars, the reviewers note that the author finds himself 'sinking into sentiments of *humanity*, incompatible with the *nobler ideas of power, war, and magnanimity*'.[132] This is quickly remedied in the next stanza, however, when the poet decides the weavers should be sent to war: 'You must vile scum, your rulers say you must / And what your Rulers say, be sure is just'.[133] The lion finds himself at sea with Lord Howe in Canto Four when another defeat against the French is lampooned: 'nought could have saved the Regicides this day, But that they happened to *get safe away*'.[134]

By Canto Eleven the lion has returned to England, having being defeated in war against the French. He appoints Pitt, Dundas and Edmund Burke as the executors of his will and asks that his tomb be inscribed with the following verse:

> Hither O curious stranger turn thine eyes,
> Beneath this stone Old England's Lion lies:
> Too long the scourge of human kind – too long
> The boastful theme of many an idle song;
> Too long of crafty Ministers, the tool –
> To say the best – a brave and gen'rous fool.[135]

Chapter One has shown how the 'Princely Song of Richard Cordelion' was interpreted as a satire in the *Collection* in order to undermine its 'boastful theme' – the heroism and chivalry of Richard the Lionheart. In the *Review*, Sampson and Russell also seek to undermine the conservative narrative of chivalry and heroism championed by Edmund Burke, who had famously lamented in the *Reflections* that 'the age of chivalry is gone'.[136] In a mocking reference to his characterization of Richard Price, Burke emerges as the 'prophet' of the 'temple of constitution' in Canto Twelve, who takes the lion on a tour of the temple showing him its regal statues. The lion is entranced by the coat of arms of three lions on the shield of Richard the Lionheart and Burke explains:

> Lo! here your mighty Ancestor you see,
> Who led the feats of holy chivalrie –
> Behold him rampant on the warriors shield,
> Protect his Sov'reign in the bloody field:
> Be there such heroes now? Alas not one!
> For why – the age of chivalrie is gone![137]

Burke also shows the lion the 'moldering' statues of the 'British Druids', the 'antient historians' who carolled forth the 'praises of the virtuous and the brave'.[138] The Lion is shown a sculpture depicting the druids of Wales being thrown down the cliffs by Edward the First and 'the prophet' assures him that 'it was an act of the most necessary severity; for that nothing so impedes the subjugation of a country as the bold and animating strains of their Poets and Orators'.[139] Following this, the commentary directly addresses the fate of Thomas Muir:

> And we would have the world to know, that such wholesome severities have never been diffused, and that hearing a seditious hurdy gurdy play CA IRA, without revealing it to the King, or his Privy Council, is at this day in a certain country, enough to ground a sentence of transportation to the *North Pole* for FOURTEEN YEARS, together with imprisonment amongst felons in the Hulks; and that in the case alluded to, the sentence, but for the tender mercies of LORD SWINTON, would have been infinitely severer.[140]

Muir was by this time waiting in the hulks to be transported for 14 years, which was a sentence tantamount to death – as meted out by King Edward to the twelfth century bards of Wales for their seditious songs and immortalized in Thomas Gray's poem *The Bard*. Lord Swinton was one of the presiding judges at the trial, and his 'tender mercies' was a sarcastic dig at the comments made upon sentencing Muir, when Swinton observed that transportation for 14 years was 'a mild punishment' for the crime which was barely distinguishable from high treason and that 'if punishment adequate to the crime of sedition were to be sought for, it could not be found in our law, now that torture is happily abolished'.[141]

William Sampson's *The Trial of the King versus Hurdy Gurdy*, where the Hurdy Gurdy is indicted for playing 'Ça Ira', also satirized the testimony of Ann Fisher in Muir's trial, as well as the use of the libel laws to censor the United Irishmen.[142] The Hurdy Gurdy was a type of barrel organ, as evident in the Dublin edition which includes Hurdy Gurdy's list of aliases: 'alias Barrel Organ, alias Grinder, alias the Seditious Organ'.[143] In the eighteenth century it was an instrument particularly associated with the street and begging. In his 1790 collection of *Ancient Songs,* Joseph Ritson noted Chaucer's reference to a type of hurdy gurdy and observed that the instrument was to be found 'so frequent[ly] at this day in the streets of London'.[144]

Hurdy Gurdy's trial begins by parodying the elaborate listing of 'innuendoes' which was the requirement for the prosecution to list an exact statement of the material alleged to constitute a seditious libel. The Lord Justice Clerk, in his summing up of Muir's trial, noted that the indictment was the longest that he had ever seen but that it was necessary 'for the benefit of the prisoner'.[145] Sampson lampoons this through his evident delight in musical puns, and 'for the benefit of the prisoner' in this context functions to show that the prosecution of Muir and Hurdy Gurdy was a persecution:

> Gentlemen this is a very long information, consisting of ninety-three counts. Some of them go as to the words, that is setting out the seditious words, in hœc verba Anglicana viz 'Ah ha Ca Ira Ca Ira!' which it is painful to me to repeat, much more to sing:

others go as to the tenor, others to the tenor and base, others to the tenor and effect, others to the base merely – and others again as to the treble: Some again are for playing others for publishing, others for causing to be published, others for causing to be played: Some are for playing a tune, others a rondeau, others a symphony, others a country-dance ; others again count upon a song: These again vary, and are multiplied by embracing every circumstance of *time*, &c.

Gentlemen, it is impossible for me to explain why it is necessary to describe this offence in so many different counts or tales. Public convenience requires that the proceedings in our criminal law should not be easily understood – the sanction of antiquity ratifies it[146]

Of course, this also had the effect of re-circulating the seditious material both in the courtroom and in print: it 'sounds' it in multiple ways. Muir's indictment, for example, reprinted specific passages from the *Patriot* and Paine's works as well as the *Address* from the United Irishmen.[147] Later in his defence, Muir also took the opportunity to once again read the *Address*.[148] In the Belfast version of the text two staves of music are printed that form the chorus of the song, while in the Dublin edition the reader is wryly informed that the musical notes of 'Ça Ira' are not set forth 'lest we should be chargeable with insidiously propagating the very thing which it was intended should be suppressed, which has happened in all the late trials of this kind'.[149]

The evidence against Hurdy Gurdy comes from 'French Horn' who, after much cajoling, eventually admits for the prosecution that he heard him play 'Ça Ira'.[150] There is not the space here to discuss the histrionic prosecution and defence speeches in which Sampson intricately develops the piece. The important point in this context is that in the judge's summation, he returns directly to Muir, informing the jury that 'one Thomas Muir' was convicted for 'causing another to play this very air' which 'was a substantive integral part of the evidence given against him'.[151] Accordingly, the judge instructs the jury that the case against Hurdy Gurdy was certainly stronger because he played it of his own 'accord'. In this passage, Sampson uses the judge to comment on the misapplication of Fox's Libel Act of 1792. This Act had clarified that juries had the power to decide upon the tendency of a publication to provoke a breach of the peace, or in other words to interpret the material.[152] Prior to this juries had often been limited to finding upon the fact of publication alone, with the judge ruling upon issues of interpretation. However Michael Lobban notes that because the Act empowered the judge to give his opinion in cases dependant upon interpretive context, they maintained a device to influence a jury.[153] The judge in the trial of Hurdy Gurdy informs the jury that he is called upon by 'the late act of parliament' to give his opinion 'as to the libel itself' and proceeds to recapitulate the case for the prosecution.[154] When he disingenuously informs the jury that if they do not believe this that they may find Hurdy Gurdy 'not guilty' and hears an echo of the words 'not guilty', he has 'echo' immediately taken into custody.[155]

Not surprisingly, given the judge's influence, the jury find Hurdy Gurdy guilty and in a clever ploy of cross-marketing, readers are referred to the *Lion of Old England* to learn of his sentence, which is provided in the second extended edition of the *Lion*.[156] There we learn that Hurdy Gurdy was sentenced to two years in the Cathedral Church of Canterbury to play 'the weekly anthem of *God Save the King*' until one day upon hearing the words from Psalm 146 'put not your trust in princes' he was 'overcome by some power of sympathy' which 'revived in the Organ all its old seditious propensities, so that it instantly played on the air of "Ça Ira"'.[157] The 'power of sympathy' that excited Hurdy Gurdy, is the power of music which was also part of Henry Redhead Yorke's 'revolution of sentiment' which, in the Sheffield context, similarly drew upon the power of the psalms to excite the people. John Barrell describes the Edinburgh trials as an important preliminary step in the development of the prosecution case against the London reformers, including Thomas Hardy, who were imprisoned and charged with treason with the suspension of Habeas Corpus in May 1794. The role of music in the trial of Muir, and the United Irish response, also forms the necessary background to understand the fate of James Montgomery. Returning now to the hymn sung at the Fast Day in Sheffield on 28 February 1794, it was in the trial of Thomas Hardy for treason that Montgomery's authorship of this hymn emerged.

Songs and Pikes in the Treason Trials of 1794

Montgomery's role as the author of the handbill hymn, sung following the delivery of the serious lecture on the fast day of 28 February 1794, was exposed in William Garrow's questioning of William Broomhead during the trial of Thomas Hardy for High Treason from 28 October to 5 November 1794. As previously mentioned, a copy of 'A Serious Lecture' had been sent to the LCS and printed along with the resolutions of Sheffield and the resolutions of support from the LCS and the SCI.[158] This pamphlet had been seized by Edward Lauzum, one of the King's messengers, during the search of Hardy's House on 12 May, and formed part of the prosecution's evidence:

> Q. After the serious lecture was read, there was an hymn prepared I believe?
> A. Yes
> Q. Who prepared that Hymn?
> A. Gale [sic] printed it
> Q. Who composed it?
> A. I believe it was composed by one Montgomery.
> Q. That was sung in full chorus by the whole assembly?
> A. Yes it was sung[159]

Broomhead and his fellow SSCI associate, William Camage, were questioned extensively about the fast day meeting and the meeting on Castle Hill on 7 April at which Henry Yorke spoke.[160] The above exchange occurred as part of the prosecution's attempt to establish that the Sheffield Society had begun to arm themselves with pikes.[161] This would go towards proving the conspiracy theory that the SSCI, in conjunction with the LCS, had hidden their treasonous designs to overthrow the King and parliament behind the pretext of 'reform'. When Camage was questioned closely about the pikes he admitted they had been made for the SSCI, but for the sole purpose of defending their right to hold meetings in *response* to a threat made by the 'opposite party'.[162] Broomhead corroborated this, testifying that the threat had been made in a malicious hand-bill that had been 'throwed about the town in the dark' shortly after the Castle Hill meeting of 7 April, which had 'caused an agitation in the minds of the people'.[163] The handbill had called for the people of Sheffield to arm against 'foreign and internal enemies' and intimated that the only way of dealing with the SSCI was by causing a riot.[164]

The testimony of Camage and Broomhead also implicated Joseph Gales and Richard Davison in the pike plot. During the raid of Hardy's house, two letters had been found from Davison to Thomas Hardy advising him that pikes might be ordered from the Secretary of the SSCI. These letters were printed as evidence in the trial:

> Fellow Citizen,
> The bare-faced aristocracy of the present administration, has made it necessary that we should be prepared to act on the defensive against any attack they may command their newly-armed minions to make upon us. – A plan has been hit upon, and if encouraged sufficiently, will, no doubt, have the effect of furnishing a quantity of pikes to the patriots great enough to make them formidable.[165]

Camage confirmed that Richard Davison had lived and worked with the Gales family, having come from Leeds where he had been secretary to the society there.[166] By this time, however, Davison, like Gales, had escaped from England for America.[167] In her memoirs, Winifred Gales also described:

> a young man who belonged to the Leeds society, came to work with us and was appointed corresponding secretary of one of the Societies. In this capacity he wrote to one of the London agents enquiring whether they would adopt the same mode of defence which the friends of reform in Sheffield meant to adopt. Of this act we knew nothing until the 'Secret Committee' found his letter amongst Hardy's papers, dated 'Gales's Printing Office'.[168]

Though the prosecution tried to use the Davison letters as evidence of a co-ordinated effort of the societies to arm, the difficulty they faced was that, as Davison's letter states, the pikes were conceived of as a 'mode of defence', and the testimony of Camage and Broomhead confirmed this.[169] Furthermore, Broomhead recounted a meeting held at his house, that included members of the public as well as the SSCI, in which Gales held the handbill and led a discussion about the need to arm for the purposes of defence.[170] Gales had then printed the resolutions to this effect in the *Sheffield Register* on 9 May 1794, so it was difficult to see a conspiracy at work in such a public act.[171]

The song evidence at Hardy's treason trial became implicated in other important questions of evidence. On the second day of the proceedings, Wednesday 29 October 1794, Mr Garrow for the prosecution questioned the Rev. Richard Williams, asking him to identify the hand writing in a letter as John Thelwall's.[172] The point of this was to introduce several addresses and seditious songs written by Thelwall which had been sung at the anniversary dinner of the LCS at the Globe Tavern on 20 January 1794.[173] The addresses and songs 'though, perhaps a subordinate and inferior branch of that conspiracy to bring all the constituent authorities in the country into contempt', and though written by Thelwall and addressed to a man named 'Vellam', were submitted as evidence by the prosecution against Hardy: 'we submit to your Lordships that any act of Mr. Thelwell's, so in furtherance of this conspiracy, is evidence against the defendant'.[174] Not surprisingly Thomas Erskine and Vicary Gibbs, acting for Hardy's defence, argued that this evidence was inadmissible because the prosecution could not show that Hardy had any knowledge of the production of the documents, and they were not addressed to him.[175] Erskine argued that the consequence of admitting this evidence was that thousands of his Majesty's subjects could be called before the court and that the conspiracy could be alleged against every single member of every one of the societies.[176] Alan Wharam has observed that this was one of the most important points of law decided upon at the trial in a debate lasting for two hours.[177] The judgement went in favour of the crown meaning that documentary evidence could be used against Hardy which he had no knowledge of at all.[178] Later, Gibbs was successful in having a song found at the apartment of an LCS member deemed inadmissible on account of the fact that it was found *after* Hardy had been taken up.[179] But when the song found at Hardy's house to the tune of the 'Vicar of Bray' with the chorus 'come rouse to arms', was read out in its entirety in court, due to the ruling for the crown on admissibility following the Thelwall letter, Erskine could only dryly, and perhaps with some exasperation, state: 'If the Jury will look at the back of it, they will see this song was sent in a letter to Mr. Hardy by somebody or other'.[180]

Songs were also referred to in the evidence of the spy John Groves who was questioned extensively about his attendance at the meeting of the Society for Constitutional Information, on their anniversary dinner of 2 May 1794. Groves testified that a song called 'Free Constitution' was delivered to him in a room adjoining the dinner room and that there were also songs on the plates in the dining room.[181] He stated that the music for 'Ça ira' was 'struck up' which was encored 'time after time' and the 'Marseillois March' was played.[182] Groves confirmed that there was a song sung to the tune of 'God Save the King' and Lord Chief Justice Eyre sought clarification that this was not the legitimate song 'God Save the King', but a song to the *tune* of 'God Save the King'.[183] It emerged that John Horne Tooke had led the singing of 'God Save the King' which contained an extra verse that Groves could not remember.[184]

In the questioning of Florimond Goddard, the first witness to give evidence for the defence, the presence of the Sheffield pikes once again emerged and eventually led the prosecution back to the songs of John Thelwall. Goddard was a member of the same division of the LCS as Hardy and was asked by Mr Gibbs, for the defence, whether Hardy 'had ever produced at the Division meeting ... any, letter, that he received from Sheffield, about pikes?' He answered, 'no never'.[185] This was the letter from Richard Davison that was central of the prosecution's case about arming. In his cross-examination the Attorney General, Sir John Scott (1751–1838) attempted to cast doubt on Goddard's denial:

> that gentleman [Mr Gibbs] asked you whether Mr. Hardy had ever communicated to you that letter from Sheffield, you immediately said no. Now I should be glad to ask you how you knew what letter it was that that gentleman alluded to – what is the letter that you mean to speak of, when you say Hardy never communicated it to you?[186]

Goddard answered 'The Sheffield letter'. At this point, however, Scott almost succeeded in confusing Goddard: when Scott again questioned 'I should be glad to know what Sheffield letter you mean', Goddard replied 'I don't know'.[187] This was obviously a way of casting doubt on Goddard's previous denial of the letter about the pikes in response to Gibbs, and Scott continued: 'Then how came you to say he never communicated the Sheffield letter, without knowing what letter it was?'[188] Goddard was aided at this point by the intervention of Felix Vaughan, the assistant counsel to Erskine and Gibbs.[189] Vaughan was sitting on the defence bench, close enough to be able to whisper so that Goddard would hear, 'the letter about pikes', thus enabling Goddard to quickly recover.[190] Scott objected that the witness had overheard this from Vaughan, before Gibbs interjected that it was *he* who had referred to the Sheffield letter as being about pikes in his former question.[191]

The importance of this complex exchange is that having failed with pikes, Scott attempted to extract from Goddard information that would show that the LCS was not a peaceable society, and it is here that his questions come to include songs. Scott asked Goddard: 'you sing some songs now and then in your society, do not you?' Goddard replied, 'never in the society', later adding 'we were a very peaceable society – songs were not generally introduced at all'.[192] This exchange recalls Davis's point that the meetings of the LCS were conducted with an emphasis on respectability. Goddard's volunteering of the adjective 'peaceable' to describe the meetings played right into Scott's hands, however, by suggesting that the songs sung at the *dinners* of the society, were not 'peaceable':

> Q. I hope you don't mean to say that there were no songs sung at your dinner?
> A. There were songs then
> Q. Did you never hear of a very good song called 'God Save the Rights of Man'
> A. I have heard of such a song[193]

Goddard eventually admitted that he had also heard of a song with the chorus 'plant plant the tree, fair freedom's tree' but was careful to state that he had 'never heard it in the society'.[194] Once again, Goddard attempted to represent the society as 'peaceable' and orderly by volunteering that 'there was a man that did attend the society with songs, a pack of idle songs, and we would not suffer him to attend the place'.[195] When Scott questioned him about John Thelwall's songs, Goddard admitted that he 'had them all' and thought 'there was no harm in them when they were sold in public shops', situating himself in the polite context of bookshops as opposed to the street and hawkers such as the man with his 'pack of idle songs'.[196] Though pressed, Goddard could not recall the titles of Thelwall's songs or agree with the prosecution that they were 'dispersed all over the country', and when he was shown a copy of 'God Save the Rights of Man' and asked whether it was one of Thelwall's songs, he replied that he could not say.[197] Erskine interjected at this point to ask, 'Is your Lordship's time to be consumed about this gentleman's opinion upon a song?'[198] As it could not be proved that the song had been sung at meetings, Erskine questioned its relevance, and this had the added effect of making the prosecution's evidence of an 'idle song' seem trivial.

Following Hardy's acquittal on 5 November, Erskine also defended Thelwall during his trial for treason from 1–5 December 1794.[199] In his analysis of John Thelwall's three songs, Michael Scrivener makes the point that while the songs were referred to as 'seditious' in the trial, their content was not actually discussed and that a reason for this was that their very existence presented enough of a threat: 'it hardly mattered what the songs actually said as long as they represented an intersection of popular oral culture that was difficult to control and radical intellectuals who could, however, be punished'.[200] As Scrivener details, following his acquittal, Thelwall indignantly republished the songs in his periodical the *Tribune* to prove that they were not in fact seditious.[201]

The point emphasised here, however, is that alongside the supposed conspiracy involving the Sheffield pikes, which failed to secure the convictions in London, was another conspiracy on the part of the government which used Sheffield songs; the government hoped, unsuccessfully, that where pikes and treason failed songs and sedition would triumph. Though there was much uncertainty over the song evidence brought to trial, one detail had emerged uncontested in the testimony of William Broomhead, and that was that James Montgomery had 'composed the hymn' that had been sung at the meeting of reformers on the fast day. Before the trial of Hardy had finished, Montgomery had been indicted on sedition on account of another song, the publication of 'A Patriotic Song by a Clergyman of Belfast'.

The Trial of James Montgomery in 1795

In a letter to Joseph Aston on 30 October, an outraged and incredulous James Montgomery described his indictment on seditious libel for publishing 'A Patriotic Song by a Clergyman of Belfast':

> I am accused of having wickedly, maliciously, seditiously and flagitiously attempted to overthrow the King and constitution by force and Arms, of what? – a halfpenny song! I am accused of having attempted to move inflame and stir up sedition amongst his majesty's liege subjects by what? – a song upon the Destruction of the bastille in France! I am further accused upon the oath of the jurors for our sovereign Lord the now King, charged with printing and publishing a scandalous false libel upon the present just and necessary war ... How? By reprinting and republishing a Patriotic song written by Mr Scot of Dromore and sung at a Festival held at Belfast in commemoration of the destruction of the Bastille, in the month of July 1792, which afterwards was printed in the Northern Star, in the Morning Chronicle on July 2nd 1792 and in the Sheffield Register of August 3rd 1792, eight months after the war commenced![202]

In Montgomery's incredulity and disbelief, are the echoes of Sampson's satire on Hurdy Gurdy. Montgomery's impending trial did not prevent him, however, from celebrating the acquittal of Hardy, Horne Tooke and Thelwall by writing a commemorative hymn that was sung at a public meeting of the Sheffield Constitutional Society on 29 December 1794, and published in the *Iris* on 2 January 1795, where it was signed J. M. G.[203] Montgomery had taken over the management of the *Sheffield Register* following Gales's departure and had tried to depoliticize the paper by styling it as the *Iris*.[204] The five Sheffield reformers arrested had also been released on 15 December 1794, though they were 'discharged on entering into recognisances to give evidence against Henry Yorke'.[205]

Montgomery's trial began on 22 January 1795, and like Muir, he had the proceedings published shortly after. Felix Vaughan, who had so cleverly come to the aid of Florimond Goddard during Hardy's trial, was the defence counsel. A protégé of John Horne Tooke, Vaughan had been heavily involved in the LCS and the reform movement and was elected as a delegate to Division 3 to help draft the constitution of the society; a point which had emerged in Hardy's trial, though which Hardy denied.[206] At the centre of the prosecution's case was that Montgomery had printed and published a song containing the following verse:

> Europe's fate on the contest's decision depends
> Most important its issue will be;
> For should France be subdued Europe's liberty ends
> If she triumphs the world will be free.[207]

The indictment stated that this had 'with the intent to degrade, vilify, and traduce our said Lord the King and his Government of this realm, and his conduct respecting the said War'.[208] As Britain had officially been at war with France since February 1793, this verse was deemed libellous for suggesting that the freedom of the world depended on Britain being *defeated*.

The main witness for the prosecution, led by 'Mr Tooker', was a song-seller named Joseph Jordan. Jordan testified that in August 1794 he had been 'crying "song-books"' in the Hartshead and was called into the printing office of the *Iris* by one of the workmen.[209] He was shown the 'printed song', which the workmen said had never been sold in Sheffield and informed that the letter-press was 'still standing' and only wanted 'working-off'.[210] Jordan asked if he could have the song printed and was told to seek the permission of the master in the shop.[211] Montgomery agreed to print six quires for threepence per quire.[212] Jordan was 'selling straws' in the street 'giving the song', when he was arrested by the constable, Samuel Hall.[213] The process of selling straws was described by Henry Mayhew in his study of the nineteenth century labouring poor:

> the strawer offers to sell any passer by in the streets a straw and to give the purchaser a paper which he dares not sell. Accordingly as he judges of the character of his audience, so he intimates that the paper is political, libelous, irreligious, or indecent.[214]

Despite selling the song as a 'straw' Jordan denied that he knew it was 'seditious' but only thought 'there was something extraordinary in it'.[215]

As Montgomery had exclaimed in his letter to Aston, the core premise of Vaughan's defence was that the song had been published before and that its meanings applied to a different context to that of 1794. He read out lengthy extracts from Arthur Young's *Travels in France During the years 1787, 1788 and 1789* which described the sufferings of the French people under the ancien régime in order to prove that the 'contest' referred to was not the current contest between Britain and France, but the July 1792 invasion of France by the Austrian and Prussian armies.[216] Had the forces of the Duke of Brunswick and his European allies prevailed, Vaughan argued, the ancien régime would have been restored and the people returned to the great suffering described by Young.[217] Vaughan went even further to suggest that such a victory would have shifted the balance of power in Europe, potentially placing Britain in danger.[218] Again, he quoted from the end of Volume Two of the *Travels* to show that this was a view that had been expressed by Young, and was one that Vaughan himself had held.[219] This led Vaughan to ask an important rhetorical question which he answered for the jury:

> And yet was Arthur Young prosecuted? No – he was rewarded with a place and pension of three hundred pounds a-year. His book is to this day sold in every bookseller's shop in the kingdom, even during the present war; and no prosecution is instituted against the vendors![220]

However the 'letter' in which Young had expressed this view was not included in the *second* edition of the *Travels*, published in 1794.[221] In any case, in his 1793 pamphlet, *The Example of France, A Warning to Britain*, Young made it clear that his sympathy for the revolution had ended:

> It is easy to see what they have lost; as to their gains, they have assignats, cocades, and the music of ci ira; it may be truly said, that they have made a wise barter: they have given their gold for paper; their bread for a ribbon, and their blood for a song. Heaven preserve us from the phrenzy of such exchanges![222]

The body politic of France, which by this time was circulating paper assignats, had irrationally, in a state of madness, exchanged all of value – gold, bread and blood – for the trivial signifiers of revolution. As with Muir's trial, this passage demonstrates the way in which songs such as 'Ça Ira' were perceived as so threatening as to lead to blood letting. Marilyn Butler notes that shortly after the publication of this pamphlet, William Pitt created a Board of Agriculture and appointed Young as secretary at £400 a year, leading to accusations that he was merely a placeman.[223] This is clearly the implication of Vaughan's remarks.

Vaughan thus used Montgomery's trial to make a political point which reached beyond the needs of providing for his defence. It is likely that Vaughan realized that, as with Muir's case, the chances were weighted against Montgomery and a conviction was a foregone conclusion. As Montgomery alluded to in his letter to Aston, the song had been published in numerous newspapers in 1792. More damagingly, however, was its circulation in the chapbooks of the United Irishmen, a fact that was not brought out during the trial, but of which Vaughan may well have been aware. When the *Sheffield Register* published the song on 3 August 1792, it was introduced as

> composed by Mr. Scot, of Dromore and presented in his name to the President of the citizens of Belfast, and their citizen soldiers of the town and neighbourhood at their commemoration of the demolition of the Bastille – the birthday of liberty in France.[224]

The United Irishmen had issued a chapbook of the songs sung, with 'A patriotic song by a Clergyman of Belfast' appearing as the 'Third Song on the French Revolution', to the tune 'Poor Jack'.[225] This was the tune to a well-known loyalist naval song by Charles Dibdin the elder.[226] As revealed in his 'Memoir', at this time Dibdin had been 'instructed to write, sing, publish, and give away what were termed war songs' by the desire of the 'then ministry', for which he received an annual gratuity.[227] The use of this tune for a revolutionary song was therefore even more subversive. Mary Helen Thuente notes that this tune was also used for later United Irish songs and that the song was also published in the *Northern Star* in July 1792 and in the 1795 *Paddy's Resource* song book.[228]

The version of the song printed in the *Sheffield Register*, at that time still run by Gales, which was ready standing in the press for his successor was:

> While Tyranny marshals his minions around,
> And bids his fierce legions advance,
> Fair Freedom! The hopes of thy sons to confound –
> To restore his old Empire in France.
>
> What Friend among men to the Rights of Mankind,
> But is fir'd with resentment to see
> The Satraps of pride and oppression combin'd
> To prevent a great Land's being free?
>
> Europe's fate on the contest's decision depends –
> Most important its issue will be –
> For should France be subdu'd – Europe's Liberty ends –
> If she triumphs – the world will be free!
>
> Then let ev'ry true Patriot unite in her cause,
> A cause of such moment to Man –
> Let all whose souls spurn at tyrannical laws,
> Lend her all the assistance they can.
>
> May the spirit of Sparta her armies inspire,
> And the Star of America guide!
> May a Washington's wisdom – a Mirabeau's fire –
> In her camps and her councils preside!
>
> May her sons fatal discord no longer divide,
> 'Mong her chiefs no dark traitors be found –
> But may the *United* resist the rough tide,
> Till their toils be with victory crown'd?
>
> And at length when sweet Peace from her sphere
> Shall descend,
> When the fiends of oppression have fled –
> Immortal renown shall those Heroes attend
> Who for Freedom sought – conquer'd – and bled
>
> Blazon'd high, then their deeds shall well History's page
> And adorn lofty Poetry's lay's;
> While the mem'ry of Tyrants – the curse of their age,
> In oblivion's dark Bastille decays.[229]

As Vaughan pointed out at Montgomery's trial, 'Tyranny' is the Duke of Brunswick 'marshalling his minions' – Francis II Emperor of Germany; Frederick William II, the King of Prussia; and Catherine II Empress of Russia.[230] The song is essentially a war song, which frames the revolutionary war in the universalist terms of the 'rights of man': 'if France triumphs the world will be free'. It is a rallying call to the friends of the 'rights of mankind' to unite behind the cause of France and of reform more generally. In this way it also speaks directly to the situation in Ireland and the cause of the United Irishmen because of its emphasis on unity – 'may her sons fatal discord no longer divide/ … may the *United* resist the rough tide'. Thuente notes that Verse Five, with its references to the spirit of Sparta, America, Washington and Mirabeau was removed from the *Northern Star* version and the version in *Paddy's Resource*.[231] The song ends by predicting a victory against 'the fiends of oppression' and the immortalization of the heroes 'who for freedom fought – conquer'd – and bled' in history and song – poetry's 'lays'. There is a sense in which Young's description of the French giving their 'blood for a song' is realized here, but rather than being worthless trivialities, songs are part of an heroic exchange which has the capacity to efface the 'mem'ry of tyrants'. These are the kind of the songs for which Edward had the Welsh bards executed and which Montgomery himself would write in his hymn on the acquittal of Hardy and the reformers.

The judge in the case, M. A. Taylor, observed in his summation 'that which was perfectly innocent in 1789 might be grossly seditious in 1794'.[232] He noted that as the facts of the printing and publication of the song were clearly proved, it was the jury's task to determine the *intent* of the song, in other words, whether its content was a seditious libel as outlined in the innuendo.[233] Jon Mee has shown that with the lapse of the Licensing Act of 1695, the law of seditious libel was the 'chief legal means by which radical writing was controlled' in the 1790s. Mee observes that the chances of acquittal were improved when the task of interpretation fell to the jury, but that evidence suggests that Fox's Libel Act did not necessarily result in more acquittals.[234] Montgomery's trial is a case in point. After an hour deliberating, the jury returned the verdict 'Guilty of Printing and Publishing', indicating that they had difficulty in deciding the issue of whether the song was a seditious libel.[235] The court refused to accept this verdict and according to the trial text they retired again and fifty minutes later returned a verdict of guilty.[236]

Following Montgomery's conviction the song was printed in the radical songster, *A Choice Collection of Civic Songs* as 'song no.xxix' without the offending verse three which was used in Montgomery's innuendo.[237] The editor intervenes at this point in a footnote asking the reader to 'excuse the ommittance' of the next 'wicked and seditious' verse on account of Montgomery's recent conviction.[238] The text in *A Choice Collection* functions as a kind of 'straw' as the omitted verse *is* in fact printed in the footnote which quotes the extract from Montgomery's indictment in which it appears. This is also an example of safe printing or a 'strategy of indirection'. Though this text appears with a London imprint, it was most likely the work of John Crome, another radical printer operating in Sheffield at this time. In the Holland and Everett biography, Montgomery relates that, shortly after his imprisonment, John Crome reprinted the song with impunity.[239]

In his discussion of United Irish ballads, and the chapbook 'Songs of the French Revolution', Tom Dunne writes:

What impact, if any, this relatively bland bourgeois propaganda had is almost impossible to assess. Some of it was certainly absorbed into popular literature, and there are some examples of broadside versions of ballads from *Paddy's Resource* being found on people arrested before and during 1798. However, we would need many more such before we could make even tentative conclusions about their spread and possible influence.[240]

The circulation of the song titled 'A Patriotic Song by a Clergyman of Belfast', also entitled 'The World Will Be Free', in English newspapers and on English streets, where it was sold by song sellers such as Joseph Jordan, provides exactly such evidence of the impact and spread of a United Irish song beyond both the 'bourgeois' sphere and Ireland. While the song has appeared in the anthology of Michael Scrivener and discussed in the work of Thuente, its influence in providing a pretext to bring Montgomery to trial for seditious libel has remained undetected.[241] It is in this context, and in connection with the treason trials of 1794, that the song's influence emerges. William Sampson's satire of Hurdy Gurdy's trial proved to be a prescient foreshadowing of Montgomery's fate. Having been found guilty, he was sentenced to 3 months in York Castle prison and a fine of twenty pounds.[242]

Remembering and Forgetting Songs

Montgomery passed his time in prison by writing the poetry that would be published under his pseudonym 'Paul Positive' as *Prison Amusements* in 1797, a work he dedicated to Felix Vaughan.[243] In a later introduction penned for this work in 1840, Montgomery would describe his encounter with the song seller Joseph Jordan who had been sent from the print room to the shop attached to the *Iris*, with the request to print the song which was 'still standing' for the press:

> Taking up the printed leaf, I perceived that it contained two copies of verses, with each of which I had been long familiar, but had never seen them coupled in that shape before; at the top of the page was the impression of a wood-cut (liberty and the British Lion) which I recognized as having figured in the frontispiece of an extinct periodical, issued by my predecessor, and entitled 'the Patriot'.[244]

The distinctive frontispiece of the *Patriot* had been the first thing Montgomery had seen upon entering the press room for the first time when the *Sheffield Register* had been under the editorship of Gales. It provides here visual continuity between the men, and a stamp of their connection through song. The other verse on the sheet was 'The Tender's Hold' a song condemning the impressment of sailors which had been printed in the *Sheffield Register* on 7 February 1794.[245] This song had also been used by the United Irishmen who changed the references to 'British Rights' to 'Irish Rights' in versions appearing in the *Northern Star* on 6 April 1793, and in the 1795 edition of *Paddy's Resource*.[246]

Figure 4.3 Woodcut detail from the title page of the *Patriot*. State Library of Victoria, Australia, Rare books, 320.5 P27

By this time Montgomery had also come into possession of a 'packet' confirming his long-held suspicion that his prosecution was 'an act of vengeance' against his predecessor, Joseph Gales, and one designed to quash the reform movement in Sheffield.[247] The packet contained a letter from the Duke of Portland to a Sheffield magistrate approving of the action against him and several letters from Joseph White, the Treasury Solicitor, instructing the prosecutor to brief three named prosecutors and to sign them 'with the Attorney-General's compliments'.[248] Montgomery learned that the trial was also paid for by Mr White from the Treasury: 'Thus I learned, that I had actually suffered, not to say enjoyed, the honor of a State prosecution.'[249] The most damning evidence of the conspiracy against him was found in a fragment of the original prosecutors' brief. Montgomery writes:

> But the most precious of these ancient manuscripts, rescued as unexpectedly from hopeless perdition as any classic treasure from the ruins of Herculaneum, is *a fragment of the original draft of the brief*, delivered to the counsel for the prosecution. From this I make the following extract. After some high-seasoned vituperation of my predecessor, the scribe proceeds thus: – 'The prisoner (myself) for a long time acted

as his (Mr. G's) amanuensis', – the next seven words express an after-thought, being interpolated in the draft, – 'and occasionally wrote essays for the newspaper. Since he has been the ostensible manager and proprietor of the *Iris*, he has pursued the same line of conduct, and his printing office has been precisely of the same stamp.' – This refers to a charge in the foregoing clause respecting Mr. G's office, that from it 'all the inflammatory and seditious resolutions, pamphlets, and papers issued' of the political societies in Sheffield. The paragraph goes on, referring to myself: – 'Without calling in question the names or characters of some of his principal supporters, who ought to act differently, suffice it to say, that *this* prosecution is carried on *chiefly* with a view of *putting a stop to the meetings of the associated clubs in Sheffield*; and it is hoped that if we are fortunate enough to succeed in convicting the prisoner, it will go a great way towards curbing the insolence they have uniformly manifested, and particularly since the late acquittals'.[250]

In a conversation as recorded with his biographers, John Holland and James Everett, Montgomery reflected: 'and thus, it may be added, do the "side-lights of history" become instructive and important'.[251] This is also a fitting reflection for the findings of this book which has shown that, rather than 'side-lights', political songs were an important and ubiquitous part of political, literary and print culture in the eighteenth-century.

The drafts of conversations Montgomery had with Holland and Everett were used towards their seven volume biography and many contained information *not* published.[252] One such conversation revealed that 'the packet' had been left in the hands of a Sheffield bookseller by the widow of John Brookfield, solicitor for the prosecution. As discussed earlier, it was Brookfield who had also sent the Treasury Solicitor a copy of the Fast-day handbill on which Montgomery's hymn appeared and the pamphlet of 'A Serious Lecture'. When Montgomery obtained the packet

> he was at first a little astonished to find the bundle labeled 'Trial of Mr Montgomery for High Treason': nor could he make out how this serious mistake could have arisen, till found two or three subpoenas addressed to himself and some of his workmen, to attend at York to give evidence against Henry Redhead Yorke, then confined on a charge of High Treason.[253]

Yorke was not tried until 10 July 1795 for conspiracy because of his role in the meeting at Castle Hill at which he called for a 'revolution of sentiment'. Joseph Gales and Richard Davison were also named on his indictment.[254] Like Montgomery, Yorke was found guilty, but owing to the more serious nature of the charge, his sentence was for two years and included a fine of one hundred pounds.[255] Yorke's trial and conviction, like Montgomery's, is only properly understood as part of the network outlined in this chapter that encompassed the treason trials in London. As the marking on the bundle indicated, Yorke was originally to be tried for High Treason, and it was only after the acquittals in London that the charge was lessened to Conspiracy.

Winifred Gales made no mention of her husband's indictment with Yorke in the memoirs she penned, though she does note that Yorke was convicted and spent four years in jail.[256] Neither does her narrative make any mention of Montgomery's trial and conviction. Writing to Montgomery from Washington in 1833, two years after she recommenced her narrative, she asks: 'judge then my dear friend, if you are not a principal and most interesting figure in the past'.[257] Though his trial occurred after her sudden departure, it is impossible that she would not have known of Montgomery's fate. Montgomery stayed on in the Hartshead with Gales's two sisters for many years and corresponded with Winifred and Joseph in America.[258] The editing of her husband's history, which was intended solely for her family, is guided by the same principles which Winifred saw in action at the meeting where she describes him calming a 'threatening mob' with reason and civility. There is no room for songs in this narrative which skirt the irrational and emotional and warlike and by extension there is no room for the 'principal' and 'most interesting' story of Montgomery. By the 1830s Winifred had internalized her own culture's attitude to political songs as being potentially as dangerous as pikes.

Holland and Everett's 1854 narrative is also edited to minimize the power of political songs in Montgomery's story. They make it clear that because Montgomery had an aptitude for poetry and found himself in a context where 'he heard the strains of his country's lyre rising around him', his mind was 'thus *accidentally* determined to political literature'.[259] By the time the biography was published, Montgomery had been successful in rehabilitating his reputation as a deeply loyal and religious man with an ambivalent attitude toward the actions of his youth.[260] He retains the status as a 'minor romantic poet', thanks to the success of works such as *The Wanderer of Switzerland* (1806), *The World Before the Flood* (1812) and *Greenland* (1819).[261] In his lifetime he achieved much acclaim as a prolific hymn writer, producing a number of enormously successful collections, including *The Christian Psalmist* (1825).[262] Montgomery also printed Thomas Cotterill's *Selection of Psalms and Hymns* in 1819 and collaborated closely with him.[263] As discussed in Chapter Two, Cotterill's text was the subject of a law suit because of the challenge it presented to the authorized status of 'Sternhold and Hopkins'. Montgomery continued then to be involved in the politics of song in its various permutations throughout his lifetime. In Sheffield, he became a pillar of the community and a statue was erected upon his death.

In concluding then, it is through a draft snippet of conversation with Holland and Everett, *not* included in the published biography, that we get an uncensored insight into the importance of political song at the heart of Montgomery's story.

Figure 4.4: Portrait of James Montgomery.

Montgomery's interlocutors record a conversation in which he reflects on 'A Patriotic Song by a Clergyman of Belfast' which interestingly, suggests Montgomery's familiarity with the song *before* his encounter with the song seller Joseph Jordan:

> 'I had at one period been exceedingly struck with the spirit of liberty and poetry which it breathed'. He then quoted the verse, with a spirit and vehemence, which showed that eight and twenty years had not sufficed to extinguish his enthusiasm in the subject to which it referred.[264]

Despite all that Montgomery had endured, twenty-eight years later, the 'spirit' of the song continued to resonate.

AFTERWORD

In 1868 when the nineteenth-century scholars Frederick Furnivall and John Hales published the old folio manuscript upon which Thomas Percy had based his *Reliques of Ancient English Poetry* (1765), they conceptualized the eighteenth-century ballad revival by drawing upon the story of Blondel's rescue of Richard the Lionheart.

> The nation lay in prison like its old Troubadour king; in its durance it heard its minstrel singing beneath the window its old songs, and its heart leapt in its bosom. It recognized the well-known, though long-neglected, strains that it had heard and loved in the days of its youth. The old love revived. The captive could not at once cast off its fetters, and go forth. But a yearning for liberty awoke in it; a wild, growing, passionate longing for liberty, for real, not artificial flowers; for true feeling, not sentimentalism; for the fresh life-giving breezes of the open country, not the languid airs of enclosed courts.[1]

In this context Percy is the minstrel who sings the 'old songs' beneath the window, awakening the nation to a consciousness of growing liberty through these songs and the creation of a new literary tradition in which poets such as Wordsworth and Coleridge, in their *Lyrical Ballads*, would play a major role. Furnivall and Hales frame the eighteenth-century ballad-revival through the lens of an intensely felt Romanticism with both affective and literary dimensions, as the feelings of love and authenticity that the 'old songs' evoke in the nation begin to displace the artifice of neo-classicism and sentimentalism. While Albert Friedman long ago called for the ballad-revival to be emancipated from the 'dead hands of the romantic critics', such as Furnivall and Hales, their narrative of the redemptive role of the ballad in English culture has proved deep and abiding.[2] The tendency to frame the eighteenth century ballad-revival in terms of the development of Romanticism and English literature as a discipline has remained dominant, naturalizing both the primacy of ballads in relation to the category of song and a conception of the ballad as timeless and apolitical.

This book has used the structuring trope of 'singing to the King', drawn from the story of Richard and Blondel, to suggest possible ways in which a 'politics of songs' could be configured with the aim of complicating and expanding this dominant narrative. Plato's cautioning against a mixing of 'song styles' has informed this discussion by highlighting the porosity and fluidity of songs and a theory of utilitarianism in which songs have the power to directly affect the constitution of the state. The book has included a consideration of the politics of the ballad revival itself and an examination of categories of songs that have conventionally been neglected as sites of analysis, including the topical political songs, the psalm and the hymn. The 'politics of songs' thus avoids the limitation of understanding political songs primarily in relation to topicality, and allows us to conceive of the way in which a variety of songs could function politically, particularly the during the French Revolution.

While the areas of study which the book canvasses are broad, this approach has been taken with a view to looking for songs in other contexts and spaces as a way of loosening the grip of the 'dead hands' of a Romanticization of the ballad, to use Friedman's image. Chapter Four has shown political songs circulating in the streets of Sheffield and sitting in the compositor's frame ready to be 'worked off' in the printing press before emerging as evidence in the treason and sedition trials of the 1790s. The flow of songs between London, Sheffield, Belfast and ultimately America, has revealed the Atlantic dimension of radical song and the way in which an intensely local topicality could resonate nationally and internationally.

The book has traced the movement of songs from the theatres into the taverns and amongst homo-social political culture at all levels of society, demonstrating that songs do not fit readily into a binary elite/popular model of culture. They circulated from the gentlemen of the Society for Constitutional Information, who reworked the classical song tradition of the 'Harmodium Melos', to the artisan membership of the radicalized Sheffield Society for Constitutional Information and the 'lower orders' that comprised the London Corresponding Society. Chapter Three situated the 'Harmodium Melos', a paradigmatic song celebrating liberty over tyranny, in reference to the texts of the Revolutionary controversy, Burke's *Reflections* and Price's *Discourse*, and the cultures of sociability that informed political life at this time.

The relationship between song and print has been foregrounded in Chapter Two in the exploration of 'Sternhold and Hopkins' as the dominant version of the psalms of David of the eighteenth century. Complementing this has been an awareness of the performance dimension of song – the significance of vocalizing, or sounding out meaning – ranging from the 'grand national chorus' that celebrated King George's recovery in 1789 to the much maligned parish clerk, who led the parochial performances of 'Sternhold and Hopkins'. Sacral song has been shown to be deeply politicized at this period, as evident when Montgomery's hymn was sung at the meeting of the Fast Day in Sheffield to the tune of the 'Old Hundredth', which had emerged from 'Sternhold and Hopkins'. Throughout the eighteenth century psalms and hymns as songs of the common people could not easily be 'laid apart' from ballads, despite a critical history which has continued to configure them in this manner. 'Sternhold and Hopkins' were closely interwoven into the fabric of everyday life and in questions of national identity.

Despite Friedman's disagreement with critics such as Furnivall and Hales and their depiction of the ballad revival, the book has shown that there is value to be found in the story of Richard and Blondel itself, as both a trope which can enable new perspectives on this period and as a way of reintroducing us to Richard the Lionheart, who has been a figure largely lost to ballad scholarship and eclipsed by the shadow of Robin Hood. Chapter One did this by investigating the transmission of 'The Princely Song of Richard the Lionheart' from the sixteenth-century garlands of Richard Johnson, to the seminal *Collection of Old Ballads* (1723); and by locating Richard the Lionheart within the complex politics of eighteenth-century ballad scholarship in the work of Thomas Percy and Joseph Ritson. The printing of the 'Princely Song' in the newspapers of 1786 presented another space in which the song circulated, connecting it both with the topicality of a particular moment in time and a broader history.

The ability to access such specific moments in time through the digital archive has played a key role in this study. Thanks to large digitisation projects, such as the Burney Collection, which provides electronic access to early English newspapers online, it is now possible to access and search eighteenth-century newspapers and other ephemeral material with a scale and speed that was hitherto impossible. The book has made extensive use of the digital archive in which the 'dungheaps' of the Roxburghe and Pepys Collections have been digitised, recalling Child's description. The digital archive will continue to play a key role in taking forward a study such as this, which has considered a range of material that falls outside the confines of 'polite literature' and has sought to create the kind of cross-disciplinary engagements advocated by both Fumerton and Guerrini in their recent statements on the state of the field of ballad scholarship, and by Fulcher in relation to the new cultural history of music.[3] Clearly there is scope for further analysis of the political song beyond 1795, together with a more comprehensive cataloguing of the generic characteristics and larger narratives that feature in political songs. The narrative of the 'Harmodium Melos' and its associated imagery has featured as one such example of a larger classical narrative that continued to function in topical political songs of the eighteenth-century. A further avenue for research might also re-connect the figures of Richard the Lionheart and Robin Hood and the mythologies that surround them in a more meaningful and comprehensive way. The trope of 'good king Richard', for example, which emerges as part of the Robin Hood tradition, remains to be explored and might be illuminated by the material brought forth in this book which reveals Richard the Lionheart to be a contested and politicized figure. This book has sought to bring together a diverse body of scholarship and to navigate its way through the endless possibilities that the digital age presents through the trope of 'singing to the King'. In this way it follows the imagining of Furnivall and Hales, but has sought a new liberty in which to understand the politics of songs.

NOTES

Introduction

1. *London Gazette*, 10 October 1789; *Public Advertiser*, 12 October 1789; *Oracle. Bell's New World*, 12 October 1789; *Diary or, Woodfall's Register*, 12 October 1789; *Argus*, 12 October 1789; *St. James's Chronicle or, British Evening-Post*, 10–13 October 1789.
2. E. Kennedy, M. Netter, J. P. McGregor and M. V. Olsen (eds), *Theatre, Opera, and Audiences in Revolutionary Paris* (Westport, CT: Greenwood Press, 1996), p. 239.
3. L. Mason, *Singing the French Revolution* (Ithaca, NY: Cornell University Press, 1996), p. 46.
4. Ibid., p. 47.
5. Ibid., p. 46.
6. M. Carlson, *The Theatre of the French Revolution* (New York: Cornell University Press, 1966), pp. 114–15; J. H. Johnson, *Listening in Paris: A Cultural History* (Berkeley, CA: University of California Press, 1995), p. 110.
7. The Larpent Catalogue lists the Covent Garden production as entry 745, with the date of October 16, 1786 and the Drury Lane production as entry 746 with the end date of October 24, 1786. D. MacMillan, *Catalogue of the Larpent Plays in the Huntington Library*, Huntington Library lists no. 4 (San Marino, CA: The Library, 1939), p. 124. See also W. A. Kinne, *Revivals and Importations of French Comedies in England 1749–1800* (New York: Ams Press, 1967), pp. 193–7.
8. Kinne, *Revivals and Importations*, p. 197.
9. E. P. Thompson, *The Making of the English Working Class* (New York: Vintage Books Random House, 1966), p. 58.
10. Francis Place Papers, Additional Manuscripts, 27825, British Library, folio 144. These songs were published in V. A. C. Gatrell's book *The Hanging Tree: Execution and the English People 1770–1868* (Oxford: Oxford University Press, 1996).
11. See also R. Darnton, *Poetry and the Police: Communication Networks in Eighteenth-Century Paris* (Cambridge, MA: Belknap, 2010).
12. I. McCalman, *Radical Underworld: Prophets, Revolutionaries and Pornographers in London, 1795–1840* (Cambridge: Cambridge University Press, 1988), p. 22; I. McCalman 'Ultra-Radicalism and Convivial Debating-Clubs in London, 1795–1838', *English Historical Review*, 102:403 (1987), pp. 309–33, on pp. 321–2. See also J. Beal, 'Why Should the Landlords have the Best Songs? Thomas Spence and the Subversion of Popular Song', in J. Kirk, A. Noble and M. Brown (eds), *United Islands? The Languages of Resistance* (London: Pickering & Chatto, 2012), pp. 51–62.

13. J. Epstein, *Radical Expression: Political Language, Ritual, and Symbol in England, 1790–1850* (Oxford and New York: Oxford University Press, 1994), p. 8.
14. M. T. Davis, '"An Evening of Pleasure Rather Than Business": Songs, Subversion and Radical Sub-Culture in the 1790s', *Journal for the Study of British Cultures*, 12:2 (2005), pp. 115–26, on p. 115.
15. M. Scrivener, 'John Thelwall and Popular Jacobin Allegory, 1793–95', *ELH*, 67: 4 (2000), pp. 951–71; M. Scrivener, *Seditious Allegories: John Thelwall & Jacobin Writing* (University Park, PA: Pennsylvania State University Press, 2001); M. Scrivener (ed.), *Poetry and Reform: Periodical Verse from the English Democratic Press 1792–1824* (Detroit, MI: Wayne State University Press, 1992).
16. M. Scrivener, 'Reading the English Political Songs of the 1790s', in Kirk, Noble and Browne, *United Islands?*, pp. 35–50.
17. M. Philp, 'Vulgar Conservatism', *English Historical Review*, 110:435 (1995), pp. 42–69.
18. M. Philp, R. Southey, C. Jackson-Houlston and S. Wollenberg, 'Music and Politics, 1793–1815 Introduction', in M. Philp (ed.), *Resisting Napoleon: The British Response to the Threat of Invasion 1797–1815* (Aldershot: Ashgate Publishing Limited, 2006), pp. 173–9, on p. 173.
19. V. Gammon, 'The Grand Conversation: Images of Napoleon in British Popular Balladry', *Journal of the Royal Society of Arts*, 137: 5398 (1989), pp. 665–74.
20. R. Ganev, *Songs of Protest, Songs of Love* (Manchester: Manchester University Press, 2009), p. 187.
21. P. Langford, *A Polite and Commercial People: England 1727–1783* (Oxford: Clarendon Press, 1989), p. 746; J. H. Jackson and S. C. Pelkey, 'Introduction', in J. H. Jackson and S. C. Pelkey (eds), *Music and History: Bridging the Disciplines* (Jackson, MS: University of Mississippi Press, 2005), pp. vii–xvii, on p. vii.
22. J. F. Fulcher, 'Introduction: Defining the New Cultural History of Music, Its Origins, Methodologies, and Lines of Inquiry', in J. F. Fulcher (ed.), *The Oxford Handbook of the New Cultural History of Music* (Oxford: Oxford University Press, 2012), pp. 3–14, on p. 9. Ashgate's 'New Cultural History of Music' series includes Vanessa Agnew's *Enlightenment Orpheus* (Oxford: Oxford University Press, 2008), a text which is discussed at greater length later.
23. P. Fumerton and A. Guerrini, 'Introduction: Straws in the Wind', in P. Fumerton and A. Guerrini (eds), and K. McAbee (asst ed.), *Ballads and Broadsides in Britain, 1500–1800* (Farnham and Burlington, VT: Ashgate, 2010), pp. 1–9, on p. 4.
24. M. Percival, 'Introduction', in *Political Ballads Illustrating the Administration of Sir Robert Walpole*, ed. M. Percival (Oxford: Clarendon Press, 1916), pp. xi–lvii, on p. xix.
25. Ibid., p. xlv.
26. P. McDowell, '"The Manufacture and Lingua-facture of *Ballad-Making*": Broadside Ballads in Long Eighteenth-Century Ballad Discourse', *Eighteenth Century: Theory and Interpretation*, 47:2–3 (2006), pp. 151–78, on p. 171.
27. A. Friedman, *The Ballad Revival: Studies in the Influence of Popular on Sophisticated Poetry* (Chicago, IL: University of Chicago Press, 1967), p. 146.
28. J. Cannon and A. Hargreaves, 'Richard I', in *The Kings & Queens of Britain* (Oxford: Oxford University Press, 2001), pp. 194–5.
29. J. Gillingham is the pre-eminent modern scholar on King Richard I. See J. Gillingham, *Richard Coeur de Lion* (London: Hambledon Press, 1994), and J. Gillingham, *Richard I* (New Haven, CT: Yale University Press, 1999). On Robin Hood see the works of Stephen Knight: S. Knight, *Robin Hood: A Mythic Biography* (Ithaca, NY: Cornell

University Press, 2003), S. Knight, *Robin Hood: A Complete Study of the English Outlaw* (Oxford: Blackwell Publishers, 1994).
30. This was a translation of a work published in 1581 by the French historian Claude Fauchet entitled *Recueil de l'Origine de la Langue et Poesie Françoises, Ryme et Romans*. A. Williams, 'Blondiaux', in *Miscellanies in Prose and Verse* (London: T. Davis, 1766), pp. 46–8.
31. Ibid., p. 48.
32. T. Percy, 'An Essay on the Ancient English Minstrels', in *Reliques of Ancient English Poetry: Consisting of Old Heroic Ballads, Songs, and other Pieces of our earlier Poets, (chiefly of the lyric kind) Together with some few of later Date*, 2nd edn, 3 vols (London: J. Dodsley, 1767), vol. 1, pp. xixl–xxvi.
33. Percy drew upon André Favyn's *Theatre of Honour and Knighthood*, the first English translation of which had appeared in 1623. Ibid., p. xxviii.
34. Ibid., p. xxvii.
35. Ibid., p. xxviii–xxix.
36. J. Hawkins, *A General History of the Science and Practice of Music*, 5 vols (London: T. Payne, 1776), vol. 2, p. 48.
37. Ibid., p. 52.
38. H. Walpole, *A Catalogue of the Royal and Noble Authors of England*, 2nd edn, 2 vols (London: R. and J. Dodsley, 1759), vol. 1, pp. 3–6.
39. Hawkins, *A General History*, vol. 2, pp. 48–9.
40. Ibid., p. 50; T. Rymer, *A Short View of Tragedy; Its Original, Excellency, and Corruption with some Reflections of Shakespear, and Other Practitioners for the Stage* (London, 1693), p. 67.
41. Hawkins, *A General History*, vol. 2, p. 58.
42. C. Burney, *A General History of Music from the Earliest Ages to the Present Period*, 4 vols (London: Printed for the Author, 1782), vol. 2, pp. 234–47.
43. Ibid., pp. 236–7.
44. Ibid., p. 237.
45. Ibid., pp. 240–1.
46. R. Eastcott, *Sketches of the Origin, Progress and Effects of Music with an Account of the Ancient Bards and Minstrels* (Bath: S. Hazard, 1793), pp. 37–8.
47. B. B. Broughton, *The Legends of King Richard I Coeur de Lion* (The Hague: Mouton & Co., 1966), pp. 70–1; Gillingham, *Richard Coeur de Lion*, pp. 184–5; Gillingham, *Richard I*, p. 233.
48. L. Harap, 'Some Hellenic Ideas on Music and Character', *Musical Quarterly*, 24:2 (1938), pp. 153–68; E. A. Lippman, *A History of Western Musical Aesthetics* (Lincoln, NE: University of Nebraska Press, 1992), pp. 3–16.
49. E. A. Lippman, *Musical Thought in Ancient Greece* (New York: Columbia University Press, 1964), p. 45.
50. Ovid, *The Metamorphoses*, trans. M. Simpson (Amherst, MA: University of Massachusetts Press, 2001), pp. 165–84.
51. Burney, *A General History of Music*, vol. 1, pp, 185–6. Burney drew upon the judgements of 'M Burette' to consider the claims made by the ancients for the medicinal properties of music noting that 'he allows it to be possible, and even probable, that music, by reiterated strokes and vibrations given to the nerves, fibres, and animal spirits, may be of use in the cure of certain diseases; yet he by no means supposes that the music of the ancients possessed this power in a greater degree than the modern'.

52. Lippman, *A History of Western Musical Aesthetics*, p. 10.
53. Plato, 'Republic, (397–401b)', in A. Barker (ed.), *Greek Musical Writings*, 2 vols (Cambridge: Cambridge University Press, 1984), vol. 1, p. 130.
54. Ibid., p. 131.
55. Plato, 'Republic, (410a–412b)', in Barker, *Greek Musical Writings*, p. 137.
56. Ibid., p. 137.
57. Ibid., p. 139.
58. Plato, 'Republic, (423d–425a)', in Barker, *Greek Musical Writings*, p. 140.
59. See Barker's notes on Damon in Barker, *Greek Musical Writings*, pp. 168–9
60. Plato, 'Laws, (700a–701b)' in Barker, *Greek Musical Writings*, p. 156.
61. Ibid., p. 156.
62. Ibid., p. 156.
63. Ibid., pp. 156–7.
64. Agnew, *Enlightenment Orpheus*, p. 6.
65. Ibid., p. 6–7.
66. Ibid., p. 7.
67. L. Goehr, *The Imaginary Museum of Musical Works: An Essay in the Philosophy of Music* (Oxford: Oxford University Press, 2007), p. 123.
68. T. Gray, 'The Bard. A Pindaric Ode ', in *The Poems of Gray, Collins and Goldsmith*, ed. R. Lonsdale (London: Longman, 1969), pp. 177–200, on pp. 185–6.
69. Ibid., p. 183.
70. Ibid., p. 180.
71. See Lonsdale's introductory note in R. Lonsdale (ed.), *The Poems of Gray, Collins and Goldsmith*, ed. R. Lonsdale (London: Longman, 1969), pp. 180–1.
72. A. Fletcher, *The Political Works of Andrew Fletcher, Esq; of Saltoun* (Glasgow: G. Hamilton and J. Balfour, 1749), p. 266.
73. D. Herd, *Ancient and Modern Scottish Songs, Heroic Ballads, etc*, 2 vols (Edinburgh: James Dickson and Charles Elliot, 1776), vol. 1, p. iii.
74. J. Addison, 'Spectator Papers Nos 70, 74 and 85', in D. F. Bond (ed.), *The Spectator*, 5 vols (Oxford: Clarendon Press, 1965), vol. 1, pp. 297–303, 315–22, 360–4.
75. Addison, 'Spectator No. 70', in Bond, *The Spectator*, p. 298; Addison, 'Spectator No. 74', in Bond, *The Spectator*, p. 316.
76. Ibid., pp. 315–22.
77. Addison, 'Spectator No. 70' in Bond, *The Spectator*, p. 297.
78. Ibid.
79. Ibid., pp. 298–9.
80. Ibid., p. 299.
81. Homer, *The Iliad*, trans. R. Fagles (New York: Viking Penguin, 1990), p. 77.
82. Addison, 'Spectator No. 70' in Bond, *The Spectator*, p. 299.
83. W. Wordsworth, 'Preface to *Lyrical Ballads*, (1802)', in S. Gill (ed.), *William Wordsworth* (Oxford: Oxford University Press, 1984), pp. 595–615, on pp. 596–97.
84. Ibid., p. 613.
85. Ibid.
86. Ibid.
87. N. Groom, *The Making of Percy's Reliques* (Oxford: Oxford University Press, 1999), pp. 148–50.

88. Letter from William Shenstone to Thomas Percy, 24 April 1761 in C. Brooks (ed.), *The Correspondence of Thomas Percy and William Shenstone* (New Haven, CT: Yale University Press, 1977), pp. 94–5.
89. C. O. Brink, *Horace on Poetry*, 3 vols (Cambridge: Cambridge University Press, 1982), vol. 3, p. 13, lines 46–7.
90. Horace, *The Satires and Epistles of Horace: A Modern English Verse Translation*, trans. S. P. Bovie (Chicago, IL: University of Chicago Press, 1969), p. 249.
91. See Brink's commentary in Brink, *Horace on Poetry*, p. 74.
92. D. Mallet, *The Works of David Mallet*, 3 vols (London: A. Millar and P. Vaillan, 1759), vol. 1, p. 7; *Lucy and Colin, A Song Written in Imitation of William and Margaret* (Dublin: Printed by Pressick Rider and Thomas Harbin, 1725).
93. [J. MacPherson], *The Poems of Ossian and Related Works*, ed. H. Gaskill (Edinburgh: Edinburgh University Press, 1996). For an account of the ancient ballad forgeries of the eighteenth century, including Ossian, see S. Stewart, 'Scandals of the Ballad', in *Crimes of Writing: Problems in the Containment of Representation* (Oxford: Oxford University Press, 1991), pp. 102–31.
94. The title of 'William and Margaret' is altered to 'Margaret's Ghost' in volume three of Percy, *Reliques*, 2nd edn, pp. 331–4.
95. Groom, *The Making of Percy's Reliques*, pp. 168–9.
96. McDowell, '"The Manufacture and Lingua-facture of *Ballad-Making*"', p. 164; P. McDowell, '"The Art of Printing was Fatal": Print Commerce and the Idea of Oral Tradition in Long Eighteenth-Century Ballad Discourse', in Fumerton and Guerrini, *Ballads and Broadsides in Britain 1500–1800*, pp. 35–56, on p. 45.
97. Letter from Percy to Shenstone, 19 July 1761 in Brooks, *The Correspondence of Thomas Percy and William Shenstone*, pp. 108–10, on pp. 108–9.
98. P. Connell, 'British Identities and the Politics of Ancient Poetry in Later Eighteenth-Century England', *Historical Journal*, 49:1 (2006), pp. 161–92.
99. W. Wordsworth, 'Essay Supplementary to the Preface to Poems (1815)', in Gill, *William Wordsworth*, pp. 640–62, on p. 645.
100. Ibid., p. 651.
101. Ibid., p. 654–6.
102. Friedman, *The Ballad Revival*, p. 94; A. B. Friedman, 'Addison's Ballad Papers and the Reaction to Metaphysical Wit', *Comparative Literature*, 12:1 (1960), pp. 1–13. McDowell has also recently acknowledged this in 'The Art of Printing was Fatal', p. 40.
103. Friedman, 'Addison's Ballad Papers', p. 13.
104. Friedman, *The Ballad Revival*, p. 94.
105. Ibid., p. 86.
106. J. W. Hales and F. J. Furnivall, 'The Revival of Ballad-Poetry in the Eighteenth Century', in *Bishop Percy's Folio MS. Ballads and Romances*, 3 vols (London: N. Trübner & Co., 1868), vol. 2, pp. v–xxxi, on p. v.
107. J. Dennis, 'Of Simplicity in Poetical Composition, in Remarks on the 70th Spectator', in *Original Letters, Familiar, Moral and Critical*, 2 vols (London: W. Mears, 1721), vol. 1, pp. 166–244, on p. 187.
108. Ibid., p. 192.
109. S. Newman, *Ballad Collection, Lyric, and the Canon: The Call of the Popular from the Restoration to the New Criticism* (Philadelphia, PA: University of Pensylvannia Press, 2007), p. 2; D. Dugaw, 'On the "Darling Songs" of poets, scholars, and singers: an introduction', *Eighteenth Century: Theory and Interpretation*, 47:2–3 (2006), pp. 97–113, on p. 98.

110. F. J. Child, 'Preface' in *The English and Scottish Ballads*, 8 vols (Boston: Little, Brown and Company, 1860), vol. 1, pp. vii–xii, on p. vii.
111. Letter from Francis Child to Sven Grundtvig dated 25 August 1872, in S. B. Hustvedt, *Ballad Books and Ballad Men: Raids and Rescues in Britain, America, and the Scandinavian North Since 1800* (Cambridge, MA: Harvard University Press, 1930), pp. 252–5, on pp. 253–4.
112. F. J. Child, 'Ballad Poetry', in *The English and Scottish Popular Ballads*, 2nd edn prepared by M. F. Heiman and L. S. Heiman, 5 vols (Northfield, MN: Loomis House Press, 2001), vol. 1, pp. xxvii–xxxiv, on p. xxvii.
113. Ibid.
114. See Dave Harker's account of the development of folksong and the ideology of 'mediation' in D. Harker, *Fakesong: The Manufacture of British 'Folksong' 1700 to the Present Day* (Milton Keynes: Open University Press), pp. i–xviii.
115. C. J. Sharp, *English Folk Song: Some Conclusions*, 4th edn (1907; London: Mercury Books, 1965).
116. See N. Leask, '"A Degrading Species of Alchymy": Ballad Poetics, Oral Tradition, and the Meanings of Popular Culture', in P. Connell and N. Leask (eds), *Romanticism and Popular Culture in Britain and Ireland* (Cambridge: Cambridge University Press, 2009), pp. 51–71.
117. R. S. Thomson, 'The Development of the Broadside Ballad Trade and Its Influence Upon the Transmission of English Folksongs' (PhD dissertation, University of Cambridge, 1974), pp. 24–5.
118. A. Fox, *Oral and Literate Culture in England, 1500–1700* (Oxford: Oxford University Press, 2002), p. 5.
119. Ibid.
120. D. Dugaw, *Warrior Women and Popular Balladry, 1650–1850* (Cambridge: Cambridge University Press, 1989), p. 1.
121. McDowell, '"The Manufacture and Lingua-facture of *Ballad-Making*"', p. 171.
122. M. Scrivener, 'Reading the English Political Songs of the 1790s', in Kirk, Noble and Browne, *United Islands?*, pp. 35–50, on pp. 37–9.
123. T. Wright, *England Under The House of Hanover: its History and Condition during the Reigns of the Three Georges*, 2 vols (London: Richard Bentley, 1848), vol. 1, p. ix.
124. W. W. Wilkins, 'Preface', in *Political Ballads of the Seventeenth and Eighteenth Centuries*, 2 vols (London: Spottiswoode and Co., 1860), vol. 1, pp. v –xii, on p. vi.
125. Ibid.
126. Ibid., p. ix.
127. Percival, 'Introduction', p. xlv.
128. Ibid., pp. xv, liv, lvi.
129. Ibid., p. xxxiv.
130. C. H. Firth, 'The Ballad History of the Reigns of Henry VII. and Henry VIII', *Transactions of the Royal Historical Society*, 2(1908), pp. 21–50, on p. 21.
131. See for example, Thompson, *The Making of the English Working Class*, pp. 292–3; E. P. Thompson, 'Rough Music', in *Customs in Common* (London: Merlin Press, 1991), pp. 467–531; T. Hitchcock, 'A New History from Below', *History Workshop Journal*, 57:1 (2004), pp. 294–8.
132. R. Palmer, *A Touch on the Times : Songs of Social Change, 1770–1914* (Harmondsworth: Penguin Education, 1974); M. Vicinus, *Broadsides of the Industrial North* (Newcastle upon Tyne: Graham, 1975).

133. W. W. Wilkins, 'Preface', in *Political Ballads*, pp. v–vi.
134. R. Blakey, *The History of Political Literature from the Earliest Times*, 2 vols (London: Richard Bentley, 1855), vol. 2, p. 189.
135. P. Burke, 'Introduction to the Third Edition', in *Popular Culture in Early Modern Europe*, 3rd edn (Farnham: Ashgate, 2009).
136. T. Harris, 'Problematising Popular Culture' in *Popular Culture in England, c. 1500–1850* (New York: St Martin's Press, 1995), pp. 1–28, on p. 26.
137. M. Butler, *Romantics, Rebels and Reactionaries English Literature and Its Backgrounds 1760–1830* (Oxford: Oxford University Press, 1981); M. Butler (ed.), *Burke, Paine, Godwin and the Revolution Controversy* (Cambridge: Cambridge University Press, 1984).
138. I. McCalman, 'Introduction: A Romantic Age Companion', in I. McCalman (ed.), *An Oxford Companion to the Romantic Age: British Culture 1776–1832* (Oxford: Oxford University Press, 1999), pp. 1–11, on pp.1–2.
139. M. McLane, *Balladeering, Minstrelsy, and the Making of British Romantic Poetry* (Cambridge: Cambridge University Press, 2008), p. 6.
140. P. Connell and N. Leask, 'What is the People?' in Connell and Leask, *Romanticism and Popular Culture in Britain and Ireland*, pp. 3–48, on p. 7.
141. *A Collection of Old Ballads. Corrected from the Best and Most Ancient Copies Extant. With Introductions Historical and Critical*, 3 vols (London: J. Roberts, 1725), vol. 3, pp. 11. Hereafter referred to as '*Collection*'.
142. E. Burke, *Reflections on the Revolution in France* (1790), ed. J. C. D. Clark (Stanford, CA: Stanford University Press, 2001), p. 156.
143. R. Lowth, *Lectures on the Scared Poetry of the Hebrews; Translated from the Latin of the Right Rev. Robert Lowth, D. D.*, trans. G. Gregory, 2 vols (London: J. Johnson, 1787), vol. 1, p. 23.
144. O. Smith, *The Politics of Language 1791–1819* (Oxford: Clarendon Press, 1984), p. ix.
145. J. Barrell and J. Mee (eds), *Trials for Treason and Sedition*, 8 vols (London: Pickering & Chatto, 2006), vol. 3, p. 186. Hereafter abbreviated as *TTS*.
146. Scrivener, *Poetry and Reform*, pp. 50–1.
147. B. T. Bennett, *British War Poetry in the Age of Romanticism 1793–1815* (New York: Garland, 1976), pp. 293, 326–7, 327–8, 357, 380–1, 387–8, 429–30.
148. J. Barrell, *Imagining the King's Death: Figurative Treason, Fantasies of Regicide 1793–1796* (Oxford: Oxford University Press, 2000), p. 40.

1 'The Heart of the Lion: The 'Princely Song' and the Transmission of Richard'

1. *Morning Post and Daily Advertiser*, 27 October 1786.
2. *Morning Chronicle and London Advertiser*, 28 October 1786.
3. 'Acon' was the anglicized name for Acre, a city in northern Israel which held strategic importance as a sea port. It had fallen under the control of the forces of the great Muslim warrior Saladin in 1187. During the third crusade in 1191, Richard I and his ally King Philip of France laid siege to the city eventually forcing its surrender. See Gillingham, *Richard I*, pp. 155–71.
4. See p. 175, n. 7. Both plays were printed: [J. Burgoyne], *Richard Coeur de Lion. An Historical Romance. From the French of Monsr. Sedaine. As Performed at the Theatre-Royal, Drury-Lane* (London: J. Debrett, 1786); Leonard MacNally, *Richard Coeur De Lion. A*

Comic Opera, As Performed at The Theatre Royal Covent Garden. Taken from a French Comedy of the Same Name, written by Monsieur Sedaine (London: T. Cadell, 1786). For discussions of the opera see D. L. Hoeveler and S. D. Cordova, 'Gothic Opera as Romantic Discourse in Britain and France: A Cross-Cultural Dialogue', in L. H. Peer and D. L. Hoeveler (eds), *Romanticism: Comparative Discourses* (Aldershot: Ashgate, 2006), pp. 11–34, on pp. 15–16, and D. Charlton, 'On Redefinitions of "Rescue Opera"', in M. Boyd (ed.), *Music and the French Revolution* (Cambridge: Cambridge University Press, 1992), pp. 169–88, on pp. 173, 178.

5. D. Dugaw, 'The Popular Marketing of "Old Ballads": The Ballad Revival and Eighteenth-Century Antiquarianism Reconsidered', *Eighteenth-Century Studies*, 21:1 (1987), pp. 71–90.
6. See p. 176, n. 29.
7. *Collection*, vol. 3, pp. 11–22.
8. M. Treadwell, 'London Trade Publishers 1675–1750', *The Library*, s6-IV: 2 (1982), pp. 99–134, on pp. 108–10.
9. Treadwell, 'London Trade Publishers 1675–1750', p. 110.
10. Dugaw, 'The Popular Marketing of "Old Ballads"', p. 83; Groom, *The Making of Percy's Reliques*, pp. 168–9.
11. W. St. Clair, *The Reading Nation in the Romantic Period* (Cambridge: Cambridge University Press, 2004), p. 345.
12. For accounts of the 'ballad partners', see W. A. Jackson, *Records of the Court of the Stationers' Company, 1602 to 1640* (London: Bibliographical Society, 1957), pp. xiii–xiv; C. Blagden, 'Notes on the Ballad Market in the Second Half of the Seventeenth Century', *Studies in Bibliography*, 6 (1954), pp. 161–80; Thomson, 'The Development of the Broadside Ballad Trade', pp. 54–80.
13. St Clair, *The Reading Nation*, p. 501.
14. *Collection*, vol. 1, pp. ii–iii.
15. P. McDowell, '"The Manufacture and Lingua-facture of *Ballad-Making*"', pp. 151–78, on p. 161.
16. The publication of the *Collection* was announced in the May edition of the *Monthly Catalogue* for 1723, see number 3 in *The First Volume of the Monthly Catalogue Containing an Exact Register of All Books, Sermons, Plays, Poetry, and Miscellaneous Pamphlets, Printed and Published in London, or the Universities, from the Beginning of March 1723, to the End of December, 1724* (London: Printed for John Wilford, 1725), p. 2. The *Collection* was advertised for 3 shillings 'bound in calf' in the *Daily Courant* on Monday, 20 May 1723 and in the *London Journal* on 8 June 1723, which also announced that a second volume was in the press.
17. *Collection*, vol. 1, p. iii.
18. Ibid., p. iii–iv.
19. Ibid., p. vi.
20. Ibid., p. vi.
21. Paula McDowell discusses a letter sent to *Applebee's Journal* in 1722 by 'Jeffrey Sing-Song', thought to be Daniel Defoe, who identifies himself as a 'ballad maker' and 'British manufacturer', see McDowell, '"The Manufacture and Lingua-facture of *Ballad-Making*"', pp. 155–9. This idea was also used by Charles Isaac Mungo Dibdin, who would come to refer to himself as a 'song smith' and titled his 1801 collection of songs *The Song Smith or Rigmarole Repository*.

22. The tune for 'Sally in the Alley' was used in Act Three of John Gay's *Beggar's Opera* as Air 18, 'Of All the Girls that are so Smart', see J. Gay, *The Beggar's Opera* (1728), eds B. Loughrey and T. O. Treadwell (London: Penguin, 1986), p. 117.
23. H. Carey, 'Preface', in *Six Songs for Conversation: The Words by Divers Hands. The Tunes Contrived to Make Agreeable Little Lessons for the Harpsichrod, Viol, Violin, and Hautboy*, 2 vols (London: 1728), vol. 2, n.p.
24. Ibid.
25. Ibid.
26. N. Bailey, *An Universal Etymological English Dictionary Comprehending the Derivations of the Generality of Words in the English Tongue either Ancient or Modern*, 25th edn (London: J. Murray, 1783).
27. R. Burn, *The Justice of the Peace, and Parish Officer*, 2nd edn, 2 vols (The Strand: A. Millar 1756), vol. 2, p. 25.
28. *Collection*, vol. 1, pp. vi–vii.
29. Ibid., title page; Nicholas Rowe, *The Tragedy of Jane Shore* (London: Bernard Lintott, 1714), n.p.
30. G. Russell, 'Keats, Popular Culture, and the Sociability of Theatre', in Connell and Leask, *Romanticism and Popular Culture in Britain and Ireland*, pp. 194–213, on p. 199.
31. *Collection*, vol. 1, p. 145.
32. Addison, 'Spectator No. 74' in Bond, *The Spectator*, p. 316.
33. *Collection*, vol. 1, n. p.
34. Ibid., vol. 2, p. v.
35. Dugaw, 'The Popular Marketing of "Old Ballads"', p. 74.
36. M. Segar, 'A Collection of Ballads', *Times Literary Supplement*, 3 March 1932, p. 154.
37. Ibid.; L. de la Torre Bueno, 'Was Ambrose Philips a Ballad Editor?' *Anglia*, LIX (1935), pp. 252–70.
38. W. T. Lowndes (ed.), *The Bibliographer's Manual of English Literature*, 4 vols (London: Henry G. Bohn, 1857), vol. 1, p. 105.
39. De La Torre Bueno, 'Was Ambrose Philips a Ballad Editor?', pp. 256–7.
40. Ibid., p. 257.
41. Thomson, 'The Development of the Broadside Ballad Trade', p. 109.
42. Ibid., p. 111; [J. Haselwood], 'Fly Leaves VII – Old Ballads', *The Gentleman's Magazine* 93 (1823), p. 24; *Collection*, vol. 3, p. 218; 'William and Margaret' had also been printed in a periodical by Aaron Hill titled the *Plain Dealer* on 24 July 1724, the year before volume three was published, in a piece that makes many observations similar to the editor of the *Collection*. The *Plain Dealer* was also printed by 'J. Roberts'.
43. *Collection*, vol. 3, pp. 16–17.
44. Ibid., pp. 21–2.
45. See also B. H. Bronson, 'The Interdependence of Ballad Tunes and Texts', in *The Ballad as Song* (Berkeley: University of California Press, 1969), pp. 37–63.
46. See the English Broadside Ballad Archive (EBBA) at the University of California. 'The Lamentations of a New Married Man' from the Roxburghe collection (British Library Roxburghe 1.216–2170) appears at http://ebba.english.ucsb.edu/ballad/30155/image; and from the Pepys collection (Magdalene College Pepys 1.380–381) at http://ebba.english.ucsb.edu/ballad/20176/image.
47. C. M. Simpson, *The British Broadside Ballad and its Music* (New Brunswick: Rutgers University Press, 1966), pp. 557–9.
48. J. H. Harvey, *The Plantagenets 1154–1485* (London: Batsford, 1948), pp. 33–4.

49. Gillingham, *Richard I*, p. 265.
50. Ibid., p. 265.
51. *Collection*, vol. 2, p. 115.
52. P. de Rapin-Thoyras, *The History of England, as Well Ecclesiastical as Civil*, trans. N. Tindal, 15 vols (London: Printed for James and John Knapton, 1728), vol. 3, p. 147.
53. L. Crompton, *Homosexuality and Civilization* (Cambridge, MA: Harvard University Press, 2003), pp. 36–9.
54. W. Blackstone, *Commentaries on the Laws of England. Book the Fourth*, 4 vols (Oxford: Clarendon Press, 1769), vol. 1V, pp. 215–16.
55. Gillingham has shown that historians such as Rapin have misinterpreted the language of the medieval chroniclers in considering Richard's sexuality. When the medieval chronicler, Roger of Howden, writes of the friendship between Richard and the French Prince, Philip Augustus, in the summer of 1187, they are described as sharing the same bed at night, In Rapin's *The History of England* this is sexualized and Philip lets Richard lie in his bed and caress him with a margin note recording '1187 Philip seduces Richard', see de Rapin-Thoyras, *The History of England*, vol. 3, p. 83. Gillingham points out however that in the context of the times, sharing a bed had a ritual political significance, signifying the alliance between Philip and Richard. Similarly, Rapin's account of the hermit upbraiding of Richard for his 'sins against nature' is a misreading of the chronicle, according to Gillingham, because 'what King Richard's alleged sins were in 1195 ... Roger of Howden does not tell us, and any guess is bound to reflect upon ourselves and upon our age rather than upon Richard's behaviour', see Gillingham, *Richard I*, p. 264–5.
56. H. Trevor-Roper, 'A Huguenot Historian: Paul Rapin', in I. Scouloudi (ed.), *Huguenots in Britain and Their French Background, 1550–1800* (Basingstoke: Macmillan, 1987), pp. 3–19.
57. Ibid., p. 5, 17.
58. See de Rapin-Thoyras, *The History of England*, vol. 1, p. i, 'The government of England is a mixt and limited Monarchy, as it is certain all the Governments in Europe establish'd by the northern nations formerly were'; and p. ii, 'The King has great prerogatives, and they were the effect or consequence of the mutual agreement of the first Anglo-Saxon Kings with their people'. See also vol. 2, 'A Dissertation on the Government, Laws. Manners, Customs, and Language of the Anglo Saxons', pp. 137–210, on p. 138.
59. C. Hill, 'The Norman Yoke', in *Puritanism and Revolution* (London: Secker & Warburg, 1958), pp. 50–122.
60. Ibid., p. 57.
61. Ibid.
62. Trevor-Roper, 'A Huguenot Historian', p. 16.
63. S. Keynes, 'The Cult of King Alfred the Great', *Anglo-Saxon England*, 28 (1999), pp. 225–356 on p. 274; de Rapin-Thoyras, *The History of England*, vol. 1, p. 341.
64. Ibid., p. 342.
65. Ibid., p. 352.
66. *Collection*, vol. 1, p. 44.
67. Langford, *A Polite and Commercial People*, pp. 19–57.
68. J. G. A. Pocock, 'The Varieties of Whiggism from Exclusion to Reform: A History of Ideology and Discourse', in *Virtue, Commerce, and History: Essays on Political Thought and History Chiefly in the Eighteenth Century* (Cambridge: Cambridge University Press, 1985), pp. 215–310.

69. C. Robbins, *The Eighteenth-Century Commonwealthman* (Cambridge, MA: Harvard University Press, 1959), pp. 3–21.
70. Langford, *A Polite and Commercial People*, p. 36.
71. C. Gerrard, *The Patriot Opposition to Walpole: Politics, Poetry, and National Myth, 1725–1742* (Oxford: Clarendon, 1994), pp. 116–17.
72. D. Hume, *The Letters of David Hume*, ed. J. Y. T. Greig, 2 vols (Oxford: Oxford University Press, 1932), vol. 1 1727–1765, p. 179.
73. D. Hume, *The History of England, the Invasion of Julius Caesar to the Revolution in 1688*, 8 vols (London: A. Millar, 1767), vol. 2, p. 3.
74. Ibid., pp. 37 and 36.
75. *A Catalogue of Maps, Prints, Copy-Books, Drawing-Books, Histories, Old Ballads, Broad-Sheet and Other Patters, Garlands, &c. Printed and Sold by William and Cluer Dicey, at Their Warehouse, Opposite the South Door of Bow-Church in Bow-Church-Yard London* (London: 1754), p. 50.
76. Sir Frederick Madden (1801–73) was Keeper of Manuscripts at the British Museum from 1837–66. Robert Thomson describes his collection, which includes 26 volumes of broadside ballads from the eighteenth and nineteenth centuries, as 'possibly the largest and most important collection of such material yet discovered', see R. S. Thomson, 'Publisher's Introduction: Madden Ballads from Cambridge University Library', at http://microformguides.gale.com/Data/Introductions/30330FM.htm [accessed 12 January 2014]. The 'Princely Song' appears at Reel 01 frame 0473 in the microfilm of the collection.
77. Dugaw, 'The Popular Marketing of "Old Ballads"', p. 76.
78. Ibid., p. 77.
79. Ibid., p. 78; *Collection*, vol. 3, p. 201.
80. V. Neuburg, 'The Diceys and the Chapbook Trade', *The Library*, XXIV:3 (1969), pp. 219–31, on p. 220.
81. Ibid.
82. Ibid., p. 221.
83. W. W. Hadley, *The Bi-centenary Record of the Northampton Mercury*, (Northampton: Mercury Press, 1920), p. 16.
84. Thomson, 'The Development of the Broadside Ballad Trade', p. 94.
85. Ibid., p. 95.
86. The advantage of this arrangement would have been the certainty of a regular income over the precarious existence of the small trader reliant upon a certain amount of capital to purchase goods wholesale. However, Thomson reports that the temptation for chapmen to abscond with the goods was too great in some instances, see Thomson, 'The Development of the Broadside Ballad Trade', p. 97.
87. Percival, 'Introduction', p. xix.
88. R. Johnson, *The Golden Garland of Princely Pleasures and Delicate Delights. Wherein is Conteined the Histories of Many of the Kings, Queenes Princes, Lords, Ladies, Knights and Gentlewomen of this Kingdom*, 3rd edn (London: Thomas Langely, 1620).
89. The three songs were 'A Lamentable Song of the Death of King Leare and his Three Daughters', to the tune of 'When Flying Fame' (first song of the *Golden Garland*, in *Collection*, vol. 2, p. 8); 'The most cruel Murther of Edward the fift, and his brother Duke of Yorke, in the towre; by their Vncle Richard Duke of Gloster', to the tune of 'Fortune my foe' (fifteenth song of the *Golden Garland*, in *Collection*, vol. 2, p. 100); and 'An excellent

song, entitled, a penny-worth of Wit' (sixteenth song of the *Golden Garland*, in *Collection*, vol. 2, p. 245).
90. R. Johnson, *A Crowne Garland of Govlden Roses. Gathered out of Englands royall garden. Being the liues and strange fortunes of many great personages of this Land. Set forth in many pleasant new songs and sonnetts neuer before imprinted*. (London: John Wright, 1612).
91. Volume One includes two songs from the 1612 *Crowne Garland*: song sixteen, 'Richard Whittington's Advancement' and song twenty-four, 'The Life and Death of the famous Thomas Stukely'. The second song of Volume One of the *Collection*, 'A lamentable ballad of Fair Rosamund, King Henry the Second's Concubine', can be found in the 1659 edition of the *Crowne Garland*. Volume Two of the *Collection* includes the following songs from Richard Johnson's *Crown Garlands*: 'The Battel of Agincourt between the French and the English'; 'The lamentable fall of the Dutchess of Glocester'; 'the Union of the red Rose and the White'; and 'The Doleful death of Queen Jane'.
92. There is no record of the Thomas Stukely song in Hyder Rollins's index of all separate ballad entries in the Stationers' Registers, see H. E. Rollins, 'An Analytical Index to the Ballad-Entries (1557–1709) in the Registers of the Company of Stationers of London', *Studies in Philology* 21:1 (1924), pp. 1–324. However, broadsides of this song may be found in the Roxburghe and Pepys Collections online at the English Broadside Ballad Archive: http://ebba.english.ucsb.edu/.
93. See also A. G. Chester, 'Richard Johnson's *Golden Garland*', *Modern Language Quarterly*, 10:1 (1949), pp. 61–7.
94. Thomson, 'The Development of the Broadside Ballad Trade', Appendix F.
95. Ibid., p. 23–4.
96. Ibid., p. 5–24.
97. T. Watt, *Cheap Print and Popular Piety 1550–1640* (Cambridge: Cambridge University Press, 1991), p. 42.
98. Ibid., p. 47.
99. R. Johnson, *The Most Famous History of the Seauen Champions of Christendome* (London: Cuthbert Burbie, 1596); R. Johnson, *The Second Part of the Famous History of the Seauen Champions of Christendome* (London: Cuthbert Burbie, 1597). The first scholarly edition of the work has been produced by Jennifer Fellows, see R. Johnson, *The Seven Champions of Christendom (1596/7) By Richard Johnson*, ed. J. Fellows (Aldershot: Ashgate, 2003).
100. N. C. Liebler, 'Bully St. George: Richard Johnson's *Seven Champions of Christendom* and the Creation of the Bourgeois National Hero', in N. C. Liebler (ed.), *Early Modern Prose Fiction: The Cultural Politics of Reading* (London and New York: Routledge, 2007), pp. 115–29.
101. J. Fellows, 'Introduction', in Johnson, *The Seven Champions of Christendom*, pp. xiii – xxxi, on p. xxviii.
102. R. Proudfoot, 'Johnson, Richard *(fl.* 1592–1622)', *ODNB* (Oxford University Press, 2004), at http://www.oxforddnb.com/view/article/14909, [accessed 14 January 2012].
103. N. C. Liebler, 'Elizabethan Pulp Fiction: The Example of Richard Johnson', *Critical Survey*, 12:2 (2000), pp. 71–87, on p. 73.
104. Franklin B. Williams pointed out that Johnson's memorial to Queen Elizabeth, *Anglorum Lacrimae*, was plagiarized from Thomas Rogers's 1598 text *Celestial Elegies of the Goddesses and the* Muses, see F. B. Williams, 'Richard Johnson's Borrowed Tears', *Studies in Philology* 34:2 (1937), pp. 186–90. Richard Hirsch also identified Johnson's 1613 text *Looke on Me London* to be plagiarized from George Whetstone's 1584 text *A Mirour for*

Magestrates of Cyties and its second part *A Touch*stone *for the Time*, see R. Hirsch, 'The Source of Richard Johnson's *Look on Me London*', *English Language Notes*, 13 (1975), pp. 107–13.
105. E. Arber (ed.), *A Transcript of the Registers of the Company of Stationers 1554–1640*, 5 vols (1876; New York: Peter Smith, 1950), vol. 3, p. 478.
106. W. Chappell, 'Introduction' in *The Crown Garland of Golden Roses Consisting of Ballads and Songs. By Richard Johnson. Author of the 'Seven Champions of Christendom' From the Edition of 1612*, ed. W. Chappell (London: Percy Society, 1842), pp. v–x, on p. ix; T. Deloney, *Strange Histories, or Songes and Sonets, of Kings, Princes, Dukes, Lordes, Ladyes, Knights, and Gentlemen* (London: W. Barley, 1607).
107. 'Saint George's Commendation', in H. E. Rollins (ed.), *The Pepys Ballads*, 8 vols (Cambridge, MA: Harvard University Press, 1929), vol. 1, pp. 39–46. The 1612 ballad was 'imprinted at London by W. W.'. and was not registered with the Stationers' Company.
108. *Collection*, vol. 1, pp. 23–7.
109. See Rollins, 'An Analytical Index to the Ballad Entries', p. 204, index entries 2364, 2365 and 2366. The first entry in the Stationers', Registers was dated 15 June 1657, see G. E. B. (ed.), *A Transcript of the Registers of the Worshipful Company of Stationers 1640–1708*, 3 vols (1913; New York: Peter Smith, 1950), vol. 2, p. 130. The second and third entries were dated 1 March as part of a large entry of ballads by the ballad partners. This entry included two versions of the ballad, 'A most excellent ballad of St George for England' and 'St. George', see Ibid., p. 497, 500.
110. Rollins, 'Saint George's Commendation', p. 43.
111. Ibid., p. 45.
112. *Collection*, vol. 1, p. 23.
113. Ibid., p. 28.
114. T. Percy (ed.), *Reliques of Ancient English Poetry: Consisting of Old Heroic Ballads, Songs, and Other Pieces of our Earlier Poets, (Chiefly of the Lyric kind.) Together with Some Few of Later Date*, 1st edn, 3 vols (London: J. Dodsley, 1765), vol. 3, pp. 286–90.
115. In the preface to volume one, Percy describes 'an ancient folio manuscript' which came into his possession, see Ibid. vol. 1, p. ix.
116. C. Brooks, 'Introduction', in C. Brooks (ed.), *The Correspondence of Thomas Percy & Richard Farmer* (Louisiana: Louisiana State University Press, 1946), pp. i–xviii, on p. ix.
117. Letter from Thomas Percy to Richard Farmer, 9 October 1763 in Brooks, *The Correspondence of Thomas Percy & Richard Farmer*, pp. 46–54, on pp. 49–50.
118. T. Percy, 'On the Ancient Metrical Romances', in Percy, *Reliques*, 1st edn, vol. iii, pp. ii–xxiv.
119. Ibid., p. ix; D. Gray, 'Lydgate, John (*c*.1370–1449/50?)', *ODNB* (Oxford University Press, 2004), at http://www.oxforddnb.com/view/article/17238 [accessed 3 April 2012]; D. Gray, 'Gower, John (*d*. 1408)', *ODNB* (Oxford University Press, 2004), at http://www.oxforddnb.com/view/article/11176 [accessed 3 April 2012].
120. Percy, 'Ancient Metrical Romances', p. ix.
121. Ibid.
122. Ibid., p. x; For a discussion of the *Romance of Richard Coeur de Lion* printed by Wynkyn de Worde in 1509 and 1528 see Broughton, *The Legends of King Richard I Coeur de Lion*, pp. 41–5.
123. Percy, *Reliques*, 1st edn, vol. 3, pp. 213–24.
124. Ibid., p. 213.
125. Ibid.

126. Ibid.; This line is from book six, satire 1 of J. Hall's *Virgidemiarum* first printed in 1597, see J. Hall, *Satires, and Other Poems*, ed. P. Hall (London: G. Willis, 1838), p. 118.
127. Percy, *Reliques*, 1st edn, vol. 3, p. 213
128. T. Warton, *Observations on the Faerie Queene of Spenser* (London: R. and J. Dodsley, 1754).
129. Percy, *Reliques*, 1st edn, vol. 3, p. 214 He quotes a long description of a dragon from 'the more ancient poem, Syr Bevis of Hampton' in order to prove 'how closely the author of the Seven Champions has followed him'.
130. Ibid., p. 216.
131. Percy, 'Ancient Metrical Romances', p. v.
132. Percy, 'Ancient Metrical Romances', p. vii.
133. T. Percy, 'An Essay on the Ancient Minstrels', in *Reliques of Ancient English Poetry: Consisting of Old Heroic Ballads, Songs, and other Pieces of our Earlier Poets (Chiefly of the lyric Kind.) Together with some few of later date*, 1st edn (London: J. Dodsley, 1765), pp. xv–xxiii, on p. xv–xvi.
134. Ibid., pp. xvi–xvii.
135. Ibid., p. xxi.
136. Ibid., p. xxii.
137. Ibid., p. xxiii.
138. McDowell, '"The Manufacture and Lingua-facture of *Ballad-Making*"', pp. 165–6.
139. Percy, 'Essay on the Ancient Minstrels', p. xxiii.
140. Percy, 'An Essay on the Ancient English Minstrels', pp. xix–lxxvi; T. Percy, 'On The Ancient English Minstrels', in *Four Essays, As Improved and Enlarged in the Second Edition of the Reliques of Ancient English Poetry* (London: Printed for J. Dodsley, 1767), pp. 3–60.
141. Percy, 'Essay on the Ancient Minstrels', pp. xxvii–xxviii.
142. H. Walpole, 'Richard The First', in *A Catalogue of the Royal and Noble Authors of With Lists of their Works* (Strawberry Hill: 1758), pp. 1–3.
143. Percy, 'Essay on the Ancient Minstrels', pp. xxviii.
144. Ibid.
145. Ibid., pp. xxviii–xxix.
146. B. Davis, *Thomas Percy: A Scholar-Cleric in the Age of Johnson* (Philadelphia PA: University of Pennsylvania Press, 1989), p. 125.
147. Williams, 'Blondiaux', in *Miscellanies in Prose and Verse*, pp. 46–8.
148. Ibid., p. 46.
149. A. Favine, 'The Order of England, called of the Blew Garter: Instituted in the yeare One thousand three hundred fortie seauen. The Fift Booke', in *The Theater of Honour and Knight-hood. Or A Compendius Chronicle and Historie of the whole Christian World.* (London: William Iaggard, 1623), pp. 33–77, on p. 49. '[Blondel] sat directly before a window of the Castell, where King Richard was kept prisoner, and began to sing a song in French, which King Richard and Blondel has sometime composed together. When King Richard heard the song, he knew it was Blondel that sung it, & when Blondel paused at halfe of the Song, the King entreated him to sing the rest'.
150. Mr Pegge, 'Observations on Dr. Percy's Account of Minstrels among the Saxons read at the Society of Antiquaries, May 29, 1766', in *Archaeologia: or Miscellaneous Tracts Relating to Antiquity* (London: Society of Antiquaries, 1773), pp. 100–6, on p. 101.
151. Pegge, 'Observations on Dr Percy's Account of Minstrels', p. 102.

152. For analyses of Ritson's cultural politics, see Butler, *Burke, Paine, Godwin*, pp. 203–5; J. Mee, *Dangerous Enthusiasm: William Blake and the Culture of radicalism in the 1790s* (Oxford: Clarendon Press, 1992), pp. 113–15; Leask, '"A Degrading Species of Alchymy"' pp. 51–71, on. p.58; P. McDowell, ' "The Art of Printing was Fatal", pp. 46–7.
153. M. Butler, 'Joseph Ritson', in Butler, *Burke, Paine, Godwin*, pp. 203–5, on p. 203.
154. J. Ritson, 'A Historical Essay on the Origin and Progress of National Song' in *A Select Collection of English Songs* (London: J. Johnson, 1783), pp. i–lxxii, on pp. li–lii; Ritson recapitulated these arguments in his later essay 'Observations on the Ancient Minstrels' in *Ancient Songs from the Time of King Henry the Third to the Revolution* (London: J. Johnson, 1790), pp. i–xxvi.
155. Ritson, 'A Historical Essay on the Origin and Progress of National Song', pp. li–lii.
156. Ibid., p. lvi.
157. Ibid., p. lviii.
158. Ibid., p. lix.
159. Ibid.
160. Connell, 'British Identities and the Politics of Ancient Poetry', pp. 161–92, on pp.183–4.
161. O. Hulme, *An Historical Essay on the English Constitution* (London: Edward and Charles Dilly, 1771), p. 3.
162. Ibid., p. 50.
163. J. Burgh, *Political Disquisitions*, 3 vols (London: E. and C. Dilly, 1774), vol. 1, p. 84.
164. *Old Ballads, Historical and Narrative, With Some of Modern Date; Now First Collected, and Reprinted from Rare Copies with Notes*, 2 vols (The Strand: T. Evans, 1777), vol. 1, p. 80–6.
165. Ibid., preface, n.p. A second edition was published by Thomas Evans in 1784 with two additional volumes. In 1810 the collection was enlarged and published by Thomas Evans's son, R. H. Evans. In his address to the reader (1810) R. H. Evans praises Percy's *Reliques* but notes that 'the venerable prelate has ascribed a false importance to the English ballad singer, who never was "High placed in hall, a welcome guest", like the more fortunate foreigner, who visited this island; but was compelled to earn a scanty subsistence, by chaunting his ballads, and playing his crowd for the amusement of the middling, and lower classes of society', see *Old Ballads, Historical and Narrative, With Some of Modern Date; Collected from Rare Copies and Mss. By Thomas Evans. A New Edition Revised and Considerably Enlarged From Public and Private Collections, by his son, R. H. Evans*, 4 vols (London: R. H. Evans, 1810), vol. 1, pp. i–ix, on pp. iv–v.
166. [J. Ritson], *Robin Hood: A Collection of all the Ancient Poems, Songs, and Ballads, Now Extant, Relative to that Celebrated English Outlaw to which are Prefixed Historical Anecdotes of his Life* (London: T. Egerton and J. Johnson, 1795).
167. MacNally, *Richard Coeur de Lion*, p. 37.
168. [Burgoyne], *Richard Coeur de Lion*, pp. 26–7.
169. *Morning Post and Daily Advertiser*, 18 October 1786.
170. *Morning Post and Daily Advertiser*, 19 October 1786.
171. *Morning Chronicle and London Advertiser*, 17 October 1786.
172. *Morning Chronicle and London Advertiser*, 20 October 1786.
173. The *Morning Post* would become a prominent opposition paper aligned with the Whigs and Carlton House during the Regency crisis of 1788–9, see A. Aspinall, *Politics and the Press c. 1780–1850* (London: Hame & Van Thal Ltd, 1949), p. 274; L. Werkmeister,

The London Daily Press 1772–1793 (Lincoln: University of Nebraska Press, 1963), pp. 201–81.
174. T. Bartlett, 'The Life and Opinions of Leonard MacNally (1752–1820): Playwright, Barrister, United Irishman, and Informer', in H. Morgan (ed.), *Information, Media and Power Through the Ages* (Dublin: University College Dublin Press, 2001), pp. 113–36; T. Bartlett *Revolutionary Dublin, 1795–1801: The Letters of Francis Higgins to Dublin Castle* (Dublin: Four Courts Press, 2004), pp. 36–46.
175. Bartlett, 'The Life and Opinions of Leonard MacNally', pp. 114–15; MacMillan, *Larpent Plays*, p. 109, entry 654.
176. Bartlett, 'The Life and Opinions of Leonard MacNally', p. 117.
177. Ibid., pp. 116–19.
178. Bartlett found that MacNally betrayed the defence strategies of William Jackson, Henry and John Sheares and Robert Emmet, who were all executed. He passed the last letters of Jackson and Emmet to the authorities rather than their families, Ibid., p. 122.
179. Ibid., pp. 124–5.
180. J. P. Eigen, 'Nicholson, Margaret (1750?–1828)', *ODNB*, at http://www.oxforddnb.com/view/article/20145 [accessed 24 April 2012].
181. *Morning Chronicle*, 20 October 1786.
182. W. O. Henderson, 'The Anglo-French Commercial Treaty of 1786', *The Economic History Review, New Series*, 10:1 (1957), pp. 104–12, on p. 104.
183. Ibid.
184. *General Advertiser*, 20 October 1786.
185. Ibid.
186. Ibid.
187. M. Donaghay, 'Calonne and the Anglo-French Commercial Treaty of 1786', *The Journal of Modern History*, 50:3 (1978), pp. 1157–1184, on p. 1173.
188. 'Airs' from the MacNally Covent Garden production were printed in the *London Chronicle*, 17–19 October, 1786 and the *Morning Chronicle* on October 17, 1786. The *Morning Chronicle* also printed airs from the Drury Lane production in the issue of 26 October. The *Daily Universal Register*, the precursor to The *Times*, printed 'specimens of the songs' from the Covent Garden version, following a review, in the issue of 17 October 1786 and airs from the Drury Lane production in the issues of 26 & 27 October, 1786. The *General Evening Post*, 24 –26 October 1786, printed songs from the Drury Lane production following a favourable review. The *General Advertiser*, which was scathing of the MacNally production, printed an 'air' from the Drury Lane production in the issue of 27 October, 1786.
189. *Songs, Duettos, Trios, Quartettos, Quintettos and Musical Dialogue, &c. in the Comic Opera of Richard Coeur de Lion. Performing at The Theatre Royal Covent Garden* (London: T. Cadell, 1786); *Songs, Chorusses, &c in Richard Coeur de Lion. From the French of Monsr. Sedaine. The Whole of the Music by Monsieur Gretry. As It is now performing at the Theatre-Royal, Drury-Lane* (London: J. Debrett, 1787); *The Banquet of Thalia, or the Fashionable Songsters Pocket Memorial, an Elegant Collection, of the Most Admired Songs from Ancient, & Modern Authors* (London,1788), pp. 196–7; *The Busy Bee, or, Vocal Repository. Being a Selection of Most Favourite Songs, &c. Contained in the English Operas, that have been Sung at the Public Gardens, and Written for Select Societies; Together with an Extensive Collection of Hunting Songs, and a Variety of Scotch and Irish ballads*, 3 vols (London: J.S. Barr, 1790), vol. 1, pp. 332–40. *The Busy Bee* includes songs from 'MacNallay' followed by songs from 'Burgoyne'.

190. M. Kassler, *Music Entries at Stationers' Hall, 1710–1818: From Lists Prepared for William Hawes, D. W. Krummel and Alan Tyson and from Other Sources* (Aldershot: Ashgate, 2004), pp. 70, 75.
191. Percival, 'Introduction', p. xix.

2 'The Psalms that Bind: 'Sternhold and Hopkins', the 'Old Hundredth' and the Ballad

1. T. Paine, 'Rights of Man (1791)', in *Thomas Paine: Rights of Man, Common Sense and Other Political Writings*, ed. M. Philp (Oxford: Oxford University Press, 2008), pp. 83–197, on p. 135.
2. L. F. Benson, *The English Hymn: Its Development and Use in Worship* (London: G.H. Doran, 1915), pp. 19–26; J. R. Watson, *The English Hymn: A Critical and Historical Study* (Oxford: Oxford University Press, 1999), pp. 42–56; M. F. Marshall and J. M. Todd, *English Congregational Hymns in the Eighteenth Century* (Lexington, KY: The University Press of Kentucky, 1982); R. Arnold, *The English Hymn: Studies in a Genre* (New York: Peter Lang, 1995), pp. 1–8; T. K. McCart, *The Matter and Manner of Praise: The Controversial Evolution of Hymnody in the Church of England 1760–1820* (Lanham, MD: Scarecrow Press, 1998), pp. 1–22.
3. E. D. Mackerness, *A Social History of English Music* (London: Routledge and Kegan Paul, 1964), p. 119.
4. The term 'West Gallery' comes from the architectural feature added to the West part of the church to accommodate the choirs. For further discussion see C. Turner (ed.), *The Gallery Tradition: Aspects of Georgian Psalmody: Papers from the International Conference Organised by The Colchester Institute* (Ketton: SG Publishing in association with Anglia Polytechnic University, 1997).
5. S. Drage, 'A Reappraisal of Provincial Church Music', in D. W. Jones (ed.), *Music in Eighteenth Century Britain* (Aldershot: Ashgate, 2000), pp. 172–90, on p.172.
6. V. Gammon, 'Problems in the Performance and Historiography of English Popular Church Music', *Radical Musicology*, 1 (2006), at http://www.radical-musicology.org.uk [accessed 21 May 2011]; V. Gammon, '"Babylonian Performances": the Rise and Suppression of Popular Church Music', in E. Yeo and S. Yeo (eds), *Popular Culture and Class Conflict 1590–1914: Explorations in the History of Labour and Leisure* (Sussex: Harvester Press, 1981), pp. 62–88, on pp. 62–4; V. Gammon, *Desire, Drink and Death in English Folk and Vernacular Song, 1600–1900* (Aldershot: Ashgate Publishing, 2008), p. 199. Gammon maintains his position with respect to parochial psalmody as a 'plebeian style' across these works.
7. W. Vincent, *Considerations on Parochial Music*, 2nd edn (London: T. Cadell, 1787), p. 6.
8. Burney, *General History of Music*, vol. 3, pp. 61.
9. Gammon, 'Babylonian Performances', p. 81; Gammon, 'Problems in the Performance', paragraph 74.
10. E. P. Thompson, 'The Patricians and the Plebs', in *Customs in Common*, pp. 16–96, pp. 56–7.
11. See Thompson, 'Rough Music', pp. 467–531.
12. Gammon, 'Babylonian Performances', p. 81.
13. Ibid.
14. Ibid., p. 82–3.

15. Ibid., p. 83.
16. Gammon, 'Problems in the Performance'.
17. Quoted in McCart, *The Matter and Manner of Praise*, p. 98.
18. Ibid., p. 93.
19. Cotterill argued against the supposition that there existed an authority for the use of the authorized versions of the psalms ('Sternhold and Hopkins'). Consequently he argued that there could be no basis for the exclusion of the hymns from the service: T. Cotterill, 'Preface', in *A Selection of Psalms and Hymns, for Public and Private Use, Adapted to the Festivals of the Church of England*, 8th edn (Sheffield: J. Blackwell, 1829), p. vii.
20. McCart, *The Matter and Manner of Praise*, pp. 93–112.
21. T. Sternhold and J. Hopkins, *The Whole Book of Psalms, Collected into English Metre* (London: H.S. Woodfall for the Company of Stationers, 1781). I am using the edition of 'Sternhold and Hopkins' from 1781, the same year in which Thomas Warton's *History of English Poetry* was published. A new edition of 'Sternhold and Hopkins' was printed every year of the eighteenth century.
22. Sternhold and Hopkins, *The Whole Book of Psalms*, psalm C.
23. J. L. Mays, *The Lord Reigns: A Theological Handbook to the Psalms* (Louisville, KY: Westminister John Knox Press, 1994), p. 72.
24. Ibid., p. 73.
25. T. Sternhold, *Certayne Psalmes Chosen out of the Psalter of David, & Drawen into English Metre* (London: E. Whitchurche, *c.* 1549). The success of Sternhold's Certayne Psalmes was such that by 1554 eleven editions of the enlarged 1549 version had been printed which were the catalyst for a host of imitators and what Zim describes as a 'vogue' for metrical psalmody: R. Zim, *English Metrical Psalms*, (Cambridge: Cambridge University Press, 1987), p. 144.
26. B. Quitslund, *The Reformation in Rhyme: Sternhold, Hopkins and the English Metrical Psalm 1547–1603* (Aldershot: Ashgate, 2008), p. 27–8.
27. Ibid., p. 20–2.
28. P. Collinson, *The Reformation* (London: Weidenfeld & Nicolson, 2003), p. 27.
29. R. Leaver, *'Goostly psalmes and spirituall songes': English and Dutch Metrical Psalms From Coverdale to Utenhove 1535–1566* (Oxford: Clarendon Press, 1991), p. 272.
30. N. Temperley, *The Music of the English Parish Church*, 2 vols (Cambridge: Cambridge University Press, 1979), vol. 1, p. 19.
31. See Temperley, *The Music of the English Parish Church*, pp. 20–1; C. Garside, Jr., 'The Origins of Calvin's Theology of Music: 1536–1543', *Transactions of the American Philosophical Society*, 69:4 (1979), pp. 1–36.
32. Coverdale's *Goostly psalmes and spirituall songes* (c.1535) is the earlier surviving example of metrical psalms in England. See Zim, *English Metrical Psalms*, p. 112 and Quitslund, *The Reformation in Rhyme*, p. 17.
33. Temperley, *The Music of the English Parish Church*, p. 24.
34. H. Smith, 'English Metrical Psalms in the Sixteenth Century and Their Literary Significance', *Huntington Library Quarterly*, 9:3 (1946), pp. 249–71, on p. 254.
35. The title of the text was amended: T. Sternhold and J. Hopkins, *Al Such Psalmes of David as Thomas Sternhold Late Grome of Kinges Maiesties Robes, Didde in his Life Time Draw into English Metre* (London: E, Whitchurch, 1549).
36. Zim, *English Metrical Psalms*, p. 124; R. Zim, 'Hopkins, John (1520/21–1570)', *ODNB* (Oxford: Oxford University Press, 2004), at www.oxforddnb.com/view/article/13748 [accessed 6 Sept 2013].

37. Zim, *English Metrical Psalms*, p. 125.
38. Quitslund, *The Reformation in Rhyme*, p. 115.
39. As Quitslund and Leaver have meticulously documented, the original forty-four psalms of 'Sternhold and Hopkins' were reprinted and added to with eight further paraphrases by William Samuel, in a text printed in the German town of Wesel in 1556. This Wesel psalter either drew upon, or was developed in parallel, with the one hundred and fifty metrical psalms printed in the Anglo-Genevan psalter which had also appeared in 1556 and had been appended to *The Form of Prayers* for the English congregation at Geneva. This was the first psalter to include musical notation. There were significant alterations to Sternhold and Hopkins's original paraphrases which appeared in the 1556 Anglo-Genevan psalter. These alterations reflected the split between those Frankfurt Protestants who wished to follow the Edwardian *Book of Common Prayer* and those who believed that the Edwardian reforms had not gone far enough. See, Quitslund, *The Reformation in Rhyme*, pp. 155–192 and Leaver, 'Goostly Psalmes', pp. 195–215.
40. M. Frost, *English and Scottish Psalm & Hymn Tunes c.1542–1677* (London: S.P.C.K. and Oxford University Press, 1953), p. 147–8.
41. Quitslund, *The Reformation in Rhyme*, appendix C.
42. Leaver, 'Goostly psalmes', p. 235; H. Hamlin, *Psalm Culture and Early Modern English Literature* (Cambridge: Cambridge University Press, 2004), p. 32; Quitslund, *The Reformation in Rhyme*, p. 169.
43. It is unclear why the attribution shifted from Kethe to Hopkins in the text. The complex issues surrounding the provenance of this psalm at this time are beyond the bounds of this book.
44. See also Rev. W. H. Havergal, *A History of the Old Hundredth Psalm Tune* (New York: Mason Brothers, 1854).
45. W. H. Frere (ed.), *Visitation Articles and Injunctions of the Period of the Reformation*, 3 vols (London: Longmans, Green & Co, 1910), vol. 3 1559–1575 p. 22–3. Leaver notes that this 'carefully worded injunction' was a compromise between the Catholic sympathies of areas of rural England and the Protestantism of London and the South East. While choral Church music was permitted the injunctions stipulated that songs must be 'modest and distinct' and plainly understood: Leaver, 'Goostly Psalmes', p. 239.
46. Temperley, *The Music of the English Parish Church*, p. 53; Quitslund, *The Reformation in Rhyme*, pp. 199–201.
47. I. Green, *Print and Protestantism in Early Modern England* (Oxford: Oxford University Press, 2000), p. 3.
48. Frere, *Visitation Articles and Injunctions*, vol. 3, p. 24–5; T. Sternhold and J. Hopkins, *The Whole Booke of Psalmes, collected into Englysh metre by T. Sternhold I. Hopkins, & others: conferred with the Ebrue, with apt notes to synge them with al, Faithfully perused and alowed according to thordre appointed in the Quenes maiesties Iniunctions. Very mete to be used of all sortes of people privately for their solace & comfort: laying apart all vngodly Songes and Ballades, which tende only to the norishing of vyce, and corrupting of youth* (London: J, Day, 1562).
49. Quitslund, *The Reformation in Rhyme*, p. 201.
50. Jackson, *Records of the Court of the Stationers' Company*, p. viii.
51. C. Blagden, *The Stationers' Company: A History, 1403–1959* (New York: Hillary House Publishers, 1960), p. 92; see also J. Doelman, 'George Wither, the Stationers Company and the English Psalter', *Studies in Philology*, 90:1 (1993), pp. 74–82.

52. Doelman writes, 'This patent, renewed in 1616 and 1634, gave them [the Stationers' Company] exclusive rights to the English metrical psalter, that versification of all the Psalms made in the 1550s and 1560s, most often referred to as 'Sternhold and Hopkins'. This Psalter was the standard in the English church at the time, and remained so until the end of the seventeenth century, despite the widespread dissatisfaction with it on the part of churchmen, poets, and even King James I himself, Ibid., p. 74.
53. P. Heylyn, *Ecclesia Restaurata; or, The History of the Reformation of the Church of England*, 2nd edn (London: H. Twyford, J. Place, T. Basset, W. Palmer, 1670), p. 127.
54. Quitslund, *The Reformation in Rhyme*, p. 262.
55. I. Gentles, 'The Iconography of Revolution: England 1642–1649', in I. Gentles, J. Morril, and B. Worden (eds), *Soldiers, Writers and Statesmen of the English Revolution* (Cambridge: Cambridge University Press, 1998), pp. 91–113, on pp. 102–4.
56. Quitslund, *The Reformation in Rhyme*, p. 273.
57. N. Tate and N. Brady, *A New Version of the Psalms of David, Fitted to the Tunes Used in Churches* (London: Printed by M. Clarke For the Company of Stationers, 1696).
58. Ibid., pp. 202–03.
59. Ibid., n.p.
60. W. Beveridge, 'A Defence of the Book of Psalms, Collected into English Metre, By Thomas Sternhold, John Hopkins, and Others. With critical observations on the late new version, compared with the old', in *The Theological Works of William Beveridge, D.D.*, 12 vols (Oxford: John Henry Palmer, 1846), vol. 8, pp. 613–54, on p. 628.
61. Ibid., p. 632.
62. Ibid., p. 649.
63. Addison, 'Spectator No. 205' in Bond, *The Spectator*, vol. 2, pp. 305–6.
64. T. McGeary, 'Music Literature', in H. D Johnstone and R. Fiske (eds), *The Blackwell History of Music in Britain: The Eighteenth Century* (Cambridge, MA: Basil Blackwell Inc, 1990), pp. 397–421, on p. 398. Several *Spectator* papers by Addison had ridiculed the Italian opera, see Addison, 'Spectator Papers Nos 5, 13, 18, 29, and 31' in Bond, *The Spectator*, vol. 1, pp. 22–7, 55–9, 78–82, 119–23, 127–32. For John Dennis's views see: J. Dennis, *An Essay on the Opera's After the Italian Manner, Which Are About to Be Establish'd on the English Stage: With Some Reflections on the Damage Which They May Bring to the Publick* (London: Printed for John Nutt, 1706).
65. G. D'Arcy Wood, 'Introduction: Opera and Romancticism', in *Romantic Circles Praxis Series* (May, 2005) at http://www.rc.umd.edu/praxis/opera/wood/intro.html [accessed 21 May 2011].
66. Richard Platt describes Nicolini Grimaldi as 'the first great castrato' heard in London whose popularity led to the establishment of the Italian opera at the Queen's theatre, see R. Platt, 'Theatre Music', in Johnstone and Fiske (eds), *The Blackwell History of Music in Britain*, pp. 96–158, on p. 109.
67. L. Colley, *Britons Forging the Nation 1707–1837* (1992; New Haven, CT: Yale University Press, 2009), p. 19.
68. A. Bedford, *The Great Abuse of Musick* (London: John Wyatt, 1711).
69. The advertisements do not appear in D. F. Bond's edition of *The Spectator*. See the original *Spectator* papers in the Burney database.
70. Bedford drew upon Collier's *A Short View of the Immorality and Profaneness of the English Stage* (1698).
71. J. Dennis, *The Grounds of Criticsm in Poetry* (London: Geo. Strahan and Bernard Lintott, 1704), n.p.

72. In his explanatory notes to this passage, E. N. Hooker writes that 'at the beginning of Anne's reign the idea of closing the theatres seems to have been seriously considered, but the policy of regulation rather than suppression was decided upon'. J. Dennis, *The Critical Works of John Dennis*, ed. E. N. Hooker, 2 vols (1939–40; Baltimore: Johns Hopkins Press, 1967), vol. 1, p. 509.
73. Dennis, *The Grounds of Criticsm in Poetry*, Preface. This was also reproduced in *The Prompter*, for 25 June, 1736 and *The London Magazine* for June 1736.
74. 'antick' in S. Johnson, *A Dictionary of the English Language*, 2nd edn, 2 vols (London: J Knapton et al., 1755–6).
75. F. Quarles, *Divine Fancies Digested into Epigrams, Meditations, and Observations*, 9th edn (London, 1722), p.152; J. Doelman, 'The Religious Epigram in Early Stuart England', *Christianity and Literature*, 54:4 (2005), pp. 497–520, on pp. 510–11.
76. Dennis, 'Of Simplicity', pp. 166–93.
77. Ibid., pp. 187–8.
78. Ibid., p. 189.
79. Ibid.
80. Ibid., pp. 189–90.
81. Ibid., p. 187.
82. Addison wrote eighteen essays on Milton's *Paradise Lost*, beginning on Saturday, 5 January 1712, in *Spectator* no. 267 and continuing on the Saturday following. See Addison, 'Spectator Nos 267 and 273', in Bond, *The Spectator*, vol. 2, p. 537 and the discussion in 'Introduction' in Bond, *The Spectator*, vol. 1, p. lxiii.
83. See Dennis, *The Critical Works of John Dennis*, vol. 2, p. 442.
84. J. Gay, 'The Shepherd's Week', in *John Gay: Poetry and Prose*, ed. V. A. Dearing and C. E. Beckwith, 2 vols (Oxford: Clarendon Press, 1974), vol. 1, pp. 90–126, on p. 120.
85. *The Parish-Clerk's Guide: or, The Singing Psalms Used in the Parish-Churches Suited to the Feasts and Fasts of the Church of England, and Most other Special Occasions* (London: Re-printed by John March, for the Company of Parish-Clerks, 1731).
86. N. Temperley, 'Music in Church', in Johnstone and Fiske (eds), *The Blackwell History of Music in Britain*, pp. 357–96, on p. 379.
87. *Rochester's Jests: or, The Quintessence of Wit*, 4th edn (London: Printed for the Proprietors, and Sold by J. Wilkie, 1770), p. 5. See also Hamlin, *Psalm Culture*, p. 22; Green, *Print and Protestantism*, p. 504.
88. Burney, *A General History of Music*, vol. 2, p. 220.
89. A. W. Rowland, '"The False Nourice Sang": Childhood, Child Murder, and the Formalism of the Scottish Ballad Revival', in L. Davis, I. Duncan and J. Sorensen (eds), *Scotland and the Borders of Romanticism* (Cambridge: Cambridge University Press, 2004), pp. 225–44, on p. 228.
90. Connell and Leask, 'What is the People?', p. 21.
91. D. Dugaw, 'Folklore and John Gay's Satire', *Studies in English Literature, 1500–1900*, 31: 3 (1991), pp. 515–33, on p. 515.
92. Gay, 'The Shepherd's Week', pp. 121–2.
93. Ibid., p. 122; J. Denham, 'News from Colchester: Or, A Proper new Ballad of certain Carnal passages betwixt a Quaker and a Colt, at Horsely, near Colchester in Essex', in *The Poetical Works of Sir John Denham* (London: Printed for John Bell, 1793), pp. 84–7.
94. Gay, 'The Shepherd's Week', p. 122.
95. I. Watts, 'A Short Essay Toward the Improvement of Psalmody: Or, An Enquiry how the Psalms of *David* ought to be translated into Christian Songs, and how lawful and neces-

sary it is to compose other Hymns according to the clearer Revelations of the Gospel, for the Use of the Christian Church', in *Hymns and Spiritual Songs* (London: John Lawrence, 1707), pp. 233–76. By 1720 Watts's *Hymns and Spiritual Songs* had reached seven editions and a total of sixteen editions were published over his lifetime. See McCart, *The Matter and Manner of Praise*, pp. 23–5.
96. Watts, 'A Short Essay Toward the Improvement of Psalmody', p. 246.
97. Ibid., p. 242–3.
98. Ibid., p. 253.
99. Ibid., p. 261.
100. [I. Watts], 'Psalm CXIV', *The Spectator*, ed. D. F. Bond, 5 vols (Oxford: Clarendon Press, 1965), vol. 4, pp. 126–8. I. Watts, *The Psalms of David Imitated in the Language of the New Testament, And Apply'd to the Christian State and Worship* (London: J. Clarke, R. Ford and R. Cruttenden, 1719), pp. 299–300.
101. [Watts], 'Psalm CXIV', p. 126.
102. J. Wesley, 'Letter XCIX. [Of Public Worship, in a Letter to a Friend, by Rev. Mr. John Wesley]', *Arminian Magazine*, 3 (February 1780), pp. 101–3, on p. 101; emphasis added.
103. Temperley, 'Music in Church', p. 387.
104. J. Wesley, 'Preface', in *A Collection of Hymns for the Use of the People Called Methodists* (London: Printed by J. Paramore, 1780), pp. iii–vi, on p. v.
105. Nicholas Temperley notes that Methodist singing was communal and 'such as people might have experienced in a tavern, a mill, or a hayfield'. It had a 'free and secular character' and made use of popular secular tunes in 'parody hymns', see N. Temperley, 'John Wesley, Music, and the People Called Methodists', in N. Temperley and S. Banfield (eds), *Music and the Wesleys* (Urbana, IL: University of Illinois Press, 2010), pp. 3–25 and N. Temperley, 'The Music of Dissent', in I. Rivers and D. L. Wykes (eds), *Dissenting Praise: Religious Dissent and the Hymn in England and Wales* (Oxford: Oxford University Press, 2011), pp. 197–228.
106. D. Fairer, 'The Formation of Warton's *History*', in *Thomas Warton's History of English Poetry*, 4 vols (1774; London: Routledge, 1998), vol. 1, pp. 1–70, on pp. 4–10.
107. T. Warton, 'Section XXVII Effects of the Reformation on Our Poetry', in *The History of English Poetry, from the Close of the Eleventh to the Commencement of the Eighteenth Century*, 4 vols (London: J.Dodsley et al., 1781), vol. 3, pp. 161–80, on p. 161.
108. Ibid., p. 173.
109. Ibid. Warton switches the Christian names of Sternhold and Hopkins and mistakenly attributes the psalm to 'Thomas Hopkins'.
110. Ibid.
111. Ibid., p. 174.
112. *The Parish-Clerk's Guide*, pp. 41–2.
113. N. Brady and N. Tate, 'Psalm LXXIV' in *A New Version of the Psalms of David, fitted to the Tunes used in Churches* (London: Richard Hett, for the Company of Stationers, 1782), pp. 111–13, on p. 112.
114. Warton, 'Section XXVII Effects of the Reformation on Our Poetry', p. 174.
115. Ibid.
116. Ibid., pp. 176–7.
117. Ibid., p. 178.
118. *Gentleman's Magazine*, 51 (June 1781), pp. 265–6, on p. 266.
119. The equivalent passage of psalm LXXIV in the updated 'old version' in the edition for 1781 (the year that Warton's *History* was published) reads: 'Why dost thou thy right

hand withdraw/ from us so long away/ Out of thy Bosom pluck it forth/ with speed thy foes to flay: T. Sternhold and J. Hopkins, 'Psalm LXXIV', in *The Whole Book of Psalms*, 1781 edn, n.p.
120. E. Miller, *Thoughts on the Present Performance of Psalmody in the Established Church of England Addressed to the Clergy* (London: W. Miller, 1791), pp. 30–1.
121. Addison, 'Spectator No. 85', in Bond, *The Spectator*, p. 361.
122. *Gentleman's Magazine*, 51 (August 1781), pp. 369–70.
123. Temperley, *The Music of the English Parish Church*, p. 227.
124. P. A. Scholes, *God Save the Queen: The History and Romance of the World's First National Anthem* (London: Oxford University Press, 1954), pp. 3–22.
125. Ibid., pp. 6–7.
126. Ibid., p. 50.
127. *Gentleman's Magazine*, 15 (October 1745), p. 552.
128. Colley, *Britons*, pp. 45, 54.
129. Ibid., p. 44.
130. Ibid., p. 45.
131. 'anthem' in Johnson, *A Dictionary*
132. Temperley, 'Music in Church', p. 364.
133. Sternhold and Hopkins, 'Psalm LXVIII', in *The Whole Book of Psalms*, 1781 edn, n.p.
134. *The Parish-Clerk's Guide*, pp. 41–2
135. F. D'Arblay, Diary entry Tuesday 30 June 1789, in *Diary and Letters of Madame D'Arblay*, ed. C. Barratt, 4 vols (London: Bickers and Son, 1876), vol. 3, p. 190.
136. For proclamation see *The London Gazette*, 4–7 April 1789.
137. *Times*, 23 April 1789.
138. *World*, 24 April 1789.
139. *London Gazette*, 21–35 April 1789.
140. *Gentleman's Magazine*, 59 (April 1789), p. 366.
141. *Gentleman's Magazine*, 59 (April 1789), p. 367.
142. *Grand Procession. The Order of Procession of the King, Queen, &c. to St. Paul's Church, (And the Whole of the Ceremony during Divine Service) On Thursday the 23d of April, 1789, being the Day appointed for a General Thanksgiving, on Account of His Majesty's Recovery* (London: 1789), p. 22.
143. *Times*, 24 April 1789.
144. *Gentleman's Magazine*, 59 (April 1789), p. 367.
145. H. Cunningham, *The Children of the Poor: Representations of Childhood since the Seventeenth Century* (Oxford: Basil Blackwell, 1991), p. 38.
146. S. Lloyd, 'Pleasing Spectacles and Elegant Dinners: Conviviality, Benevolence, and Charity Anniversaries in Eighteenth-Century London', *Journal of British Studies*, 41:1 (2002), pp. 23–57, on p. 27.
147. Sir G. Elliot, Letter dated 25 April 1789, in *Life and Letters of Sir Gilbert Elliot First Earl of Minto from 1751 to 1806*, ed. N. Minto, 3 vols (London: Longmans, Green, and Co., 1874), vol. 1, pp. 302–6, on p. 303.
148. Ibid., Letter dated 25 April 1789, p. 304.
149. Ibid.
150. Ibid.
151. Ibid., p. 305.
152. Ibid.

153. D. Fairer, 'Experience Reading Innocence: Contextualizing Blake's Holy Thursday', *Eighteenth-Century Studies* 35:4 (2002), pp. 535–62, on p. 540.
154. Ibid., p. 540. Fairer's wider frame of reference is Blake's poem 'Holy Thursday' from *Songs of Innocence and Experience* which describes the charity children's procession to St. Paul's on the anniversary day and their singing. Rather than a pageant of innocence Fairer reads the poem as an ironic comment on the narratives of order, discipline and regulation which compromised this innocence.
155. Ibid.
156. *Psalms and Anthem to be Sung at the Anniversary Meeting of the Charity Children, At the Cathedral Church of St. Paul, on Thursday, May 26, 1785* (London: John Rivington, Jun. Printer to The Society for Promoting Christian Knowledge, 1785). Along with the one hundred and thirteenth psalm and the one hundred and fourth psalm.
157. V. Knox, 'On The Amusement of Music', in *Essays Moral and Literary* (London: Charles Dilly, 1793), pp.107–115, on p. 110.
158. T. Paine, *The Age of Reason Part the Second Being an Investigation of True and Fabulous Theology* (London: Daniel Isaac Eaton, 1796), p. 31.
159. Ibid.
160. Ibid.

3 Songs as Philippics: The 'Harmodium Melos' and the 'Io Paean' of Revolution.

1. In 1606 James the First had passed 'An Act for a Publick Thanksgiving to Almighty God Every Year on the Fifth Day of November' (3 James I, c. I.), which, in addition to thanksgiving and prayer, required the Act to be read aloud following the service, see *The Statutes at Large, from Magna Charta, to the thirtieth year of King George the Second, inclusive*, 6 vols (London: Printed by Thomas Baskett, 1758), vol. 2, pp. 530–1. By the time of George III's accession in 1760, the religious calendar included two more significant dates: 30 January, a day of fasting to commemorate the 'martyrdom' of Charles I; and 29 May, a day of thanksgiving to commemorate the restoration of the royal family in 1660. The proclamation of 7 October 1761 added 25 October as another date of observation which was the date George III came to the throne in 1760, and required the publishing and binding of the four forms of prayer associated with these days with the *Book of Common Prayer*. For a notice of the declaration see the *London Gazette*, 6–10 October, 1761.
2. *The Book of Common Prayer, and administration of the Sacraments, and other Rites and Ceremonies of the Church According the the Use of the Church of England: Together with the Psalter or Psalms of David Pointed as they are to be sung or said in Churches* (Cambridge: John Archdeacon, Printer to the University, 1789), n.p.; emphasis added.
3. This text is also known as *The Deipnosophistae*, the title of C. B. Gulick's 1941 translation. The most recent translation uses the title *The Learned Banqueters*, which is the edition used in this chapter. Athenaeus, *The Learned Banqueters*, trans. and ed. S. Douglas Olson, 8 vols (Cambridge Mass: Harvard University Press, 2006–12).
4. A. Goodwin, *The Friends of Liberty: The English Democratic Movement in the Age of the French Revolution* (London: Hutchinson, 1979), p. 19.
5. Ibid., p. 19–20.
6. K. Wilson, 'Inventing Revolution: 1688 and Eighteenth-Century Popular Politics', *Journal of British Studies*, 28:4 (1989), pp. 349–86, on pp. 352–3. See also L. G. Schwo-

erer, 'Celebrating the Glorious Revolution, 1689–1989', *Albion: A Quarterly Journal Concerned with British Studies* 22:1 (1990), pp. 1–20; R. Quinault, 'The Cult of the Centenary, c.1784–1914', *Historical Research*, 71:176 (1998), pp. 303–23; S. Pincus, *1688: The First Modern Revolution* (New Haven, CT: Yale University Press, 2009), p. 14.

7. E. C. Black, *The Association: British Extraparliamentary Political Organization 1769–1793* (Cambridge, MA: Harvard University Press, 1963), pp. 214–16.
8. G. Russell and C. Tuite, 'Introducting Romantic Sociability', in G. Russell and C. Tuite (eds), *Romantic Sociability: Social Networks and Literary Culture in Britain 1770–1840* (Cambridge: Cambridge University Press, 2002), p. 4.
9. Ibid., pp. 6–7.
10. British Library, Additional Manuscript, 64814, *Revolution Society: Minute-book of the Revolution Society 16 June 1788–4 November 1791*, folio 13/7. The 'Character of King William' was a set piece extolling the virtues of the King that was read every year at the anniversary celebration.
11. 'Daniel Arrowsmith (fl. 1783–1794)', in P.H. Highfill (ed.) et al., *A Biographical Dictionary of Actors, Actresses, Musicians, Dancers, Managers & Other Stage Personnel in London 1660–1800*, 16 vols (Carbondale: Southern Illinois University Press, 1973–93), vol. 1, pp. 128–9 (hereafter *BDA*); 'Charles Dignum (1765–1827)' in *BDA*, vol. 4, pp. 416–20, on p. 418.
12. Ibid.
13. Quoted in Ibid.
14. *Morning Post and Daily Advertiser*, 1 November 1788.
15. *Public Advertiser*, 6 November 1788.
16. See Pincus, *1688*, pp. 366–7.
17. 'Russel' refers to Edward Russell, Earl of Orford (1652–1727) who had been one of the 'immortal seven', the group of signatories who invited William of Orange to invade England in 1688. See D. D. Aldridge, 'Russell, Edward', *ODNB*, at www.oxforddnb.com/view/article/24304 [accessed 4 Aug 2012]; 'Rook' refers to Sir George Rooke (1650–1709), a naval commander who was part of the squadron that escorted Queen Mary from the Netherlands to England in 1689. See J. B. Hattendorf, 'Rooke, Sir George', *ODNB*, at www.oxforddnb.com/view/article/24059 [accessed 4 Aug 2012]; 'Marlbro' refers to John Churchill, the first Duke of Marlborough (1650–1722), an army officer and courtier loyal to James who changed his allegiance to William of Orange in November 1688. See J. B. Hattendorf, 'Churchill, John', *ODNB*, at www.oxforddnb.com/view/article/5401 [accessed 4 Aug 2012].
18. *Pocock's Everlasting Songster, containing a selection of the most approved songs which have been and are likely to be sung for ever with universal applause. Also a collection of toasts & sentiments upon a plan perfectly new to which is added original rules of behaviour* (Gravesend: Printed by R. Pocock, 1800), p. iii.
19. See, for example, *The Toast Master, Being a Collection of Sentiments & Toasts Calculated for the most polite circles to heighten social mirth and to add fresh charms to the chearful Glass* (London: Printed for W. Thiselton, 1791); *The Royal Toast Master containing many thousands of the best toasts Old and New to give brilliancy to Mirth & make the joys of the glass supremely agreeable also the Seaman's Bottle Companion, being a Selection of Exquisiste modern Sea Songs* (London: J. Roach, 1793).
20. *Pocock's Everlasting Songster*, p. ii.
21. Ibid., p. v.

22. *An Abstract of the History and Proceedings of the Revolution Society, in London to which is annexed a copy of the Bill of Rights* (London: Printed by Order of the Committee, 1789). There were three versions of this Abstract printed in 1789. The first version, evidently printed earlier in the year, contained the toast list from the celebration of 4 November 1788.
23. Wilson, 'Inventing Revolution', p. 360.
24. J. Epstein, 'Rituals of Solidarity: Radical Dining, Toasting, and Symbolic Expression', in *Radical Expression*, pp. 147–65, on p. 150.
25. Ibid., p. 149.
26. P. Waddington, 'Morris, Charles (1745–1838)', *ODNB*, at www.oxforddnb.com/view/article/19300 [accessed 20 Aug 2012].
27. Wright, *England Under the House of Hanover*, vol. 2, p. 145.
28. *History of the Westminster Election, Containing Every Material Occurrence, From Its Commencement on the First of April, to the Final Close of the Poll, on the 17th of May* (London: Printed for the Editors, and sold by J. Debrett, 1784), pp. 506–7.
29. 'English Convivial Song Writers', *The Irish Quarterly Review*, III:IX (1853), pp. 120–51, on p. 140.
30. *History of the Westminster Election*, p. 73. At the meeting at Willis's Rooms on 19 March 1784, Captain Morris sang 'his Constitutional Song, which got so much applause at the Shakespeare', p. 76. At the meeting at the Crown and Anchor Tavern on April 26, following a speech by Fox, 'several constitutional healths were drunk till about six o'clock, when Captain Morris made his appearance in the room ... the whole assembly, in one universal clamour, called out for the *Baby and Nurse*; Capt. Morris sung it with uncommon spirit and exertion; the tumult of applause was beyond all belief', p. 338.
31. W. Arnold, *The Life and Death of the Sublime Society of Beef Steaks* (London: Bradbury, Evans, & Co., 1871), p. xx.
32. Ibid., p. 3. Arnold reprints a selection of Captain Morris's songs, at pp. 47–77.
33. See 'The Toper's Apology' in Ibid., pp. 51–53; *The Festival of Anacreon. Containing a Collection of Modern Songs, Written for the Anacreontic Society, The Beef-Steak, and Humbug Clubs. By Captain Morris, Mr. Brownlow, Mr Hewerdine, Sir John Moore, Capt. Thompson, and other Lyric Writers, whose Compositions are the delight of the Festive Board!*, 7th edn (London: George Peacock, *c.*1790).
34. Captain Morris's songs in praise of drinking, 'The Choice Spirits' and 'When the Fancy Stirring Bowl' were printed in numerous editions of the songster, *The Festival of Momus, a Collection of Comic Songs, including the Modern and a Variety of Originals* (London: W Lane, *c.*1780). The drinking song, 'The Rosy Bowl' was printed in *The Bull-Finch: Being a Choice Collection of the Newest and most Favourite English Songs which have been Sung at the Public Theatres & Gardens* (London: G. Robinsons, R. Baldwin and G & J Wilkie, *c.* 1781), pp. 202–3. Two well-known Morris songs satirizing William Pitt, 'Bow Wow Wow', and 'Billy's Too Young to Drive us' were printed in *The New Vocal Enchantress: Containing an Elegant Selection of all the Newest Songs Lately Sung* (London: Printed for C. Stalker, A. Cleugh & C. Couch, 1788), pp. 134–40.
35. *A Collection of Songs, by the Inimitable Captain Morris. Part the First* (London: James Ridgeway, 1786). The fifteenth edition of Morris's songs appeared in 1798, C. Morris, *A Collection of Political and Other Songs*, 15th edn (London: Printed for T. Lewis, 1798). In 1840 the complete collection of Captain Morris's songs was published as C. Morris, *Lyra Urbanica; or the Social Effusions of the Celebrated Captain Charles Morris of the Late Life-Guards*, 2 vols (London: Richard Bentley, 1840).

36. *Catalogue of Personal and Political Satires Preserved in the Department of Prints and Drawings in the British Museum*, ed. M. D. George, 11 vols (London: The Trustees of the British Museum by British Museum Publications Limited, 1978), vol. 7, p. 356 (satire no. 9023).
37. *General Evening Post*, 4–6 November 1788; *London Chronicle* 4–6 November, 1788; *Whitehall Evening Post* 4–6 November 1788, which also printed the last two stanzas of a song by Mr Hewerdine sung at the anniversary celebration of the Constitutional Club. William Hewerdine was also known for his political songs at this time, see *BDA*, vol. 7, pp. 280–1.
38. *General Evening Post*, 4–6 November 1788.
39. *Abstract of the History and Proceedings of the Revolution Society*, pp. 8–9.
40. *The Parliamentary History of England from the Norman Conquest in 1066 to the year 1803*, 36 vols (London, 1806–20), vol. 27, col. 1332. (Hereafter cited as *PH*)
41. Ibid., cols. 1334–5.
42. Ibid., col. 1335.
43. Ibid., col. 1335.
44. Ibid., vol. 28, col. 297.
45. Ibid., col. 295.
46. Ibid., col. 295.
47. Ibid., col. 296.
48. Goodwin refers to the Bill briefly in *Friends of Liberty*, p. 86.
49. *PH*, vol. 28, pp. 1–41.
50. R. Price, *A Discourse on the Love of Our Country, Delivered on Nov. 4, 1789, at the Meeting-House in the Old Jewry, to the Society for Commemorating the Revolution in Great Britain*, 3rd edn (London: T. Cadell, 1790), p. 33, 35.
51. Ibid., p. 37; Goodwin, *Friends of Liberty*, p. 81;
52. Price, *A Discourse,* 3rd edn, p. 39.
53. Ibid., p. 41.
54. See J. C. D. Clark's timeline of events for 1789 in Burke, *Reflections on the Revolution in France (1790)*, 2001 edn, p. 19.
55. Paine, 'Rights of Man (1791)', pp. 161–4.
56. Ibid., p. 162.
57. Ibid., p. 163.
58. Edmund Burke to Richard Bright, 18 February 1790, in A. Cobban and R. A. Smith (eds), *The Correspondence of Edmund Burke*, 10 vols (Cambridge: Cambridge University Press, 1967), vol. VI, pp. 82–5, on pp. 83–4.
59. Ibid., p. 83.
60. Burke, *Reflections on the Revolution in France (1790)*, 2001 edn, pp. 153–4.
61. Price's *Discourse* was first printed with an appendix containing the 'report of the committee' of the Revolution Society, 'an account of the population of France', and 'the declaration of rights by the National Assembly of France'. The third edition of the *Discourse* added to the appendix the 'communications from France occasioned by the congratulatory address of the Revolution Society to the National Assembly of France, with the Answers to them'. An enlarged version of *Abstract of the History and Proceedings of the Revolution Society* also printed the congratulatory address from the Revolution Society sent to the National Assembly and the ensuing communications.
62. Burke, *Reflections*, 2001 edn, pp. 147–8.
63. Ibid., pp. 145 and 148.

64. Ibid., pp. 148–9.
65. Ibid., p. 148.
66. Ibid., pp. 155 and 156.
67. Goodwin, *Friends of Liberty*, pp. 131–2.
68. Archbishop of Aix, President of the National Assembly, to Lord Stanhope Chairman of the Revolution Society, 5 December 1789, see 'Appendix' in Price, *A Discourse*, 3rd edn, p. 20.
69. J. C. D. Clark, in Burke, *Reflections*, 2001 edn, p. 15 n. 35.
70. C. C. O'Brien, in E. Burke, *Reflections on the Revolution in France* (1790), ed. C. C. O'Brien (1968; London: Penguin Books, 2004), p. 379 n.7.
71. Demosthenes delivered his first 'Philippic' in 351 BC, see D. M. MacDowell, *Demosthenes the Orator* (Oxford: Oxford University Press, 2009), 210–18.
72. H. Bowden, *Classical Athens and the Delphic Oracle* (Cambridge: Cambridge University Press, 2005), p. 18.
73. Peter Hunt points to Book Five, Section Ninety of Herodotus's *History of the Peloponnesian War*, in which the Lacedaemonians learn that the Pythian priestess has been bribed, P. Hunt *War, Peace, and Alliance in Demosthenes' Athens* (Cambridge: University of Cambridge Press, 2010), p. 88, n. 111.
74. Aeschines, 'The Speech Against Ctesiphon', in *The Speeches of Aeschines*, trans. C.D. Adams (London: William Heinemann, 1919), pp. 305–511, on p. 411.
75. Plutarch, 'Demosthenes', in *The Age of Alexander: Nine Greek Lives*, trans I. Scott-Kilvert (Harmondsworth: Penguin Books, 1973), pp. 188–217, on p. 205.
76. M. T. Cicero, *Philippics*, trans. and ed. D. R. Shackleton Bailey (Chapel Hill: University of North Carolina Press, 1986).
77. 'Philippick' in Johnson, *A Dictionary*.
78. H. Blair, 'Lecture XXVII Different Kinds of Public Speaking – Eloquence of Popular Assemblies – Extracts from Demosthenes', in *Lectures on Rhetoric and Belles Lettres* (Dublin: Whitestone et al., 1783), pp. 221–55, on p. 225.
79. J. Swift, 'A Discourse of the Contests and Dissentions between the Nobles and the Commons in Athens and Rome; with the Consequences they had upon both those States', in *The Works of the Rev. Dr. Jonathan Swift, Dean of St. Patrick's Dublin*, ed. T. Sheridan, 17 vols (London: W. Strahan, 1784), vol. 2, pp. 365–423, on p. 384.
80. *Several Orations of Demosthenes, Exciting the Athenians to Oppose the Exorbitant Power of Philip King of Macedon* (London: J. and R. Tonson and S. Draper, 1744), n.p.
81. Plutarch, 'The Oracles at Delphi no Longer Given in Verse', in *Plutarch's Moralia*, trans. F. C. Babbitt, 14 vols (London: William Heinemann Ltd, 1935), vol. V, pp. 259–409.
82. Plutarch, 'The Oracles', pp. 321–23.
83. J. Burgh, *The Art of Speaking*, 7th edn (London: T. Longman and J. Buckland et al., 1787), p. 8.
84. 'Unison', in Johnson, *A Dictionary*.
85. Lowth delivered seventeen lectures in all as part of his appointment to Professor of Poetry, see Lowth, *Lectures on the Scared Poetry of the Hebrews*, vol. 1, pp. 1–2.
86. A. Cullhed, 'Original Poetry: Robert Lowth and Eighteenth-Century Poetics', in J. Jarick (ed.), *Sacred Conjectures: The Context and Legacy of Robert Lowth and Jean Astruc* (New York: T&T Clark, 2007), pp. 25–47, on p. 31.
87. R. Lowth, 'Lecture 1. Of the Uses and Design of Poetry' in Lowth, *Lectures on the Scared Poetry of the Hebrews*, p. 8, 13.
88. Ibid., p. 22.

89. The song is also known as the 'Song to Harmodius' and the 'Ode to Harmodius and Aristogeiton'.
90. Lowth, 'Of the Uses and Design of Poetry', p. 23.
91. Ibid., p. 26.
92. The banquet is hosted by a wealthy Roman named Larensis who owns an extensive library. The text comprises several different narrative frames and an internal dialogue between the banqueters. In the conversations that occur in these frames the speakers canvas many issues and quote a range of works to demonstrate their knowledge and learning. See P. Ceccarelli, 'Dance and Desserts: An Analysis of Book Fourteen', in D. Braund and J. Wilkins (eds), *Athenaeus and His World* (Exeter: University of Exeter Press, 2000), pp. 272–91; C. Jacob, 'Athenaeus the Librarian', in Braund and Wilkins (eds), *Athenaeus and his World*, pp. 85–110.
93. O. Murray, 'Sympotic History', in Murray (ed.), *Sympotica: A Symposium on the Symposion* (Oxford: Clarendon Press, 1990), pp. 3–13. Murray points out that the symposium in its strict sense referred to that part of the evening following the meal at which alcohol was consumed. In the late classical and Hellenic period there were strict rules governing the conduct and order of proceedings at a symposium which included the mixing of wine with water and an order of proceedings governing the way songs were to be sung, p. 6.
94. Athenaeus, *The Learned Banqueters*, vol. 8, p. 157.
95. Ibid., p. 159. In Charles Burton Gulick's 1941 translation, the third type of skolion sung is sung 'only by those who enjoyed the reputation of being specially skilled at it, and in whatever part of the room they happened to be', see Athenaeus, *The Deipnosophists*, trans. C. B. Gulick, 7 vols (London: William Heinemann, 1941), vol. 7, p. 217.
96. Athenaeus, *The Learned Banqueters*, vol. 8, p. 165. For an alternative translation see *Greek Lyric*, ed. and trans. D. A. Campbell, 5 vols (Cambridge, MA: Harvard University Press, 1993), vol. 5, pp. 286–7.
97. C. Burney, 'Of the Scolia, or Songs, of the Ancient Greeks', in C. Burney, *A General History of Music from the Earliest Ages to the Present Period*, 2nd edn, 4 vols (London: Printed for the Author, 1789), vol. 1, pp. 453–61, on p. 455.
98. Ibid., p. 455. The classical scholar, T. J. Mathiesen, believes that the 'Harmodium Melos' was performed in the second manner, with the verses of the song being passed along with the branch of myrtle: 'Athenaeus's arrangement of the text into four separate pieces provides a clear example of the way in which the verses of a traditional song could be passed from guest to guest', see T. J. Mathiesen, *Apollo's Lyre: Greek Music and Music Theory in Antiquity and the Middle Ages* (Lincoln, NE: University of Nebraska Press, 1999), pp. 146–7.
99. Burney, 'Of the Scolia', pp. 455–9.
100. Ibid., p. 458.
101. Lowth, 'Of the Uses and Design of Poetry', p. 24.
102. *The Myrtle. Being a Favourite Collection of Above Two Hundred of the Newest and Best English and Scotch Songs* (London: J. Fuller and S. Neale, 1755); R. Hudson, *The Myrtle: A Collection of New English Songs for the Violin, German Flute or Harpsichord* (London: for the author, c. 1755); *The Myrtle of Venus: Containing the Following Much Admired Songs* (London: C. Sheppard, c. 1798–1800); *The Myrtle of Venus. Being a Choice Collection of the Most Favourite Songs, Sung This and the Last Season at Vauxhall, Ranelagh, Apollo Gardens, Sadler's Wells, the Theatres &c.* (London: printed and sold by J. Evans,

c. 1791–1800); C. H. Wilson, *The Myrtle and Vine; or Complete Vocal Library*, 4 vols (London: West and Hughes, 1800).
103. Burney, 'Of the Scolia', p. 460.
104. 'Peisistratus', in M. C. Howatson (ed.), *The Concise Oxford Companion to Classical Literature*, 3rd edn (Oxford: Oxford University Press, 2011), at http://www.oxfordreference.com/view/10.1093/acref/9780199548545.001.0001/acref-9780199548545-e-2280?rskey=4P0tKa&result=2240 [accessed 11 December 2013]
105. See E. W. Robinson (ed.), 'The Beginnings of Athenian Democracy: Who Freed Athens?' in *Ancient Greek Democracy: Readings and Sources* (Oxford: Blackwell, 2004), pp. 76–95.
106. Though debate continues as to when democracy exactly began in classical Athens, following the fall of the Peisistraid tyranny in 510 BC, the reforms of Cleisthenes from the Alcmaeonid family in 507 BC are generally taken as either the beginning of democracy or at the very least a major development, see R. Osborne, 'When was the Athenian Democratic Revolution', in S. Goldhill and R. Osborne (eds), *Rethinking Revolutions Through Ancient Greece* (Cambridge: Cambridge University Press, 2006), pp. 10–28.
107. Thucydides, *The Peloponnesian War*, trans. W. Blanco and eds W. Blanco and J. T. Roberts (New York and London: W. W. Norton & Company, 1998), p. 10.
108. Ibid. According to Thucydides, Harmodius and Aristogeiton had planned to kill Hippias but on the day of the assassination they suspected that he had learned of the plot. Determined to do something before they were captured, they decided to kill Hipparchus.
109. Ibid., pp. 253–6.
110. Ibid., p. 253.
111. Ibid., p. 255.
112. Burney, 'Of the Scolia', p. 458.
113. See chapter 1, pp. 53–6.
114. Ritson, 'A Historical Essay on the Origin and Progress of National Song', pp. ix–x.
115. S. Mandelbrote, 'Lowth, Robert (1710–1787)', *ODNB*, at www.oxforddnb.com/view/article/17104 [accessed 9 Aug 2013].
116. R. Lowth, *A Sermon Preached at the Chapel Royal of St. James's Palace, on Ash-Wednesday* (London: J. Dodsley and T. Cadell, 1779), p. 17.
117. Ibid. In the second edition of Lowth's pamphlet, he attempted to qualify his note by stating that the first part of the quoted passage, before the sentence beginning 'by assuming', was not meant to refer to Price. However, in this edition he quoted even *more* extensively from Price's *Observations*, noting that Price 'frequently' represents the government 'as not being a Free Government' and that the principal part of the book is a 'defence' of the 'American Rebellion', see R. Lowth, *A Sermon Preached at the Chapel Royal of St. James's Palace, on Ash-Wednesday*, 2nd edn (London: J. Dodsley and T. Cadell, 1779), pp. 25–6.
118. R. Price, 'Postscript to Dr. Price's Sermon on the Fast Day; Containing Remarks on a Passage in the Bishop of London's sermon preached at the Chapel Royal on Ash-Wednesday last', in *A Sermon Delivered to a Congregation of Protestant Dissenters, at Hackney, On the 10th of February last, Being the Day appointed for a General Fast* (London: Printed for T. Cadell, 1779), pp. 1–8, on p. 8. [pagination is separate from the sermon].
119. W. Jones, 'An Ode in Imitation of Callistratus', in *The New Annual Register, or General Repository of History, Politics, and Literature, for the year 1782* (London: G. Robinson, 1783), pp. 181–2.
120. S. M. Farrell, 'Wentworth, Charles Watson, Second Marquess of Rockingham (1730–1782), Prime Minister', *ODNB*, at http://www.oxforddnb.com/index/28/101028878/

[accessed 12 Dec 2013]; W. C. Lowe, 'Lennox, Charles, Third Duke of Richmond', *ODNB*, at http://www.oxforddnb.com/index/16/101016451/ [accessed 12 Dec 2013]; J. Cannon, 'Petty [formerly Fitzmaurice], William, Second Earl of Shelburne and First Marquess of Lansdowne (1737–1805), Prime Minister', *ODNB*, at http://www.oxforddnb.com/index/22/101022070/, [accessed 12 Dec 2013].
121. Burke, *Reflections*, 2001 edn, p. 146.
122. *An Address to the Public, from the Society for Constitutional Information* (London, c. 1780), p. 1; Black, *The Association*, pp. 174–80.
123. M. J. Franklin, *'Orientalist Jones': Sir William Jones, Poet, Lawyer, and Linguist, 1746–1794* (Oxford: Oxford University Press, 2011), p. 149; W. Jones, 'An Ode in Imitation of Callistratus', in *The Works of Sir William Jones*, 6 vols (London: G. G. and J. Robinson and R. H. Evans, 1799), vol. 4, pp. 573–5; Black notes that Burney had set the ode to music for the occasion, since lost, see Black, *The Association*, p. 190, n. 34.
124. Jones, 'An Ode in Imitation of Callistratus', p. 573.
125. W. Jones, 'An Ode in Imitation of Alcaeus', in *The Works of Sir William Jones*, vol. IV, pp. 571–2; W. Jones, 'The Principles of Government, in a Dialogue Between a Gentleman and a Farmer' in *The Works of Sir William Jones*, vol. IV, pp. 569–76. These publications were first published in 1782 for the Society for Constitutional Information. They were 'printed and distributed gratis anonymously by a member of the Society for Constitutional information'. The 1782 version of the dialogue carried the slightly different title: *The Principles of Government, in a Dialogue between a Scholar and a Peasant*.
126. Jones, 'An Ode in Imitation of Alcaeus', vol. 4, pp. 571–2.
127. *Pigs' Meat; or, Lessons for the Swinish Multitude. Published in Weekly Penny Numbers*, 3rd edn, 2 vols (London: T. Spence, c.1795), vol. 1, p. 59.
128. V. Knox, 'The Effects of Songs', in *Winter Evenings: Or Lucubrations on Life and Letters*, 3 vols (London: Charles Dilly, 1788), vol. 1, pp. 223–29, on p. 223.
129. J. Bell, *Bell's New Pantheon; or, Historical Dictionary of the Gods, Demi-gods, Heroes, and Fabulous Personages of Antiquity*, 2 vols (London: John Bell, 1790), vol. 2, p. 8.
130. C. Burney, 'The History of Greek Music', in Burney, *A General History of Music*, 2nd edn, vol. 1, p. 282.
131. Ibid., p. 292.
132. M. De Chastellux, *Travels in North-America, in the years 1780, 1781, and 1782 Translated from the French by an English Gentleman*, 2 vols (London: G. G. J. and J. Robinson, 1787), vol. 1, p. 52. In a songster from 1797 entitled *The Political Harmonist*, a 'Cosmopolite' writes that 'the Americans obtained their liberty by the heart-chearing sound of yankee-doodle, and the French by the more exhilarating ones of ca ira and the Marseillois', see *The Political Harmonist; or, Songs and Poetical Effusions Sacred to the Cause of Liberty. By A Cosmopolite* (Holborn: T. Williams, 1797), p. v.
133. Price, *A Discourse*, 3rd edn, pp. 49–50. Luke 2: 29–32 describes Simeon's response when he sees Jesus presented by Mary and Joseph in the Temple, in fulfilment of a promise made to him by the Holy Ghost.
134. Burke, *Reflections*, 2001 edn, pp. 233–4.
135. Ibid., p. 235. See Ian Newman's excellent article 'Edmund Burke in the Tavern', for a nuanced discussion of Burke's attitudes to tavern sociability in terms of the threat of an increasingly influential commercial class, a point obscured by the focus of much scholarship on plebeian radicalism in the context of the tavern. I. Newman, 'Edmund Burke in the Tavern', *European Romantic Review*, 24:2 (2013), pp. 125–48.
136. Ibid., p. 234.

137. R. Price, *A Discourse on the Love of Our Country, Delivered on Nov. 4, 1789, at the Meeting-House in the Old Jewry, to the Society for Commemorating the Revolution in Great Britain*, 4th edn (London: T. Cadell, 1790), p. vii.
138. F. P. Lock, *Edmund Burke*, 2 vols (Oxford: Clarendon Press, 2006), vol. 2, p. 295.
139. *PH,* vol. 28, col. 439.
140. Ibid., cols 439–40.
141. Ibid., col. 452.
142. J. Priestley, 'Genuine Copy of the Introduction to a Toast, proposed by Dr. Price on Wednesday, the 14 of July, at the Feast for celebrating the first Anniversary of the Revolution in France', in J. Priestley, *The Theological and Miscellaneous Works of Joseph Priestley*, ed. by J. T. Rutt, 25 vols (London: Printed by G. Smallfield, 1817–32), vol. 1, part 2, pp. 79–81.
143. Priestley, 'Letter from Joseph Priestley to Dr Price, 29 August 1790' in Priestley, *The Theological and Miscellaneous Works of Joseph Priestley*, p. 79.
144. *Times*, 15 July 1790; *Gazetteer and New Daily Advertiser*, July 15 1790.
145. *Gazetteer and New Daily Advertiser*, 15 July 1790.
146. D. O. Thomas, *The Honest Mind: The Thought and Work of Richard Price* (Oxford: Oxford University Press, 1977), pp. 309–42; H. T. Dickinson, 'Richard Price on Reason and Revolution', in W. Gibson and R. G. Ingram (eds), *Religious Identities in Britain, 1669–1832* (Aldershot: Ashgate, 2005), pp. 231–54, on pp. 231–2.
147. C. Reid, 'Burke, the Regency Crisis, and the "Antagonist World of Madness"', *Eighteenth-Century Life*, 16 (1992), pp. 59–75.
148. Barrell, *Imagining the King's Death*, pp. 90–1.
149. G. Russell, 'Burke's Dagger: Theatricality, Politics and Print Culture in the 1790s', *British Journal for the Eighteenth Century*, 20 (1997), pp. 1–16, on p. 2.
150. Philip Francis to Edmund Burke, 19 February 1790, in *The Correspondence of Edmund Burke*, vol. VI, p. 85.
151. Ibid., pp. 86–7.
152. 'Philip Francis to Edmund Burke, 3/4 November 1790', in *The Correspondence of Edmund Burke*, vol. VI, p. 151.
153. Ibid., p. 155.
154. *PH,* vol. 29, pp. 416–26.
155. 'It must be proved that his construction is in perfect harmony with that of the ancient Whigs, to whom, against the sentence of the modern on his part I here appeal', E. Burke, 'An Appeal from the New to the Old Whigs (1791)', in *The Works of Edmund Burke*, 8 vols (London: George Bell, 1901), vol. 3, pp. 1–115, on p. 42.
156. Ibid., p. 115.
157. Ibid., p. 13.
158. Ibid., p. 87.
159. 'Thus the leaders are at first drawn to a connivance with sentiments and proceedings, often totally different from their serious and deliberate nations. But their acquiesence answers every purpose', Ibid., p. 97.
160. For an account of the formation of the Association of the Friends of the People see F. O'Gorman, *The Whig Party and the French Revolution* (London: Macmillan, 1967), pp. 82–121.
161. M. Butler, 'Tom Paine (1737–1809)', in Butler, *Burke, Paine, Godwin,* pp. 107–9, on p. 108.

162. *The Muses Banquet or Vocal Repository for the year 1791 being the newest and most modern collection of songs, duets, trios, &c* (London: Printed by R. Bassam, 1791), p. 48.
163. *The Correspondence of the Revolution Society in London, with the National Assembly, and with Various Societies of the Friends of Liberty in France and England* (London: 1792), pp. 224–5.
164. Colley, *Britons*, p. 5.
165. *The Muses Banquet*, n.p.
166. Ibid., pp. 59–60.
167. British Library, Political Broadsides, shelfmark 648.c.26.(6) & 648.c.26.(7).
168. Black, *The Association*, p. 216.
169. F. K. Donnelly, 'The Foundation of the Sheffield Society for Constitutional Information', *Labour History Review*, 56:2 (1991), pp. 51–53; F. K. Donnelly and J. L. Baxter, 'Sheffield and the English Revolutionary Tradition', *International Review of Social History*, 20:3 (1975), pp. 398–423.
170. See Thomas Hardy's account of the formation of the LCS in M. Thale (ed.), *Selection from the Papers of the London Corresponding Society 1792–1799* (Cambridge: Cambridge University Press, 1983), pp. 5–9, on p. 7.
171. And they collected subscriptions for Paine's defence against the libel charge.
172. For the full text of the proclamation see *London Gazette*, 22 May 1792.
173. J. Graham, *The Nation, the Law and the King, Reform Politics in England 1789–1799*, 2 vols (New York: University Press of America, 2000), vol. 1, p. 342.
174. Goodwin, *Friends of Liberty*, p. 241.
175. Ibid., p. 240.
176. *St. Cecilia; or, the Lady's and Gentleman's Harmonious Companion* (Edinburgh: C. Wilson, 1779), pp. 14–15. This song became popular after it was sung by Mrs Abington in productions of *Twelfth Night* at Drury Lane during the 1770s. The music for this tune can be found in *Calliope: or the Musical Miscellany. A Select Collection of the Most Approved English, Scots, and Irish Songs, Set to Music* (London: C. Elliot and T. Kay, 1788).
177. See J. C. D. Clark, 'Chronological Table', in Burke, *Reflections on the Revolution in France*, p. 21.
178. C. Morris, *A Complete Collection of Songs, by Captain Morris*, 3rd edn (London: James Ridgeway, 1786), pp. 18–19.
179. Treasury Solicitor's Papers, National Archives, Kew, Surrey, 24/3/168 and 24/3/174 (hereafter TS). Thelwall's songs appear in TS 24/3/169. Michael Scrivener analyses these songs in the context of Jacobin allegory in Scrivener, 'John Thelwall and Popular Jacobin Allegory, 1793–95', pp. 951–71.
180. British Library, Additional manuscript, 16920, Letters from various writers, relating to the 'Association for Preserving Liberty and Property against Republicans and Levellers', vol. 2, folio 51.

4 Songs and Pikes in Sheffield: The Trial of James Montgomery.

1. Burney, *A General History of Music*, vol. 2, p. 239.
2. On the prison literature of this period see M. T. Davis, I. McCalman, and C. Parolin (eds), *Newgate in Revolution: An Anthology of Radical Prison Literature in the Age of Revolution* (London: Continuum, 2005). On John Thelwall's prison poems see J. Mee, 'The Dungeon and the Cell: The Prison Verse of Coleridge and Thelwall', in S. Poole (ed.),

John Thelwall: Radical Romantic and Acquitted Fellon (London: Pickering & Chatto, 2009), pp. 107–16.
3. Montgomery was imprisoned twice for seditious libel. This chapter will deal with his first imprisonment in 1795.
4. Enid C. Gilthorpe notes that Gales was involved in a range of activities, reflected on a billhead from 1791 where he describes himself as 'Printer, bookbinder, stationer, bookseller, music, map and printseller, vender of genuine medicines, auctioneer and appraiser and printer and proprietor of "The Sheffield Register"', see E. C. Gilthorpe, *Book Printing at Sheffield in the Eighteenth Century*, Sheffield City Libraries Local Studies Leaflet (Sheffield: City of Sheffield Printing Department, 1967), n.p. The engraver David Martin was co-owner of the *Register* with Gales.
5. J. Holland and J. Everett, *Memoirs of the Life and Writings of James Montgomery*, 7 vols (London: Longman, Brown, Green, and Longmans, 1854), vol. 1, p. 132.
6. D. Read, *Press and People, 1790–1850: Opinion in Three English Cities* (London: Edward Arnold Ltd, 1961), p. 68–9.
7. The first issue of the *Patriot* was dated 3 April 1792. Holland and Everett record that the first time Montgomery entered the printing-office of the *Register* the press was at work printing this title, see Holland and Everett, *Memoirs*, p. 159. The Sheffield Central Library contains the first volume of the *Patriot* with a note bound into the volume recording this.
8. The aim of dissemination is reflected in the full title, *The Patriot: or, Political, Moral, and Philosophical Repository, Consisting of Original Pieces, and Selections from Writers of Merit. A Work Calculated to Disseminate These Branches of Knowledge Among All Ranks of People, at a Small Expence. By a Society of Gentlemen*, vol. 1 (London: G. G. J. and J. Robinson, 1792), p. 9. The *Patriot* did not carry Gales's printer's imprint, but that of 'G. G. J. and J. Robinson' in London. George Robinson was known to be sympathetic to the radical movement, see G. E. Bentley Jr., 'Copyright Documents in the George Robinson Archive: William Godwin and Others 1713–1820', *Studies in Bibliography*, 35 (1982), pp. 67–110, on pp. 79–81.
9. The *Patriot*, p. 10.
10. M. Philp, 'Paine, Thomas (1737–1809)', *ODNB*, at http://www.oxforddnb.com/view/article/21133, [accessed 13 Aug 2012].
11. G. Claeys, *Thomas Paine: Social and Political Thought* (Boston: Unwin Hyman, 1989), p. xiii.
12. T. Paine, 'Rights of Man Part the Second Combining Principle and Practice (1792)', in Paine, *Thomas Paine,* pp. 263–326.
13. Ibid., p. 208.
14. Thompson, *The Making of the English Working Class*, p. 94.
15. See chapter 3, p. 113.
16. J. Stevenson, *Artisans and Democrats: Sheffield in the French Revolution, 1789–97* (Sheffield: Sheffield History Pamphlets, 1989), p. 10. Wentworth House was the home of Fitzwilliam. Charles Howard, the eleventh Duke of Norfolk (1746–1815), was the other main landowner.
17. Papers of William Wentworth-Fitzwilliam, 2nd Earl Fitzwilliam (1748–1833), Wentworth Woodhouse Muniments, Sheffield Archives, F 44/2 (hereafter WWM). (The signature of the correspondent has been effaced.)
18. WWM, F 44/7.
19. Graham, *The Nation, the Law and the King*, vol. 1, p. 16.

20. Ibid., p. 110.
21. Ibid., p.111.
22. W. H. G Armytage, 'The Editorial Experience of Joseph Gales', *North Carolina Historical Review*, 28 (1951), pp. 332–61; Donnelly, 'The Foundation of the SSCI', pp. 51–53.
23. Ibid., p. 51.
24. Ibid.
25. This letter was confiscated as part of the papers seized at Hardy's house upon his arrest in 1794.
26. TS 11/958/3503.
27. The speech was enclosed with the letter but was not present in the archives.
28. TS 11/958/3503.
29. J. Wilson (ed.), *The Songs of Joseph Mather to which are added a Memoir of Mather and Miscellaneous Songs relating to Sheffield* (Sheffield: Pawson and Brailsford, Printers High Street, 1862), pp. 35–6. Wilson notes that the antics of Russell of Dronfield were also reported in the *Sheffield Register*. He does not provide the tune for the song.
30. Ibid., p. 35.
31. Ibid., pp. 35–6.
32. C. Hobday, 'Two Sansculotte Poets: John Freeth and Joseph Mather', in J. Lucas (ed.), *Writing and Radicalism* (London and New York: Longman, 1996), pp. 61–84, on p. 80.
33. T. Paine, 'Letter Addressed to the Addressers On the Late Proclamation (1792)' in Paine, *Thomas Paine*, pp. 354–6.
34. J. Ritson, 'A Historical Essay on the Origin and Progress of National Song', p. lii.
35. J. Wilson, 'Memoir of Mather', in *Songs of Joseph Mather*, pp.vii–x, on pp. viii–x.
36. Wilson, 'Preface', in *Songs of Joseph Mather*, p. iii.
37. Thompson quotes from one of Mather's other well-known songs, 'The Jovial Cutlers', which describes the observance of 'Good Saint Monday' and a wife admonishing her husband Jack for leading a 'plaguy drunken life', see Thompson, *Customs in Common*, pp. 352–403, on p. 375.
38. P. C. Garlick, 'The Sheffield Cutlery and Allied Trades and their markets in the Eighteenth and Nineteenth Centuries' (Master of Arts Thesis, University of Sheffield, 1951), p. 15.
39. R. Leader, *Sheffield in the Eighteenth Century* (Sheffield: W. C. Leng & Co., 1905), p. 36; Goodwin, *Friends of Liberty*, p. 163.
40. Wilson, *Songs of Joseph Mather*, p. 63. This song was printed as a broadside, see Plate Two in M. Vicinus, *The Industrial Muse: A Study of Nineteenth Century British Working-Class Literature* (London: Croom Helm, 1974), pp. 192–3.
41. Wilson gives an account of overhearing the song as boy, which he relates in a note: 'I can never forget the impression made on my mind when a boy on hearing it sung by an old cutler. This event happened on a "good saint Monday" during a "foot ale" which was drank in the workshop'. Wilson, *Songs of Joseph Mather*, pp. 63–4.
42. A. L. Lloyd, *Folk Song in England* (London: Panther Arts, 1969), p. 394; G. Porter, *The English Occupational Song* (Umea: University of Umea, 1992), p. 15; Vicinus, *The Industrial Muse*, pp. 23–4; J. L. Baxter and D. E. Martin, 'Mather, Joseph (1737–1804) Radical Songwriter and Singer', in J. M. Bellamy and J. Saville (eds), *Dictionary of Labour Biography* (London: Macmillan Press, 1987), pp. 161–5.
43. Wilson, *Songs of Joseph Mather*, p. 35.
44. Ibid., pp. 35, 56.
45. TS 11/958/3503.

46. WWM, F 44/20. The signature on this letter is illegible.
47. WWM, F 44/20.
48. Wilson, *Songs of Joseph Mather*, pp. 56–7.
49. G. Russell, *The Theatres of War: Performance, Politics, and Society, 1793–1815* (Oxford: Clarendon Press, 1995), p. 11.
50. Home Office Papers, National Archives, Kew, Surrey, 42/20/386–95.
51. W. Gales, 'Reminiscences of our Residence in Sheffield', Gales Family Papers, p.47 #02652-z, Southern Historical Collection, Wilson Library, University of North Carolina at Chapel Hill. Hereafter abbreviated as GFP.
52. The memoir was written in two stages, beginning in 1815 and followed on in 1831 at which time she wrote of the meeting.
53. 'Lord Effingham' being Richard Howard, fourth Earl of Effingham (1748–1816), and MP for Steyning who resided at Thundercliffe Grange in Rotherham, six miles from Sheffield, see T. Langdale, *A Topographical Dictionary of Yorkshire*, 2nd edn (Northallerton: J. Langdale, 1822), p. 429. It is not stated why his 'land agent' was visiting Gales at this time.
54. Marcus Tullius Cicero was known as 'Tully' to English readers until the early nineteenth century.
55. GFP, pp. 42–5.
56. M. T. Davis, 'The Mob Club? The London Corresponding Society and the Politics of Civility in the 1790s', in M.T Davis and P. Pickering (eds), *Unrespectable Radicals?: Popular Politics in the Age of Reform* (Aldershot: Ashgate, 2008), pp. 21–40, on pp. 25–6.
57. Stevenson, *Artisans and Democrats*, p. v.
58. Ibid., p. 19; Graham, *The Nation, the Law and the King*, vol. 1, pp. 378–9.
59. The procession is described in detail in the *Manchester Herald*, 1 December 1792 which is reproduced in Stevenson, *Artisans and Democrats*, pp. 59–60.
60. Thompson, *Customs in Common*, p. 525–6.
61. F. O'Gorman, 'The Paine Burnings of 1792–1793', *Past and Present*, 193 (2006), pp. 111–55, on p. 122.
62. Ibid., pp. 121–2.
63. *Sheffield Register*, 4 January 1793.
64. *Sheffield Register*, 18 January 1793.
65. For Burke's speech see *PH*, vol. 27, col. 1213: 'Did they recollect that they were talking of a sick King, of a Monarch smitten by the hand of Omnipotence, and that the Almighty had hurled him from his throne, and plunged him into a condition which drew upon him the pity of the meanest peasant in his kingdom'.
66. Barrell, *Imagining the King's Death*, pp. 90–1.
67. N. K. Robinson, *Edmund Burke: A Life in Caricature* (New Haven: Yale University Press, 1996), pp. 39–40.
68. Burke wrote that 'Along with its natural protectors and guardians, learning will be cast into the mire, and trodden down under the hoofs of a swinish multitude', see Burke, *Reflections*, 2001 edn, p. 242.
69. James T. Boulton catalogues the play on this phrase in numerous radical publications, including Daniel Isaac Eaton's *Hog's Wash, or Salmagundy for Swine* (1793) and Thomas Spence's *One Pennyworth of Pig's Meat; or, Lessons for the Swinish Multitude* (1793–95) which also contained numerous political songs, see J. T. Boulton, *The Language of Politics in the Age of Wilkes and Burke* (London: Routledge & Kegan Paul, 1963), pp. 259–60.
70. Thompson, *Customs in Common*, p. 524.

71. Holland and Everett, *Memoirs*, vol. 1, p. 168.
72. GFP, p. 34.
73. Goodwin, *Friends of Liberty*, pp. 332–3.
74. Graham, *The Nation, The Law and the King*, vol. 2, p. 612.
75. Goodwin, *Friends of Liberty*, p. 334.
76. Montgomery wrote a letter dated 3 October 1848 to Robert Leader, printer of newspaper *The Independent*, to correct an account that had been printed of Gales fleeing 'half dressed' when the King's messengers had arrived to make arrests in 1794. Setting the record straight, Montgomery wrote: 'Mr Gales on the previous day had gone to Derby on some family affairs, without any personal apprehension for his safety at that time'. The letter is held at the Sheffield Archives at MD 2104–40. In their *Memoirs*, vol. 1, p. 171, Holland and Everett intimate that the 'family affairs' concerned a romantic entanglement between Gales's sister Sarah and Henry Redhead York, who had left Sheffield for Derby 'in an unsatisfactory manner, so far as his intentions towards the lady were concerned'. Gales then followed him to Derby.
77. Winifred Gales writes in her 'Reminiscences' that her husband was simply 'absent on a visit to Derby' and gives an account of the search of the home and printery, GFP, pp. 59–64.
78. TS 11/1071
79. TS 11/1071
80. For the Proclamation see *London Gazette*, 14–18 January 1794.
81. J. Wesley, *Hymns for Times of Trouble and Persecution* (1744), pp. 25–6, on p. 26.
82. *Abstract of the Form of Prayer, to Be used in all Churches & Chapels throughout England, On Friday the 28th Day of February, 1794 Being the Day Appointed for a General Fast* (Sheffield: J. Northall, 1794).
83. *Sheffield Register*, 7 March 1794.
84. For its publication in the *Cambridge Intelligencer* see J. J. McGann's notes in *The New Oxford Book of Romantic Period Verse* (Oxford: Oxford University Press, 1993), p. 791. For the LCS publication see 'Fast Day as Observed at Sheffield (1794)', in M. T. Davis (ed.), *London Corresponding Society, 1792–1799*, advisory eds J. Epstein, J. Fruchtman and M. Thale, 6 vols (London: Pickering & Chatto, 2002), vol. 1, pp. 257–71. The publication is also referred to in meetings of the LCS, see Thale, *Selections from the Papers of the LCS*, pp. 123, 126.
85. McGann, *The New Oxford Book of Romantic Period Verse*, p. 114; Bennett, *British War Poetry in the Age of Romanticism*, p. 111.
86. Goodwin, *Friends of Liberty*, p. 325.
87. *Proceedings of the Public Meeting Held at Sheffield, in the Open Air, on the Seventh of April, 1794; and Also An Address to the British Nation, Being An Exposition of the Motives which have, Determined The People of Sheffield to Petition the House of Commons No More On the Subject of Parliamentary Reform* (Sheffield: Printed for the Sheffield Constitutional Society, 1794).
88. GFP, p. 38. On Yorke see Y. Amnon, 'Between Heroism and Acquittal: Henry Redhead Yorke and the Inherent Instability of Political Trials in Britain during the 1790s', *Journal of British Studies*, 50:3 (2011), pp. 612–38.
89. Thale, *Selections from the Papers of the LCS*, p. 101. The government spy, Groves, reported that 'the crowds that packed there were inconceivable & beyond all my ideas', p. 136.
90. Privy Council Papers, National Archives, Kew, Surrey, 1/21/35b (hereafter PC).

91. PC 1/21/35b. Broomhead describes being in Gales's shop after he had printed the speech Yorke had delivered on Castle Hill where he was given 'fifty or sixty' pamphlets with directions to send them to Daniel Adams, Secretary of the Constitutional Society in London and Thomas Hardy.
92. *PH*, vol. 30, col. 775.
93. Ibid. cols 779–86. The petition was rejected with 108 noes to 29 yeas. Olivia Smith discusses petitioning in Smith, *The Politics of Language*, pp. 31–4.
94. Resolutions on the question of the other two matters were passed: to petition the King for the emancipation of the Negro Slaves; and to address the King on behalf of the Scottish prisoners.
95. *Proceedings of the Public Meeting Held at Sheffield ... on the Seventh of April, 1794*, p. 11.
96. Ibid.
97. Ibid., p. 12.
98. Ibid., pp. 12–13.
99. Ibid., pp. 14–15.
100. Barrell, *Imagining the King's Death*, p. 188.
101. *Proceedings of the Public Meeting Held at Sheffield ... on the Seventh of April, 1794*, p. 36.
102. Ibid., p. 10.
103. *Trial of William Skirving, Secretary to the British Convention, Before the High Court of Justiciary, on the 6th and 7th of January 1794; for Sedition* (Edinburgh: William Skirving, 1794); *The Trial of Maurice Margarot, before the High Court of Justiciary, at Edinburgh, on the 13th and 14th of January, 1794, on an indictment for Seditious Practices* (London: M. Margarot, 1794); *The Trial of Joseph Gerrald, Delegate from the London Corresponding Society, to the Edinburgh Convention, before the High Court of Justiciary, at Edinburgh. on the 3rd, 10th, 13th, and 14th of March 1794. For Sedition* (Edinburgh: James Robertson, 1794).
104. The Scottish Friends of the People held a second convention in April and May of 1793 and a third convention on 19 October 1793 at which it was decided that a *British* convention would be held. This was the last convention which began on 19 November 1793. See G. Pentland, 'Patriotism, Universalism and the Scottish Conventions, 1792–1794', *History*, 89:295 (2004), pp. 340–60 and K. R. Johnston, 'The First and Last British Convention', *Romanticism*, 13:2 (2007), pp. 99–132.
105. Goodwin, *Friends of Liberty*, pp. 298–304; Graham, *The Nation, The Law and the King*, vol. 2, pp. 559–67; Pentland, 'Patriotism, Universalism and the Scottish Conventions, 1792–1794', pp. 341–2.
106. See chapters four and nine of Barrell, *Imagining the King's Death*.
107. C. Bewley, *Muir of Huntershill* (Oxford: Oxford University Press, 1981), pp. 8, 30–4.
108. An account of the trial of Thomas Muir Esq. Younger, of Huntershill, before the High Court of Justiciary, at Edinburgh on the 30 and 31 days of August, 1793, for sedition ([Edinburgh, 1793]), pp. 5–20.
109. M. Elliott, *Partners in Revolution The United Irishmen and France* (New Haven: Yale University Press, 1982), pp. 22–3; N. J. Curtin, *The United Irishmen: Popular Politics in Ulster and Dublin* (Oxford: Clarendon Press, 1994), pp. 43–5.
110. T. W. Tone, 'Declaration and Resolutions of the Society of United Irishmen', in J. Killen (ed.), *The Decade of the United Irishmen: Contemporary Accounts 1791–1801* (Belfast: Blackstaff Press, 1997), pp. 20–1.
111. K. Whelan, *The Tree of Liberty: Radicalism, Catholicism and the Construction of Irish Identity 1760–1830* (Notre Dame: University of Notre Dame Press, 1995), p. 100.

112. The address is printed in full in Appendix 2 in E. W. McFarland, *Ireland and Scotland in the Age of Revolution* (Edinburgh: Edinburgh University Press, 1994), pp. 248–52.
113. N. Leask, 'Thomas Muir and The Telegraph: Radical Cosmopolitanism in 1790s Scotland', *History Workshop Journal*, 63:1 (2007), pp. 48–69.
114. *The Trial of Thomas Muir*, 2nd edn (Edinburgh: printed by Alexander Scott, c. 1793), p. 50.
115. Leask, 'Thomas Muir', p. 57.
116. *The Trial of Thomas Muir*, p. 46
117. Ibid., pp. 116–17
118. The pantomime was written by Robert Merry. For further analysis see J. Mee, '*The Magician No Conjurer*: Robert Merry and the Political Alchemy of the 1790s', in Davis and Pickering (eds), *Unrespectable Radicals*, pp. 41–55.
119. H. M. Williams, *Letters Written in France, in the Summer 1790, to a Friend in England*, 2nd edn (London: T. Cadell, 1791), p. 91.
120. See Introduction, p. 1.
121. British Library Additional Manuscript 16920, Letters from various writers, relating to the 'Association for Preserving Liberty and Property against Republicans and Levellers', vol. 2, f. 99.
122. Russell, *Theatres of War*, p. 109.
123. R. Thompson, *A Tribute to Liberty. Or, New Collection. of Patriotic Songs; Entirely Original* (London: 1793), pp. 79–80.
124. Leask, 'Thomas Muir', p. 55.
125. Bewley, *Muir of Huntershill*, p. 70.
126. On increasing levels of surveillance see the case of John Frost in J. Epstein, '"Equality and No King": Sociability and Sedition: The Case of John Frost', in Russell and Tuite, *Romantic Sociability*, pp. 43–61 and J. Barrell, *The Spirit of Despotism Invasions of Privacy in the 1790s* (Oxford: Oxford University Press, 2006).
127. *The Trial of Thomas Muir*, p. 116–7.
128. Ibid., p. 70.
129. Mary Thuente reports that *The Lion* was serialized from 4 September through to 26 December 1793 in the *Northern Star*, and was published as a pamphlet in two editions, the second with additions, in 1794 under the title *Review of The Lion of Old England*, see M. Thuente, 'William Sampson: United Irish Satirist and Songwriter', *Eighteenth Century Life*, 22:3 (1998), pp. 19–30, on p. 30. The *Trial of Hurdy Gurdy* was serialized in the *Northern Star* beginning 31 July 1794 with the second installment on 4 August and the final on 11 August. It was republished in Belfast and Dublin as a pamphlet in 1794, and in New York in 1806 and 1807 see M. Thuente, '"The Belfast Laugh": the Context and Significance of United Irish Satires', in J. Smyth (ed.), *Revolution, Counter-Revolution and Union: Ireland in the 1790s* (Cambridge: Cambridge University Press, 2000), pp. 67–83.
130. *Review of the Lion of Old England; or the Democracy Confounded as it Appeared from Time to Time in A Periodical Print*, 2nd edn (Belfast 1794), p. 6–7. J. Ralfe, 'Historical Memoirs of Admiral Lord Gardner', in *The Naval Biography of Great Britain*, 4 vols (London: Whitmore & Fenn, 1828), vol. 1, pp. 407–12, on p. 411.
131. *Review of the Lion of Old England*, p. 7.
132. Ibid., p. 9
133. Ibid.
134. Ibid., p. 10.

135. Ibid., p. 30.
136. Burke, *Reflections*, 2001 edn, p. 238.
137. *Review of the Lion of Old England*, p. 46.
138. Ibid., pp. 39–40.
139. Ibid.p. 40.
140. Ibid., p. 41.
141. T. J. Howell (ed.), *A Complete Collection of State Trials and Proceedings for High Treason and Other Crimes and Misdemeanors*, 33 vols (London: Longman, Hurst, Rees, Orme and Brown, 1817), vol. 28, col. 234. Hereafter *ST.*
142. *Report of the Trial of the King versus Hurdy Gurdy, alias Barrel Organ, alias Grinder, alias the Seditious Organ* (Dublin 1794). Thuente notes that the text also consciously parodies the trials for seditious libel of the proprietors of the *Northern Star* in May 1794 and the United Irishmen leader Dr William Drennan in June 1794. Sampson had acted as a junior counsel in the *Northern Star* trial and when he published the pamphlet in full later that year, it carried the same date as the May trial, see Thuente, 'William Sampson', p. 24.
143. *Report of the Trial of the King versus Hurdy Gurdy*.
144. [J. Ritson], 'Dissertation on the Songs, Music, and Vocal and Instrumental Performance of the Ancient English', in *Ancient Songs from the Time of King Henry the Third, to the Revolution* (London: J. Johnson, 1790), pp. xxvii–lxxvi, on p. xlii.
145. *The Trial of Thomas Muir*, p. 81; *ST*, vol. 28, col. 229.
146. *A Faithful Report of the Trial of Hurdy Gurdy, at the Bar of the Court of King's Bench, Westminster on the — , of — , 1794 on an Information, filed ex-officio, by the Attorney General* (Belfast: Printed by John Rabb, 1794), p. 4.
147. *The Trial of Thomas Muir*, pp. 5–20; *ST*, vol. 28, cols 119–126.
148. *The Trial of Thomas Muir*, pp. 125–8; *ST*, vol. 28, cols 224–6.
149. *A Faithful Report of the Trial of Hurdy Gurdy*, p. 3; *Report of the Trial of the King Versus Hurdy Gurdy*, p. 5–6.
150. *A Faithful Report of the Trial of Hurdy Gurdy*, pp. 13–15.
151. Ibid., p. 34.
152. On Fox's libel act see M. Lobban, 'From Seditious Libel to Unlawful Assembly: Peterloo and the Changing Face of Political Crime c.1770–1820', *Oxford Journal of Legal Studies* 10:3 (1990), pp. 307–52; J. Mee, '"Examples of Safe Printing" : Censorship and Popular Radical Literature in the 1790s' in N. Smith (ed.), *Essays and Studies Collected on Behalf of the English Association* (Cambridge: D. S. Brewer, 1993), pp. 81–96; Barrell and Mee, 'Introduction', in *TTS*, pp. ix–xli, on pp. xiii–xviii.
153. Lobban, 'From Seditious Libel to Unlawful Assembly', p. 321. Jon Mee's article on 'safe printing' also highlighted the ways in which the act was used to the advantage of reformers of trial, Mee, '"Examples of Safe Printing"', pp. 81–96.
154. *A Faithful Report of the Trial of Hurdy Gurdy*, p. 28–9.
155. Ibid., p. 37.
156. Ibid., p. 41.
157. *Review of the Lion of Old England*, p. 72.
158. p. 147, n. 84.
159. *TTS*, vol. 3, p. 186.
160. PC 1-21-35b; PC 1-22-36A.
161. *TTS*, vol. 3, pp. 146–87.
162. Ibid., p. 164.
163. Ibid., p. 178.

164. Ibid., p. 209. Under cross-examination by Vicary Gibbs, Broomhead stated that 'It [the handbill] was given out, by various people in the town of Sheffield, we can never do any thing against these people, against the society [the SSCI], till we ourselves cause a riot'.
165. *TTS*, vol. 3, pp. 144–5.
166. Ibid., p. 153.
167. M. Durey, *Transatlantic Radicals and the Early American Republic* (Lawrence: University Press of Kansas, 1997), p. 137. Durey notes that Gales re-employed Davison in Philadelphia and helped him establish a newspaper in Warrenton, North Carolina.
168. GFP, p. 58.
169. In addition to the pikes, the prosecution also put a line of questioning to Camage and Broomhead about a weapon known as the 'night cat', which was a spike designed to be thrown down on the ground to injure the cavalry. Both men admitted to seeing the instrument, but only as a model. Camage maintained that none were made for the Society and Broomhead testified that the instrument was shown to him as 'a toy' and discussed laughingly. For Camage's testimony on the night-cat see *TTS*, vol. 3, pp. 158–9, 166–7; for Broomhead's see Ibid., pp. 179–81.
170. Ibid., p. 178, 210.
171. *Sheffield Register*, 9 May 1794. 'Sheffield Constitutional Society. Committee Room May 6 1794. At a Special Meeting of the Committee of the above Society held this Day it Sat. Resolved, 1. That War of every Kind, but particularly Civil war, is the greatest calamity which can befall a Nation. 2. That a number of Inhabitants of this Town having agreed to arm and accouter themselves, for the Purpose of "augmenting the internal strength of the Country, to co-operate with the Civil Magistrate in enforcing Obedience to the Laws, in apprehending all disturbers of the public Peace; and at his Requisition in preventing or suppressing all riotous, disorderly and unlawful Meetings and Assemblies", not wishing to be behind hand with any of our townsmen in our Exertions in the cause of our common Country, and in our efforts to preserve the Peace and Order of our Town, we also recommend to every Member of this society to be prepared to defend himself'.
172. *TTS*, vol. 2, p. 370.
173. Thale, *Selections from the Papers of the LCS*, pp. 106–8. Copies of the songs appear in TS 24/3/172.
174. *TTS*, vol. 2, p. 370.
175. Ibid., pp. 371–3.
176. Ibid., p. 402.
177. A. Wharam, *The Treason Trials, 1794* (Leicester University Press: Leicester, 1992), p. 153.
178. Ibid., p. 154.
179. *TTS*, vol. 3, pp. 371–2.
180. Ibid., vol. 4, p. 10. This song was referred to in the introduction.
181. Ibid., vol. 3, pp. 398–403. The song which Grove could not recall the name of is most likely that held in TS 24/3/171. This is a slip song without a title as such, being simply introduced as 'Song, sung at the Anniversary of The Society for Constitutional Information, held at the Crown-and-Anchor Tavern, London; May 2, 1794. The Words and music composed By a Citizen Visitor'. On the back of the song is a note by William Ross, 'Found the inclosed printed songs &c &c in Jeremiah Joyce's House this 14 Day of May 1794'. Jeremiah Joyce was a Unitarian minister and member of the SCI who was arrested on 4 May and charged with High Treason on 6 October 1794.
182. *TTS*, vol. 3, p. 401.

183. Ibid., p. 403.
184. Ibid.
185. Ibid., vol. 4, p. 303.
186. Ibid.
187. Ibid.
188. Ibid.
189. John Barrell and Jon Mee note that Vaughan was a 'key player' in the radical movment in London. He had written a bill on behalf of the LCS criticizing John Reeves and his association which resulted in the prosecution of Carter the 'bill sticker', see their 'Introduction', in *TTS*, vol. 1, p. xxi.
190. Ibid., vol. 4, p. 303.
191. Ibid., p. 304. Lord Chief Justice Eyre confirmed that Gibbs was correct: 'I had really taken down the answer of the witness before any part of this conversation arose – "that he had never heard of any letter from Sheffield about pikes"', p. 305.
192. *TTS*, vol. 4, pp. 309–10.
193. Ibid., p. 310.
194. Ibid., p. 311.
195. Ibid.
196. Ibid.
197. Ibid., p. 312.
198. Ibid.
199. Ibid., vol. 8.
200. Scrivener, 'John Thelwall and Popular Jacobin Allegory, 1793–95', pp. 951–71, on p. 956.
201. Scrivener, 'John Thelwall and Popular Jacobin Allegory', p. 951. See Volume One of *The Tribune, A Periodical Publication, Consisting Chiefly of the Political Lectures of J. Thelwall*, 3 vols (London 1795), vol. 1, pp. 165–7, 190–2 and 338–40.
202. Sheffield Literary and Philosophical Society, Correspondence of James Montgomery (hereafter SLPS), 37 (1)–3. See also Holland and Everett, *Memoirs*, vol. 1, p. 198.
203. Ibid., pp. 187–8. Holland and Everett quoted the last five stanzas of this hymn.
204. The first issue of the *Iris* appeared on 4 July 1794. See also P. Isaac and T. Schmoller, 'Letters from a Newspaperman in Prison', *The Library*, 4:2 (2003), pp. 150–167.
205. PC 1/22/37.
206. *TTS*, vol. 2, p. 99. On Vaughan's involvement see Goodwin, *Friends of Liberty* pp. 195–6. He also acted as the defence counsel in the seditious libel trial of Daniel Isaac Eaton for publishing the second part of *Rights of Man*, and with Erskine at the trial of Thomas Walker of Manchester in 1794. He acted as assistant counsel for John Horne Tooke's treason trial and was listed as the defence counsel for Jeremiah Joyce's treason trial, which was abandoned following the acquittals. See *TTS*, vol. 1 for Eaton's trial, and vol. 8 for Joyce's 'arrest for treasonable practices'.
207. *The Trial of James Montgomery for a Libel on the War, By Reprinting and Republishing a Song Printed and Published long before the War begun; at Doncaster Sessions, January 22, 1795* (Sheffield: James Montgomery, 1795), p. 5.
208. Ibid., p. 3.
209. Ibid., p. 10.
210. Ibid.
211. Ibid., p. 11.
212. Ibid.

213. Ibid.
214. H. Mayhew, *London Labour and the London Poor; A Cyclopaedia of the Condition and Earnings of Those That Will Work, Those That Cannot Work, and Those That Will Not Work*, 4 vols (1861–2; New York: Dover Publications, 1968), vol. 1, p. 239.
215. *Trial of James Montgomery*, p. 12.
216. Ibid., pp. 17–24.
217. Ibid., pp. 24–5.
218. Ibid., pp. 25–6.
219. Ibid., pp. 27–8. The passage by Young that Vaughan referred to was: 'Is an unforeseen union of two or three great powers to protrude through Europe a predominancy dangerous to all. Gentlemen which indulge their wishes for a counter-revolution in France do not, perhaps, wish to see the Prussian colours at the Tower not the Austrian at Amsterdam'. See A. Young, *Travels During the Years 1787, 1788 and 1789, Undertaken More Particularly with a View of Ascertaining the Cultivation, Wealth, Resources, and National Prosperity, of the Kingdome of France*, 2 vols (Dublin: Messrs. R.Cross et al, 1793), vol, 2, p. 571.
220. *Trial of James Montgomery*, p. 28.
221. A. Young, *Travels During the Years 1787, 1788, & 1789, Undertaken More Particularly with a View of Ascertaining the Cultivation, Wealth, Resources, and National Prosperity of the Kingdom of France*, 2nd edn, 2 vols (London: W. Richardson, 1794), vol. 1.
222. A. Young, *The Example of France, A Warning to Britain* (London: W. Richardson, 1793), p. 39.
223. M. Butler, 'Arthur Young', in Butler, *Burke, Paine, Godwin*, pp. 96–106, on p. 102.
224. *Sheffield Register*, 3 August 1792.
225. *Songs on the French Revolution that Took Place at Paris, 14th July, 1789; Sung at the Celebration thereof at Belfast on Saturday 14th July, 1792* (Belfast, 1792).
226. T. Dibdin (ed.), *Songs, Naval and National, of the Late Charles Dibdin* (London: John Murray, 1844), pp. 1–2.
227. T. Dibdin, 'Memoir of Charles Dibdin', in T. Dibdin (ed.), *Songs, Naval and National* (London: John Murray, 1844), pp. ix–xv, on p. xii.
228. M. Thuente, *The Harp Re-strung. The United Irishmen and the Rise of Literary Nationalism* (Syracuse, NY: Syracuse University Press, 1994), p. 126. The song appears under the title 'The World will be Free' in *Paddy's Resource: Being A Select Collection of Original and Modern Patriotic Songs, Toasts and Sentiments, Compiled for the use of the People of Ireland* (Belfast, 1795), pp. 86–7. Two other songs in *Paddy's Resource* to the tune of 'Poor Jack' are 'The Progress of Reason', on p. 24, and 'Freedom's the Work', on pp. 70–1.
229. *Sheffield Register*, August 3 1792.
230. *Trial of James Montgomery*, p. 24. William Sampson had facetiously dedicated the *Lion of Old England* to Catherine II – 'Most Mighty and Most Terrible Czarina'.
231. Thuente, *The Harp Re-strung*, p. 126.
232. *Trial of James Montgomery*, p. 34.
233. Ibid., p. 36.
234. Mee, 'Safe Printing', p. 84.
235. *Trial of James Montgomery*, p. 37.
236. Ibid., p. 37.
237. *A Choice Collection of Civic Songs Part 1* (London, 1795), p. 42.
238. Ibid., p. 42.
239. Holland and Everett, *Memoirs*, vol. 1, p. 206.

240. T. Dunne, 'Popular Ballads, Revolutionary Rhetoric and Politicisation', in H. Gough and D. Dickson (eds), *Ireland and the French Revolution* (Dublin: Irish Academic Press, 1990), pp. 139–55, on p. 145.
241. Scrivener, *Poetry and Reform Periodical Verse from the English Democratic Press 1792–1824*, pp. 50–1.
242. *Trial of James Montgomery*, p. 44.
243. [J. Montgomery], *Prison Amusements* (London: J. Johnson, 1797). Tragically, Felix Vaughan died at the young age of 33 in 1799.
244. J. Montgomery, 'Introduction to Prison Amusements', in *The Poetical Works of James Montgomery. With A Memoir of the Author*, 5 vols (Boston: Little, Brown and Company, 1860), vol. 1, pp. 237–66, on p. 239.
245. *Sheffield Register*, 7 February 1794.
246. Thuente, *The Harp Re-strung*, p. 103; *Paddy's Resource*, pp. 45–6.
247. Montgomery, 'Introduction to Prison Amusements', p. 254.
248. Ibid., p. 255. By January 1794, the Duke of Portland, formerly a Whig, had completely separated from Fox and his former political allies, accepting a position in Pitt's ministry as Home Secretary.
249. Montgomery, 'Introduction to Prison Amusements', vol. 1, p. 255.
250. Ibid., pp. 255–6.
251. Holland and Everett, *Memoirs*, vol. 1. p. 212.
252. The manuscripts of these draft conversations are part of the archives of the Sheffield Literary and Philosophical society, held in the Sheffield archives.
253. Drafts of Holland and Everett, *Memoirs*, SLPS 47 / (see folder labelled '1794 88–91')
254. *The Trial of Henry Yorke, for a Conspiracy, &c. Before the Hon. Mr. Justice Rooke, at the Assizes Held for the County of York on Saturday July 10* (1795).
255. H. T. Blethen, 'Henry Redhead Yorke', in J.O. Baylen and N. J. Grossman (eds), *Biographical Dictionary of Modern British Radicals* (Sussex: Harvester Press, 1979), pp. 561–62. For a recent reading of Yorke's trial see Amnon, 'Between Heroism and Acquittal', pp. 612–38.
256. GFP, p. 79. Yorke was actually sentenced to two years' jail rather than four, Amnon, 'Between Heroism and Acquittal', p. 635.
257. SLPS 36 – 988.
258. Such was their attachment that Montgomery and the Gales sisters resided together in the Hartshead for 40 years. In 1836 he moved from the Hartshead to 'the Mount' with Joseph Gales's only sister then living, see Holland and Everett, *Memoirs*, vol. 1V, p. 169.
259. Ibid., vol. 1, pp. 181–2; emphasis added.
260. In 1803 at the height of fears of French invasion, Montgomery wrote his 'Ode to the Volunteers', a deeply patriotic work, see Holland and Everett, *Memoirs*, vol. 2, p. 36.
261. For a study of Montgomery's life and a bibliography of his enormous literary output see H. F. Beutner, 'With Fraternal Feeling Fired: The Life and Work of James Montgomery' (PhD. Dissertation, Northwestern University, 1967).
262. J. Montgomery, *The Christian Psalmist; or Hymns, Selected and Original*, 3rd ed. (Glasgow: William Collins, 1826). *The Christian Psalmist* includes 'Angels from the Realms of Glory' which was set to music and became a popular Christmas carol, see p. 401.
263. T. Cotterill, *A Selection of Psalms and Hymns, for Public and Private Use, Adapted to the Festivals of the Church of England*, 8th edn (Sheffield: J. Montgomery, 1819). See Holland and Everett, *Memoirs,* vol. 3, pp. 158–60 for Montgomery's account of Cotterill and the case. Thomas McCart notes that Montgomery edited Cotterill's collection and

attributes the success of the work to his abilities, see McCart, *Matter and Manner of Praise,* p. 94.
264. SLPS 45–23.

Afterword

1. Hales and Furnivall, 'The Revival of Ballad Poetry in the Eighteenth Century', pp. v–xxxi, on p. xxix.
2. Friedman, *The Ballad Revival,* p. 86.
3. Fulcher, 'Introduction: Defining the New Cultural History of Music, Its Origins, Methodologies, and Lines of Inquiry', p. 9; Fumerton and Guerrini, 'Introduction: Straws in the Wind', p. 4.

WORKS CITED

Abstract of the Form of Prayer, to Be Used in All Churches & Chapels Throughout England, On Friday the 28th Day of February, 1794 Being the Day Appointed for a General Fast, (Sheffield: J. Northall, 1794).

An Abstract of the History and Proceedings of the Revolution Society, in London to Which Is Annexed a Copy of the Bill of Rights, (London: Printed by Order of the Committee, 1789).

An Account of the Trial of Thomas Muir Esq. Younger, of Huntershill, before the High Court of Justiciary, at Edinburgh on the 30th and 31st days of August, 1793, for sedition ([Edinburgh, 1793]).

An Address to the Public from the Society for Constitutional Information (London, c. 1780).

Addison, J. *The Spectator*, ed. D. Bond, 5 vols (Oxford: Clarendon Press).

Aeschines, *The Speeches of Aeschines*, trans. C. D. Adams (London: William Heinemann, 1919), pp. 305–511.

Agnew, V. *Enlightenment Orpheus: The Power of Music in Other Worlds* (Oxford: Oxford University Press, 2008).

Aldridge, D. D. 'Russell, Edward', *ODNB*, at www.oxforddnb.com/view/article/24304 [accessed 4 Aug 2012].

Amnon, Y. 'Between Heroism and Acquittal: Henry Redhead Yorke and the Inherent Instability of Political Trials in Britain during the 1790s', *Journal of British Studies*, 50:3 (2011), pp. 612–38.

Arber, E. (ed.), *A Transcript of the Registers of the Company of Stationers 1554–1640*, 5 vols (1876; New York: Peter Smith, 1950).

Argus

Armytage, W. H. G. 'The Editorial Experience of Joseph Gales', *North Carolina Historical Review*, 28 (1951), pp. 332–61.

Arnold, R. *The English Hymn: Studies in a Genre* (New York: Peter Lang, 1995).

Arnold, W. *The Life and Death of the Sublime Society of Beef Steaks* (London: Bradbury, Evans, & Co., 1871).

Aspinall, A., *Politics and the Press c. 1780–1850* (London: Hame & Van Thal Ltd, 1949).

Athenaeus, *The Deipnosophists*, trans. C. B. Gulick, 7 vols (London: William Heinemann, 1941).

—, *The Learned Banqueters*, trans. and ed. S. Douglas Olson, 8 vols (Cambridge, MA: Harvard University Press, 2006–12).

Bailey, N., *An Universal Etymological English Dictionary Comprehending the Derivations of the Generality of Words in the English Tongue Either Ancient or Modern*, 25th edn (London: J. Murray, 1783).

Barker, A. (ed.), *Greek Musical Writings*, 2 vols (Cambridge: Cambridge University Press, 1984).

The Banquet of Thalia, or the Fashionable Songsters Pocket Memorial, an Elegant Collection, of the Most Admired Songs from Ancient, & Modern Authors (London, 1788).

Barrell, J., *Imagining the King's Death: Figurative Treason, Fantasies of Regicide 1793–1796* (Oxford: Oxford University Press, 2000).

—, *The Spirit of Despotism Invasions of Privacy in the 1790s* (Oxford: Oxford University Press, 2006).

— and J. Mee (eds), *Trials for Treason and Sedition 1792–1794*, 8 vols (London: Pickering & Chatto, 2006).

Bartlett, T., 'The Life and Opinions of Leonard MacNally (1752–1820): Playwright, Barrister, United Irishman, and Informer', in H. Morgan (ed.), *Information, Media and Power Through the Ages* (Dublin: University College Dublin Press, 2001), pp. 113–36.

— (ed.), *Revolutionary Dublin, 1795–1801: The Letters of Francis Higgins to Dublin Castle* (Dublin: Four Courts Press, 2004).

Baxter, J. L. and D. E. Martin, 'Mather, Joseph (1737–1804) Radical Songwriter and Singer', in J. M. Bellamy and J. Saville (eds), *Dictionary of Labour Biography* (London: Macmillan Press, 1987), pp. 161–5.

Beal, J., 'Why Should the Landlords have the Best Songs? Thomas Spence and the Subversion of Popular Song', in J. Kirk, A. Noble and M. Brown (eds), *United Islands? The Languages of Resistance* (London: Pickering & Chatto, 2012), pp. 51–62.

Bedford, A., *The Great Abuse of Musick* (London: John Wyatt, 1711).

Bell, J., *Bell's New Pantheon; or, Historical Dictionary of the Gods, Demi-Gods, Heroes, and Fabulous Personages of Antiquity*, 2 vols (London: John Bell, 1790).

Bennett, B. T., *British War Poetry in the Age of Romanticism 1793–1815* (New York: Garland, 1976).

Benson, L. F., *The English Hymn: Its Development and Use in Worship* (London: G. H. Doran, 1915).

Bentley Jr., G. E., 'Copyright Documents in the George Robinson Archive: William Godwin and Others 1713–1820', *Studies in Bibliography*, 35 (1982), pp. 67–110.

Beutner, H. F., 'With Fraternal Feeling Fired the Life and Work of James Montgomery', (PhD dissertation, Northwestern University, 1967).

Beveridge, W., 'A Defence of the Book of Psalms, Collected into English Metre, By Thomas Sternhold, John Hopkins, and Others. With critical observations on the late new version, compared with the old', in *The Theological Works of William Beveridge, D.D.*, 12 vols (Oxford: John Henry Parker, 1842–8), pp. 613–54.

Bewley, C., *Muir of Huntershill* (Oxford: Oxford University Press, 1981).

Black, E. C., *The Association: British Extraparliamentary Political Organization 1769–1793* (Cambridge, MA: Harvard University Press, 1963).

Blackstone, W., *Commentaries on the Laws of England. Book the Fourth*, 4 vols (Oxford: The Clarendon Press, 1769).

Blagden, C., 'Notes on the Ballad Market in the Second Half of the Seventeenth Century', *Studies in Bibliography*, 6 (1954), pp. 161–180.

—, *The Stationers' Company: A History, 1403–1959* (New York: Hillary House Publishers, 1960).

Blair, H., 'Lecture XXVII Different Kinds of Public Speaking – Eloquence of Popular Assemblies – Extracts from Demosthenes' in *Lectures on Rhetoric and Belles Lettres* (Dublin: Whitestone et al., 1783), pp. 221–55.

Blakey, R., *The History of Political Literature from the Earliest Times*, 2 vols (London: Richard Bentley, 1855).

Blethen, H. T., 'Henry Redhead Yorke', in J. O. Baylen and N. J. Gossman (eds), *Biographical Dictionary of Modern British Radicals* (Sussex: Harvester Press, 1979), pp. 561–2.

Bond, D. F. (ed.) *The Spectator*, 5 vols (Oxford: Oxford Clarendon Press, 1965).

The Book of Common Prayer, and Administration of the Sacraments, and Other Rites and Ceremonies of the Church According the Use of the Church of England: Together with the Psalter or Psalms of David Pointed as They Are to Be Sung or Said in Churches (Cambridge: John Archdeacon, Printer to the University, 1789).

Boulton, J. T., *The Language of Politics in the Age of Wilkes and Burke* (London: Routledge & Kegan Paul, 1963).

Bowden, H., *Classical Athens and the Delphic Oracle* (Cambridge: Cambridge University Press, 2005).

Brink, C. O., *Horace on Poetry*, 3 vols (Cambridge: Cambridge University Press, 1982).

Brooks, C. (ed.), *The Correspondence of Thomas Percy & Richard Farmer* (Louisiana: Louisiana State University Press, 1946).

—, *The Correspondence of Thomas Percy and William Shenstone* (New Haven, CT: Yale University Press, 1977).

Bronson, B. H., 'The Interdependence of Ballad Tunes and Texts', in *The Ballad as Song* (Berkeley: University of California Press, 1969), pp. 37–63.

Broughton, B. B., *The Legends of King Richard I Coeur De Lion* (The Hague: Mouton & Co., 1966).

The Bull-Finch: Being a Choice Collection of the Newest and Most Favourite English Songs Which Have Been Sung at the Public Theatres & Gardens (London: G. Robinsons, R. Baldwin and G & J Wilkie, c. 1781).

Burgh, J., *Political Disquisitions*, 3 vols (London: E. and C. Dilly, 1774).

—, *The Art of Speaking*, 7th edn (London: T. Longman and J. Buckland et al., 1787).

[Burgoyne, J.] *Richard Coeur De Lion. An Historical Romance. From the French of Monsr. Sedaine. As Performed at the Theatre-Royal, Drury-Lane* (London: J. Debrett, 1786).

Burke, E., 'An Appeal from the New to the Old Whigs (1791)', in *The Works of Edmund Burke*, 8 vols (London: George Bell, 1901), vol. 3, pp. 1–115.

—, *Reflections on the Revolution in France* (1790), ed. C. C. O'Brien (Harmondsworth: Penguin Books, 1968).

—, *Reflections on the Revolution in France* (1790), ed. J. C. D. Clark (Stanford, CA: Stanford University Press, 2001).

Burke, P., *Popular Culture in Early Modern Europe*, 3rd edn (Farnham: Ashgate, 2009).

Burn, R., *The Justice of the Peace, and Parish Officer*, 2nd edn, 2 vols (The Strand: A. Millar, 1756).

Burney, C., *A General History of Music from the Earliest Ages to the Present Period*, 4 vols (London: Printed for the author, 1776).

—, 'The History of Greek Music', in C. Burney, *A General History of Music from the Earliest Ages to the Present Period*, 2nd edn, 4 vols (London: Printed for the author, 1789), vol. 1, pp. 258–301

—, 'Of the Scolia, or Songs, of the Ancient Greeks', in *A General History of Music*, 2nd edn, vol. 1, pp. 453–61, on p. 455.

The Busy Bee, or, Vocal Repository. Being a Selection of Most Favourite Songs, &c. Contained in the English Operas, That Have Been Sung at the Public Gardens, and Written for Select Societies; Together with an Extensive Collection of Hunting Songs, and a Variety of Scotch and Irish Ballads, III vols (London: J. S. Barr, 1790).

Butler, M., *Romantics, Rebels and Reactionaries English Literature and Its Backgrounds 1760–1830* (Oxford: Oxford University Press, 1981).

— (ed.), *Burke, Paine, Godwin, and the Revolution Controversy* (Cambridge: Cambridge University Press, 1984).

Calliope: or the Musical Miscellany. A Select Collection of the Most Approved English, Scots, and Irish Songs, Set to Music (London: C. Elliot and T. Kay, 1788).

Campbell, D. A. (ed. and trans.), *Greek Lyric*, 5 vols (Cambridge, MA: Harvard University Press, 1993).

Cannon, J., 'Petty [formerly Fitzmaurice], William, Second Earl of Shelburne and First Marquess of Lansdowne (1737–1805), Prime Minister', *ODNB*, at http://www.oxforddnb.com/index/22/101022070/, [accessed 12 Dec 2013].

— and A. Hargreaves, *The Kings & Queens of Britain* (Oxford: Oxford University Press, 2001).

Carey, H., 'Preface', in *Six Songs for Conversation: The Words by Divers Hands. The Tunes Contrived to Make Agreeable Little Lessons for the Harpsichrod, Viol, Violin, and Hautboy.*, 2 vols (London: 1728), vol. 2, n.p.

Carlson, M., *The Theatre of the French Revolution* (New York: Cornell University Press, 1966).

A Catalogue of Maps, Prints, Copy-Books, Drawing-Books, Histories, Old Ballads, Broad-Sheet and Other Patters, Garlands, &c. Printed and Sold by William and Cluer Dicey, at Their Warehouse, Opposite the South Door of Bow-Church in Bow-Church-Yard London (London: 1754).

Catalogue of Personal and Political Satires Preserved in the Department of Prints and Drawings in the British Museum, ed. M. D. George, 11 vols (London: The Trustees of the British Museum by British Museum Publications Limited, 1978).

Ceccarelli, P., 'Dance and Desserts: An Analysis of Book Fourteen', in D. Braund and J. Wilkins (eds), *Athenaeus and His World* (Exeter: University of Exeter Press, 2000) pp. 272–91.

Chappell, W. (ed.), *The Crown Garland of Golden Roses Consisting of Ballads and Songs. By Richard Johnson. Author of the 'Seven Champions of Christendom' From the Edition of 1612* (London: The Percy Society, 1842).

Charlton, D., 'On Redefinitions of "Rescue Opera"', in M. Boyd (ed.), *Music and the French Revolution* (Cambridge: Cambridge University Press, 1992), pp. 169–88.

Chester, A. G., 'Richard Johnson's *Golden Garland*', *Modern Language Quarterly*, 10:1 (1949), pp. 61–7.

Child, F. J., 'Preface', in *The English and Scottish Ballads*, 8 vols (Boston: Little, Brown and Company, 1860), vol. 1, pp. vii–xii.

—, 'Ballad Poetry', in F. J. Child (ed.), *The English and Scottish Popular Ballads*, 2nd edn prepared by M. F. Heiman and L. S. Heiman. (Northfield, MN.: Loomis House Press, 2001), pp. xxvii–xxxiv.

A Choice Collection of Civic Songs Part 1, (London, 1795).

Cicero, M. T., *Philippics*. Translated by and edited by D. R. Shackleton Bailey (Chapel Hill, NC: The University of North Carolina Press, 1986).

Claeys, G., *Thomas Paine: Social and Political Thought* (Boston, MA: Unwin Hyman, 1989).

Cobban, A. and R. A. Smith (eds), *The Correspondence of Edmund Burke*, vol. 6 (Cambridge: Cambridge University Press, 1967).

A Collection of Old Ballads. Corrected from the Best and Most Ancient Copies Extant with Introductions Historical, Critical, or Humorous, 3 vols (London: J. Roberts, 1723–25).

A Collection of Songs, by the Inimitable Captain Morris. Part the First, (London: James Ridgeway, 1786).

Colley, L., *Britons Forging the Nation 1707–1837* (1992; New Haven, CT: Yale University Press, 2009).

Collinson, P., *The Reformation* (London: Weidenfeld & Nicolson, 2003).

Connell, P., 'British Identities and the Politics of Ancient Poetry in Later Eighteenth-Century England', *The Historical Journal*, 49:1 (2006), pp. 161–92.

— and N. Leask, 'What is the People?' in P. Connell and N. Leask (eds), *Romanticism and Popular Culture in Britain and Ireland* (Cambridge: Cambridge University Press, 2009), pp. 3–48.

The Correspondence of the Revolution Society in London, with the National Assembly, and with Various Societies of the Friends of Liberty in France and England (London, 1792).

Cotterill, T., *A Selection of Psalms and Hymns, for Public and Private Use, Adapted to the Festivals of the Church of England*, 8th edn (Sheffield: J. Montgomery, 1819).

—, *A Selection of Psalms and Hymns, For Public and Private Use, Adapted to the Festivals of the Church of England*, 8th edn (Sheffield: J. Blackwell, 1829)

Crompton, L., *Homosexuality and Civilization* (Cambridge, MA: Harvard University Press, 2003).

Cullhed, A., 'Original Poetry: Robert Lowth and Eighteenth-Century Poetics', in J. Jarick (ed.), *Sacred Conjectures: The Context and Legacy of Robert Lowth and Jean Astruc* (New York: T&T Clark, 2007), pp. 25–47.

Cunningham, H., *The Children of the Poor: Representations of Childhood since the Seventeenth Century* (Oxford: Basil Blackwell, 1991).

Curtin, N. J., *The United Irishmen: Popular Politics in Ulster and Dublin* (Oxford: Clarendon Press, 1994).

Daily Universal Register.

Darnton, R., *Poetry and the Police: Communication Networks in Eighteenth Century Paris* (Cambridge, MA: The Belknap Press, 2010).

D'Arblay, F., *Diary and Letters of Madame D'Arblay*, ed. C. Barratt, 4 vols (London: Bickers and Son, 1876).

D'Arcy Wood, G., 'Introduction', *Romantic Circles Praxis Series: Opera and Romanticism*, (May 2005), at http://www.rc.umd.edu/praxis/opera/wood/intro.html [accessed 21 May 2012].

Daily Courant.

Davis, M. T., '"An Evening of Pleasure Rather Than Business": Songs Subversion and Radical Sub-Culture in the 1790s', *Journal for the Study of British Cultures*, 12:2 (2005), pp. 115–26.

—, 'The Mob Club? The London Corresponding Society and the Politics of Civility in the 1790s', in M. T. Davis and P. Pickering (eds), *Unrespectable Radicals?: Popular Politics in the Age of Reform*, (Aldershot: Ashgate, 2008), pp. 21–40.

—, I. McCalman, and C. Parolin (eds), *Newgate in Revolution: An Anthology of Radical Prison Literature in the Age of Revolution* (London, New York: Continuum, 2005).

Davis, B., *Thomas Percy: A Scholar Cleric in the Age of Johnson* (Philadelphia, PA: University of Pennsylvania Press, 1989).

de Chastellux, M., *Travels in North-America, in the Years 1780, 1781, and 1782 Translated from the French by an English Gentleman*, 2 vols (London: G. G. J. and J. Robinson, 1787).

de la Torre Bueno, L., 'Was Ambrose Philips a Ballad Editor?' *Anglia*, LIX (1935), pp. 252–70.

de Rapin-Thoyras, P., *The History of England, as Well Ecclesiastical as Civil*, trans. N. Tindal, 15 vols (London: James and John Knapton, 1728).

Deloney, T., *Strange Histories, or Songes and Sonets, of Kings, Princes, Dukes, Lordes, Ladyes, Knights, and Gentlemen*, (London: W. Barley, 1607).

Denham, J., 'News from Colchester: Or, A Proper new Ballad of certain Carnal passages betwixt a Quaker and a Colt, at Horsely, near Colchester in Essex', in *The Poetical Works of Sir John Denham* (London: Printed for John Bell, 1793), pp. 84–7.

Dennis, J., *The Grounds of Criticism in Poetry* (London: Geo. Strahan and Bernard Lintott, 1704).

—, *An Essay on the Opera's after the Italian Manner, Which Are about to Be Establishe'd on the English Stage: With Some Reflections on the Damage which They May Bring to the Publick* (London: John Nutt, 1706).

—, 'Of Simplicity in Poetical Composition, in Remarks on the 70th Spectator', in *Original Letters, Familiar, Moral and Critical*, 2 vols (London: W. Mears, 1721), vol. 1, pp. 166–224.

—, *The Critical Works of John Dennis*, ed. E. N. Hooker, 2 vols (Baltimore, MD: The Johns Hopkins Press, 1943).

Diary; or Woodfall's Register.

Dibdin, T. (ed), *Songs, Naval and National, of the Late Charles Dibdin*, (London: John Murray, 1844).

—, '"Memoir of Charles Dibdin", in *Songs, Naval and National*, pp. ix–xv.

Dickinson, H. T., 'Richard Price on Reason and Revolution', in W. Gibson and R. G. Ingram (eds), *Religious Identities in Britain, 1669–1832* (Aldershot: Ashgate, 2005), pp. 231–54.

Doelman, J., 'George Wither, the Stationers Company and the English Psalter', *Studies in Philology*, 90:1 (1993), pp. 74–82.

—, 'The Religious Epigram in Early Stuart England', *Christianity and Literature*, 54:4 (2005), pp. 497–520.

Donaghay, M., 'Calonne and the Anglo-French Commercial Treaty of 1786', *The Journal of Modern History*, 50:3 On Demand Supplement (1978), pp. D1157–D84.

Donnelly, F. K., 'The Foundation of the Sheffield Society for Constitutional Information', *Labour History Review*, 56:2 (1991), pp. 51–3.

— and J. L. Baxter, 'Sheffield and the English Revolutionary Tradition', *International Review of Social History*, 20:3 (1975), pp. 398–423.

Drage, S., 'A Reappraisal of Provincial Church Music', in D. W. Jones (ed.), *Music in Eighteenth Century Britain* (Aldershot: Ashgate, 2000), pp. 172–90.

Dugaw, D., 'The Popular Marketing of "Old Ballads": The Ballad Revival and Eighteenth-Century Antiquarianism Reconsidered', *Eighteenth-Century Studies*, 21:1 (1987), pp. 71–90.

—, *Warrior Women and Popular Balladry, 1650–1850* (Cambridge: Cambridge University Press, 1989).

—, 'Folklore and John Gay's Satire', *Studies in English Literature 1500–1900*, 31:3 (1991), pp. 515–33.

—, 'On the "Darling Songs" of Poets, Scholars, and Singers: An Introduction', *Eighteenth Century: Theory and Interpretation*, 47: 2–3 (2006), pp. 97–113.

Dunne, T., 'Popular Ballads, Revolutionary Rhetoric and Politicisation', in H. Gough and D. Dickson (eds), *Ireland and the French Revolution* (Dublin: Irish Academic Press, 1990), pp. 139–55.

Durey, M., *Transatlantic Radicals and the Early American Republic* (Lawrence, KS: University Press of Kansas, 1997).

Eastcott, R., *Sketches of the Origin, Progress and Effects of Music with an Account of the Ancient Bards and Minstrels* (Bath: S. Hazard, 1793).

Eigen, J. P., 'Nicholson, Margaret (1750?–1828)', ONDB, at http://www.oxforddnb.com/view/article/20145 [accessed 24 April 2012].

Elliott, M., *Partners in Revolution: The United Irishmen and France* (New Haven, CT: Yale University Press, 1982).

'English Convivial Song Writers', *The Irish Quarterly Review*, III:IX (1853), pp. 120–51.

Epstein, J., *Radical Expression: Political Language, Ritual, and Symbol in England, 1790–1850* (Oxford: Oxford University Press, 1994).

—, '"Equality and No King": Sociability and Sedition: The Case of John Frost', in G. Russell and C. Tuite (eds), *Romantic Sociability: Social Networks and Literary Culture In Britain: 1770–1840* (Cambridge: Cambridge University Press, 2002), pp. 43–61.

Eyre, G. E. B. (ed.), *A Transcript of the Registers of the Worshipful Company of Stationers 1640–1708*, 3 vols (1913; New York: Peter Smith, 1950).

A Faithful Report of the Trial of Hurdy Gurdy, at the Bar of the Court of King's Bench, Westminster on the — , of — , 1794 on an Information, filed ex-officio, by the Attorney General, (Belfast: Printed by John Rabb, 1794).

Fairer, D., 'The Formation of Warton's History' in *Thomas Warton's History of English Poetry*, 4 vols (London: Routledge, 1998), vol. 1, pp. 1–70.

—, 'Experience Reading Innocence: Contextualizing Blake's Holy Thursday', *Eighteenth-Century Studies*, 35:4 (2002), pp. 535–62.

Farrell, S. M., 'Wentworth, Charles Watson, Second Marquess of Rockingham (1730–1782), Prime Minister', *ODNB*, at http://www.oxforddnb.com/index/28/101028878/, [accessed 12 Dec 2013].

'Fast Day as Observed at Sheffield (1794)' in M. T. Davis (ed.), *London Corresponding Society, 1792–1799*, advisory eds J. Epstein, J. Fruchtman and M. Thale, 6 vols (London: Pickering & Chatto, 2002), vol. 1, pp. 257–71.

Favine, A., 'The Order of England, called of the Blew Garter: Instituted in the yeare One thousand three hundred fortie seauen. The Fift Booke', in *The Theater of Honour and Knight-Hood. Or a Compendius Chronicle and Historie of the Whole Christian World* (London: William Iaggard, 1623), pp. 33–77.

Fellows, J., 'Introduction', in R. Johnson, *The Seven Champions of Christendom (1596/7) By Richard Johnson*, ed. J. Fellows (Aldershot: Ashgate, 2003), pp. xiii–xxxi.

The Festival of Anacreon. Containing a Collection of Modern Songs, Written for the Anacreontic Society, the Beef-Steak, and Humbug Clubs. By Captain Morris, Mr. Brownlow, Mr Hewerdine, Sir John Moore, Capt. Thompson, and Other Lyric Writers, Whose Compositions Are the Delight of the Festive Board!, 7th edn (London: George Peacock, c.1790)

The Festival of Momus, a Collection of Comic Songs, Including the Modern and a Variety of Originals, 7th edn (London: W. Lane, c. 1780)

The First Volume of the Monthly Catalogue Containing an exact register of all books, sermons, plays, poetry, and miscellaneous pamphlets, printed and published in London, or the Universities, from the beginning of March 1723, to the End of December, 1724 (London: Printed for John Wilford, 1725).

Firth, C. H., 'The Ballad History of the Reigns of Henry VII. And Henry VIII', *Transactions of the Royal Historical Society*, 2 (1908), pp. 21–50.

Fletcher, A., *The Political Works of Andrew Fletcher, Esq; of Saltoun* (Glasgow: G. Hamilton and J. Balfour, 1749).

Fox, A., *Oral and Literate Culture in England, 1500–1700* (Oxford: Oxford University Press, 2002).

Franklin, M. J., '*Orientalist Jones*': *Sir William Jones, Poet, Lawyer, and Linguist, 1746–1794* (Oxford: Oxford University Press, 2011).

Frere, W. H. (ed.), *Visitation Articles and Injunctions of the Period of the Reformation*, 3 vols (London: Longmans, Green & Co, 1910).

Friedman, A. B., 'Addison's Ballad Papers and the Reaction to Metaphysical Wit', *Comparative Literature*, 12:1 (1960), pp. 1–13.

—, *The Ballad Revival: Studies in the Influence of Popular on Sophisticated Poetry* (Chicago, IL: University of Chicago Press, 1967).

Frost, M., *English and Scottish Psalm & Hymn Tunes c. 1542–1677* (London: S.P.C.K., 1953).

Fulcher, J. F., 'Introduction: Defining the New Cultural History of Music, Its Origins, Methodologies, and Lines of Inquiry', in J. F. Fulcher (ed.), *The Oxford Handbook of the New Cultural History of Music* (Oxford: Oxford University Press, 2012), pp. 3–14.

Fumerton, P. and A. Guerrini, 'Introduction: Straws in the Wind', in P. Fumerton, A. Guerrini and K. McAbee (eds), *Ballads and Broadsides in Britain, 1500–1800* (Farnham and Burlington, VT: Ashgate, 2010), pp. 1–9.

Gammon, V., '"Babylonian Performances": The Rise and Suppression of Popular Church Music', in E. Yeo and S. Yeo (eds), *Popular Culture and Class Conflict 1590–1914: Explorations in the History of Labour and Leisure* (Sussex: The Harvester Press, 1981), pp. 62–88.

—, 'The Grand Conversation: Images of Napoleon in British Popular Balladry', *Journal of the Royal Society of Arts*, CXXXVII: 5398 (1989), pp. 665–74

—, 'Problems in the Performance and Historiography of English Popular Church Music', *Radical Musicology*, 1 (2006), at http://www.radical-musicology.org.uk [accessed 21 May 2013].

—, *Desire, Drink and Death in English Folk and Vernacular Song, 1600–1900* (Aldershot: Ashgate Publishing, 2008).

Ganev, R., *Songs of Protest, Songs of Love* (Manchester: Manchester University Press, 2009).

Garlick, P. C. 'The Sheffield Cutlery and Allied Trades and Their Markets in the Eighteenth and Nineteenth Centuries', (Master of Arts dissertation, University of Sheffield, 1951).

Garside Jr., C., 'The Origins of Calvin's Theology of Music: 1536–1543', *Transactions of the American Philosophical Society*, 69: 4 (1979), pp. 1–36.

Gatrell, V. A. C., *The Hanging Tree: Execution and the English People 1770–1868* (Oxford: Oxford University Press, 1996).

Gay, J., 'The Shepherd's Week', in *John Gay: Poetry and Prose*, eds V. A. Dearing and C. E. Beckwith, 2 vols (Oxford: Clarendon Press, 1974), vol. 1, pp. 90–126.

—, *The Beggar's Opera* (1728), eds B. Loughrey and T. O. Treadwell (London: Penguin, 1986).

Gazetteer and New Daily Advertiser
General Advertiser
General Evening Post
The Gentleman's Magazine.

Gentles, I., 'The Iconography of Revolution: England 1642–1649', in I. Gentles, J. Morrill and B. Worden (eds), *Soldiers, Writers and Statesmen of the English Revolution* (Cambridge: Cambridge University Press, 1998), pp. 91–113.

Gerrard, C., *The Patriot Opposition to Walpole: Politics, Poetry, and National Myth, 1725–1742* (Oxford: Clarendon, 1994).

Gill, S. (ed.), *William Wordsworth* (Oxford: Oxford University Press, 1984).

Gillingham, J., *Richard Coeur De Lion* (London: The Hambledon Press, 1994).

—, *Richard I* (New Haven, CT: Yale University Press, 1999).

Gilthorpe, E. C. *Book Printing at Sheffield in the Eighteenth Century,* Sheffield City Libraries Local Studies Leaflet (Sheffield: City of Sheffield Printing Department, 1967).

Goehr, L., *The Imaginary Museum of Musical Works: An Essay in the Philosophy of Music* (Oxford: Oxford University Press, 2007).

Goodwin, A., *The Friends of Liberty: The English Democratic Movement in the Age of the French Revolution* (London: Hutchinson, 1979).

Graham, J., *The Nation, the Law and the King, Reform Politics in England 1789–1799*, 2 vols (New York: University Press of America, 2000).

Grand Procession. The Order of Procession of the King, Queen, &C. To St. Paul's Church, (And the Whole of the Ceremony during Divine Service) On Thursday the 23d of April, 1789, being the Day Appointed for a General Thanksgiving, on Account of His Majesty's Recovery, (London, 1789).

Gray, D., 'Gower, John (*d.* 1408)', *ONDB* (Oxford University Press, 2004), at http://www.oxforddnb.com/view/article/11176 [accessed 3 April 2012].

—, 'Lydgate, John (*c.*1370–1449/50?)', *ONDB* (Oxford University Press, 2004), at http://www.oxforddnb.com/view/article/17238 [accessed 3 April 2012].

Gray, T., 'The Bard. A Pindaric Ode', in *The Poems of Gray, Collins and Goldsmith*, ed. R. Lonsdale (London: Longman, 1969), pp. 177–200.

Green, I., *Print and Protestantism in Early Modern England* (Oxford: Oxford University Press, 2000).

Groom, N., *The Making of Percy's Reliques* (Oxford: Oxford University Press, 1999).

Hadley, W. W., *The Bi-Centenary Record of the Northampton Mercury with an Historical Introduction by Sir Ryland Adkins. K.C. M.P., and Contributions by Professor A. V. Dicey, & Others* (Northampton: The Mercury Press, 1920).

Hales, J. W. and F. J. Furnivall, 'The Revival of Ballad-Poetry in the Eighteenth Century', in *Bishop Percy's Folio MS. Ballads and Romances*, 3 vols (London: N. Trubner & Co., 1868), vol. 2, pp. v–xxxi.

Hall, J., *Satires, and Other Poems*, ed. P Hall (London: G. Willis, 1838).

Hamlin, H., *Psalm Culture and Early Modern English Literature* (Cambridge: Cambridge University Press, 2004).

Harap, L., 'Some Hellenic Ideas on Music and Character', *The Musical Quarterly*, 24: 2 (1938), pp. 153–68.

Harker, D., *Fakesong: The Manufacture of British 'Folksong' 1700 to the Present Day* (Milton Keynes: Open University Press, 1985).

Harris, T., 'Problematising Popular Culture', in T. Harris (ed.), *Popular Culture in England, c. 1500–1850* (New York: St. Martin's Press, 1995), pp. 1–28.

Harvey, J. H., *The Plantagenets 1154–1485* (London: Batsford, 1948).

[Haselwood, J.] 'Fly Leaves VII – Old Ballads', *The Gentleman's Magazine*, 93 (January 1823), p. 24.

Hattendorf, J. B., 'Churchill, John', *ODNB*, at www.oxforddnb.com/view/article/5401 [accessed 4 Aug 2013].

—, 'Rooke, Sir George', *ODNB*, at www.oxforddnb.com/view/article/24059 [accessed 4 Aug 2013].

Havergal, Rev. W. H., *A History of the Old Hundredth Psalm Tune* (New York: Mason Brothers, 1854).

Hawkins, J., *A General History of the Science and Practice of Music*, 5 vols (London: T. Payne, 1776).

Henderson, W. O., 'The Anglo-French Commercial Treaty of 1786', *The Economic History Review, New Series*, 10:1 (1957), pp. 104–12.

Herd, D., *Ancient and Modern Scottish Songs, Heroic Ballads, etc*, 2 vols (Edinburgh: James Dickson and Charles Elliot, 1776).

Heylyn, P., *Ecclesia Restaurata; or, the History of the Reformation of the Church of England*, 2nd edn (London: H. Twyford, J. Place, T. Basset, W. Palmer, 1670).

Highfill, P. H., K. A. Burnim, and E. A. Langhans (eds), *A Biographical Dictionary of Actors, Actresses, Musicians, Dancers, Managers & Other Stage Personnel in London, 1660–1800*, 16 vols (Carbondale, IL: Southern Illinois University Press, 1973–1993).

Hirsch, R., 'The Source of Richard Johnson's *Look on Me London*', *English Language Notes*, 13 (1975), pp. 107–13.

History of the Westminster Election, Containing Every Material Occurrence, From Its Commencement on the First of April, to the Final Close of the Poll, on the 17th of May, (London: Printed for the Editors, and sold by J. Debrett, 1784).

Hitchcock, T., 'A New History from Below', *History Workshop Journal*, 57: 1 (2004), pp. 294–8.

Hobday, C., 'Two Sansculotte Poets: John Freeth and Joseph Mather', in J. Lucas (ed.), *Writing and Radicalism* (London and New York: Longman, 1996), pp. 61–83.

Hoeveler, D. L. and S. D. Cordova, 'Gothic Opera as Romantic Discourse in Britain and France: A Cross-Cultural Dialogue', in L. H. Peer and D. L. Hoevler (eds), *Romanticism: Comparative Discourses* (Aldershot: Ashgate, 2006), pp. 11–34.

Holland, J. and J. Everett, *Memoirs of the Life and Writings of James Montgomery*, 7 vols (London: Longman, Brown, Green, and Longmans, 1854–6).

Homer, *The Iliad*, trans. R. Fagles (New York: Viking Penguin, 1990).

Horace, *The Satires and Epistles of Horace: A Modern English Verse Translation*, trans. S. P. Bovie (Chicago: University of Chicago Press, 1969).

Howatson M.C. (ed.), *The Concise Oxford Companion to Classical Literature*, 3rd edn (Oxford: Oxford University Press, 2011), at http://www.oxfordreference.com/view/10.1093/acref/9780199548545.001.0001/acref-9780199548545-e-2280?rskey=4P0tKa&result=2240 [accessed 11 December 2013].

Howell, T. J. (ed.), *A Complete Collection of State Trials and Proceedings for High Treason and Other Crimes and Misdemeanors*, 33 vols (London: Longman, Hurst, Rees, Orme and Brown, 1817).

Hudson, R., *The Myrtle: A Collection of New English Songs for the Violin, German Flute or Harpsichord* (London: for the author, c. 1755).

Hulme, O., *An Historical Essay on the English Constitution* (London: Edward and Charles Dilly, 1771).

Hume, D., *The History of England, the Invasion of Julius Caesar to the Revolution in 1688*, 8 vols (London: A. Millar, 1767).

—, *The Letters of David* Hume, ed. J. Y. T. Greig, 2 vols (Oxford: Oxford University Press, 1932).

Hunt, P., *War, Peace, and Alliance in Demosthenes' Athens* (Cambridge: University of Cambridge Press, 2010).

Hustvedt, S. B., *Ballad Books and Ballad Men: Raids and Rescues in Britain, America, and the Scandinavian North Since 1800* (Cambridge, MA: Harvard University Press, 1930).

Isaac, P. and T. Schmoller, 'Letters from a Newspaperman in Prison', *The Library*, 4:2 (2003), pp. 150–167.

Jackson, J. H., and S. C. Pelkey, 'Introduction', in J. H. Jackson and S. C. Pelkey (eds), *Music and History Bridging the Disciplines* (Jackson, MS: University of Mississippi Press, 2005), pp. vii–xvii.

Jackson, W. A. (ed), *Records of the Court of the Stationers' Company, 1602 to 1640* (London: Bibliographical Society, 1957).

Jacob, C., 'Athenaeus the Librarian', in D. Braund and J. Wilkins (eds), *Athenaeus and His World: Reading Greek Culture in the Roman Empire* (Exeter: University of Exeter Press, 2000), pp. 85–110.

Johnson, J. H., *Listening in Paris: A Cultural History* (Berkeley, CA: University of California Press, 1995).

Johnson, R., *The Most Famous History of the Seauen Champions of Christendome* (London: Cuthbert Burbie, 1596).

—, *The Second Part of the Famous History of the Seauen Champions of Christendome*. (London: Cuthbert Burbie, 1597).

—, *A Crowne Garland of Govlden Roses. Gathered out of Englands Royall Garden. Being the Liues and Strange Fortunes of Many Great Personages of This Land. Set Forth in Many Pleasant New Songs and Sonnetts Neuer before Imprinted*, (London: John Wright, 1612).

—, *The Golden Garland of Princely Pleasures and Delicate Delights. Wherein Is Conteined the Histories of Many of the Kings, Queenes Princes, Lords, Ladies, Knights and Gentlewomen of This Kingdom Being Most Pleasant Songs and Sonnets to Sundry New Tunes and Most in Use: The Third Time Imprinted, Enlarged and Corrected by Rich. Iohnson. Deuided into Two Parts*, 3rd edn (London: Thomas Langely, 1620).

—, *The Seven Champions of Christendom (1596/7) By Richard Johnson*, ed. J. Fellows (Aldershot: Ashgate, 2003)

Johnson, S., *A Dictionary of the English Language*, 2nd edn, 2 vols (London: J Knapton et al., 1755–6).

Johnston, K. R., 'The First and Last British Convention', *Romanticism*, 13:2 (2007), pp. 99–132.

Jones, W., 'An Ode in Imitation of Callistratus', in *The New Annual Register, or General Repository of History, Politics, and Literature, for the Year 1782* (London: G. Robinson, 1783), pp. 181–2.

—, *The Works of Sir William Jones*, 6 vols (London: G. G. and J. Robinson and R. H. Evans, 1799).

—, 'An Ode in Imitation of Alcaeus', in *The Works of Sir William Jones*, vol. 4, pp. 571–2.

—, 'An Ode in Imitation of Callistratus', in *The Works of Sir William Jones*, vol. 4, pp. 573–5.

—, 'The Principles of Government, in a Dialogue Between a Gentleman and a Farmer' in *The Works of Sir William Jones*, vol. 4, pp. 569–76.

Kassler, M., *Music Entries at Stationers' Hall, 1710–1818: From Lists Prepared for William Hawes, D. W. Krummel and Alan Tyson and from Other Sources* (Aldershot: Ashgate, 2004).

Kennedy, E., M. Netter, J. P. McGregor, and M. V. Olsen, *Theatre, Opera, and Audiences in Revolutionary Paris* (Westport, CT: Greenwood Press, 1996).

Keynes, S., 'The Cult of King Alfred the Great', *Anglo-Saxon England*, 28 (1999), pp. 225–356.

Kinne, W. A., *Revivals and Importations of French Comedies in England 1749–1800* (New York: Ams Press, 1967).

Knight, S., *Robin Hood: A Mythic Biography* (Ithaca, NY: Cornell University Press, 2003).

—, *Robin Hood: A Complete Study of the English Outlaw* (Oxford: Blackwell Publishers, 1994).

Knox, V., 'The Effects of Songs', in *Winter Evenings: Or Lucubrations on Life and Letters*, 3 vols (London: Charles Dilly, 1788).

—, 'On The Amusement of Music', in *Essays Moral and Literary* (London: Charles Dilly, 1793).

The Lamentation of a New Married Man, Briefely Declaring the Sorrow and Grief That Comes by Marrying a Young Wanton Wife (c. 1619–29).

The Lamentation of a New Married Man, Briefely Declaring the Sorrow and Grief That Comes by Marrying a Young Wanton Wife (London: Printed by A. M., c. 1630).

Langdale, T., *A Topographical Dictionary of Yorkshire*, 2nd edn (Northallerton: J. Langdale, 1822).

Langford, P., *A Polite and Commercial People: England 1727–1783* (Oxford: Clarendon Press, 1989).

Leader, R., *Sheffield in the Eighteenth Century* (Sheffield: W. C. Leng & Co, 1905).

Leask, N., 'Thomas Muir and the Telegraph: Radical Cosmopolitanism in 1790s Scotland', *History Workshop Journal*, 63:1 (2007), pp. 48–69.

—, '"A Degrading Species of Alchymy": Ballad Poetics, Oral Tradition, and the Meanings of Popular Culture', in Connell and Leask, *Romanticism and Popular Culture in Britain and Ireland*, pp. 51–71.

Leaver, R., *'Goostly psalmes and spirituall songes': English and Dutch Metrical Psalms from Coverdale to Utenhove 1535–1566* (Oxford: Clarendon Press, 1991).

Liebler, N. C., 'Elizabethan Pulp Fiction: The Example of Richard Johnson', *Critical Survey* 12:2 (2000), pp. 71–87.

—, 'Bully St. George: Richard Johnson's *Seven Champions of Christendom* and the Creation of the Bourgeois National Hero', in N. C. Liebler (ed.), *Early Modern Prose Fiction: The Cultural Politics of Reading* (London: Routledge, 2007), pp. 115–29.

Lippman, E. A., *Musical Thought in Ancient Greece* (New York: Columbia University Press, 1964).

—, *A History of Western Musical Aesthetics* (Lincoln, NE: University of Nebraska Press, 1992).

Lloyd, A. L., *Folk Song in England* (London: Panther Arts, 1969).

Lloyd, S., 'Pleasing Spectacles and Elegant Dinners: Conviviality, Benevolence, and Charity Anniversaries in Eighteenth-Century London', *Journal of British Studies*, 41:1 (2002), pp. 23–57.

Lobban, M., 'From Seditious Libel to Unlawful Assembly: Peterloo and the Changing Face of Political Crime c1770–1820', *Oxford Journal of Legal Studies*, 10:3 (1990), pp. 307–52.

Lock, F. P., *Edmund Burke*, 2 vols (Oxford: Clarendon Press, 2006).

London Chronicle.

London Gazette.

London Journal.

London Magazine.

Lonsdale, R. (ed.), *The Poems of Gray, Collins and Goldsmith* (London: Longman, 1969).

Lowe, W. C., 'Lennox, Charles, Third Duke of Richmond', *ODNB*, at http://www.oxforddnb.com/index/16/101016451/, [accessed 12 Dec 2013].

Lowndes, W. T. (ed.), *The Bibliographer's Manual of English Literature*, 4 vols (London: Henry G. Bohn, 1857).

Lowth, R., *A Sermon Preached at the Chapel Royal of St. James's Palace, on Ash-Wednesday* (London: J. Dodsley and T. Cadell, 1779).

—, *A Sermon Preached at the Chapel Royal of St. James's Palace, on Ash-Wednesday*, 2nd edn (London: J. Dodsley and T. Cadell, 1779).

—, *Lectures on the Sacred Poetry of the Hebrews; Translated from the Latin of the Right. Rev. Robert Lowth D. D.*, trans. G. Gregory, 2 vols (London: J. Johnson, 1787).

—, 'Lecture 1. Of the Uses and Design of Poetry' in *Lectures on the Sacred Poetry of the Hebrews; Translated from the Latin of the Right Rev. Robert Lowth D. D.*, trans. G. Gregory, 2 vols (London: J. Johnson, 1787), vol. 1, pp. 1–40.

Lucy and Colin, A Song Written in Imitation of William and Margaret, (Dublin: Printed by Pressick Rider and Thomas Harbin, 1725).

MacDowell, D. M., *Demosthenes the Orator* (Oxford: Oxford University Press, 2009).

Mackerness, E. D., *A Social History of English Music* (London: Routledge and Kegan Paul, 1964).

MacMillan, D., *Catalogue of the Larpent Plays in the Huntington Library*, Huntington Library Lists No. 4 (San Marino, CA: The Library, 1939).

MacNally, L., *Richard Coeur De Lion. A Comic Opera, as Performed at the Theatre Royal Covent Garden. Taken from a French Comedy of the Same Name, Written by Monsieur Sedaine* (London: T. Cadell, 1786).

[MacPherson, J.], *The Poems of Ossian and Related Works*, ed. H. Gaskill (Edinburgh: Edinburgh University Press, 1996).

Mallet, D., *The Works of David Mallet*, 3 vols (London: A. Millar and P. Vaillan, 1759).

Mandelbrote, S., 'Lowth, Robert (1710–1787)', *ODNB*, at www.oxforddnb.com/view/article/17104 [accessed 9 Aug 2013].

Marshall, M. F., and J. M. Todd, *English Congregational Hymns in the Eighteenth Century* (Lexington, KY: The University Press of Kentucky, 1982).

Mason, L., *Singing the French Revolution* (Ithaca, NY: Cornell University Press, 1996).

Mathiesen, T. J., *Apollo's Lyre: Greek Music and Music Theory in Antiquity and the Middle Ages* (Lincoln, NE: University of Nebraska Press, 1999).

Mayhew, H., *London Labour and the London Poor; a Cyclopaedia of the Condition and Earnings of Those That Will Work, Those That Cannot Work, and Those That Will Not Work*, 4 vols (1861–2; New York: Dover Publications, 1968).

Mays, J. L., *The Lord Reigns: A Theological Handbook to the Psalms* (Louisville, KY: Westminster John Knox Press, 1994).

McCalman, I., 'Ultra-Radicalism and Convivial Debating-Clubs in London, 1795–1838', *The English Historical Review*, 102:403 (1987), pp. 309–33.

—, *Radical Underworld Prophets, Revolutionaries and Pornographers in London, 1795–1840* (Cambridge: Cambridge University Press, 1988).

—, 'Introduction: A Romantic Age Companion', in I. McCalman (ed.), J. Mee, G. Russell, and C. Tuite (assoc. eds), K. Fullagar and P. Hardy (assist. eds), *An Oxford Companion to the Romantic Age: British Culture 1776–1832* (Oxford: Oxford University Press, 1999), pp. 1–11.

McCart, T. K., *The Matter and Manner of Praise: The Controversial Evolution of Hymnody in the Church of England 1760–1820* (Lanham, MD: Scarecrow Press, 1998).

McDowell, P., '"The Manufacture and Lingua-Facture of *Ballad-Making*": Broadside Ballads in Long Eighteenth-Century Ballad Discourse', *Eighteenth Century: Theory and Interpretation*, 47: 2–3 (2006), pp. 151–78.

—, '"The Art of Printing was Fatal": Print Commerce and the Idea of Oral Tradition in Long Eighteenth-Century Ballad Discourse', in P. Fumerton, A. Guerrini and K. McAbee (eds), *Ballads and Broadsides in Britain 1500–1800*, pp. 35–6.

McFarland, E. W., *Ireland and Scotland in the Age of Revolution* (Edinburgh: Edinburgh University Press, 1994).

McGann, J. J. (ed.), *The New Oxford Book of Romantic Period Verse* (Oxford: Oxford University Press, 1993).

McGeary, T. 'Music Literature', in H. D. Johnstone and R. Fiske (eds), *The Blackwell History of Music in Britain: The Eighteenth Century* (Cambridge, MA: Basil Blackwell Inc., 1990), pp. 397–421.

McLane, M. *Balladeering, Minstrelsy, and the Making of British Romantic Poetry* (Cambridge: Cambridge University Press, 2008).

Mee, J., '"Examples of Safe Printing": Censorship and Popular Radical Literature in the 1790s', in N. Smith (ed.), *Essays and Studies Collected on Behalf of the English Association* (Cambridge: D. S. Brewer, 1993), pp. 81–96.

—, *Dangerous Enthusiasm: William Blake and the Culture of Radicalism in the 1790s* (Oxford: Clarendon Press, 1992).

—, '*The Magician No Conjurer*: Robert Merry and the Political Alchemy of the 1790s', in M. T. Davis and P. Pickering (eds), *Unrespectable Radicals* (Aldershot: Ashgate, 2007), pp. 41–55.

—, 'The Dungeon and the Cell: The Prison Verse of Coleridge and Thelwall', in S. Poole (ed.), *John Thelwall: Radical Romantic and Acquitted Felon* (London: Pickering & Chatto, 2009), pp. 107–16.

Miller, E., *Thoughts on the Present Performance of Psalmody in the Established Church of England Addressed to the Clergy* (London: W. Miller, 1791).

Minto, N. (ed.), *Life and Letters of Sir Gilbert Elliot First Earl of Minto from 1751 to 1806, When His Public Life in Europe Was Closed by His Appointment to the Vice-Royalty of India. Edited by His Great-Niece the Countess of Minto*, 3 vols (London: Longmans, Green, and Co., 1874).

[Montgomery, J.] *Prison Amusements* (London: J. Johnson, 1797).

—, *The Christian Psalmist; or Hymns, Selected and Original*, 3rd edn (Glasgow: William Collins, 1826).

—, 'Introduction to Prison Amusements', in *The Poetical Works of James Montgomery. With a Memoir of the Author*, 5 vols (Boston, MA: Little, Brown and Company, 1860).

Morning Chronicle and London Advertiser

Morning Post and Daily Advertiser

Monthly Catalogue.

Morris, C., *A Complete Collection of Songs, by Captain Morris*, 3rd edn (London: James Ridgeway, 1786).

—, *A Collection of Political and Other Songs*, 15th edn (London: T. Lewis, 1798).

—, *Lyra Urbanica; or the Social Effusions of the Celebrated Captain Charles Morris of the Late Life-Guards*, 2 vols (London: Richard Bentley, 1840).

Murray, O., 'Sympotic History', in O. Murray (ed.), *Sympotica: A Symposium on the Symposion* (Oxford: Clarendon Press, 1990), pp. 3–13.

The Muses Banquet or Vocal Repository for the Year 1791 Being the Newest and Most Modern Collection of Songs, Duets, Trios, (London: Printed by R. Bassam, 1791).

The Myrtle. Being a Favourite Collection of Above Two Hundred of the Newest and Best English and Scotch Songs (London: J. Fuller and S. Neale, 1755).

The Myrtle of Venus: Containing the Following Much Admired Songs (London: C. Sheppard, c. 1798–1800).

The Myrtle of Venus. Being a Choice Collection of the Most Favourite Songs, Sung This and the Last Season at Vauxhall, Ranelagh, Apollo Gardens, Sadler's Wells, the theatres &c. (London: printed and sold by J. Evans, c. 1791–1800).

Neuburg, V., 'The Diceys and the Chapbook Trade', *The Library*, XXIV:3 (1969), pp. 219–31.

The New Vocal Enchantress: Containing an Elegant Selection of All the Newest Songs Lately Sung, (London: Printed for C. Stalker, A. Cleugh & C. Couch, 1788).

Newman, I., 'Edmund Burke in the Tavern', *European Romantic Review*, 24:2 (2013), pp. 125–48.

Newman, S., *Ballad Collection, Lyric, and the Canon the Call of the Popular from the Restoration to the New Criticism* (Philadelphia, PA: University of Pensylvannia Press, 2007).

O'Gorman, F., *The Whig Party and the French Revolution* (London: MacMillan, 1967).

—, 'The Paine Burnings of 1792–1793', *Past and Present*, 193:1 (2006), pp. 111–55.

Old Ballads, Historical and Narrative, with Some of Modern Date; Now First Collected, and Reprinted from Rare Copies with Notes, 2 vols (The Strand: T. Evans, 1777).

Old Ballads, Historical and Narrative, with Some of Modern Date; Collected from Rare Copies and Mss. By Thomas Evans. A New Edition Revised and Considerably Enlarged from Public and Private Collections, by his Son, R. H. Evans, 4 vols (London: R. H. Evans, 1810).

Oracle. Bell's New World.

Osborne, R., 'When was the Athenian Democratic Revolution', in S. Goldhill and R. Osborne (eds), *Rethinking Revolutions through Ancient Greece* (Cambridge: Cambridge University Press, 2004), pp. 10–28.

Ovid, *The Metamorphoses*, trans. M. Simpson (Amherst, MA: University of Massachusetts Press, 2001).

Paddy's Resource: Being a Select Collection of Original and Modern Patriotic Songs, Toasts and Sentiments, Compiled for the Use of the People of Ireland (Belfast, 1795).

Paine, T., *The Age of Reason Part the Second Being an Investigation of True and Fabulous Theology* (London: Daniel Isaac Eaton, 1796).

—, *Thomas Paine: Rights of Man, Common Sense and Other Political Writings*, ed. M. Philp (1995; Oxford: Oxford University Press, 2008).

—, 'Letter Addressed to the Addressers On the Late Proclamation (1792)', in *Thomas Paine: Rights of Man, Common Sense and Other Political Writings*, pp. 333–84.

—, 'Rights of Man (1791)', in *Thomas Paine: Rights of Man, Common Sense and Other Political Writings*, pp. 83–197.

—, 'Rights of Man Part the Second Combining Principle and Practice (1792)', in *Thomas Paine: Rights of Man, Common Sense and Other Political Writings*, pp. 263–326.

Palmer, R., *A Touch on the Times: Songs of Social Change, 1770–1914* (Harmondsworth: Penguin Education, 1974).

The Parish-Clerk's Guide: Or, the Singing Psalms Used in the Parish-Churches Suited to the Feasts and Fasts of the Church of England, and Most Other Special Occasions (London: Re-printed by John March, for the Company of Parish-Clerks, 1731).

The Parliamentary History of England from the Norman Conquest in 1066 to the Year 1803, ed. W. Cobbett, 36 vols (London, 1806–20).

The Patriot: Or, Political, Moral, and Philosophical Repository, Consisting of Original Pieces, and Selections from Writers of Merit. A Work Calculated to Disseminate These Branches of Knowledge Among All Ranks of People, at a Small Expence. By a Society of Gentlemen (London: G. G. J. and J. Robinson, 1792).

Pegge, Mr. 'Observations on Dr. Percy's Account of Minstrels among the Saxons. Read at the Society of Antiquaries, May 29, 1766', in *Archaeologia: Or Miscellaneous Tracts Relating to Antiquity. Published by the Society of Antiquaries of London* (1773), pp. 100–6.

Pentland, G., 'Patriotism, Universalism and the Scottish Conventions, 1792–1794', *History*, 89:295 (2004), pp. 340–60.

Percival, M. (ed.), *Political Ballads Illustrating the Administration of Sir Robert Walpole* (Oxford: Clarendon Press, 1916).

Percy, T. (ed.), *Reliques of Ancient English Poetry: Consisting of Old Heroic Ballads, Songs, and Other Pieces of Our Earlier Poets, (Chiefly of the Lyric Kind.) Together with Some Few of Later Date*, 1st edn, 3 vols (London: J. Dodsley, 1765).

—, 'An Essay on the Ancient Minstrels', in *Reliques,* 1st edn, vol. 1, pp. xv–xxiii.

—, 'On the Ancient Metrical Romances', in *Reliques,* 1st edn, vol. 3, pp. ii–xxiv.

—, *Reliques of Ancient English Poetry: Consisting of Old Heroic Ballads, Songs, and other Pieces of our Earlier Poets, (Chiefly of the Lyric Kind.) Together with some few of later Date*, 2nd edn, 3 vols (London: J. Dodsley, 1767).

—, 'An Essay on the Ancient English Minstrels', in *Reliques*, 2nd edn, vol. 1, pp. xix–lxxvi.

—, 'On the Ancient English Minstrels' in *Four Essays, as Improved and Enlarged in the Second Edition of the Reliques of Ancient English Poetry* (London: Printed for J. Dodsley, 1767), pp. 1–60.

Philp, M., 'Vulgar Conservatism', *The English Historical Review*, 110:435 (1995), pp. 42–69.

—, 'Paine, Thomas (1737–1809)', *ODNB*, at http://www.oxforddnb.com/index/21/10102 1133/ [accessed 13 Dec 2013].

—, R. Southey, C. Jackson-Houlston and S. Wollenberg, 'Music and Politics, 1793–1815 Introduction', in M. Philp (ed.), *Resisting Napoleon: The British Response to the Threat of Invasion 1797–1815* (Aldershot: Ashgate, 2006), pp. 173–9.

Pigs' Meat; or, Lessons for the Swinish Multitude. Published in Weekly Penny Numbers, 3rd edn, 2 vols (London: T. Spence, *c.*1795)

Pincus, S., *1688: The First Modern Revolution* (New Haven, CT: Yale University Press, 2009).

Platt, R., 'Theatre Music', in H. D. Johnstone and R. Fiske (eds), *The Blackwell History of Music in Britain: The Eighteenth Century*, pp. 96–158.

Plutarch, 'Demosthenes', in *The Age of Alexander: Nine Greek Lives*, trans. I. Scott-Kilvert (Harmondsworth: Penguin Books, 1973), pp. 188–217.

—, 'The Oracles at Delphi no Longer Given in Verse', in *Plutarch's Moralia*, trans. F. C. Babbitt, 14 vols (London: William Heinemann Ltd, 1935), pp. 259–409.

Pocock, J. G. A., 'The Varieties of Whiggism from Exclusion to Reform: A History of Ideology and Discourse', in *Virtue, Commerce, and History: Essays on Political Thought and History Chiefly in the Eighteenth Century* (Cambridge: Cambridge University Press, 1985), pp. 215–310.

Pocock's Everlasting Songster, Containing a Selection of the Most Approved Songs Which Have Been and Are Likely to Be Sung for Ever with Universal Applause. Also a Collection of Toasts & Sentiments Upon a Plan Perfectly New to Which Is Added Original Rules of Behaviour, (Gravesend: Printed by R. Pocock, 1800).

The Political Harmonist; or, Songs and Poetical Effusions Sacred to the Cause of Liberty. By a Cosmopolite (Holborn: T. Williams, 1797).

Porter, G., *The English Occupational Song* (Umea: University of Umea, 1992).

Price, R., 'Postscript to Dr. Price's Sermon on the Fast Day; Containing Remarks on a Passage in the Bishop of London's sermon preached at the Chapel Royal on Ash-Wednesday last', in *A Sermon Delivered to a Congregation of Protestant Dissenters, at Hackney, On the 10th of February Last, Being the Day Appointed for a General Fast* (London: Printed for T. Cadell, 1779), pp. 1–8.

—, *A Discourse on the Love of Our Country, Delivered on Nov. 4, 1789, at the Meeting-House in the Old Jewry, to the Society for Commemorating the Revolution in Great Britain*, 3rd edn (London: T. Cadell, 1790).

—, *A Discourse on the Love of Our Country, Delivered on Nov. 4, 1789, at the Meeting-House in the Old Jewry, to the Society for Commemorating the Revolution in Great Britain*, 4th edn (London: T. Cadell, 1790).

Priestley, J., *The Theological and Miscellaneous Works of Joseph Priestly*, ed. J. T. Rutt, 25 vols (London: Printed by G. Smallfield, 1817–32).

— 'Genuine Copy of the Introduction to a Toast, proposed by Dr. Price on Wednesday, the 14 of July, at the Feast for celebrating the first Anniversary of the Revolution in France', in *The Theological and Miscellaneous Works of Joseph Priestly*, vol. 1, part 2, pp. 79–81.

— 'Letter from Joseph Priestly to Dr Price, 29 August 1790' in *The Theological and Miscellaneous Works of Joseph Priestly*, vol. 1, part 2, pp. 79–81.

Prompter.

Proudfoot, R., 'Johnson, Richard (*fl.* 1592–1622)', *ODNB* (Oxford University Press, 2004), at http://www.oxforddnb.com/view/article/14909 [accessed 14 January 2014].

Proceedings of the Public Meeting Held at Sheffield, in the Open Air, on the Seventh of April, 1794; and Also an Address to the British Nation, Being an Exposition of the Motives Which Have, Determined the People of Sheffield to Petition the House of Commons No More on the Subject of Parliamentary Reform, (Sheffield: Printed for the Sheffield Constitutional Society, 1794).

Psalms and Anthem to Be Sung at the Anniversary Meeting of the Charity Children, at the Cathedral Church of St. Paul, on Thursday, May 26, 1785: When a Sermon Will Be Preached by the Hon. And Right Rev. Father in God, James, Lord Bishop of Ely (London: John Rivington, Jun. Printer to The Society for Promoting Christian Knowledge, 1785).

Public Advertiser

Quarles, F., *Divine Fancies Digested into Epigrams, Meditations, and Observations*, 9th edn (London, 1722).

Quinault, R., 'The Cult of the Centenary, c.1784–1914', *Historical Research*, 71:176 (1998), pp. 303–23.

Quitslund, B., *The Reformation in Rhyme: Sternhold, Hopkins and the English Metrical Psalm 1547–1603* (Aldershot: Ashgate, 2008).

Ralfe, J., 'Historical Memoirs of Admiral Lord Gardner', in *The Naval Biography of Great Britain*, 4 vols (London: Whitmore & Fenn, 1828), vol. 1, pp. 407–12.

Read, D., *Press and People, 1790–1850: Opinion in Three English Cities* (London: Edward Arnold Ltd, 1961).

Reid, C., 'Burke, the Regency Crisis, and the "Antagonist World of Madness"', *Eighteenth-Century Life*, 16 (May 1992), pp. 59–75.

Report of the Trial of the King Versus Hurdy Gurdy, Alias Barrel Organ, Alias Grinder, Alias the Seditious Organ, (Dublin, 1794).

Review of the Lion of Old England; or, the Democracy Confounded. As It Appeared from Time to Time in a Periodical Print. Second Edition. With Considerable Additions and Amendments from the First Edition, by the Reviewers (Belfast, 1794).

Ritson, J., 'A Historical Essay on the Origin and Progress of National Song', in J. Ritson, *A Select Collection of English Songs*, 3 vols (London: J. Johnson, 1783), vol. 1, pp. i–ixxii.

—, 'Observations on the Ancient Minstrels', in *Ancient Songs from the Time of King Henry the Third, to the Revolution* (London: J. Johnson, 1790), pp. i–xxvi.

—, 'Dissertation on the Songs, Music, and Vocal and Instrumental Performance of the Ancient English', in *Ancient Songs*, pp. xxvii–xxvi.

—, *Robin Hood: A Collection of All the Ancient Poems, Songs, and Ballads, Now Extant, Relative to That Celebrated English Outlaw to which are Prefixed Historical Anecdotes of his Life* (London: T. Egerton and J. Johnson, 1795).

Robbins, C., *The Eighteenth-Century Commonwealthman* (Cambridge, MA: Harvard University Press, 1959).

Robinson, E. W. (ed.), *Ancient Greek Democracy: Readings and Sources* (Oxford: Blackwell, 2004).

Robinson, N. K., *Edmund Burke: A Life in Caricature* (New Haven, CT: Yale University Press, 1996).

Rochester's Jests: or, the Quintessence of Wit, fourth edn (London: Printed for the Proprietors, and Sold by J. Wilkie, 1770).

Rollins, H. E. (ed.), *The Pepys Ballads*, 8 vols (Cambridge, MA: Harvard University Press, 1929–32).

Rollins, H. E., 'An Analytical Index to the Ballad-Entries (1557–1709) in the Registers of the Company of Stationers of London', *Studies in Philology*, 21:1 (1924), pp. 1–324.

Rowe, N., *The Tragedy of Jane Shore* (London: Bernard Lintott, 1714).

Rowland, A. W., '"The False Nourice Sang": Childhood, Child Murder, and the Formalism of the Scottish Ballad Revival', in L. Davis, I. Duncan and J. Sorensen (eds), *Scotland and the Borders of Romanticism* (Cambridge: Cambridge University Press, 2004), pp. 225–44.

The Royal Toast Master Containing Many Thousands of the Best Toasts Old and New to Give Brilliancy to Mirth & Make the Joys of the Glass Supremely Agreeable Also the Seaman's Bottle Companion, Being a Selection of Exquisiste Modern Sea Songs (London: J. Roach, 1793).

Russell, G., *The Theatres of War: Performance, Politics, and Society, 1793–1815* (Oxford: Clarendon Press, 1995).

—, 'Burke's Dagger: Theatricality, Politics and Print Culture in the 1790s', *British Journal for the Eighteenth Century*, 20 (1997), pp. 1–16.

— and C. Tuite, 'Introducing Romantic Sociability', in G. Russell and C. Tuite (eds), *Romantic Sociability: Social Networks and Literary Culture in Britain 1770–1840* (Cambridge: Cambridge University Press, 2002), pp. 1–23.

—, 'Keats, Popular Culture, and the Sociability of Theatre', in Connell and Leask, *Romanticism and Popular Culture*, pp. 194–213.

Rymer, T., *A Short View of Tragedy; Its Original, Excellency, and Corruption with Some Reflections of Shakespear, and Other Practitioners for the Stage* (London, 1693).

St. Cecilia; or, the Lady's and Gentleman's Harmonious Companion (Edinburgh: C. Wilson, 1779), pp. 14–15.

'Saint George's Commendation', in H. E. Rollins (ed.), *The Pepys Ballads*, 8 vols (Cambridge, MA: Harvard University Press, 1929), vol. 1, pp. 39–46.

Scholes, P. A., *God Save the Queen: The History and Romance of the World's First National Anthem* (London: Oxford University Press, 1954).

Schwoerer, L. G., 'Celebrating the Glorious Revolution, 1689–1989', *Albion: A Quarterly Journal Concerned with British Studies*, 22:1 (1990), pp. 1–20.

Scrivener, M. (ed.), *Poetry and Reform: Periodical Verse from the English Democratic Press 1792–1824* (Detroit, MI: Wayne State University Press, 1992).

—, 'John Thelwall and Popular Jacobin Allegory, 1793–95', *ELH*, 67: 4 (2000), pp. 951–71.

—, *Seditious Allegories: John Thelwall & Jacobin Writing* (University Park, PA: Pennsylvania State University Press, 2001).

—, 'Reading the English Political Songs of the 1790s', in J. Kirk, A. Noble and M. Browne (eds), *United Islands? The Languages of Resistance* (London: Pickering & Chatto, 2012).

Segar, M., 'A Collection of Ballads', *Times Literary Supplement* (3 March 1932).

Several Orations of Demosthenes, Exciting the Athenians to Oppose the Exorbitant Power of Philip King of Macedon (London: J. and R. Tonson and S. Draper, 1744).

Sharp, C. J., *English Folk Song: Some Conclusions*, 4th edn (1907; London: Mercury Books, 1965).

Sheffield Register

Simpson, C. M., *The British Broadside Ballad and Its Music* (New Brunswick: Rutgers University Press, 1966).

Smith, H., 'English Metrical Psalms in the Sixteenth Century and Their Literary Significance', *Huntington Library Quarterly*, 9:3 (1946), pp. 249–71.

Smith, O., *The Politics of Language 1791–1819* (Oxford: Clarendon Press, 1984).

Songs on the French Revolution That Took Place at Paris, 14th July, 1789; Sung at the Celebration Thereof at Belfast on Saturday 14th July, 1792, (Belfast 1792).

Songs, Chorusses, &c in Richard Coeur De Lion. From the French of Monsr. Sedaine. The Whole of the Music by Monsieur Gretry. As It Is Now Performing at the Theatre-Royal, Drury-Lane (London: J. Debrett, 1787).

Songs, Duettos, Trios, Quartettos, Quintettos and Musical Dialogue, &c. In the Comic Opera of Richard Coeur De Lion. Performing at the Theatre Royal Covent Garden (London: T. Cadell, 1786).

St. Clair, W., *The Reading Nation in the Romantic Period* (Cambridge: Cambridge University Press, 2004).

St. James's Chronicle; or, British Evening-Post.

The Statutes at Large, from Magna Charta, to the Thirtieth Year of King George the Second, inclusive, 6 vols (London: Printed by Thomas Baskett, 1758).

Sternhold, T., *Certayne Psalmes Chosen Out of the Psalter of David, & Drawen into English Metre*, (London: E. Whitchurche, c. 1549)

— and J. Hopkins, *Al Such Psalmes of David as Thomas Sternhold Late Grome of Kinges Maiesties Robes, Didde in His Life Time Draw into English Metre*, (London: E, Whitchurch, 1549).

—, *The Whole Booke of Psalmes, Collected into Englysh Metre, by T. Sternhold I. Hopkins, & others: conferred with the Ebrue, with apt notes to synge them with al, Faithfully perused and alowed according to thordre appointed in the Quenes maiesties Iniunctions. Very mete to be used of all sortes of people privately for their solace & comfort: laying apart all vngodly Songes and Ballades, which tende only to the norishing of vyce, and corrupting of youth* (London: J. Day, 1562).

—, *The Whole Book of Psalms, Collected into English Metre* (London: H.S. Woodfall, for the Company of Stationers, 1781).

— 'Psalm LXXIV' in *The Whole Book of Psalms*, n.p.

Stevenson, J., *Artisans and Democrats: Sheffield in the French Revolution, 1789–97* (Sheffield: Sheffield History Pamphlets, 1989).

Stewart, S., 'Scandals of the Ballad', *Crimes of Writing: Problems in the Containment of Representation* (Oxford: Oxford University Press, 1991), pp. 102–131.

Swift, J., 'A Discourse of the Contests and Dissentions between the Nobles and the Commons in Athens and Rome; with the Consequences They Had Upon Both Those States', in *The Works of the Rev. Dr. Jonathan Swift, Dean of St. Patrick's Dublin*, ed. T. Sheridan (London: W. Strahan, 1784), pp. 365–423.

Tate, N., and N. Brady, *A New Version of the Psalms of David, Fitted to the Tunes Used in Churches* (London: Printed by M. Clarke: For the Company of Stationers, 1696).

—, *A New Version of the Psalms of David, fitted to the Tunes used in Churches* (London: Richard Hett, for the Company of Stationers, 1782)

Temperley, N., *The Music of the English Parish Church*, 2 vols (Cambridge: Cambridge University Press, 1979).

—, 'Music in Church', in H. D. Johnstone and R. Fiske (eds), *The Blackwell History of Music in Britain: The Eighteenth Century*, (Oxford: Basil Blackwell, 1990), pp. 357–96.

—, 'John Wesley, Music, and the People Called Methodists', in N. Temperley and S. Banfield (eds), *Music and the Wesleys* (Urbana: University of Illinois Press, 2010), pp. 3–25.

—, 'The Music of Dissent', in I. Rivers and D. L. Wykes (eds), *Dissenting Praise: Religious Dissent and the Hymn in England and Wales* (Oxford: Oxford University Press, 2011), pp. 197–228.

Thale, M. (ed.), *Selection from the Papers of the London Corresponding Society 1792–1799* (Cambridge: Cambridge University Press, 1983).

Thomas, D. O., *The Honest Mind: The Thought and Work of Richard Price* (Oxford: Oxford University Press, 1977).

Thompson, E. P., *Customs in Common* (London: Merlin Press, 1991).

—, 'Rough Music', in *Customs in Common* (London: The Merlin Press, 1991), pp. 467–538.

—, 'The Patricians and the Plebs', in *Customs in Common*, pp. 16–96.

—, *The Making of the English Working Class* (New York: Vintage Books, 1966).

Thomson, R., *A Tribute to Liberty. Or, New Collection. Of Patriotic Songs; Entirely Original* (London, 1793), pp. 79–80.

Thomson, R. S., 'The Development of the Broadside Ballad Trade and Its Influence Upon the Transmission of English Folksongs', (PhD. dissertation, University of Cambridge, 1974).

—, 'Publisher's Introduction: Madden Ballads from Cambridge University Library'. See http://microformguides.gale.com/Data/Introductions/30330FM.htm: Gale Cengage Learning [accessed 12 January 2014].

Thuente, M., '"The Belfast Laugh": The Context and Significance of United Irish Satires', in J. Smyth (ed.), *Revolution, Counter-Revolution and Union: Ireland in the 1790s* (Cambridge: Cambridge University Press, 2000), pp. 67–83.

—, 'William Sampson: United Irish Satirist and Songwriter', *Eighteenth Century Life*, 22:3 (1998), pp. 19–30.

—, *The Harp Re-Strung. The United Irishmen and the Rise of Literary Nationalism* (Syracuse, NY: Syracuse University Press, 1994).

Thucydides, *The Peloponnesian War*, trans. W. Blanco and eds W. Blanco and J. T. Roberts. (New York and London: W. W. Norton & Company, 1998).

The Times.

The Toast Master, Being a Collection of Sentiments & Toasts Calculated for the Most Polite Circles to Heighten Social Mirth and to Add Fresh Charms to the Chearful Glass (London: Printed for W. Thiselton, 1791).

Tone, T. W., 'Declaration and Resolutions of the Society of United Irishmen', in J. Killen (ed.), *The Decade of the United Irishmen: Contemporary Accounts 1791–1801* (Belfast: The Blackstaff Press, 1997), pp. 20–1.

Treadwell, M., 'London Trade Publishers 1675–1750', *The Library*, s6-IV:2 (1982), pp. 99–134.

Trevor-Roper, H., 'A Huguenot Historian: Paul Rapin', in I. Scouloudi (ed.), *Huguenots in Britain and Their French Background, 1550–1800* (Basingstoke: Macmillan, 1987), pp. 3–19.

The Trial of Henry Yorke, for a Conspiracy, &c. Before the Hon. Mr. Justice Rooke, at the Assizes Held for the County of York on Saturday July 10 (1795).

The Trial of James Montgomery for a Libel on the War, by Reprinting and Republishing a Song Printed and Published Long before the War Begun; at Doncaster Sessions, January 22, 1795 (Sheffield: James Montgomery, 1795).

The Trial of Joseph Gerrald, Delegate from the London Corresponding Society, to the Edinburgh Convention, before the High Court of Justiciary, at Edinburgh. On the 3rd, 10th, 13th, and 14th of March 1794 For Sedition (Edinburgh: James Robertson, 1794).

The Trial of Maurice Margarot, before the High Court of Justiciary, at Edinburgh, on the 13th and 14th of January, 1794, on an Indictment for Seditious Practices (London: M. Margarot, 1794).

The Trial of Thomas Muir, 2nd edn (Edinburgh: printed by Alexander Scott, c. 1793).

The Tribune, a Periodical Publication, Consisting Chiefly of the Political Lectures of J. Thelwall, 3 vols (London, 1795).

Trial of William Skirving, Secretary to the British Convention, Before the High Court of Justiciary, on the 6th and 7th of January 1794; for Sedition (Edinburgh: William Skirving, 1794).

Turner, C. (ed.), *The Gallery Tradition: Aspects of Georgian Psalmody: Papers from the International Conference Organised by the Colchester Institute* (Ketton: SG Publishing in association with Anglia Polytechnic University, 1997).

Vicinus, M., *Broadsides of the Industrial North* (Newcastle upon Tyne: Graham, 1975).

—, *The Industrial Muse: A Study of Nineteenth Century British Working-Class Literature* (London: Croom Helm, 1974).

Vincent W., *Considerations on Parochial Music*, 2nd edn (London: T. Cadell, 1787).

Waddington, P., 'Morris, Charles (1745–1838)', *ODNB*, at www.oxforddnb.com/view/article/19300 [accessed 20 Aug 2012].

Walpole, H., *A Catalogue of the Royal and Noble Authors of England*, 2nd edn, 2 vols (London: R and J Dodsley, 1759).

Warton, T., *Observations on the Faerie Queene of Spenser* (London: R. and J. Dodsley, 1754).

—, 'Section XXVII Effects of the Reformation on Our Poetry', in *The History of English Poetry, from the Close of the Eleventh to the Commencement of the Eighteenth Century*, 4 vols (London: J. Dodsley et al., 1774–81), pp. 161–80.

Watson, J. R., *The English Hymn: A Critical and Historical Study* (Oxford: Oxford University Press, 1999).

Watt, T., *Cheap Print and Popular Piety 1550–1640* (Cambridge: Cambridge University Press, 1991).

Watts, I., 'A Short Essay toward the Improvement of Psalmody: Or, an Enquiry How the Psalms of *David* Ought to be Translated into Christian Songs, and How Lawful and Necessary It Is to Compose Other Hymns according to the Clearer Revelations of the Gospel, for the Use of the Christian Church', in *Hymns and Spiritual Songs* (London: John Lawrence, 1707), pp. 257–98.

[Watts, I.], 'Psalm CXIV' in *The Spectator*, ed. D. F. Bond, 5 vols (Oxford: Clarendon Press, 1965), vol. IV, pp. 127–8.

Watts, I., *The Psalms of David Imitated in the Language of the New Testament, And Apply'd to the Christian State and Worship* (London: J. Clarke, R. Ford and R. Cruttenden, 1719).

Werkmeister, L., *The London Daily Press 1772–1793* (Lincoln: University of Nebraska Press, 1963).

Wesley, J., *Hymns for Times of Trouble and Persecution*, (1744).

—, 'Letter XCIX. [Of Public Worship, in a Letter to a Friend, by Rev. Mr. John Wesley]', *Arminian Magazine*, 3 February (1780), pp. 101–3.

—, *A Collection of Hymns for the Use of the People Called Methodists* (London: Printed by J. Paramore, 1780).

Wharam, A., *The Treason Trials, 1794* (Leicester University Press: Leicester, 1992).

Whelan, K., *The Tree of Liberty: Radicalism, Catholicism and the Construction of Irish Identity 1760–1830* (Notre Dame, IN: University of Notre Dame Press, 1995).

Whitehall Evening Post

Wilkins, W. W. (ed.), *Political Ballads of the Seventeenth and Eighteenth Centuries* (London: Spottiswoode and Co., 1860).

Williams, A., 'Blondiaux', in *Miscellanies in Prose and Verse* (London: T. Davis, 1766), pp. 46–8.

—, *Miscellanies in Prose and Verse* (London: T. Davis, 1766).

Williams, H. M., *Letters Written in France, in the Summer 1790, to a Friend in England*, 2nd edn (London: T. Cadell, 1791).

Williams, F. B., 'Richard Johnson's Borrowed Tears', *Studies in Philology*, 34:2 (1937), pp. 186–90.

Wilson, C. H., *The Myrtle and Vine; or Complete Vocal Library*, 4 vols (London: West and Hughes, 1800).

Wilson, J. (ed.), *The Songs of Joseph Mather to Which Are Added a Memoir of Mather and Miscellaneous Songs Relating to Sheffield* (Sheffield: Pawson and Brailsford, 1862).

—, 'Memoir of Mather' in Songs of Joseph Mather, pp.vii–x

Wilson, K., 'Inventing Revolution: 1688 and Eighteenth-Century Popular Politics', *Journal of British Studies*, 28:4 (1989), pp. 349–86.

World.

Wright, T., *England under the House of Hanover; Its History and Condition During the Reigns of the Three Georges, Illustrated from the Caricatures and Satires of the Day*, 2 vols (London: Richard Bentley, 1848).

Young, A., *Travels During the Years 1787, 1788 and 1789, Undertaken More Particularly with a View of Ascertaining the Cultivation, Wealth, Resources, and National Prosperity, of the Kingdome of France*, 2 vols (Dublin: Messrs. R. Cross et al, 1793).

—, *Travels During the Years 1787, 1788, & 1789, Undertaken More Particularly with a View of Ascertaining the Cultivation, Wealth, Resources, and National Prosperity of the Kingdom of France*, 2nd edn, 2 vols (London: W. Richardson, 1794).

—, *The Example of France, a Warning to Britain* (London: W. Richardson, 1793).

Zim, R., *English Metrical Psalms* (Cambridge: Cambridge University Press, 1987).

—, 'Hopkins, John (1520/21–1570)', *ODNB* (Oxford: Oxford University Press, 2004), at www.oxforddnb.com/view/article/13748 [accessed 6 Sept 2013].

Manuscripts and Archives

British Library, Additional Manuscripts:

16920, Letters from various writers, relating to the 'Association for Preserving Liberty and Property against Republicans and Levellers'.

27825, Francis Place. Collections relating to manners and morals.

64814, Revolution Society: Minute-book of the Revolution Society 16 June 1788–4 November 1791.

Political Broadsides, shelfmarks 648.c.26.(6) & 648.c.26.(7).

National Archives, Kew, Surrey:

Home Office Papers, 42/20/386–95.

Treasury Solicitor's Papers, 24/3/168, 24/3/169, 24/3/171, 24/3/172, 24/3/174, 11/958/3503, 11/1071.

Privy Council Papers, 1/21/35b, 1–22–36A, 1/22/37.

Sheffield Archives:

Papers of William Wentworth-Fitzwilliam, 2nd Earl Fitzwilliam (1748–1833), Wentworth Woodhouse Muniments, Sheffield Archives, F 44/2

Correspondence of James Montgomery MD 2104–40

Sheffield Literary and Philosophical Society (SLPS), 37 (1)–3, 36–988, correspondence of James Montgomery).

SLPS 45–23, 47, Drafts of J. Holland and J. Everett's *Memoirs of the Life and Writings of James Montgomery*.

University of North Carolina at Chapel Hill:

Gales, W., 'Reminiscences of our Residence in Sheffield', Gales Family Papers, p.47 #02652-z, Southern Historical Collection, Wilson Library.

INDEX

Achilles, 13
Act of Toleration (1689), 72, 97, 102
Act of Union (1707), 13, 78
Acts of Uniformity, 66, 67
Adam and Eve, 74–5
Adams, Daniel, 144
Addison, Joseph, 5, 6, 12–13, 14, 16–17, 34, 64, 71–2, 73, 74, 75, 76, 79, 84, 85
Address to the Addressers (Paine), 135–6
Adkins, Sir Ryland, 42
'Admiral Hosier's Ghost', 39
Aeneid (Virgil), 12, 17, 74
Aeschines, 105
Agamemnon, 13
Age of Reason (Paine), 92
Agnew, Vanessa, 10, 11
Aikin, John, 20
Aix, Archbishop of, 103, 104
Alcaeus, 107, 108
Alexander the Great, 105
Alfred, King, 30, 38–9, 40, 51, 53, 56, 60, 148
Alfred (masque), 39
Alien Bill (1792), 120
America
    representative republican government, 131
    and transmission of radical song, 172
American Revolutionary War, 98, 111, 113, 115, 116, 119, 165
Anacreon, 33, 109
Anacreontic Society, 96, 123
Ancient Songs (Ritson), 154
Anglo-French Treaty (1786), 58–9, 60
Anglo-Genevan Psalter, 67
Anglo-Saxons
    freedom of, 122
    minstrels under, 53
    Norman conquest, 38, 55
    parliaments, 39
anniversary celebrations
    1788, 94–102
    1792, 94
anniversary songs, 94–102, 128
anthems
    national, 25, 85–92, 145, 151, 156
    proto-national, 39, 64
    religious meaning in 18th century, 86–8
    revolutionary, 151
    royalist, 1, 151
anti-aestheticism, 68
anti-theatrical movement, 73
Antony, Mark, 105, 108
Apollo, 115
Appeal from the Old to the New Whigs (Burke), 25, 94, 120, 128
Ariosto, Ludovico, 49
Aristogeiton, 25, 109, 110, 111, 112, 113, 117–19, 123, 152
Aristotle, 107
Arminian Magazine, 79
Armytage, W.H., 133
Arne, Thomas, 85
Arrowsmith, Daniel, 95, 96
The Art of Speaking (Burgh), 106
Artemon, 108
Ash Wednesday, 111–12
Ashton, Samuel, 134, 137
Aspinall, Arthur, 57
Association for Preserving Liberty and Property against Republicans and Levellers, 3, 127, 151
Aston, Joseph, 143, 161, 162, 163

– 247 –

Athenaeus, 25, 94, 108–9
Athens, 25, 94, 105, 109–11, 113, 114
August Revolution (1792), 126
Augustus, Emperor, 14
Austria, Duke of, 6, 29, 36, 47
Austria, French Revolutionary Wars, 126, 139, 162
autonomous music, 10–11

'Baby and Nurse', 98
Babylonian Captivity, 82, 92
Bailey, Nathan, 33
Baldwin, Richard and Abigail, 31
ballad partners, 16
ballad revival, 4, 5, 6, 12–18, 30, 73, 171, 172, 173
ballad scholarship, 4, 6, 17, 18, 22, 29, 31, 94, 173
ballad-makers, professional, 18
ballad-singers, 75–7
ballads
    18th-century trade in, 41–2
    apolitical, 19
    Carey's definition of, 33
    Child's definition of, 19
    distinction between songs and, 14–15
    metre, 66
    and psalms, 18, 66, 77
    and Sternhold and Hopkins, 61
    two classes of, 18
bands, church, 62, 63
Bank of England, 97
Banquet of Thalia, 59
'Barbara Allen', 23
'The Bard' (Gray), 11, 154
bards
    function at court, 50
    minstrels as successors to, 51
    Provençal, 7, 52
    Welsh, 11, 154, 165
barracks, program of building, 139, 143–4
Barrell, John, 3, 27, 119, 142, 148, 149, 156
Bartlett, Thomas, 58
Bastille, fall of the, 1, 25, 103, 117, 119, 123, 145, 151, 161, 163
Bates Pectoral Drops, 42
bawdy songs, 2
Beaufoy, Henry, 101, 127

Bedford, Arthur, 72–3, 77
Beef Steak Club, 123
Belfast, 26
Bell, John, 115
Bennett, Betty T., 26–7, 147
Berengaria, Queen of Navarre, 24, 35, 36, 37, 56
Beveridge, William, Bishop of St Asaph, 70–1, 83
Bewley, Christina, 152
Bible, psalms paraphrased from vernacular, 66
Bill of Rights, 100, 101, 102
'Billy's Too Young to Drive Us', 98
Birmingham, 139
'The Birth of St George', 50, 52
bishops, and French Revolution, 116
Blackstone, William, 37
Blair, Hugh, 105
Blakey, Robert, 22
Blondel, 1, 2, 6–9, 30, 53, 56–7, 129, 171, 173
Bonaparte, Napoleon, 3
Book of Common Prayer, 24, 66
    annexation of forms of prayer with thanksgiving, 93
Book of Psalms, 61, 73
Brady, Nicholas, 70
Bright, Richard, 103
Brink, C.O., 15
'Britons Awake' (Mather), 134–6, 137
broadside ballads, 15–16, 18–19, 20, 30, 36–7, 56
    'Harmodium Melos', 112
    'The Princely Song', 40–3, 47, 57
Brookfield, John, 144–5, 147, 168
Brooks, Cleanth, 48–9
Broomhead, William, 144, 147–8, 156–7, 158, 160
Brown, Matthew Campbell, 131
Browne, Dr, 135
Brunswick, Duke of, 141, 162, 164
Brutus, 120
Buckingham, Duke of, 22
Burgh, James, 56, 106
Burgoyne, John, 2, 29, 56
Burke, Edmund, 25, 39, 93–4, 99, 102, 103–4, 105–7, 113, 115, 116–17, 119–21, 122–3, 128, 131, 148, 153, 172
    effigies of, 142–3

Burke, Peter, 22
Burn, Richard, 33
Burney, Charles, 7, 8, 10, 62, 76, 88, 109, 110–11, 129
Burney, Frances, 88–9
Burney Collection, 173
Burns, Robert, 23
The Busy Bee, 59
Butler, Marilyn, 23, 54, 163

'Ça Ira', 2, 3, 26, 130, 150–2, 154, 155, 156, 159, 163
Caesar, Julius, 105, 108, 120
Callimachus, 115
Callistratus, 25, 107, 108, 111, 114, 117
Calvin, John, 66, 84
Calvinism, 84, 85
Camage, William, 144, 157, 158
Cambridge Intelligencer, 147
canonicity, 23
Carey, Henry, 33, 35, 36
Carlson, Marvin A., 2
Carte, Thomas, 11
castratos, 72
A Catalogue of Royal and Noble Authors (Walpole), 7, 8, 52, 129
Catherine II, Empress of Russia, 164
Catholicism
  Catholic absolutism, 97
  and voting rights, 150
censorship, 151
Certayne Psalms Chosen out of the Psalter of David, & Drawen into English Metre (Sternhold), 65–6
chapbooks, 18, 26, 42, 163, 165
chapmen, 42
Chappell, William, 46
charity schools, 90, 91
Charlotte, Queen, 88, 91
Chastellux, Marquis de, 115
Chaucer, Geoffrey, 49, 154
chaunting, 25, 93, 104, 106, 119
Cheap Repository Tracts, 4
'Chevy Chase', 4, 5, 12, 13, 17, 19, 23, 34, 41, 74, 75, 84
Child, Francis James, 18–19, 20, 22, 66, 173
'The Children in the Wood', 4, 5, 12, 13–14, 77, 84
chivalric songs, 130
chivalry, 7, 36, 49, 51, 153
A Choice Collection of Civic Songs, 165
choirs, church, 62, 63, 67, 72, 85
Christian State, 78
church
  Act of Toleration (1689), 97
  blurring of boundaries between theatre and, 90, 91
Church of England, 24, 25
  leading dissenting preachers as enemies of, 117
  and Reformation, 66
  and Sternhold and Hopkins, 67, 72, 80, 88
  text of psalms authorized by, 61, 63
church music
  church loses control over performance of, 62, 63
  Elizabethan permission for, 67
  influence of theatre on, 72
  vernacular, 62–3
Cicero, 105, 108, 114
Clarke, J.C.D., 104
classical songs, 5, 102
classicism, fusion of topicality with, 94
Clerk, Lord Justice, 154
Clifton, Francis, 20
clubs, 95
  radical, 126
Cobban, Alfred, 103
Coleridge, Samuel Taylor, 13, 171
A Collection of Hymns for the use of Pople Called Methodists (Wesley), 80
Collection of Old Ballads (anon.), 5, 30, 110
  anonymous editor's identity, 32, 35, 39, 60
  Dicey draws broadside of 'Princely Song' from, 40–1, 42, 47
  draws on Johnson's *Garlands*, 43–4
  historical songs from Volume Three, 44–5
  Percy's reference to, 48, 50, 52
  and 'The Princely Song', 31–40, 43, 57, 58, 59–60, 153, 173
A Collection of Psalms and Hymns (Wesley), 80
Colley, Linda, 86, 88, 89, 122

Collier, Jeremy, 72, 73
Comédie-Italienne, 1, 2
common metre, 66
common people
    literature of the, 13
    music of the, 22, 85
Commonwealthman tradition, 27, 39, 131
A Complete Collection of Songs (Morris), 127
Congregationalists, 77, 84
Connell, Philip, 16, 23, 55, 76
constitution
    attacks on the, 27
    French, 121
    power of song to affect, 172
    and Saxons, 55, 113
Constitutional Liberty Press, 123
Constitutional Whigs, 127
Convention of the Scottish Friends of the People, 149
Cook, Captain James, 10
Cooper, Benjamin, 122
copyright law, 31
Cotterill, Thomas, 63, 169
Cotterill *v* Holy and Ward, 63
Covent Garden, 2, 29, 56, 57, 58, 86, 151
Coverdale, Miles, 66
Cowley, Abraham, 12, 33
Crescimbeni, Giovanni, 7
Crome, John, 165
Cromwell, Henry, 17, 74
Cromwell, Oliver, 68, 88, 101
The Crowne Garland (Johnson), 30, 43, 46, 52
Crusades, 29, 40
Cullhed, Anna, 107
cultural alignment, 23
cultural politics, 6
cutlers, Sheffield, 131, 136, 137

Damon, 10
Danes, 51, 53, 148
D'Arcy Wood, Gillian, 72
David, King, 18, 24, 78
    Psalms of, 66, 74, 92, 172
Davis, Michael T., 3, 140, 141, 159
Davison, Richard, 157–8, 159, 168
Day, John, 67, 68
de la Torre Bueno, Lillian, 35
De Lancey, Colonel, 139

De sacra poesi Hebraeorum (Lowth), 107, 111
debating societies, 3
Declaration of Rights (1689), 148
Declaration of the Rights of Man and of the Citizen, 102
Deeble, Mr, 95, 96
Deloney, Thomas, 46, 52, 55
Delphic Oracle, 25, 104, 105, 106
Demosthenes, 25, 104–6, 119, 122
Denham, John, 77
Dennis, John, 17, 24, 64, 72, 73, 74–6, 77, 80, 82
Dibdin, Charles, 123, 163
Dicey, Cluer, 15–16, 40, 42
Dicey, William, 30, 40–2, 43, 47, 57
Dicey family, 41–2
Dickinson, H.T., 119
Dignum, Charles, 95, 96, 122, 123, 125, 127
dinner rituals, 95, 97–8, 99
A Discourse of the Contests and Dissentions between the Nobles and Commons in Athens and Rome (Swift), 105
A Discourse on the Love of Our Country (Price), 25, 101–2, 103, 104, 115–17, 119, 172
Dissenting sects/Dissenters, 25, 72, 77, 79, 80, 95, 117
    leading preachers enemies of the Church of England, 117
    right to worship and opinions, 10203
    and Test and Corporation Acts, 102, 117
    and Toleration Act, 97, 102
Dobson, Susanna, 8
Doelman, James, 68
doggerel, 17–18, 27, 64
Donaghy, Marie, 59
Donnelly, F.K., 133
Dorian song style, 30, 36, 40
Douce, Francis, 35
Douglas family, 13
Drage, Sally, 62
Drennan, Dr William, 150
drinking songs, 99
Dronfield, 141, 142
Drury Lane, 2, 29, 56, 85
Dugaw, Dianne, 18, 20, 31, 34, 41, 48, 77
Dunbar, Battle of, 68
Dundas, Henry, 142, 143, 148, 153

Dunne, Tom, 165–6

Eastcott, Rev. Richard, 8
Echard, Laurence, 37
Eden, William, 58, 59
Eden Treaty (1786), 58–9, 60
Edict of Nantes, revocation of, 38
Edward I, King, 11, 153, 154, 165
Edward VI, King, 65, 66, 68, 84
'The Effects of Songs' (Knox), 114
effigy burnings, 142–3
Effingham, Richard Howard, 4th Earl of, 139
elections, 1784, 98–9
Elizabeth I, Queen, 51, 55, 67
Elizabethan period
  ballad-writers, 51, 60
  minstrelry, 55
Elliot, Sir Gilbert, 90–1
English Broadside Ballad Archive (University of California), 37
English Civil War, 64, 68, 88, 116, 147
English Revolution (1641), 98
English Revolution (1688), 25, 38, 93, 111, 115, 148
  celebration of in light of French Revolution, 102
  centenary celebrations, 94–102
  commemoration of, 108
  songs sung at anniversary of, 124, 125–6
  Whig account of, 97
English and Scottish Ballads (Child), 18
Epstein, James, 3, 98
Erskine, Henry, 151
Erskine, Thomas, 151, 158, 159, 160
'Essay on Ancient Metrical Romances' (Johnson), 30, 49, 52
'Essay on the Origin and Progress of National Song' (Ritson), 111
'Essays on the English Minstrels' (Percy), 7, 30, 49, 51, 52
Eurydice, 8
Evans, Thomas, 56, 60
Everett, John, 130, 165, 168, 169–70
Everlasting Songster (Pocock), 97–8
exiles, Marian, 67
Exodus, 145
Eyre, Lord Chief Justice, 159

Faidit, Guacelm Anselm, 8
Fairer, David, 81, 91
fanaticism, religious, 116
Farmer, Richard, 35, 49
Fauchet, Claude, 7, 53
Favyn/Favine, André, 7, 53
Fawkes, Guy, 141
Firth, Charles Harding, 21–2
Fisher, Anne, 150–1, 152, 154
Fitzwilliam, William Wentworth Fitzwilliam, 2nd Earl, 133, 137
flash ballads, 2
Fletcher of Saltoun, Andrew, 11–12
Flower, Benjamin, 147
folklore studies, 5, 19
folksong, 19, 45
  hymns to tunes of, 66
Four Essays (Percy), 52
Fox, Adam, 19
Fox, Charles James, 98–9, 100, 117, 120, 121, 141, 155, 165
Fox-North coalition, 98
France
  ancien régime, 162
  August Revolution (1792), 126
  British relations with, 31, 58–9, 106, 117, 119, 122
  declaration of French Republic, 127
  fear of invasion by, 130
  fear of revolutionary ideas spreading from, 119, 123
  September massacres, 126
  war with, 139, 143, 162
Francis II, Emperor of Germany, 164
Francis, Philip, 120
Franklin, Benjamin, 119
Frederick, Prince of Wales, 39
Frederick William II, King of Prussia, 164
'Free Constitution', 158
'free and easy' taverns, 3
free trade, 59
freedom
  demands for rights of man, 122, 164
  erosion of popular liberties, 148
  and 'Harmodium Melos', 107, 110–11, 152, 172
  revolution and spreading of, 116
freemasons, 33

French Genevan psalter, 67
French Republic, declaration of, 127
French Revolution, 1, 2, 3, 5, 31, 102, 103, 116, 117, 119, 120, 123, 126–7, 128, 131, 162–3, 172
    and 'Ça Ira', 151
    and 'Harmodium Melos', 93
    and *Io Paean*, 116
    and spirit of internationalism, 150, 164
French Revolutionary Wars, 3, 26, 59, 126, 130, 141, 152–3, 162–3, 164
    song and loyalty during, 3, 141, 142, 143, 145, 162
Friedman, Albert B., 16–17, 23, 32, 171, 172, 173
Friends of the People, 121
Fulcher, Jane, 4, 173
Fumerton, Patricia, 4, 6, 173
Furnivall, Frederick, 17, 171, 173

Gales, Joseph, 26, 129, 130–1, 133–4, 137, 139, 140–5, 147–8, 157, 158, 161, 164, 166, 167–8, 169
Gales, Winifred, 26, 139–41, 144, 147, 157, 169
Gammon, Vic, 3, 62–3, 64, 72, 85
Ganev, Robin, 3–4
Gardner, Admiral, 152–3
garland collections, 51–2, 55, 60
The Garlands (Johnson), 24, 30, 52, 55
    and 'The Princely Song', 43–8, 60
Garlick, Peter, 136
Garrick, David, 85
Garrow, William, 156, 158
Gay, John, 75–7
Gazetteer and New Daily Advertiser, 117, 123
gender, and culture, 23
General Advertiser, 59
General Evening Post, 99
General Fast, 26, 145, 146, 147, 156, 161, 172
Gentleman's Magazine, 35, 71, 83, 86, 87, 89, 90
gentlemen reformers, 131, 133
Gentles, Ian, 68
George I, King, 39, 85, 86, 88
George III, King, 57, 113, 119, 139
    assassination attempt on, 58
    illness and recovery of, 25, 88–91, 119, 142, 145, 172
    treasonous designs against, 157
George, Dorothy M., 99
George, Prince of Wales (later King George IV), 89
George, St, 45–8
Gerrald, Joseph, 149
Gerrard, Christine, 39
Gibbs, Vicary, 158, 159
Gillingham, John, 37
Gillray, James, 99, 100
Glaucon, 9
Glorious Revolution *see* English Revolution
Glover, Richard, 39
'God Save Great Thomas Paine' (Mather), 26, 137, 138–9, 143, 144
'God Save the King', 2, 12, 13, 39, 130, 145, 151, 159
    as printed in *Gentleman's Magazine*, 87
    and psalmic context, 85–92
    subversive extra verse added to, 142, 143
    words of, 86
'God Save the Rights of Man', 160
Goddard, Florimond, 159–60, 161
Goehr, Lydia, 10–11
The Golden Garland (Johnson), 30, 43, 52
Goodwin, Albert, 94, 104, 147
Gower, John, 49
Graham, Jenny, 133
Gray, Thomas, 11, 154
The Great Abuse of Musick (Bedford), 72
'Great Bible' (1539), 66
Great Britain, creation of, 13, 78, 86
Greeks, Ancient, 8, 9–10, 13, 25, 94, 104–6, 107–11, 114
Green, Ian, 67
Gregory, C., 107
Grétry, André-Ernest-Modeste, 1
Grey, Charles, 121
Grey, Dr, 51
Groom, Nick, 14, 31, 48
Grounds for Criticism in Poetry (Dennis), 73
Groves, John, 158–9
grub street brotherhood, 21
Grundtvig, Sven, 18
Guerrini, Anita, 4, 6, 173
Gunpowder Plot, 93, 101

Habeas Corpus, suspension of, 144, 156
Hales, John, 17, 161, 173
Hall, Samuel, 162
Hampden, John, 119
handbill hymns, 144–7, 149, 156, 160
Hanoverian dynasty, 88, 97, 101
Harap, Louis, 8
Hardy, Thomas
   acquittal of, 160, 165
   arrest of, 144, 156
   and London Corresponding Society, 126, 134
   treason trial of, 26, 27, 130, 156, 157, 158, 159, 161
'Harmodium Melos', 25–6, 93–4, 107–14, 121, 123, 128, 152, 172, 173
   radicalization of, 94
   as symbol of national political freedom, 111
   text of, 109, 112–13
Harmodius, 25, 109, 110, 111, 112, 113, 117–19, 123, 152
harmony
   national, 121
   Plato's view of, 9
Harris, Tim, 22–3
Harvey, J.H., 37
Haslewood, Joseph, 35
Hawes, Robert, 123, 126, 127, 128
Hawkins, John, 7–8
Hayley, Mr, 95
Hayward, Richard, 2
Henderson, W.O., 58
Henigan, Julie, 20
Henry VII, King, 21
Henry VIII, King, 21, 54, 65, 101
Herd, David, 12
heroic poetry, 12–13
Hervey, John, Lord, 21
Heylyn, Peter, 68, 71, 83
Hill, Christopher, 38
Hill, Henry, 144
Hipparchus, 25, 109–11, 113
Hippias, 110
Historical Dictionary of the Gods (Bell), 115
'A Historical Essay on the Origin and Progress of National Song' (Ritson), 53–6
historical scolia, 111

historiography of music, 11
history
   from below, 22
   interchange with musicology, 4
History of English Poetry (Warton), 81–5
Hobday, Charles, 135
Hogarth, William, 76
Holland, John, 130, 165, 168, 169–70
Holy, Daniel, 63
Homer, 12, 13, 32, 33, 34
homosexuality, oppression of, 37
homosocial culture, importance of song in, 128, 172
Hood, Lord, 99
Hood, Robin, 6, 18, 31, 39, 41, 56, 173
Hooker, Edward Niles, 75
Hopkins, John, 17, 61, 66, 67
   see also Sternhold and Hopkins
Horace, 14–15, 33, 107
House of Commons, representation in, 148, 149
Hoveden, Roger of, 7, 8
'How Perfect is Expression', 123, 126
Howe, Lord, 153
Huguenots, 37, 38
Hulme, Obadiah, 55
Hume, David, 38, 39–40
Humphrey, Hannah, 100
Hunt, Peter, 105
'Hymn to Apollo' (Callimachus), 115
hymns, 5, 17, 25, 172
   development of, 61
   flourish after Cotterill ruling, 63
   handbill, 144–7, 149, 156, 160
   and language of revolution, 149
   Luther's collection, 66
   Wesleyan, 80
Hymns and Spiritual Songs (Watts), 77

Iliad (Homer), 13, 16, 32
imagining, and treason, 27
Injunctions, Elizabethan, 67, 68
intellectuals, involvement in radical movement, 133
internationalism, 150
Io Paean, 115–21, 128
   Burke on, 121, 122
   as song of triumph, 115, 121

Ireland
    Irish song, 20
    legislative independence for, 113
    reform societies in, 130, 150
    see also United Irishmen
Irish Volunteers, 113
Israel
    history of, 82
    Jewish nation, 78, 79, 92
Israelites
    and Egyptian Yoke, 145
    and Judaism, 65
Italian opera, 72

Jackson, Jeffrey, 4
Jacobean ballad-writers, 51
Jacobites, invasion threat, 85, 88, 106
James I, King, 51
James II, King, 38, 77, 85, 97, 106
Jane Shore (Rowe), 34
'Jemmy Dawson', 15
Jenkins, Mr, 95
Jewish state, 78, 79, 92
'Joe Miller's Jests', 18
Johnson, James H., 2
Johnson, Richard, 24, 30, 35, 43–8, 50, 52, 55, 60, 173
Johnson, Samuel, 6, 14, 19, 53, 73, 86, 107
Johnstone, Mr, 99
Jones, William, 113–14, 119, 126
Jordan, Joseph, 136, 162, 166, 170
journeymen, 136
Judaism, 65, 78, 82, 92

Kethe, William, 67
Keynes, Simon, 38
'King Alfred and the Shepherd', 40
King John (Shakespeare), 49
kings, divine right of, 88
King's Proclamation against Seditious Writings (1792), 134, 135
Kippis, Rev. Dr, 95
Kittredge, George, 22
Knox, Henry, 139
Knox, Vicesimus, 91, 114

Langford, Paul, 4
Lansdowne, William Petty-Fitzmaurice, 1st Marquess of, 104, 113
Lauzum, Edward, 156
Laws (Plato), 10
LCS *see* London Corresponding Society
Le Bossu, René, 13
The Learned Banqueters (Athenaeus), 94, 108–9
Leask, Nigel, 23, 150
Leaver, Robin, 66
Levellers/levelling, 85, 88
Libel Act (1792), 155, 165
liberty *see* freedom
Licensing Act (1695), 165
Liebler, Naomi, 45
'The Lion of Old England', 152–3
Lippman, Edward, 8, 9
literary ballads, 4, 12, 130
literary studies, and political song, 4
Lloyd, Sarah, 90
Lobban, Michael, 155
Lock, F.P., 117
London Corresponding Society (LCS), 2, 3, 114, 126, 131, 134, 140, 144, 147, 156, 158, 159–60, 161, 172
London Gazette, 1, 89
Longman and Broderip, 59, 151
Lonsdale, Roger, 11
Louis XIV, King of France, 106
Louis XVI, King of France, 1, 2, 3, 116, 117, 126, 151
Lowndes, William, 35
Lowth, Bishop Robert, 25, 26, 94, 107, 109, 110, 111, 114
    and 'Harmodius Melos', 107–8, 111, 114
loyalty, and song, 3, 123, 141, 142, 143, 163
Lucian, 109
'Lucy and Colin', 15
Luther, Martin, 66
Lydgate, John, 49
'Lylly bullero', 77
Lyrical Ballads (Coleridge/Wordsworth), 13, 14, 16, 171

Macaulay, Thomas, 21
McCalman, Iain, 3, 23
McCart, Thomas, 63

McDowell, Paula, 4, 16, 20, 32, 48, 51–2
McGann, Jerome, 147
Mackerness, E.D., 62
McLane, Maureen, 11, 23
MacNally, Leonard, 29, 31, 56, 57, 58
MacPherson, James, 15
Madden Collection (Cambridge), 40
Magna Carta, 38, 101, 131
Mallet, David, 15, 35, 39
Manchester, 139
Margarot, Maurice, 149
Marie Antoinette, Queen of France, 1, 120, 126
Marlborough, John Churchill, 1st Duke of, 97
Marseillaise, 2, 159
Martinique, 153
martyrs, Scottish, 149
Mary I, Queen, 66–7
Mary II, Queen, 111–12
Mason, Laura, 1, 2
Mather, Joseph, 26, 129, 134–8, 142, 144
'Maudlin, the Merchant's Daughter of Bristol', 41
Mayhew, Henry, 162
Mays, James Luther, 65
Mee, Jon, 165
melodies
    adapting well-known, 3, 4, 10
    hymns sung to folksong, 66
    psalm, 24, 25
    revolutionary songs sung to loyalist, 163
    revolutionary songs sung to popular, 127
    shared between ballads and psalms, 66
'Memoir of Mather' (Wilson), 136
metre
    ballads, 66
    psalms, 66
    Sternhold's, 66
Methodism, 25, 79, 80, 81, 84
metrical psalter/psalmody, 61, 63, 66
    as part of Reformation, 66
middle class, involvement in radical movement, 133
Miller, Edward, 83–4
Milton, John, 17–18, 74–5, 119, 142
minstrelsy
    court and 'vulgar', 54

Percy's theory of, 7, 16, 24, 51, 52–6, 60, 111, 136, 171
    post Norman conquest, 53, 60
Mirabeau, Honoré Gabriel Riqueti, comte de, 165
monarchy
    divine right of kings, 88
    and political song, 26, 77
    toasts to, 98
    see also national anthem
Montgomery, James, 26–7, 129–31, 144, 170, 172
    accused of sedition, 161
    composition of handbill hymn, 156, 160
    imprisonment of, 166–8
    poetry and hymns of, 169
    portrait of, 170
    trial of, 161–6, 169
Montgomery, Richard, 119
Moody, Robert, 144
Moore, Hannah, 4
Morning Chronicle and London Advertiser, 29, 57, 58
Morning Post and Daily Advertiser, 29, 57, 58, 96
Morris, Charles, 98–9, 127
'A most rare and excellent History of the Dutchess of Suffolks Calamity', 46
Muir, Thomas, 26, 130, 149–56, 161, 163
The Muses Banquet or Vocal Repository for the Year 1791, 122–3, 128
'Music as Amusement' (Knox), 91
music-making, elite forms of, 4
musicology, interchange with history, 4
The Myrtle and Vine: A Complete Vocal Library, 109

Napoleon I, Emperor, 3
narrative ballads, 5
narrative, impersonal, 22
national anthems, 25, 39, 85–92, 145, 151, 156
National Assembly of France, 102, 103, 116, 117
national identity, 172
    and religion, 86
    war with France and British, 122

national songs
    'Harmodius Melos', 108, 111
    psalms as, 92
National Thanksgiving ceremony, 89–91
natural aristocracy, 148
navy songs, 21
neo-classicism, 171
'New Song', 127
A New Version of the Psalms of David, Fitted to the Tunes Used in Churches (Tate and Brady), 70
New Whigs, 25, 120, 121
Newcastle Chronicle, 141
Newman, Steve, 18
'News from Colchester', 77
newspapers
    delivery and sales of, 42–3
    expense of, 21
    and 'Princely Song', 56–9, 173
Niccolini, Grimaldi, 72
Nicholson, Margaret, 58
Normans
    and minstrelry, 52, 53, 54, 60
    yoke of the, 16, 30, 38, 51, 55–6, 148
Northall, John, 147
Northampton Mercury, 41, 42
Northern Star, 152, 163, 165, 166
Northumberland, Countess of, 53

'O Richard, ô mon Roi', 1–2, 3, 151
O'Brien, Conor Cruise, 104
Observations on Civil Liberty (Price), 111
'Ode in Imitation of Alcaeus' (Jones), 114
Ode in Imitation of Callistratus (Jones), 112–14, 119, 126
'Ode to Harmodion and Aristogeiton' (Callistratus), 117–18
Odyssey (Homer), 32
O'Gorman, Frank, 141
Old Ballads, Historical and Narrative (Evans), 56, 60
'Old Hundredth', 24, 25, 61, 64, 85, 93, 172
    emerges during Marian exile, 67
    entrenched in song culture of the state, 70
    handbill hymn to tune of, 145–7
    as proto-national anthem, 64, 85, 90–1, 92, 145
    text altered in Tate and Brady, 70
    text of, 65
'old Stock ballads', 15–16
Old Whigs, 39, 60, 120

opera, Italian, 72
oracles, delivery in verse, 106
oral tradition, 16, 18, 19, 45, 55, 110
Orford, Edward Russell, Earl of, 97
Orpheus, 8, 10
'Orphic' politics of song, 18, 21
Oswald, James, 39
Oxford movement, 63

Paddy's Resource, 163, 165, 166
Paine, Thomas, 3, 26, 61, 64, 92, 102, 121, 126, 131, 133, 134, 135–6, 139, 141, 143, 144, 145, 155
    burning of effigies of, 141–2
Paineite radicalism, 126
Palmer, Roy, 22
Paradise Lost (Milton), 17, 74–5, 119, 142
parish clerks, 76, 79, 80, 91, 172
Parish Clerk's Guide, 82, 88
Parker, Martin, 52
parliament
    demand for annual, 148
    greater popular representation in, 95, 111, 148, 149
    reform of, 27, 39, 95, 103, 111, 121, 126, 131, 147, 148, 149, 150
    Saxon, 56
parochial psalmody, 62, 63, 64, 80
Patisson, Mamert, 53
patrician-plebian model of social relations, 62
Patriot, 131, 150, 155, 166
    title page, 132, 167
patriot songs, 109
Patriot Whigs, 39
'A Patriotic Song by a Clergyman of Belfast', 26, 129, 161, 163–5, 166, 170
Pegge, Mr, 53
Peisistratus, 107, 110
Pelkey, Stanley, 4
Pepys Collection, 16, 18, 19, 37, 46, 47, 48, 55, 173
Percival, Milton, 4, 21, 22, 43, 59
Percy, Thomas, 6, 7, 8, 13, 14, 15–16, 17, 19, 20, 24, 40, 41, 48, 73, 85, 111, 136, 171
    reproductions from *Collection*, 48, 50
    transmission of 'Princely Song', 30, 31, 48–56, 60, 173
Percy family, 13
Percy Society, 46
performance dimension of song, 172
Peters, Hugh, 104

Philip II, King of France, 129
Philip II, King of Macedon, 25, 104–5, 106
philippizing/philippics, 25, 93–4, 104–7, 108, 114, 115, 116, 119, 120, 122
Philips, Ambrose, 35
Philp, Mark, 3
The Picture of Paris, 151
Pig's Meat, 114
pikes, 157–8, 159, 160, 169
Pindar, 33, 34
Pitt, William the Younger, 153, 163
    becomes Prime Minister, 98
    green bag, 26
    reform proposals (1785), 94
Place, Francis, 2–3
plagiarism, 46
Plantagenet, Richard *see* Richard I (the Lionheart)
Plato, 6, 9–10, 11, 18, 23, 26, 30, 88, 127, 130, 171–2
plebian behaviours, 62
'The Plenipotentiary', 99
Plutarch, 105, 106, 109
Pocock, J.G.A., 39
Pocock, R., 97–8
Poems Written in Close Confinement (Thelwell), 129
poetry
    ancient, 14–15
    Lowth's lectures on, 107
    necessary to religion, 73
police in radical towns, 139
political ballads, 22, 39, 114
    journalistic function of, 21
    Percival's three categories of, 21
    relationship with literary ballads, 4
    scholarship on, 4, 20
Political Ballads of the Seventeenth and Eighteenth Centuries (Wilkins), 20–1
political resistance, songs as tools of, 3
political song, 130
    and ballad tunes, 3, 5
    conceptualizing, 11
    as dangerous as pikes, 169
    and hymn tunes, 5
    importance of, 169–70
    and literary studies, 4
    long duration of, 5
    malleability of, 6
    radicalization of, 121
    in scholarship gap, 4

politicians, as ballad writers, 21, 22
politics
    interface between musicology and history of, 3
    of song, 9–12
Polynesian music, 10
'Poor Jack', 163
Pope, Alexander, 16
popular ballads, 18–19
popular culture, 22–3
Porteous, Bielby, Bishop of London, 4
Portland, Duke of, 167
Positive, Paul (pseud.) *see* Montgomery, James
Praxilla of Sicyon, 108
Preston, John, 59
Price, Richard, 25, 93, 94, 101–2, 103, 104, 106, 111, 112, 115–17, 119, 122, 123, 128, 153, 172
Priestley, Joseph, 117
'The Princely Song of Richard Cordelion', 5, 24, 29–60, 153, 173
'The Principles of Government, in a Dialogue between a Scholar and a Peasant' (Jones), 114
print culture, 19, 24, 45
    and political song, 94, 127, 128, 172
    power of, 144
    and 'The Princely Song', 30
    and radicalization of political song, 121
Prison Amusements (Montgomery), 129, 166
professional ballad-makers, 18
protectionism, 58–9
Protestantism
    divisions within, 88
    and national anthem, 86
    restoration under Elizabeth I, 67
    under Mary I, 66–7
Prussia, French Revolutionary Wars, 162
Psalm Forty, 93, 108
Psalm One Hundred, 61, 64, 70, 72, 85, 90–1, 92, 93
Psalm One Hundred and Eight, 17, 74
Psalm One Hundred and Four, 91
Psalm One Hundred and Fourteen, 79
Psalm One Hundred and Thirty Four, 67
Psalm One Hundred and Thirty Seven, 92
Psalm Seventy Eight, 82
Psalm Seventy Four, 82, 83
Psalm Sixty-Eight, 88

psalms, 5, 17–18, 24, 60, 130, 172
　association with Puritanism, 68, 85, 88
　association with republicanism, levelling and Calvinism, 85, 88
　and chaunting, 106
　of David, 66, 74, 92, 172
　as form of entertainment, 77
　inter-relationship with ballads, 66, 77
　and language of revolution, 149
　metrical psalmody as natural development of Reformation, 66
　and national anthem, 85–92
　as national songs, 92
　New Version, 70
　parochial psalmody, 62, 63, 64, 80
　politicization of, 64
　and radical cause, 145–7, 152
　and secular song traditions, 61, 66
　Sternhold and Hopkins, 61–90
　true comprehension of, 78
　as war songs, 64
　Watts' objections to, 78–9
　Wesley's objections to, 79–81
　as word of God, 25, 78, 81, 93
　see also Sternhold and Hopkins; Tate and Brady
Psalms of David Imitated in the Language of the New Testament (Watts), 79
Public Advertiser, 96
Pulteney, William, 21
Puritans
　fanaticism of, 25, 85
　and singing of psalms, 68, 85, 88
　and Sternhold and Hopkins, 83
Pythagoras, 8
Pythia, 105, 106
Python, 115

quack medicine, 42
Quarles, Francis, 73
Quebec Government Bill (1791), 120
Quitslund, Beth, 66, 67–8

Radford, Rev., 140
radical movement, 113, 144–9
　objectives of, 147–8
　Paineite radicalism, 126
　radical political songs, 56, 172
　social classes involved in, 131–3
　toasting and dining, 3, 97–8, 99–100
　transmission of ideas, 3

Raikes, Robert, 41, 42
Rapin-Thoyras, Paul de, 24, 30, 32, 37–40, 52, 53, 55, 95
Read, Donald, 130
Rees, Rev. Dr, 95
Reeves, John, 127, 151
Reflections on the Revolution in France (Burke), 25, 93, 102, 103, 106, 113, 117, 119, 120, 128, 131, 142, 153, 172
reform societies, 130, 150
Reformation, 66, 81, 83
Reformation of Manners movement, 72
Regency, 91
Regency crisis, 89, 91, 119, 142
regicide, 104, 120, 153
regional identity, and culture, 23
Reid, Christopher, 119
religion
　and culture, 23
　and national identity, 86
religious ballads, 45
Reliques of Ancient English Poetry (Percy), 7, 13, 14, 15–16, 17, 19, 30, 31, 40, 48, 73, 171
　and 'Princely Song', 48–56, 60
'Reminiscences of our Residence in Sheffield' (W. Gales), 139–41, 144
Republic (Plato), 9
Review of The Lion of Old England (Sampson), 130, 152–4, 156
revolution
　commemoration of, 94
　fear of spreading of, 119, 123, 163
　future, 127
　and 'Io Paean', 115–16, 121
　promotion of international, 126, 127
　of sentiment, 148–9
Revolution Commemoration Bill, 100–1, 126
Revolution Society, 25, 26, 93, 94, 95–100, 101, 102, 103, 116, 121, 122, 123
　addresses National Assembly of France, 103, 104
　Burke questions legitimacy of, 103
　radicalization of, 126
　songs sung at anniversary of 1688 Revolution, 124–6, 128
revolutionary songs, 1–2, 12, 126, 145–7, 151, 163
Richard Coeur de Lion (opera/play), 1, 2, 29, 31, 56–7, 58, 59, 60, 96, 151

Index

Richard I (the Lionheart), King, 1, 2, 5, 6–9, 11, 16, 24, 29–60, 130, 171, 173
    as hero of chivalry, 7, 36, 40, 52, 153
    relations with his wife, 24, 35, 36–7
    sexuality of, 24, 30, 37, 40
    'Song of Complaint', 129
Richmond, Charles Lennox, 3rd Duke of, 113
The Rights of Man (Paine), 3, 61, 92, 102, 121, 126, 131, 150
riot, incitement to, 157
Ritson, Joseph, 6, 16, 24, 30, 35, 53–6, 60, 111, 112, 136, 154, 173
ritual burnings, 142–3
Roach, John, 96
Roberts, James, 31, 32, 34, 43
Robin Hood, 58
Rochefoucault, Duke de, 103
Rochester, Duke of, 22
Rochester, John Wilmot, Earl of, 76
Rochester's Jests, 76
Rockingham, Thomas Watson-Wentworth, 2nd Marquess of, 113
Rollins, Hyder, 47
Romans, 14–15, 25, 105, 108
Romantic poetry, 23
Romanticism, 5, 11, 16, 17, 20, 23, 95, 171, 172
Rooke, Sir George, 97
rough music, 22, 62, 63, 64, 143, 144
Rowe, Nicholas, 34
Rowland, Anne Weirda, 76
Roxburghe Collection, 16, 18, 19, 37, 46, 173
Royal Proclamation (1761), 93
royalist anthems, 1, 151
'Rule Britannia', 39
Russell, Gillian, 3, 34, 95, 120, 139, 151
Russell, Thomas, 152
Russell, William, Lord, 119
Russell of Dronfield, 134, 135, 141
Rymer, Thomas, 7

St Clair, William, 31
'St George and the Dragon', 46, 47–8
'St George for England', 48
'Saint George's Commendation', 46, 47, 48
St Paul's Cathedral, 90–1
Sainte-Pelaye, Jean-Baptiste de, 8
'Sally in the Alley', 33
Sampson, William, 152–6, 161, 166
'Saturday' (Gay), 75

Saxons, 53
    debt to, 55–6, 60
scalds, 50
Scholes, Percy, 85, 86, 88
SCI *see* Society for Constitutional Information
Scot of Dromore, Mr, 161, 163
Scotland
    patriots imprisoned in, 147
    reform societies, 130, 150
    Scottish song, 12
    trials of Scottish martyrs, 149–56
Scott, Sir John, 159–60
Scottish Society of the Friends of the People, 149, 150
Scrivener, Michael, 3, 5, 20, 26, 160, 166
sectarianism, 68, 88
Sedaine, Jean Michael, 1, 29
Sedgewich, Mr, 95, 96
sedition/seditious libel, 26, 126, 129, 130, 135, 139, 144, 150, 154, 160, 161, 165, 166
Seditious Writings, King's Proclamation against (1792), 134, 135
Segar, Mary, 35
Selection of Psalms and Hymns (Cotterill), 63, 169
sentimentalism, 171
Septennial Act (1716), 39
'A Serious Lecture', 144–9, 156, 168
The Seven Champions of Christendom (Johnson), 45–6, 48, 50, 52
Several Orations of Demosthenes, 106
Shakespeare, William, 30, 46, 49, 50, 126
Sharman, Colonel, 113
Sharp, Cecil, 19
sheepshearing songs, 127
Sheffield
    clash of radical and loyalist song in, 144
    political songs in, 128, 129–70, 172
    radical movement, 26, 129–49, 167–8
    support for Republican France, 141
    trial of James Montgomery, 161–6
    troops stationed in, 139, 143–4
Sheffield Iris, 26, 161, 166
Sheffield Register, 129, 130, 133, 141–2, 143, 144, 147, 158, 161, 163, 164, 166
Sheffield Society for Constitutional Information (SSCI), 126, 131–4, 137, 139, 141, 147, 161, 172
    arrest of leading members for treason, 144

pikes acquired by members of, 157–8, 159, 160
treason trials, 156–61
Shelburne, William Petty-Fitzmaurice, 2nd Earl of, 113
Shelley, Percy Bysshe, 23
Shenstone, William, 14–15, 16, 21, 22
The Shepherd's Week (Gay), 75–7
Sheridan, Richard, 99, 100, 121, 126
Shield, William, 151
Shore, Jane, 34, 41
'A Short Essay Towards the Improvement of Psalmody' (Watts), 77
silk workers, 59
singing to the king, 26, 27, 60, 149, 171, 173
Skimmington rides, 62, 143
Skirving, William, 149
skolion, 107, 108, 109, 110, 111, 112
slavery, abolition of, 147
slip-songs, 94, 99, 123
Smith, Hallett, 66
Smith, Olivia, 26
sociability, 3, 33, 94, 95, 116, 119, 172
social relations, patrician-plebian, 62
societies
radical, 126, 128
reform, 130
Society of Antiquaries, 60
Society for Constitutional Information (SCI), 94, 103, 112, 113, 114, 119, 126, 131, 144, 156, 158, 172
Society for Promoting Christian Knowledge, 72, 90
Socrates, 9–10
sodomy, criminalization of, 37
'Song of Complaint', 8, 129
song, politics of, 9–12
'A Song on the Revolution' (Arrowsmith), 96–7
song-enditers, 33–4
song-forms, 5
malleability and intersection of, 5–6, 130, 172
'Songs of the French Revolution', 165
Sparta, 110, 165
Spectator, 5, 12, 16, 34, 64, 71–2, 73, 79
Spence, Thomas, 3, 114
Spenser, Edmund, 49, 50
SSCI *see* Sheffield Society for Constitutional Information

stage performances, 56, 57, 60
stamp acts, 21
Stanhope, Lord, 101, 126
state poetry, 22
state, power of song to affect, 172
Stationer's Company
monopoly, 24, 68, 70, 71
records, 19, 30, 45, 46
Steele, Richard, 72, 75
Sternhold, Thomas, 17, 61, 65–6
Sternhold and Hopkins, 17–18, 23, 24–5, 60, 61–92, 147, 172
association with Puritanism and radicalism, 68
authorized status of, 61, 63–4, 67–8, 70, 89, 169
and chaunting, 106
defence of, 70–1
dissemination of, 71
as doggerel, 64, 68, 73–7, 80, 83
doubts about, 68, 71, 77, 78, 79
entrenched place in Church of England, 88
increased identification with secular song, 77
legality questioned, 77, 78–9, 80, 83
and 'Old Hundredth', 64–71, 90, 91, 92
origins of, 65–6
Paine's disparaging reference to, 61, 92
reshaping of original paraphrases in exile, 67, 68
ridiculed, 72
title page, 69
two versions of, 71
Warton's criticism of, 81–5
Watts' and Wesley's criticism of, 78–81, 84
Sternhold's metre, 66
Stevenson, John, 141
stock ballads, 19
Stott of Dromore, Thomas, 26
street ballads, 4
Stuart, Charles Edward (Bonnie Prince Charlie), 85
Stuart dynasty, 85, 88, 101
Stukely, Thomas, 43
style, mixing of song, 171–2
Sublime Society of Beef Steaks, 99
Suckling, Sir John, 33
suffrage
general, 148
Irish, 150

sumptuary laws, 59
Swift, Johathan, 105
Swinton, Lord, 154
Sydney, Algernon, 119

Tanner, Bishop Thomas, 7
Tasso, Torquato, 49
Tate, Nahum, 70
Tate and Brady, 63, 70, 82
Taylor, M.A., 165
'The Tear that Bedews Sensibility's Shrine', 123, 127
Temperley, Nicholas, 76, 85, 86–8
'The Tender's Hold', 166
Test and Corporations Acts, 25, 101, 102, 103, 117, 120
theatre
    blurring of boundaries between church and, 90, 91
    influence on church music, 72
    and transmission of song, 172
Thelwall, John, 3, 127, 129, 144, 158, 159, 160, 161
Thesaurus Musicus, 86
Thessalus, 110
Thomas, D.O., 119
Thomason, James, 16, 39
Thompson, E.P., 2, 3, 22, 62, 131, 141, 143
Thompson, R., 151
Thomson, Robert, 19, 35, 42, 45
Thucydides, 110, 121
Thuente, Mary Helen, 163, 165, 166
Tickell, Thomas, 15
Tijou, Mr, 2
Tilley, Mr, 95, 96
The Times, 89, 90, 117
Timocrates, 108
'To the Delegates for Promoting a reform in Scotland' (Muir), 150
toasts, 3, 97–8, 99–100
    ambiguous, 117, 119
Toleration Act (1689), 72, 97, 102
Tollendal, Lally, 116
Tone, Theobald Wolfe, 150
Tooke, John Horne, 144, 159, 161
Tooker, Mr, 162
'The Toper's Apology' (Morris), 99
topical songs, 5, 172
topicality, fusion of classicism with, 94
Towers, Rev. Dr, 95

transmission
    dual, 19–20, 45
    oral, 19, 55
    oral manuscript, 55
    of 'The Princely Song', 29–60, 173
    print, 19, 55
    of radical/revolutionary songs, 127, 172
transportation, 154
travelling agents, 42
Treadwell, Michael, 31
treason, 26
    hiding behind pretext of reform, 157
    new interpretation of, 27
    political reformers arrested for, 144
    trials, 130, 156–61
Trevor-Roper, Hugh, 38
Trial of the King versus Hurdy Gurdy, 130, 152, 154–6, 161, 166
trials
    of James Montgomery, 161–6
    political songs as evidence in, 26, 130, 149, 152, 156, 158–60, 161–2, 163–6
    of Scottish martyrs, 149–56
    treason trials (1794), 156–61
Tribune, 160
Tribute to Liberty, 151
troubadours, 7, 8
Trumpener, Katie, 11
Tuite, Clara, 95
tunes *see* melodies
tyranny, and 'Harmodius Melos', 107, 108, 110, 113, 172

United Irishmen, 26, 58, 130, 150, 152–6, 163, 164, 165, 166
utilitarianism, 172
Utrecht, Treaty of (1713), 58

Valmy, Battle of, 141
Vatican Library, 8, 10
Vaughan, Felix, 159, 161, 162, 163, 164, 166
'Vicar of Bray', 27, 158
Vicinus, Martha, 22
Victor, Benjamin, 85
Vikings, 51, 53, 148
Vincent, William, 62
Virgil, 12, 13, 17, 74, 75
vocalization, 172

Wagstaff, William, 17
Wales, 11, 153, 154, 165

Walpole, Horace, 7, 8, 52, 129
Walpole, Sir Robert, 4, 21, 39
War of the Austrian Succession, 106
War of the Spanish Succession, 106
Ward, Samuel Broomhead, 63
Warren, John, Bishop of Bangor, 101
Warren, Joseph, 119
warrior woman motif, 20
Warton, Thomas, 24–5, 50, 54, 64, 71, 88
    and Sternhold and Hopkins, 81–5
Wary, Sir Cecil, 99
Washington, George, 165
Watkinson, James, 136
'Watkinson and his Thirteens' (Mather), 136–7
Watt, Tessa, 45
Watts, Isaac, 64, 77–9, 80–1, 84, 92
Webb, Mr, 112
Werkmeister, Lucyle, 57
Wesley, Charles, 80
Wesley, John, 64, 79–81, 83, 84, 145
West Gallery music, 62
West Riding of Yorkshire, 133
Wharam, Alan, 158
Whelan, Kevin, 150
Whig Club, 99–100
Whigs
    account of Glorious Revolution, 97
    break of Fox with, 120
    court, 39
    and French Revolution, 120
    historiography, 30, 38, 60
    patriot heroes, 119
    and publishing business, 31, 32
    and Regency, 91
    and Revolution Society, 126
    thought, 55
    varieties of, 39
Whitchurch, Edward, 66
White, Joseph, 144, 167
Whole Book of Psalms (Sternhold and Hopkins), 17, 67, 71, 83
    title page, 69
    see also Sternhold and Hopkins

Widdeson, George, 144
Wilberforce, William, 148
Wilkins, William Walker, 20–1, 22
Wilkite campaigns, 98
William III, King, 25, 38, 70, 85
    accepts throne, 111–12
    birthday of, 25, 95, 102
    and Glorious Revolution, 97, 98, 101
    prayer for arrival of, 93
    toasts to, 99
William the Conqueror, 38, 51, 55–6
William Dicey imprint, 40
'William and Margaret', 14, 15, 35
William of Orange *see* William III, King
Williams, Anna, 6–7, 53
Williams, Helen Maria, 151
Williams, Rev. Richard, 158
Wilson, John, 134, 136, 137, 138, 141
Wilson, Kathleen, 94–5, 98
women
    ballad-singers, 76
    exclusion from societies, 98
Wood, George, 135
Wordsworth, William, 6, 13–14, 16, 17, 23, 171
working class
    consciousness, 22
    membership of SSCI, 131–3, 172
    radicalization of, 126
    and radicalization of political song, 121
    songs, 2
The World, 89
'The World Will Be Free', 166
Wright, Thomas, 20, 98
Wrighte, John, 46

Yankee Doodle, 115
Yorke, Henry, 147–9, 156, 161, 168–9
'You Batchelors that Brave it', 43
Young, Arthur, 162–3, 165
Young Pretender *see* Stuart, Charles Edward (Bonnie Prince Charlie)

Zouch, Henry, 133